How to Profit from the Y2K Recession

How to Profit from the Y2K Recession

... by Converting the Year 2000 Crisis into an Opportunity for Your Investments and Business

JOHN MAULDIN

St. Martin's Press ❧ New York

Text design by Stanley S. Drate/Folio Graphics Co. Inc.

ISBN 0-312-20706-9

First U.S. Edition: March 1999

10 9 8 7 6 5 4 3 2 1

I have to thank my children, Tiffani, Melissa, Henry, Abigail, Amanda, Chad, and Trey for letting Dad write and not complaining about all the time I spent at the office. No man has ever been blessed by God with greater kids.

Acknowledgments

There are so many people who have been a big part of making this book possible. Words cannot express my gratitude to those who graciously allowed me to intrude upon their busy schedules when I needed data, statistics, feedback, and comments.

I need to thank Capers Jones for his help and time and updating tables for me. Gary Shilling graciously let me bounce ideas off him and provided critical economic insights. Dr. Leon Kappelman spent hours providing resources, information, introductions to important sources, and encouragement. Congressman Pete Sessions and his staff were extremely helpful. Y2K consultant Colonel Doner provided long hours and critical commentary, and guided me to numerous quotes and sources. John Dawson and Bob Mumford were instrumental in helping me think through the social and religious implications of Y2K. Don Peters took a lot of his valuable time helping me develop bond tables and strategies.

I have obviously relied upon the foundational research of Capers Jones, The GartnerGroup (and especially Lou Marcoccio), Triaxsys Research, Ed Yourdon, Dr. Ed Yardeni, Michael Curtiss, and many others. Their research stands on its own. They are not responsible for any flaws in my interpretation of their valuable work.

Michael Williams did a great deal of the research on chapters 3 through 8. His input and advice were invaluable, as well as helping me think through the practical aspects of Y2K. Trey Johnson often did late-night work with me finding the economic statistics I needed but didn't have at my fingertips.

The staff at ProFutures Investments had to pick up the slack while I went away to write. Martin Weiss shared the burden on my newsletter while I wrote this book. I want to thank Mac Ross, Mike Posey, Tony Keyes, Colonel Doner, Professor Ryan Amacher, and Renda Combs for the comments on various chapters. Martin Weiss, Bill Miller, and Stephen Montalvo read the edited manuscripts and made many helpful corrections and suggestions. My assistant, Nancy Blackman, who suffered through my schedules and problems needs special prayers. I could not have done this without my daughter Tiffani taking much of the personal burdens and doing charts late at night. Mutual fund guru Tony Sagami helped me with the mutual fund information. I want to publicly acknowledge the help and time that Gary North provided me in my research, even though we disagree over the nature of the Y2K crisis. Too many people take his research on a variety of topics and never acknowledge it because they disagree with him.

Super-agent Kathy Yanni believed in this project from the start and found the perfect publishing company in St. Martin's Press. Lynn Barrington made me realize I could write this book. From the first interview at St. Martin's, I knew I wanted these professionals to do this book. A special thanks to senior editor George Witte and his staff: the extent to which this book is readable is due in no small part to their efforts. The fact that it was published in just a few months is testimony to their organizational skills.

And finally, this book would not have been possible without the many hours of help, feedback, and encouragement from Gary Halbert.

Contents

How to Profit from the Y2K Recession

Traffic Jam on the Information Superhighway

What is Y2K?

Two little digits.

Two little digits that should trigger the turning of 1999 into 2000 on every computer in the world—but won't do so, because of a thirty-year-old miscalculation.

It is difficult to believe that just two little digits could cause the havoc being forecast for the beginning of the year 2000. The problem appears so simple that it seems patently ludicrous that the software can't be fixed quickly and that life won't go on as usual.

But it isn't simple, the software won't be fixed quickly, and your life is going to be impacted—perhaps significantly—by the Y2K problem.

Unless billions of lines of software are fixed so that they can recognize what year it is, computers all over the world will simply stop, or worse, give us wrong information.

Everything that we do is dependent upon computers and computer chips. We have come to depend upon them because our experience tells us that we can. We have come to expect technology to deliver what to our grandparents seems like miracle after miracle.

The *information superhighway* is more than just the Internet. It is every computer and computer chip, every software program and electronic controller, every ATM and telephone. Today, we expect to get on that highway with no problems and cruise along quickly to our destination. Occasionally, we have a wreck like the 1998 breakdown of the satellite Galaxy IV, which knocked out 90 percent of the pagers in this country for a day. But for the most part, everything works.

Everyone has experienced the results of a major wreck at rush hour on a main freeway. Traffic slows or comes to a stop until the wreckage is cleared. Schedules are shot to heck, tempers flare, and meetings are missed. If you add up the lost time caused by some major wrecks, I am sure that the dollar cost is significant.

The Y2K problem is going to be the cause of the mother of all traffic jams on the information highway.

Our technological wonders are at risk, all because programmers over thirty years ago decided that it was too expensive to use four digits instead of two when they wanted to know what year it was. So 99 means 1999, but 00 means . . . 1900, instead of 2000. In order to save a lot of dollars on disk storage, they decided to leave the problem for a future generation.

We are that future generation. The most respected research firms in the world tell us that decision, made by a few computer designers, is now going to cost the world over *$600 billion* to fix and, to add insult to injury, another *$1 trillion* in legal costs, plus hundreds of billions in lost productivity and unemployment, not to mention untold problems and skyrocketing costs as governments, power companies, telephone companies, and a host of businesses around the world cease to operate.

Two little digits.

The Internet is full of stories about the Millennium Bug. Television, magazines, and newspapers are joining the chorus with ever-increasing coverage. Some of the them predict the End of Western civilization. Others assure us that there will be no problems. And both sides seem so *sure* that they are right.

The question is, "How do you get a true understanding of how the Year 2000 computer problem will affect your family, your job, and your money? Is this a pending disaster, as some suggest? Is it a problem that will have no effect on the economy and your family as others hope?"

Or is the answer somewhere in the middle? But since the opposing sides are so far apart, the middle ground is a huge territory. Exactly where in the middle is the correct position? And what exactly, if anything, should you do?

The latest data from the world's leading research firms now allow us to get a picture of how serious the problem is, not only in the United States, but around the world. What it reveals is a problem that is quite serious. The Y2K problem is going to cause major complications for those who choose to ignore the implications of the research.

Because much of the world has waited until the eleventh hour to address the problem, we will enter the next millennium with much of the repair work left to be finished. The data shows that there simply isn't enough time or aren't enough programmers available to get it all done properly. The result will be that many products or services dependent upon correctly programmed computers will not be available in the early part of 2000. As we will see, this directly translates into higher unemployment, lower profits, and lack of some government services.

The result of this worldwide epidemic of procrastination is in all likelihood going to be the first significant recession in the U.S. economy in over twenty-five years—*the Y2K Recession.* Within eighteen months I believe we will have double-digit unemployment, a stock market down 50 percent from its highs, and hundred-billion-dollar deficits. Many of the countries around the world will be in far worse shape, facing depression and massive unemployment.

These are not pleasant predictions, but as you study the data presented by governments and the leading research firms in the world, it is difficult to come to any other conclusion.

It Is Not All Bad News

I don't think that you need to sell your home and move to the country, as some suggest. I don't think that we will see the electrical power grid go down for a significant amount of time, if at all. Most businesses and services in this country will be fine. But there will be enough problems to cause a recession. And if you don't take certain steps to protect your family, your investments, and your money from the effects of the Y2K Recession, you put yourself in a position where you could experience some severe losses and problems.

That is the bad news. The good news is that we can see this recession coming. And frankly, I think that it will be a severe, but short, recession. The bull market that will follow will be exhilarating. If you prepare now, the Y2K Recession doesn't have to threaten your lifestyle or your future. *You will be able to go into the new millennium with confidence.* In fact, it will be possible to be better off financially in two years than you are today.

What I want to do in this book is give you the information and the tools that you need to prepare yourself and your family. We are going to look in detail at the most important areas of our economy, and see what shape our power, telephone, government, and financial institutions are in. We will examine how the rest of the world is doing.

After we have this foundation, we will move on to look at why there will be a Y2K Recession. We will look at the data compiled by the leading institutions in the world, and analyze the results in terms of our economy.

And then we will look at what we can do to not only protect our investments and families, but *learn how to profit from the Y2K Recession.*

But first, we need to look at why there is such a wide range of opinions on the Y2K problem. If you can get an understanding of why this exists, it will help you keep your balance as you try to decide for yourself where you come out on the issue.

The Doomsday Versus the Pollyanna Camps

As noted above, there are two widely divided camps when it comes to assessing how bad the Y2K problem will be. Some believe that it will be a mere hiccup that will hardly be felt, while others believe that it will be the end of Western civilization as we know it. For this discussion, I will refer to these groups as the *doomsday* and the *Pollyanna* camps. Simply put, the crux of the argument from both camps on the edge of the Y2K debate is that *the division of labor is either the problem or the solution.* Keep that thought in mind as you read what follows.

(To put it simply, the *division of labor* allows an individual to cooperate with others in order to survive. In primitive societies, some would hunt and some would farm and others would make pottery, each trading for or sharing in the results of the combined effort. The basic tasks of life were divided up among the tribe members. In advanced societies, the division becomes much more highly specialized. I do not have to grow food or build cars or design airplanes or build roads or perform any of the approximately 1 million other jobs it takes to make our country work, with the exception of my own. I do a few specialized tasks for which I earn dollars that buy the goods or services of other specialized workers.)

Those who foresee a Y2K apocalypse rightly point out that society is so interconnected and that we depend on each other to such an extreme that a major breakdown in the ability of the division of labor to function will either severely impair or collapse society. For example, if the banking system were to collapse or if the utilities do shut down, we would probably drift into a panicked barter period that could take years, if not decades, to recover from.

Their argument is that the systems are *so* complex and that time is *so* short and that there is *so much more* to do than can possibly be done that there is *no way* that the problem can be fixed in time. Even if *most* companies and services get their act together, the doomsday camp contends, we are so interdependent that *most* is not good enough to keep economic civilization—by today's standards—intact. They argue that we depend on each other for food, power, jobs, and basic goods, and that a breakdown in the delivery systems that bring them to our communities and to our doors would be a disaster of biblical proportions, especially in the cities.

The Pollyanna camp replies that it is precisely the division of labor that will save us. Since it is in each person's self-interest to make sure that their jobs and businesses are secure and that their systems work, it seems reasonable to assume that the vast majority of people will do whatever it takes to be ready for January 1, 2000. For systems not ready, there will be work-arounds, contingency plans, or "whatever it takes" in order to assure that customers are serviced and that life goes on. Eventually, the systems will get fixed or replaced, and things will get back to what we think of as normal. (Think about twenty-five years ago versus today—the definition of "normal" has undeniably changed!)

They would further argue that the systems that do break down will cause inconvenience but not disaster. If one company cannot deliver the goods, then we can go to another. Even if random utilities are struck, it will only be for a relatively short time (hours, days, a month in the odd site) that some people will be without electricity. Plane schedules might become inconvenient, but planes will run. Finally, some have pointed out that we are not as dependent upon software as we might think. For most people computers are a convenience, not a necessity.

The Middle Ground: The Y2K Recession

The reality is, as usual, somewhere in the middle. And if it is anywhere actually close to the middle, the consequences of the Y2K problem will have a serious impact on our economy and on our investments. *I am in this middle camp: I don't expect a breakdown of society, but neither do I think that this is a trivial exercise.*

The Pollyanna Perspective

Let's look at four of the ways that Pollyannas approach this problem, the reasons that they give to support their rose-colored view of Y2K, and why you should reject these positions.

THE DENIAL APPROACH:
This is a problem dreamed up by consultants to make lots of money.

I had heard this excuse bantered about, but never really believed that anyone seemingly credible would use it, until I opened my *Wall Street Journal* one morning, and there, on the op-ed page, was a piece by a professor from a recognized university telling us that the Y2K problem was a hoax perpetrated by consultants and Year 2000 "fix-it" companies to soak money from naïve, unsuspecting companies. (I won't embarrass him by printing his name.)

As I travel and speak at conferences, I hear this article cited as "proof" of this position by those who share it. When I get the opportunity, I always ask the following questions. (I never get answers.)

If it is not a problem, why would Citicorp spend $300 million, General Motors $500 million, and the world a collective $600 billion to solve it? What naïve manager authorized those expenditures? (To top it off, the companies get absolutely no increase in productivity or any technological benefit—they only get to survive into the next millennium!)

Exactly how do these consultants get tens of thousands of companies to spend collectively $600 billion on a nonexistent problem?

If it is not a problem, why does Lloyd's of London estimate that the legal bill will be over $1 trillion? (If you see the lawyers circling, you can guarantee that it is going to be a big problem!)

If it is just a problem created by consultants to milk naïve companies, which powerful consultant got the North American Electric Reliability Council to say that if the problem is not fixed, the power grid will fail?

Why do so many government figures, industry leaders, and major research houses assert that this is one of the most serious problems to confront our culture?

Where is the *first* report from a credible research firm or government agency that says the Year 2000 problem is not serious?

Those who believe in this assertion must believe that there is some vast worldwide computer conspiracy among technology managers, software programmers, information specialists, and computer companies to scare us into spending hundreds of billions of dollars.

The answer is that no one could make Citicorp or General Motors spend hundreds of millions of dollars on a nonexistent problem, let alone tens of thousands of other companies. These companies realize that their computers will not work if their software is not fixed.

As we will see in the next chapter, the problem *is* serious. Those who think that it is a problem created by consultants and software companies have simply not done their homework. They give a whole new meaning to the concept of wishful thinking.

THE FAITH APPROACH:
Bill Gates (or somebody) will fix it.

I have actually had people on several occasions tell me that Bill Gates will fix the Millennium Bug. Others state that some genius somewhere will figure out how to solve it.

Peter de Jager, one of the earliest computer professionals to warn of the Y2K problem, tells us of a recent press conference in Washington, D.C. Attorney General Janet Reno was being questioned about the government's lawsuit against Microsoft and Bill Gates. One reporter seriously asked her whether she would back off if Bill Gates fixed the Y2K problem.

Such faith in technology and genius is going to be sorely tested in the next few years. The fact is that no "silver bullet" is possible. The problem is far too complex and widespread to be solved by one "superprogram."

There *are* lots of software tools that have been developed by clever programmers to help the process. But the Millennium Bug has infected hundreds of computer languages on hundreds of computer platforms running millions of software programs. Unique solutions must be developed for every "platform" (the term for the computers and the languages that run them).

Much of the code that runs our largest and most complex programs was written over twenty years ago, and in some cases over thirty years ago! In many cases, the original documentation of what the code actually does no longer exists. Evidently, some early programmers were an eccentric lot, using cryptic names to describe certain sections or modules of code that they understood but that have no meaning to anyone today.

Today's programmers, when trying to decipher what is happening inside a program that may have been written before they were born, have to have the skills of an archeologist, looking for clues as they dig deeper and deeper into the jungle of code, trying not to disturb the main process even as they change bits and bytes to fix the problems.

At the end of the day, this is a job that requires brute strength. It takes time and people to check every infected line of code. Admittedly, it is not difficult to fix any one line. But the problem becomes vastly more complex when there are 1 million or 100 million lines to check and fix. And experience is showing us that when a program is "fixed," it will have errors caused by the fixes that have to be fixed all over again. And again. And again.

Those who believe that Bill Gates or his counterparts will fix this problem do so because of a simple, but misplaced, faith in technology. In their lives, technology has worked because some brilliant person somewhere else made it work. They now expect that this chain of events will continue.

Those who expect some miracle cure are living in a technological fantasy world. They simply have not studied the issue. They can cite no credible source to support their position.

A long, detailed description of why a silver-bullet, one-size-fits-all approach will not work is beyond the scope of this book. But for those who are interested, I have listed a number of books that can offer detailed explanations of the problem in appendix A. These books are written by nationally recognized software experts with many years of experience. Many of them offer relatively dire predictions along with their solutions.

Unfortunately, I can find no books that tell us how and why the problem is easy to fix, or that offer a single, simple solution. The book does not exist, and there will not be one written.

Reality, like software, is sometimes quite hard.

THE OPTIMISM APPROACH:
There is still plenty of time to get the computers fixed.

In the first week of November 1998 two notices were sent to me. China had awakened to the Year 2000 Crisis. Its leaders, duly alarmed, issued decrees that all software be fixed by November of 1999. Failure to comply would result in criminal prosecution.

Kenya was even more ambitious. Its leaders decided to have their projects finished by April of 1999.

People who research such things tell us that less than 50 percent of software projects are finished on time and within budget.

The reality is that the code is flawed, and we have an immovable deadline and an industry populated with optimists who have a history of missing deadlines.

Recently, I was speaking at a Y2K conference for programmers. (I was talking about the economic consequences of Y2K, not the programming questions!) I slipped into a session conducted by Peter de Jager. He asked a room of several hundred programmers and information managers how many of them worked in companies where even 50 percent of projects were completed on time.

There was not one hand raised! He later told me that this was typical. I thought that it was one of the scariest things that I had ever witnessed.

The Kenya Factor

What happens in the typical software project is somewhat like the process for fixing the code in Kenya. Management decides how much time is available to do the job and then tells the programmers to develop a schedule and make sure they get the job done on time. Damn the torpedoes and full speed ahead!

One nationally known Y2K expert, Bill Ulrich, has stated that one of his major concerns is the lack of resources available to finish the job in time. When companies begin to panic, they are going to go to outside consulting services for the code changes. Many of these services have set up shop, hiring programmers and waiting for a crush of Y2K-related business. These "factories" (although they do not like to be called that, I am told) are operating at about 50 percent of capacity, on average. Ulrich notes that if you add up all the spare capacity and then look at the amount of work to be done, there is only enough capacity to handle about 20 to 25 percent of the problem.

I checked this with a senior manager at one of the largest Y2K-software consulting firms in the world, with over twenty different software factories around the world doing Y2K conversion. They are indeed operating well below capacity. When asked if he agreed with Ulrich, he said that he thought the situation was not as bad as Ulrich claimed, but that if there is not a rush within the next few months, it could get that bad quickly.

Those who say that there is plenty of time may be right about any one particular company. Given enough resources, most companies could finish on time. But there are not enough programmers for every company to institute a last-minute effort. It is like the child's game of musical chairs, in which there are not enough chairs for everyone to sit down. There are not enough programmers for everything to get fixed.

The United States is short over 300,000 software professionals today. Because of this, companies are aggressively recruiting programmers, offering bonuses and ever-higher salaries and perks. Programmers are leaving government jobs for more lucrative consulting offers. Employee turnover is becoming a serious problem. The work loads are causing an epidemic of burnout.

But throwing more bodies at the problem is not necessarily the answer. Computer programming expert Ed Yourdon tells us:

> When software project schedule delays first began to be noticed over thirty years ago, there was a common tendency to add more programmers to a project, in the optimistic hope that the additional personnel could help speed things up. But in a classic software-engineering book, first published in 1975, Dr. Fred Brooks articulated what has come to be known as "Brooks' law": *Adding more people to a late software project just makes it later.*[1] [Emphasis added.]

He notes that you can produce software more quickly by adding people, doubling overtime, and other measures, but that the law of diminishing returns sets in much more quickly than lay people would think. This won't keep senior management from attempting to refute Brooks' Law by throwing large numbers of programmers at the project as the December 31, 1999 deadline looms nearer and nearer.

We are already seeing salaries for qualified programmers reach levels not dreamed of a few years ago. They will go much higher as 2000 approaches and panic sets in. Small companies on limited budgets will simply not be able to compete with large corporations. Corporations with lots of cash get programmers and compliant systems. Cash-strapped companies won't get either.

Procrastination kills.

THE OSTRICH APPROACH:
It doesn't affect me. I don't use computers.

"There are two types of people, those who aren't working on it and aren't worried, and those who are working on it [Y2K] and are terrified."[2]

---

[1]*Time Bomb 2000,* Ed Yourdon and Jennifer Yourdon, Prentice Hall, p. 381. The book cited in Yourdon's text is *The Mythical Man-Month.*

[2]Nigel Jones of Data Dimensions, *Newsweek,* June 2, 1997.

It is very difficult to find someone not affected by computers. We use ATMs and telephones and shop at grocery stores. We stop at red lights, switch on lights, and shop at Wal-Mart. All of these are controlled by computers.

We pay rent or mortgages, buy gas, and send packages, all with the aid of computers. Many of those who receive government aid might not think that they depend upon computers, but without computers it would be impossible to administer the government programs that serve them.

In 1973, OPEC decided to reduce the world's supply of oil. This shock to the world's economy produced a major recession. Our country's economy shrank by almost 4 percent, unemployment jumped dramatically, and it took years before the market recovered and went on to new highs. Most economists view the 1973 to 1974 recession as caused by a disruption in the oil supply.

The Y2K Recession will be caused by a disruption in the information supply. As computers break down or refuse to give us useful information, crippling our industry and causing numerous hassles, we will see a loss of productivity, businesses failing, and a host of other problems.

Let's go back to the image of the traffic jam on the information superhighway. It won't be just one wreck. The freeways will be littered with wrecks. The off-ramps will be blocked. The side streets will be backed up for miles, and even the alleys will be closed off. And in a few cases, the bridges and overpasses will collapse, forcing people to go miles out of their way just to get across the river.

People are going to miss meetings, not get products delivered on time, lose clients, and worse. It will take days and months to completely clear the wrecks and rebuild the information paths. We will cope by getting up two hours earlier, figuring out alternate routes to get to work, and getting used to taking three hours to get home when it used to take thirty minutes. (This was the case in some parts of California after the last major earthquake.)

The costs of all this information wreckage will be enormous. One estimate, which we will examine in detail in later chapters, is that the Y2K problem will directly result in the loss of 3 million jobs. When you add the indirect losses, the number could easily double that, pushing us to double-digit unemployment.

This recession is going to affect everyone. There will be less money spent on goods and services, because an extra 5 percent of our country will be unemployed. Jobs will be lost, and companies will go bankrupt, not because their computers failed, but from the ripple effects of the failures of computers that these companies were never aware of. When Wall Street crashed in 1987, New York limousine drivers were put out of work as their former high-flying clients went back to the subways.

The Doomsday Perspective

The next time you read one of these gloom and doom Y2K scenarios, think of it this way. I tell you that the next airliner you get on is going to crash and all aboard will be killed. No question about it. The problem is that you cannot prove me wrong until you take the flight, land safely at your destination and call me to announce that I was an idiot, and that I unnecessarily worried you half to death.[3]

The doomsday perspective is in many ways the mirror opposite of the Pollyanna perspective. And just as no one in the Pollyanna crowd holds all the viewpoints that I mentioned above, so no one in the doomsday camp holds all the positions mentioned below.

Frankly, while I don't agree with the conclusions that either camp has come to, I can more easily understand the doomsday perspective. Instead of burying their heads in the sand, many doomsdayers have shown remarkable zeal in analyzing and studying this problem. To a significant extent, their activities have brought about an increased awareness of the Y2K crisis, which is very important. It is far easier to become pessimistic about Y2K after you have looked at it than to maintain a Pollyanna perspective.

But I don't think that the facts warrant extreme pessimism.

Apocalypse Now

The old line goes that some people say that the glass of water is half-full and others say that it is half-empty. Then there are some who say that the glass is half-empty, that the water is evaporating rapidly, that it contains fluorides and is full of bacteria, and that the government is going to tax the use of the glass.

Many of those in the doomsday camp take the statistics we have, extrapolate them to the worst-possible scenario, and then assume that will be the case. And I agree that if everyone stands by and does nothing, it will be The End.

The reality is that at some point every business is going to realize that there is a problem. I expect that 1999 will see a mad scramble as companies start looking to see what their problems are and try to correct them. For some, it will be too late. They will die.

But most businesses in the U.S. will figure out something or some way to keep delivering their products or services. It may not be pretty or ele-

[3]Quote from correspondence by Gary Halbert, President, ProFutures, Inc.

gant. The businesses may not be as profitable, or they might even be unprofitable in the short run, but most of them will find some way to keep things going.

American entrepreneurs have never been content to just sit around and wait for someone else to bring them a solution. And not all entrepreneurial activity is done at the small-company level. There are a lot of entrepreneurial employees at large firms. Americans in general are very creative and industrious, and we seem to do well in crisis mode.

As I said at the beginning, the division of labor is either the problem or the solution, depending upon your view of the world. It is true that we are all interdependent and that to the extent that some companies are not capable of providing services, there will be inconveniences and/ or disruptions. But the reality is that, at some point, every business is going to realize that there is a difficulty.

A large part of my quarrel with the gloom-and-doom proponents is that they assume the worst. And this means that they also assume the worst about the American worker, manager, and entrepreneur. We can all gripe and complain about various aspects of our society, but no country or system has ever produced more for its people. On an individual basis, we have all dealt with personal or business challenges just as difficult as Y2K. Admittedly, we have not all dealt with as large a problem all at the same time, but I see no reason why we will not rise to meet the challenge. There is nothing about this problem that will cause everyone to get overwhelmed and sit back and give up.

Because they assume the worst, many doomsday proponents are preparing for the worst-case outcome instead of the likely outcome.

I agree that if the electric grid, telephones, and financial system were all to go down for months or years, it would mean chaos. The current thinking of the most-respected independent analysts is that we won't lose these services for months. In most cases we are talking hours or days, if any time at all. If some of us lose our power or phones for small lengths of time, it will be much less of a problem, but a problem nonetheless. It will be inconvenient, cost us time and money, and, in a few rare cases, could contribute to serious injury or loss of life.

I think that the first few weeks of January 2000 are going to be chaotic. The way that I am going to deal with the potential chaos is to plan to go through it in a place where I want to live, rather than try to become self-sufficient in an isolated location. If I truly thought that the loss of power, telephones, and services would last for months or even years, I would move my family.

The worst effects of the Millennium Bug are going to be economic. It will cause the *Y2K Recession.* If the best place for you to be during a recession is in the country, then by all means move. But most of us will want to be where we can find jobs and provide for our families.

The doomsday approach takes our eye off the real problems. "The end of civilization as we know it" is not where we should be looking. The challenges that we need to focus on are the loss of millions of jobs in the U.S., the postponement of savings and retirement plans as the stock market crashes, a global recession, the crippling of government services, and the collapse of government budgets.

It is certain that the Y2K Crisis is going to disrupt our lives. The two questions that we have to deal with are:

1. To what extent will Y2K cause problems?
2. What actions should I take to minimize the effect of those problems?

The first parts of this book are designed to help you understand what difficulties we will probably be facing. As you will see, they are serious. You cannot ignore them and expect life to continue as always. There will be unpleasant consequences for those who do.

The second part of the book deals with what actions you can take to minimize the impact of those difficulties, especially on your business, investments, and money, because ultimately that is where the most serious economic impacts will fall.

If you prepare, I think that it will be possible for you to survive and prosper during the Y2K Recession.

Just the Facts

Until now, however, there has been little factual basis on which doomsayers and apocalyptic fear mongers could spread their gospel. After studying the potential impact of Y2K on the telecommunications industry, health care, economy, and other vital sectors of our lives, I would like to warn that we have cause for fear. For the failure to address the Millennium Bug could be catastrophic.

—Senator Patrick Moynihan, October 7, 1998

When I began seriously looking into Y2K problems in mid-1997, there was a great deal of speculation about it. Since that time much has been written about Y2K: how much will it cost, how much progress is or is not being made, which specific industries are or are not doing something about it, who is going to be ready and who isn't, and what will be the likely results of this massive effort?

There are huge web sites with links to thousands of articles, research papers, and stories about almost any Y2K topic you could care to research. I and my staff have looked at mountains of documents.

In this chapter, I am going to reproduce and comment on what I believe to be some of the more important or interesting items from among those thousands of documents. (For those who want to do research on their own, I will tell you in appendix A where to look.)

It is very important that you do not skip this chapter. This material, some of which I will comment on at length in later chapters, forms much of the basis for my conclusions about why we are facing the Y2K Recession. As you read, remember that these documents and articles are from some of the most respected research firms in the world.

My hope is that as you read this chapter, you will get a sense of urgency. I want you to understand the seriousness of what lies before us, and to realize that you need to make plans and take action—soon—to make sure that you do not have to suffer from the consequences of the Y2K Crisis.

(This chapter is divided into sections by the sources of the material. The order of the material does not reflect its importance or that of its authors. I will offer summary commentary either at the end of the chapter or in subsequent chapters.)

Software Productivity Research, Capers Jones, Chairman

Capers Jones is the dean of research on software productivity. He is the highly respected chairman and founder of Software Productivity Research, is the author of the book *The Year 2000 Software Problem: Quantifying the Costs and Assessing the Consequences,* and also has conducted a study entitled "The Economic Impact of the Year 2000 Computer Software Problem." Capers Jones probably knows more about the actual inner workings of software projects and information-technology departments than anyone in the world. He has spent decades researching the productivity of programmers. If you want data on what percentage of software projects is delivered on time, what it costs, and what it actually produces for a particular area of industry, he is the man who has the data. If there is any criticism of Jones's work or his analysis of Y2K matters, I have not been able to find it. The respect of his peers for his research is universally high.

One of the biggest problems in addressing the impact of Y2K on business and the economy is trying to figure out how much will actually get done and how much will not get done by 2000. If you ask any specific company today, its CEO will tell you that the company will be compliant and that the Y2K problem will have minimal impact on its business.

And I believe that companies really think that they will be fine. Further, I think that most of them will be. But the data from Capers Jones tell us that most software projects are not completed on time, and certainly not on budget. Here are some things gleaned from the volumes of research he has done.

The average software development firm gets rid of only 85 percent of bugs, and that percentage should hold true when eradicating Y2K bugs. With possibly 5 percent to more than 20 percent of the Year 2000 problems still unrepaired and remaining in software after the century ends, the probability of significant damages is alarmingly high.[1]

This first table highlights some of the problems businesses and governments will probably face in 2000. It goes into the implications of having bugs still in software after 2000. *It's a long list, but you need to read it. It will tell you what type of problems you will be facing.*

Let me quote directly a few selected paragraphs from this report. The

---

[1]This material by Capers Jones is from an abstract located at *http://www.year2000.com/ archive/proby2k.html.*

T A B L E   2 - 1

Year 2000 Damage Probabilities Assuming Latent Date Problems

Year 2000 Problem	Probability of Occurrence	Year 2000 Problem	Probability of Occurrence
Bad credit reports due to Year 2000 errors	70%	Reduction in stock values	20%
Cancellation of Year 2000 liability insurance	60%	Errors in 2000 tax reporting (W2 forms)	15%
Loss of local electric power (> 1 day)	55%	Errors in bank-account balances	15%
Litigation against corporate officers	55%	Disruption of stock-market trading	15%
Loss of regional electric power (> 1 day)	40%	Shutdown of pharmaceutical manufacturing	15%
Loss of international telephone services	35%	Errors in hotel/motel reservations	12%
Errors in 2000 tax reporting (1099 forms)	35%	Delays or cancellations of shipping	10%
Errors with Social-Security payments	35%	Errors in prescription dates	10%
Errors in first January paycheck	30%	Delays in UPS, FedEx deliveries	10%
Errors or delays in tax refunds	30%	Delays or cancellations of rail shipments	10%
Delays or cancellations of airline flights	25%	Urban bankruptcy due to Year 2000	7%
Loss of local telephone services	20%	Water shortages/rationing	7%
Errors with motor-vehicle records	20%	Corporate bankruptcy due to Year 2000	5%
Medical or hospital billing errors	20%	Food shortages/rationing	3%
Manufacturing shutdowns (> 1 day)	20%	Escheatment of bank accounts	2%
Process control shutdowns (> 1 day)	20%	Deaths or injuries due to Year 2000	1%

web-site location is in footnote 1 for those who would like to view the whole report.

The highest probability is that we will have bad credit reports filed against us due to year 2000 problems which make us seem to be late in payments. This problem is almost certain to occur because there are just too many credit cards and billing systems in the United States for all of them to be fixed. . . .

Another very high probability risk is that we will lose electric power for at least a day, and possibly for more than a week. Electric power plants in the United States are highly computerized and the year 2000 problem is endemic within this industry. Worse, experiments by electric companies to test out their year 2000 repairs have indicated worse problems and longer outages than anyone envisioned. These date problems are found in every form of electric generation: hydroelectric, coal, and nuclear. They are often obscure and difficult to both find and fix. . . .

In sum, there is no reason at all to assume that year 2000 defect removal efficiency levels will be any higher than the ranges for other kinds of software errors. Software quality has been a major embarrassment to the software industry for 50 years. It is naïve to think that thousands of companies who were never very good in software quality control before the year 2000 problem will suddenly achieve higher than average defect removal rates for one of the toughest software problems in history. [Emphasis added.]

Go back and read that last paragraph again. And while you are reading it, remember that this is Capers Jones making that statement. But the reality is any one of a dozen experts just as respected, just as thorough in their research, and just as thoughtful would say the same thing. I can find NO authority who disagrees with Jones's statement. Jones has gone into his mountains of data and looked at programming development and repair success levels on an industry-by-industry basis to develop the table above.

What we are going to learn, time and time again, is that much of the software responsible for almost everything we do is not going to be repaired on time. That doesn't mean that we are facing the end of the world. It doesn't mean that it won't eventually get fixed. It doesn't mean that we won't somehow figure out how to make things work while we are waiting to get things fixed. *It does mean problems, delays, cost overruns, missed shipments, and lost jobs.*

In 1997, Jones published estimates of the number of businesses subject to failure due to Y2K problems and the corresponding job losses. I visited with him over the phone briefly in late 1998. He graciously agreed to update those numbers for me based on his latest data.

These numbers (Table 2-2) are more optimistic than those of 1997

T A B L E   2 - 2 ▬▬▬▬▬▬▬▬▬▬▬▬▬▬▬▬▬▬▬▬▬▬▬▬▬▬▬

Business Size by Employees	No. of Businesses in Category	Bankruptcies	Job Loss
1	5,000,000	300,000	300,000
2–10	1,000,000	50,000	200,000
11–100	350,000	17,500	525,000
101–1,000	75,000	3,000	900,000
1,001–10,000	10,000	300	1,050,000
10,001–100,000	1,000	1	25,000
>100,000	25	0	0
Totals	**6,436,025**	**370,801**	**3,000,000**

and reflect a growing belief, shared by several other research firms, that the larger businesses in the U.S. are making good progress in their compliance efforts, but that midsize and smaller companies are lagging. The key statistic to keep in mind is the number of job losses. We will be looking in depth at this statistic and what it will mean to the economy in chapter 9.

Why will so many companies go out of business? I think that the easiest way to explain this is to relate a story from a software-engineer friend who works for a large (nine-figure) consumer-products company that sells to major retail outlets all over the country. This fall, the company is working overtime to make a software conversion from one "platform" to another. When it is finished, this company will be Y2K compliant. The company started this project several years ago.

But the project is behind schedule. The "inventory and shipping" module in the total software package is having major difficulties. Consequently, the company is not on-line with major vendors, not totally aware of how much or where its inventory is, and is having problems shipping products in time for Christmas. It has had to slow down manufacturing, because its warehouses are full. It has orders in hand that could empty the warehouses. It is having to process and ship *by hand* hundreds of thousands of items.

The company manufactures and sells hundreds of items, with dozens of "models" of each item. No one store buys more than a few items, and any given store only takes certain models. With thousands of stores, it gets very complicated to fill any order by hand, as a human being must go into a cavernous warehouse, find the products, gather them into boxes and onto pallets, and then ship them, all the while making sure he or she documents what gets shipped so that the company can bill, and thereby alert manufacturing to make some more products to replace what was shipped.

According to my friend, the company's Christmas sales are going to be down 40 percent from what they should be. Sometime late in 1998 the system was expected to be working, and things would go back to normal. But shareholders are going to get a nasty shock from fourth-quarter sales. Fortunately for the shareholders and employees, the company is financially strong enough to cope with its losses. It is likely it will lose market share, though, as its customers go to its competitors and buy products. Most will probably return, but you can bet their competitors are going to do everything they can to show the Wal-Marts and Searses of the world how well *they* can deliver and try to hold onto the business.

Many companies are not going to have the cash and credit sources to survive a 40-percent drop in sales in their most important quarter of the year. They will simply go bankrupt. In 2000, there are going to be literally thousands of companies having shipping problems. Most will cope. But a few, no matter what they do, will not be able to survive. It only takes a few midsize and small companies to add up to 3 million lost jobs. It is not so difficult to come to 3 million lost jobs when one considers the massive number of software programs which need fixing.

According to Capers Jones's 1996 analysis of over seven thousand software projects from over six hundred organizations, in the worst-managed information systems (IS) shops a project with 5000 function points (about 525,000 COBOL source-code statements) has an 85 percent probability of being late and a 40 percent probability of being completely canceled—not particularly viable options with Year 2000 projects. *Yet even in the very best-managed shops, the probability of being late is still 22 percent, with total cancellation down to 1 percent.* But even a 1 percent overall failure rate of Year 2000 projects could have profoundly negative economic consequences given that even those enterprises that solve their own Year 2000–related problems will face injury from the errors or failures of those that do not.

Commenting on these numbers, Professor Leon Kappelman, chairman of the Society for Information Management (SIM) Year 2000 Working Group wrote:

> To make matters worse, most Year 2000 projects will be many, many times that size. And IS professionals know all too well that increased size increases project risk and the likelihood of problems keeping projects on time, on budget, and as specified. According to a benchmarking study conducted by SIM during August and September 1996 and including over two hundred organizations representing most sectors of the economy, about 75 percent of Year 2000 projects will be larger than 50,000 function points in size, with nearly 20 percent exceeding 1.9 million function points. The SIM study also indicates (differences by industry, size, enterprise age, and IS management practices aside) that about two-thirds of all applications are affected, about one-third of data

files will be modified, nearly 4 percent of all source code is missing, and the cost will be about 25 percent of the annual IS operating budget, with some estimates exceeding annual budgets several times.[2]

Comment: read that statistic-filled paragraph again. Software engineers measure the size of programs in function points. Roughly, a function point is about one hundred lines of code. To give you an idea of relative size, this fairly complex word processing program that I am using is only about 5,000 function points. What Kappelman is saying is that the software programs running the computers for the largest businesses in our country are huge; 20 percent are four hundred TIMES the size of the program for the word processor I am using. And I can tell you that all the bugs are not out of this program!

When you couple Kappelman's statement with Jones's comments about an 85 percent bug-removal success rate, you can begin to get some idea of the scope of the problem. The only way to cut the problem rate is to test, find the problems, test again, find the remaining problems, test, find the problems you created, test, fix more problems, put the software into production, find the really nasty hidden problems, fix them, and so on. Normally, you do not change 10 percent of the code (as is common in Y2K fixes) in a program and throw it back into production. You do a little at a time, constantly testing to make sure that you have not created more problems than you fixed.

What we will find is that too many companies have waited too long to start the process, so that there is not going to be adequate time to test. Testing should consume 50 percent of the process. Large programs will take over a year to test. Many companies and governments simply do not have a year. Some will not even have a few months. The consequences to those companies will not be good.

In a lengthy study called "The Global Economic Impact of the Year 2000 Software Problem," Jones stated that even with sophisticated software repair tools, if a midsized company wants to be compliant, it will need to have started no later than 1997 in order to finish by 2000. If it started in 1998, it will only have 85 percent of its applications fixed, and if it starts in 1999, the percentage will only be 60 percent. I will later cite studies that show that a significant number of companies are just now starting their Y2K projects. While any one company may beat the odds and become compliant through Herculean efforts, Jones's research suggests that a significant number of them will not. It is difficult to believe that somehow all companies will succeed with their Y2K fixes when the average software-development project is months late.

[2]Year 2000 problem: Strategies and Solutions from the Fortune 100, page 74–75, available at *http://www.year2000.unt.edu*.

In Table 2-3[3] Jones provides an overview of the probable consequences for the best-case, expected-case, and worst-case scenarios. This abstract (sources in footnotes) is worth reading in its entirety. I have extracted the following list which summarizes Jones's thinking about some of the possible effects as of September 17, 1998. The major variables in these scenarios are:

1. The number of software applications in the United States with date problems;
2. The average defect-removal efficiency rate for repairing those date problems; and
3. The number of unrepaired, latent date problems that will still be present on 1/1/2000.

The best-case scenario features a reduced estimate of 10 million software applications for Year 2000 problems coupled with 95 percent defect-removal efficiency. The expected-case scenario assumes 12 million applications with date problems, coupled with 85 percent removal efficiency. The worst case assumes 15 million applications with date problems, coupled with only 75 percent removal efficiency. (Incidentally, these assumptions are for the United States. For much of the world, the worst-case scenario may not be bad enough, and removal efficiencies could even drop below 65 percent, with disastrous consequences.)

What this tells us, among other things, is that Jones realistically expects that 15 percent of the country will experience five days of power loss, that 350 cities will file for bankruptcy, and that we will see loss of telephones, transportation services, and other services. He does not expect the problems to last for long.

▬▬▬▬▬▬

GartnerGroup

The GartnerGroup is one of the largest technology research firms in the world. Its client list is a who's who of the business world. It has been making projections about the Y2K problem for several years, and is probably the most quoted authority on the problem. I found 127 references to GartnerGroup on one Y2K site alone. I am going to cite some of the quotes and discuss at length the U.S. Senate testimony of GartnerGroup executive Lou Marcoccio. (The italic highlights are my additions.) Here is the first quote:

> Worldwide costs are estimated between $300 billion and $600 billion, according to the GartnerGroup, an information technol-

[3]From an abstract titled "The Aftermath of the Year 2000 Software Problem," dated September 17, 1998. Software Productivity Research, Inc. an Artemis Company, 1 New England Executive Park, Burlington, MA 01803-5005

T A B L E   2 - 3

Year 2000 Recovery Scenarios for the United States

	Best Case	Expected Case	Worst Case
Software applications	10,000,000	12,000,000	15,000,000
Removal efficiency	95.00%	85.00%	75.00%
Unrepaired dates	500,000	1,800,000	3,750,000
Months to repair	3.00	6.00	18.00
Final repair date	April 1, 2000	July 1, 2000	July 1, 2001
Number of lawsuits	47,500	171,000	356,250
Cost per lawsuit	$526,316	$584,795	$842,105
Software damages	$23,215,125,000	$116,075,625,000	$ 348,226,875,000
Software recovery	$42,175,312,500	$281,168,750,000	$ 702,921,875,000
Litigation costs	$25,000,000,000	$100,000,000,000	$ 300,000,000,000
Post-2000 Total	$90,390,437,500	$497,244,375,000	$1,351,148,750,000
Cost per capita	$322.82	$1,775.87	$4,825.53
Power failure (days)	3	5	15
Power failure (%)	5.00%	15.00%	75.00%
Transport failure (days)	3	7	15
Transport failure (%)	5.00%	12.00%	50.00%
Telephone failure (days)	1	3	12
Telephone failure (%)	5.00%	15.00%	65.00%
City bankruptcies	35	350	963

ogy consulting firm. And that's just for correcting the software. The costs jump to trillions when delays in business operations, hardware and litigation expenses are factored in. GartnerGroup estimates that worldwide, 30 percent of companies have not even addressed the problem. The Office of Management and Budget's estimate for fixing federal government computers is $4.7 billion. Estimates for correcting state government computer systems, compiled by NASIRE, range from $1.5 million to more than $250 million per state.

Fifty-five percent of government enterprises will not be ready when the calendar hits 2000 and it could have political ramifications for lawmakers, say members of the GartnerGroup. The 2000 dilemma has such serious consequences that it could unseat politicians who don't demonstrate effective leadership, warns Jim Cassell, a Gartner vice president. Because the public is very much aware of the problem, Cassell predicts that leaders who don't try to resolve the issue "during their watch" will be held responsible.[4]

And here is the second:

> *One shocking conclusion Marcoccio reached, especially given that companies have tended to be unduly optimistic in their projections, was that fully half of those surveyed won't perform a lick of Y2K testing.* Their day of reckoning will arrive and they won't know what will happen. It's a circumstance that Marcoccio compared to developing a software application and shipping it to customers without doing any quality assurance work.[5]

The GartnerGroup warned this week that 80 percent of companies predicting millennium compliance by the end of this year will fall short by at least three months because of unrealistic planning.

The risk, warns Gartner and analyst Andy Kyte, is that companies will not adequately budget for the ongoing requirements if they believe the project will be completed by the end of this year.

"When we question Year 2000 program managers about their deadlines, it is clear that most of them recognize already that they have no realistic possibility of delivering to their current end date," warned Kyte.

"However, they appear able to suspend their logical and critical faculties when reporting program status, maybe either through fear of the anger that a more realistic date might bring, or in the blind hope that a miracle might occur," he added.

Such a policy only ends up disappointing users by failing to achieve compliance by the deadline, and forcing difficult reassigning of resources. Year 2000 program managers should review projects, ideally with an external agency, and communicate costs and dates to all parts of the business.

"Delaying the pain associated with bad news nearly always results in an increased level of pain," said Kyte.

European governments are failing to protect their citizens against fallout from the millennium computer bomb, and the consequences of their inaction are likely to start at the end of this year in hospitals and welfare systems, a conference was told yesterday.

"European governments and public sector organizations have only spent between 5 and 10 percent of what it needs to fix their

---

[4]From a web site of the National Conference of State Legislatures: *http://www.ncsl.org/programs/lis/y2k/Resources.htm#count* referencing an article from *State Legislatures Magazine,* May, 1998, "Countdown to 2000" by Joanne Bourguard.

[5]*Wired News,* "All Is Not A-OK on Y2K" by Pete Danka (8/5/98).

systems," Andy Kyte told a press briefing. "The public sector is the biggest danger here. They're not doing the work at all," he told Reuters.

"The millennium computer problem is going to start manifesting itself as we cross into 1999. There will also be clusters of problems at key dates like the end of the first quarter," another Gartner analyst, Matthew Hotle, told the briefing.

Kyte said that European governments were saying plenty but doing little. "The federal government in the U.S. has not done a great job either, but at least it has been open about it," he said.[6]

One of the best assessments of potential Y2K costs is contained in senate testimony by Lou Marcoccio, director of Y2K research at the GartnerGroup.[7] Gartner did a survey of fifteen thousand companies in eighty-seven countries. Although we are going to look at the implications of this report in detail in later chapters, a few of the facts gleaned from it deserve to be highlighted here. This report is dated October 7, 1998.

> Twenty-three percent of all companies and government agencies have not started any Year 2000 effort. 83% of these are small companies with fewer than 2000 employees. . . .
>
> In April 1997, 50% of companies, across all industries, had not started Year 2000 efforts. By November 1997, the number dropped to 30%. By October 1, 1998, 23% of companies throughout the world had not started. 83% of those are small companies. *We predict that in January 2000, nearly 20% will still not be started, and they will mostly be small companies and companies in lagging countries (0.8 probability). . . . [Emphasis added.]*
>
> Thirty to fifty percent of companies and government agencies worldwide will experience at least one mission critical system failure (includes all sizes, all industries, all countries) through Q1 2000. In the U.S., 15% of companies and government agencies will experience a mission critical system failure (also see section on country status for status of U.S. versus all other countries). 10% of failures will last 3 days or longer. The cost of recovering from a single failure after it occurs will range from US $20,000–$3.5 million. . . .
>
> Sixty-five percent of U.S. cities and towns do not have Year

---

[6]From the VNU web site. An article entitled "Bad Planning Means Most Companies Will Slip Y2K Deadlines" by Jonathon Lambeth. VNU is a large publisher of business publications. *http://webserv.vnunet.com/www_user/plsql/pkg_vnu_news.right_frame ?p_story = 59943*

[7]*http: // gartner3.gartnerweb.com / public / static / aboutgg / pressrel / testimony1098.html#top.* Testimony of GartnerGroup's Lou Marcoccio to the Senate Special Committee on the Year 2000 Technology Problem, 10/7/98.

2000 projects. Many midsize and smaller cities and towns are lagging far behind or have not started.

Marcoccio divides the eighty-seven countries into four categories, with 1 being the best and 4 the worst. Over half the world's population lives in Status 4 countries. Japan, Germany, and Argentina are in Status Group 3. Status 3 countries will see significant disruptions in power, air transportation, and government services, among many other problems. A significant portion of our exports go to Status 3 and 4 countries.

The U.S. is in Status Group 1. Most readers, having looked at Jones's estimates of U.S. problems, would rate his projections as serious for the U.S. In later chapters, we will look in detail at what Gartner expects for other countries.

Here is an excerpt from an article in the *Ottawa Citizen*. Marcoccio is quoted as stating:

> "The largest risk for Canada is what is happening in other countries that don't have time to get their systems fixed before 2000," said Lou Marcoccio, director of Y2K research at the GartnerGroup, the leading firm tracking the world's Year 2000 preparedness.
>
> "We're going to have bank unrest, power and telecommunications failures happening in about 20 countries that will affect the rest of the world in the long term. We're going to have major inflation, the cost of goods rise and shortages of key resources." But he warns the Canadian economy will feel the rippling effects of a global recession that will be created by the computer failures of other countries who are months, if not years, behind Canada, in repairing their systems.
>
> He expects major problems from Russia and China, along with many nations in Latin America, Central Africa, and Southeast Asia. These problems could fuel a global recession that lasts four to six years.
>
> "Countries already plagued with financial woes, sharp increases in inflation, limited monetary reserves and high unemployment are some of the same countries farthest behind on Year 2000 compliance," Mr. Marcoccio wrote in a recent report.

Incidentally, the article also says that the Canadian military has been ordered to plan for the worst—the preparations have been dubbed Operation Abacus—with troops and frigates ready to be deployed across the country to provide emergency services should computer foul-ups in 2000 create civil chaos.[8]

---

[8]From "Year 2000 Bug Can Bite Canada Across Borders" by Kathryn May, *Ottawa Citizen*, 10/29/98, *http://www.ottawacitizen.com/national/981029/1973780.html.*

Ed Yourdon

Ed Yourdon is the author of two dozen books on programming. He is coauthor (with his daughter, Jennifer) of a book on the Y2K problem, *Time Bomb 2000.* This is an excellent book, and I recommend it for those interested in a programmer's perspective on the problem. There are few men in the world who can claim to know as much about programming as Yourdon. He has been warning the world of the Y2K problem for years. The following quotations are from an article posted on the Internet from October 13, 1997. I could summarize his words, but they have a great deal more force coming from him. I have found that this line of thinking is quite prevalent among the speakers (and therefore presumably knowledgable Y2K experts) at the numerous Y2K conferences I have attended.

The issue of project management is one that has been mentioned in various writings about Y2000, but it's often glossed over or dismissed—and yet it's the primary basis of my technical concerns about the risk of Y2000 projects all over the world. Here it is, in a nutshell: the software industry has accumulated metrics from tens of thousands of projects (that's a literal number, not hyperbole) over the past 30–40 years, which tell us, statistically, that approximately 15% of all software projects are delayed (behind schedule), and approximately 25% are canceled before completion.

Statistics like this have been gathered and published over a long period of time, by well-respected software metrics professionals, long before Y2000 was on anyone's radar screen. One of the sources of information in this area is "Patterns of Software Systems Failure and Success," by Capers Jones (International Thomson Press, 1996—and probably available from Capers's web site at www.spr.com). But if you don't like the numbers from Capers, you can find almost identical numbers from the research carried out by Dr. Howard Rubin (head of the Computer Science Department at Hunter College in NYC, author of several worldwide software benchmarking metrics studies, and developer of the highly regarded ESTIMACS software-estimating product now marketed by Computer Associates) or Larry Putnam's company, Quantitative Software Management (Larry has also been in the software industry for 30 years, and is the coauthor of a book called *Measures for Success: Delivering Software On Time, Within Budget* [Prentice-Hall, 1992]). The Standish Group, the GartnerGroup, the GAO, *Scientific American*, and several other reputable sources have confirmed that our track record for delivering software on time is lousy, and has been for a long, long time.

The situation is substantially worse for large projects. In the Capers Jones book referenced above, approx. 24% of all 10,000 function-point (FP) projects are finished behind schedule, and approx. 48% are canceled. For 100,000 FP projects, approx. 21% are behind schedule, and approx. 65% are canceled. If you're not familiar with function points: 1 FP is approx. equal to 100 COBOL statements; you can do the rest of the arithmetic. The point is that many of the large, mission-critical legacy systems that are the subject of Y2000 remediation fall into this category.

A related issue: just how late are the projects that are "delayed"? *It turns out that the experience of the software industry, over the last 30–40 years, is that the average software project is approximately 6–7 months late* [emphasis added]. Again, the situation is much worse on the big projects: the 10,000 FP projects, according to the Capers Jones statistics, are an average of 13.8 months behind schedule, and the 100,000 FP projects are an average of 25.8 months behind schedule. Note that this doesn't include the projects that were canceled!

And later on Yourdon says:

What's taking place on almost all Y2000 projects is NOT estimating, but rather a form of "backwards wishful thinking." It starts as follows: everyone knows what the "ultimate" deadline is for Y2000—we can't negotiate or ignore that fact. Indeed, most organizations have arbitrarily decreed that their Y2000 projects WILL, by golly, be finished on Dec 31, 1998. Not because anyone did any project-level estimating, or planning with Pert charts and Gantt charts, but simply because that's when management has decreed that things will be done. So if that's the deadline, then a rational project manager has to work backwards, leading to a train of thought that says, "If we have to be done by 12/31/98, that means we have to start testing by 12/31/97, which means that we have to be done with all of the planning and analysis by 6/30/97 . . . whoops! Omygosh, we're already 3 months behind schedule. Well, we'll make it up somehow by working very hard and convincing ourselves that we're not going to make any mistakes!" This is NOT a new phenomenon: we've been doing it for 30 years, every time management imposes an arbitrary deadline on project managers, because nobody has the guts to stand up and say, "Hell no!"

If you want to see a mind-boggling example of backwards wishful thinking, take a look at the published plans for Y2000 projects by the major Federal government agencies; I believe it's still available at *www.cio.fed.gov/ y2krev.htm*. Note how many of them have an arbitrarily decreed deadline of 12/31/98 for finishing their work. Note also that the publicly stated schedule says, among other things, that 12 of the agencies are planning to devote either ZERO months, or ONE month, for the testing of all the Y2000 remediation work they've done on their schedule. And as I assume you've heard, four of the agencies were recently given "flunking" grades by Congressman Stephen Horn (a former university president, which may or may not be relevant) because they're so far behind schedule on the planning and assessment phase of their work, which is estimated by most Y2000 experts to represent approx. 5% of the overall task. The typical reaction to such criticism: "Oh, well, we'll catch up by working harder, and we won't make any mistakes, which is why we can get away with so little testing." Maybe so, but such a statement contradicts the cumulative evidence of 30–40 years of work in the software field. Privately and off-the-record, the project managers (who get all the heat and the pressure from high-level managers when unpleasant news like this is made known) mutter to themselves, "We'll fudge the numbers on the next progress report, so that we can get these idiots off our back, and get some work done." This is not a new phenomenon; this is what's been happening to large software projects since I got into the field, and probably long before that. And there is good reason to believe (based on first-hand reports from such project managers, which I'm not allowed to describe in detail because of non-disclosure agreements I've signed) that there are several of these situations underway in the government right now. Hence my conclusion: all of the available evidence strongly suggests that we're not going to finish our Y2000 projects. We'll certainly get 50% of them done, probably 80%, possibly 90%— but nowhere near 100%. Sure, some organizations will finish 100% of their systems (indeed, a few organizations have been Y2000 compliant all along); but some won't finish ANY of their Y2000 work, because they haven't heard about it yet, or because they haven't gotten around to funding and staffing it yet. To ignore the significant likelihood that 10% or 20% or more of the mission-critical Y2000 projects in this country won't be finished is irresponsible, in my opinion, not to mention imprudent. On a national level: sooner or later (probably later) someone at a high level is going to have to confront the significant likelihood that 900 or 1000 or more of the government's mission-critical systems will not be remediated in time. Unpleasant news, to be sure, but to ignore it is something I'm not willing to do.[9]

[9]http://www.garynorth.com/y2k/detail_.cfm/540.

The National Federation of Independent Business

William Dennis, Jr., of the National Federation of Independent Business did a very comprehensive and lengthy study on the awareness and impact of the Y2K problem on small business. I will give some of the more interesting facts and conclusions.

1. Eighty-two percent of small business (over 4,750,000) are directly exposed to the Y2K problem, yet just 41 percent have taken action or plan to take action.
2. Only one-quarter of the group that believes that its sales or production would be down by 71 percent or more if its systems malfunction have taken action, although another 40 percent plan it. But the numbers do suggest that far from all who depend significantly on their computers and automated systems are convinced that Y2K is worth addressing.
3. Eighty-one percent of small business owners have updated their most-critical software in the last two years.
4. Seventy-five percent of small businesses with a computer deal electronically with important business partners.
5. Eight percent of employers are "not very aware" and 10 percent are "not at all aware." That means more than 1 million employers have limited or no awareness of Y2K.
6. Only 41 percent plan to check out the Y2K preparedness of their key vendors.

Finally, quoting directly from the study,

7. *"Conclusion: even if all those planning to take action follow through and another million (about one in five of the exposed population) eventually make plans and carry out preventive measures, over 1 million small, employing businesses will be directly exposed to the Y2K problem without having taken any precautions."* [Emphasis added.]

In a story by the *Los Angeles Times*,[10] the NFIB is quoted as having a worst-case scenario of as many as 330,000 failures among small businesses.

Forrester Research

Y2K program office managers and CIOs are in denial. Why? Forrester Research, a Cambridge, Mass., technology research firm, believes that large

---

[10]*Los Angeles Times*, September 18, 1998.

companies have underestimated the impact of Y2K assessment, repair, and testing work by a factor of 25 percent (see Graph 2-1 below). This means that when they make their estimates of how much work they must do in order to be ready, they will be 25 percent short in needed manpower, money, and time. So, instead of being nearly done, large companies are on average only 68 percent through the job as of January 1999.

This point is crucial. It should reinforce what the rest of this chapter is telling you. The experts tells us that software is not delivered on time. Forrester tells us that one of the reasons is that project managers underestimate the amount of time that it takes to complete a project.

This is not just a problem in computer-systems development. It is part of the human condition. I bet that if someone did a study on book writers and when they promised that a book would be ready and when it actually was delivered, the results might look something like the numbers for software development. Whatever industry you are in, whatever you do, you will find that humans are optimists about deadlines and how much work they can do. But what happens is that additional, unforeseen new problems crop up that push schedules back.

We should mention one more item from Forrester Research. The im-

GRAPH 2-1

Projected Year 2000 Progress

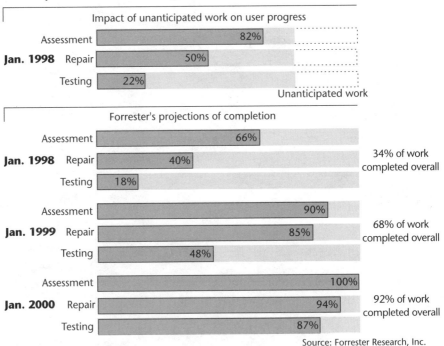

Source: Forrester Research, Inc.

pact on large businesses could even be greater than anticipated by Capers Jones. George Colony of Forrester Research gave a speech that divided the Fortune 1000 into three groups:

"A" companies will fix their critical computing systems in time. They will thrive because of Y2K. This category accounts for 35 percent of the Fortune 1000.

"B" companies will experience failures of some of their critical computing systems. Most, but not all, will manage to survive Y2K. Fifty percent of the Fortune 1000 will fall into this group.

"C" companies will not repair their critical computers in time. Most will fail. Fifteen percent of the Fortune 1000 will end up in this trash heap.

Dr. Ed Yardeni

Dr. Yardeni is the chief economist of Deutsche Bank and one of the most widely respected economists on Wall Street. He was an early predictor of the latest bull market and has had an enviable track record of making correct predictions. He is also one of the few major Wall Street figures addressing the Y2K problem and its consequences. He has written a great deal on the topic, and as of this writing allows a 70 percent chance of a Year 2000 Recession, although I am told by numerous sources that privately he feels it is much closer to 100 percent. He has been raising the likelihood of a recession over the year from a low of 30 percent to the current 70 percent, and I would suspect that that number will continue to rise. Most Wall Street analysts choose to consciously ignore Y2K, as the prospective consequences to their firms of predicting a bear market are not pleasant. Yardeni is to be highly commended for his courage and leadership on this issue. I quote some of his thoughts from his web site and articles at *www.yardeni.com.*

> In a Y2K scenario, corporate earnings are likely to fall dramatically, but so are interest rates on U.S. Treasury securities. I expect that both the federal funds rate and the 30-year Treasury yield could fall to 3% in 2000. For the stock market, the drop in rates should offset some, but not all of the bad news on earnings. I expect that stock prices could fall at least 30%. I am not sure when investors will start to discount Y2K in stock prices, but it will be by the summer of 1999. . . .
>
> The Year 2000 Problem (Y2K) is a very serious threat to the U.S. economy. Indeed, it is bound to disrupt the entire global economy. If the disruptions are significant and widespread, then a global recession is likely. Currently, I believe there is a 70% chance of such a worldwide recession, which could last at least 12 months

starting in January 2000 and could be at least as severe as the 1973–74 global recession. . . .

The recession could begin before January 1, 2000, perhaps during the second half of 1999, if the public becomes alarmed and takes precautions. If stock prices fall sharply in 1999, in anticipation of a recession in 2000, the resulting loss in confidence could cause consumers to retrench in 1999 and trigger a recession sooner as well. It could start in 1999 if bankers cause a credit crunch by refusing to lend to companies that are most at risk of failing in 2000. If these companies are not bailed out by their key vendors or customers, they might start failing during 1999. . . .

In the United States, real GDP dropped 3.7% from peak to trough during 1973–74. I estimate that an identical drop, starting in 2000, would reduce real GDP by $300 billion, back to where it was in early 1998, or three years prior to the end of 2000.

Is this too pessimistic, or realistic? Actually, in my opinion, it might be too optimistic to believe that the information gridlock won't be even more damaging, sending us further back in time, when the level of GDP that our information systems supported was even lower. Therefore, I predict that, in the United States, real GDP could fall 5% from peak to trough over a 12–24 month period starting late in 1999.

If a Y2K recession is coming, it will be deflationary, unlike the 1973–74 recession, in which many prices and wages increased sharply, led by soaring oil prices. Economists labeled the subsequent period of slow growth and high inflation "stagflation." With inflation rates falling close to zero in most industrial nations, a 2000 recession could easily push us over the edge into deflation.[11]

Other Voices

Cap Gemini (CG is one of the world's largest software development companies):

Services supplier Cap Gemini America is tracking the Y2K progress of 127 public and private sector organizations and last week announced *90 percent had missed deadlines* [emphasis added],

[11]Dr. Yardeni maintains a web site on Y2K at *www.Yardeni.com,* along with a large database of economic statistics. He has been one of the seminal thinkers on Y2K and the economy. I highly recommend his work and writings. If you are researching the Y2K status of larger companies, his web site is the place to start. He frequently writes on the larger economic and structural implications of Y2K, and I consider his "web-book" on Y2K essential reading if you want to understand the broader issues surrounding Y2K.

up from 78 percent in April. Forty-four percent of respondents have experienced 2000-related failures in the form of processing disruptions or financial miscalculations. In April, only 40 percent reported such failures.[12]

IBM:

> Many published reports point to concerns about the readiness of small businesses for the Year 2000. The GartnerGroup and others are often quoted as saying small businesses are lagging behind. *Our own contact with customers suggests that so far only about 25% of small businesses worldwide are moving to deal with the issue* [emphasis added]. When we speak to small business owners, there is a surprising lack of urgency. Some think they are ready, some think they have plenty of time, and some feel the issue is all hype and they will not be affected. Others have realized the importance of being prepared and are taking action. We have learned a lot from the experiences of those who have moved to deal with the issue.[13]

The Software Engineering Institute at Carnegie Mellon University in Pittsburgh estimates that *67 percent of organizations have no formal Y2K testing program in place.* Even the praiseworthy 33 percent are finding Y2K testing to be knottier and more problematic than anything they've done before. "Dates are just so all-encompassing that when you start messing with them, every aspect of the system—and all the interrelationships between systems—needs [sic] to be tested," says Albert Kern, an assistant vice president and the Y2K project leader at Boston's Commercial Union Insurance.[14]

Dr. Howard A. Rubin, a professor of computer science at Hunter College in New York, has said that "over the next three years five hundred thousand to seven hundred thousand additional programmers will need to go to work in the United States alone to handle date-conversion." His numbers are based on a study conducted by himself. "There should have been a code conversion event at the Olympics because we're going to have to start setting new records," he said.[15]

At a Y2K conference in April 1998 I did an informal survey of approximately twenty companies exhibiting at the conference. These were companies that sold software solutions or services for Y2K problems. My

---

[12]*The Financial Review of Australia,* November 3, 1998: *http://www.afr.com.au/content/981103/inform/inform7.html.*

[13]Congressional testimony of Debra W. Taufen, manager, Global Small and Medium Business Initiatives, International Business Machines *http://www.house.gov/smbiz/leg/hearings/hearing_11/taufen.html,* July 15, 1998.

[14]"Test Patterns" by Scott Kirsner, from *CIO Magazine,* March 1, 1998. From the web site of CIO, Chief Information Officer: *http://www.cio.com/archive/030198_y2k_content.html.*

[15]*Washington Post,* March 2, 1997 in an article entitled "Old Programmers May Fix Future."

presupposition was that because they deal with hundreds of companies on an intimate basis, they are in a position to have a realistic idea as to what is really happening. And while one company might have a bias as to the particular types of companies that they service, I thought that a survey of the entire group would yield some insight. I asked three questions:

A. What percentage of the mission-critical software of the Fortune 1000 companies will be ready by January 2000?
B. What percentage of the mission-critical software of all U.S. companies will be ready by January 2000?
C. What percentage of the mission-critical software of government entities will be ready by January 2000?

The average answers were: A. 90 percent, B. 75 percent, C. 40 percent.

It is interesting to note that even though most of the people I questioned acknowledged the lateness of large corporations getting into action (confirmed in the Triaxsys study), they expected most large corporations to be 90 percent ready. These are the people who are actually doing the work for these corporations.

The scary part is that they think that only 40 percent of government software will be ready. Most of the people whom I interviewed rolled their eyes when asked about government preparedness. Pulling the number up to 40 percent was a significant number of people who said 50 percent, but were clearly trying to be generous or hopeful. The numbers from those whom I could tell actually did work with governments were lower than 40 percent.

I conducted the same survey in early July and in September at another conference. The overall numbers from the exhibitors were slightly lower, but the expectations from the software companies that deal with the largest companies were slightly higher or more optimistic. I conclude that the above numbers are still a reasonable measure of sentiment among Y2K-software vendors.

At the April conference, one speaker questioned an audience containing some 350 people representing a wide variety of companies. Over 80 percent raised their hands when asked if they were either beginning their Y2K program or in the assessment phase. Of course, you would expect a larger-than-normal number at a conference of this type, which attracted a significant number of companies beginning the process, but 80 percent was a little unnerving, even for the speaker. Only a few people, less than five that I could see, raised their hands when asked if they were in the testing phase.

There are three basic phases to achieving Y2K compliance: assessment, conversion/remediation (actually changing the code), and testing. According to experts, testing should be allotted the most time, but clearly there are going to be a number of programs put back into service without adequate testing time.

National banks worldwide are printing extra money

The Bank of Canada plans to print extra banknotes in the coming year, anticipating a run on cash by people living in fear of the Year 2000 computer bug. A number of banks are expecting that nervous customers will sock away more bills than usual as 2000 approaches. As a result, the central bank is working with financial institutions to determine exactly how much extra money it will need to print. Here are some excerpts from a *Globe and Mail* article:

> "I think people might think it is prudent to hold a bit more cash," a Bank of Canada spokesman said. "We are, as other central banks, looking ahead and saying there could be some additional demands as Y2K [the year 2000] approaches. . . ."
>
> The Bank of Canada is not alone in its decision to print more money. In a report published this month, the Bank of England said it will run off extra cash in the run-up to January 2000.
>
> And in New Zealand, the Reserve Bank said it will keep old bank notes—which are due to be replaced next year by flexible plastic ones—in vaults instead of destroying them to ensure there will be enough cash available to its customers into 2000.
>
> As well, the U.S. Federal Reserve Board announced last month it will have an extra $50 billion in cash on hand, just in case there is a run on money. The Fed usually keeps $150 billion in currency in reserve within government vaults. However, it plans to raise the amount it keeps in reserve to $200 billion over the next year.[16]

"Why Can't They Just Do . . . ?"

The following is from the Y2K Newswire web site and is one of the best explanations in simple terms that I have read for just one aspect of why fixing the code is so difficult. It is longer than some of the other quotes in this chapter, but I think that it will help you understand the nature of the programming problem. Remember, there are answers just like this for almost every question that begins, "Why can't they just do . . . ?"

[16]*The Globe and Mail,* November 2, 1998, at *http://www.theglobeandmail.com/docs/news/19981102/GlobeFront/UBANKN.html.*

WHY CAN'T WE JUST ROLL THE CLOCKS BACK?

Perhaps the most frequently asked question we receive at Y2K NEWSWIRE.COM is, "Why can't we all just roll the clocks back on the mainframes?"

This is a reasonable question. Lots of people ask it. There are perhaps a hundred reasons why you can't do this, though, and we'll cover a few here.

First, realize that if this were the solution, and if it were this simple, companies wouldn't be spending hundreds of billions of dollars fixing the bug. So right off the bat, you know there must be a reason why this won't work.

To suppose that we could roll the clocks back to 1999 and re-live 1999 all over again means that we would essentially lose the meaning of time. After all, the four digits representing the year are not just there for fun: they "represent" something. They represent the real-world calendar. Now, if you just go tweaking the years in the mainframes, changing them at random, you essentially lose all relevancy with the years. If a record comes up in the database saying 1999, how does anybody know whether it means the first 1999 or the second, repeated 1999?

That, essentially, is the problem. The years stand for something, and you can't just roll them back.

Here are some specific examples of this. Suppose you're a lonely banking computer and your job is to calculate interest payments. You come across a record that says the loan originated on January 1, 1999. But how would you know "which" 1999 they were talking about? You wouldn't, and thus all date-sensitive calculations would be rendered useless. In this way, this "solution" creates new problems.

But there are many more reasons why the rollback won't work. For one, the days of the week are different in 1999 than 2000. So if you have a day of the week calculation, based on whether it's Monday, Tuesday, and so on, it won't work if you have a "fake" 1999.

Another reason is that even if you fix the problem once, you can't keep rolling the clocks back to 1999 forever. Sooner or later, you'll have to agree to go to 2000. And when that happens, everybody would have to code some kind of software patch that would count 1999 multiple times, depending on how many times the year was repeated. In other words, you'd be doing math, saying, "What is 2001 minus 1999?" The correct answer might actually be FIVE, depending on how many times you rolled everything back to 1999. And obviously, "five" is the wrong answer from a mathematical point of view, so you'd have to reprogram all the computers to make an exception for this year. Now, come to think of it, THAT job is harder than reprogramming the computers to simply work with 2000!

Another reason the one-year rollback idea won't work is that some companies are going to make it to 2000. These companies will never agree to throw away all their renovation efforts just to save the companies that started too late. Y2K has become a competitive issue. The companies that succeed in fixing the problem would frankly rather see their competition go out of business. Why save the companies that procrastinated?

And yet another reason (like we said, there are probably a hundred) is that embedded systems have no rollback feature. Their clocks are hard-coded. You simply can't go in and change them.

Finally, there's the whole idea of getting everybody to agree with the rollback. From a political point of view, it would be impossible. You simply can't get the whole world to agree on something like that without a LOT of effort and a powerful leader who can kick everybody else into action.

VARIATIONS ON THE ROLLBACK IDEA

There are plenty of other variations on this idea. Some people ask, "Why can't we just roll the clocks to 2100?" Okay, that one should be obvious. 2100 also has two zeroes just like 2000. Other people have said, "Why don't we just have a 1999A and a 1999B?" That is essentially the same as the 1999 rollback idea mentioned above.

Yet other people suggest we roll the clocks back to 1900. Again, this ends with two zeroes. And one person even suggested we just start over with the year "1." Neat idea, but it won't work either. The programming required to tell computers how to interpret the year "1" is even more than the programming required to tell computers how to recognize "2000."

In every case, time after time, the suggestions on fixing this that come from the general public—while certainly put forth out of genuine concern—would actually result in more code repair than what's required for the regular 2000 fix. Remember, the problem we're talking about here has a relatively simple concept: we just need our computers to work with four-digit years rather than two-digit years. See, the problem is NOT the actual four digits it's dealing with. The problem, essentially, is that the computers aren't dealing with four digits at all. That's why the suggestions of 2100, 2200, and so on just don't cut it.

THERE IS NO MAGIC BULLET

Many people have theorized that at some point, some genius is going to come up with some brilliant idea that will solve all the

Y2K problems. This just "ain't gonna happen," folks. There is no magic bullet unless God himself wants to get involved and magically repair all the code. You know why there is no magic bullet? Because we're not talking about one computer language here. We're talking about "hundreds." And we're talking about hardcoded systems (embedded systems) with hard-coded clocks that must be entirely replaced. They simply can't be reprogrammed.

There are "workaround" schemes that have been devised to work with two-digit dates, of course. One such scheme is called "pivot dates" or "date windowing." It assumes that any two-digit year under, say, "50" must mean it's in the 2000 range. And any number greater than "50" must be in the 1900 range. So if you take the year 02 and subtract 98, you get four because you're actually taking 2002 minus 1998, and that's four.

But this solution is a stopgap measure at best, and it doesn't comply with the new date formats that have been suggested. Oh yes, that's one more angle to this problem. Did you know there is no globally–agreed upon date format? You might think it should be mm/dd/yyyy right? Well, that isn't so. Since the current format in the United States is mm/dd/yy and now they're trying to add a century to it, some people are putting the century at the front, like this: cc/mm/dd/yy. So January 1, 2000, would look like this:

20/01/01/00

But other people are putting it near the end, using: mm/dd/ccyy, like this:

01/01/2000

But Europe does things a little differently. Even in 1998, they put the day first. For example, October 5, 1998, would look like:

05/10/98

Where, in America, it would look like:

10/05/98

Now, when you get the two combinations of the century placement and combine them with the two combinations of possible century placements, here are the four possibilities you get for new, Y2K-compliant dates representing October 5, 2000:

20/10/05/00
20/05/10/00
10/05/2000
05/10/2000

These four different formats represent the same date, see?

Now here's part of the problem: when these computers start EXCHANGING this data, the receiving computer might think it represents May 10, 2000 instead of October 5, 2000.

You might even get a computer trying to read the century date in the wrong place. It might see 20/10/05/00 and think it is really the 10th day of the 20th month of the year 2005. But there IS no 20th month, right? So the computer generates an error, maybe even stops the execution of the routine.

THIS IS THE NITTY GRITTY OF IT

Even if you don't have a programming background, you can hopefully begin to see some of the complexity of what's being faced here. You can also realize one IMPORTANT point that is hardly being talked about these days: the compliance of the "data exchanges." See, it's not enough for your own computer system to be compliant. Your computers have to exchange data with the supplier's computers, with the government's computer, and perhaps with customer's computers. And here we are at the end of 1998, and while the NIST has put forth a "standard" on the new date format, some companies are not following that standard. So we are going to have computers talking to each other but speaking different date languages. One computer is going to say, "Why does this other computer keep sending me data about the 20th month? There is no 20th month!" . . . and it's going to reject all that data.

Rejected data is no good. That computer might as well not operate at all.[17]

In Summary

I could spend the rest of this book quoting articles like the ones above. Every day more information comes out, and I am sure that we will see an avalanche of information as 2000 approaches.

But the point is very clear. No matter what anyone says, there is going to be a lot of software not fixed on January 1, 2000. It is not a matter of desire, or even of money. It is just that writing and fixing software are very difficult things to do. They are time-consuming processes. For companies that started late, it is likely that their software will not all be ready in time. The critical issue for many companies in 1999 is going to be

---

[17]The e-mail letter of November 5, 1998 from *www.y2knewswire.com*. They have a (mostly) daily service that comments on various news items about Y2K. They are more pessimistic than I am, but the editor (who is anonymous) does find some very interesting items.

how to survive in 2000 while their systems are being fixed. It is called *contingency planning.*

A well-known consultant has numerous international (non-U.S.) banks as clients. Many are late coming to the remediation process. His advice to them is to start figuring out how to survive on limited computer systems. The process is called *triage,* just like the process in hospital emergency rooms. The goal is to keep the patient alive until the doctors can fix the problem.

Many businesses are going to be in triage mode in 2000. Some will only be there for a day or two, but for some it will be months. And sadly, for some, all the emergency efforts will be for naught. They will fail.

At this point, I should tell you that even after reading what you have read (and countless articles more), *I remain an optimist today.* While I believe that there is very little chance for our nation to avoid a serious recession, we must keep in mind that *this is just a recession.* It is not the end of the world, nor does it have to be a depression.

We have survived recessions before and will do so this time. The Y2K dilemma may not even be the largest problem that we face during this upcoming generation. For example, the looming Medicare and Social Security crisis has the potential to create a debt scenario that will make our previous budget problems seem minuscule in comparison.

The advantage to this being an event-driven recession is that unlike most recessions, this one is coming with some advance notice. Therefore, individuals can do more to protect themselves now and to mitigate the effects on their lives. And, as I will discuss in later chapters, there are ways to make a profit from a recession and a falling stock market.

In the next six chapters, we are going to look at the most important sectors of our economy: power, telecommunications, banking and finance, government, businesses, and the international situation.

There are actually some areas about which we can be optimistic, as we will see. There are others that are quite grim. But before we can begin to look at the economic effects of the Y2K Crisis on our lives, we need to know what is happening in each of these sectors. And then we can begin to make informed decisions about what we can and must do.

3

"The Night the Lights Went Out in Georgia"

To give us some perspective, let's look at a few quotes from my files about the electric-power industry:

According to Senator Bob Bennett, chairman of the Senate Special Committee on the Year 2000 Technology Problem, only 20 percent of utilities had even finished their assessments by early 1998. None had developed a "Y2K plan." Consequently Bennett rates chance of a total blackout at 40 percent.[1]

Democratic Senator Chris Dodd, cochairman of the Senate Y2K Committee with Senator Bennett says: "Outages are inevitable, the question is how long? How widespread? No one knows."

GartnerGroup: "One-third of utilities [has] barely begun Y2K work."

Dr. Ed Yardeni: "Plans for rationing utility should be prepared."

CIA: "We're concerned about a disruption of the power grid, telecommunications, and banking."

San Jose Mercury News, quoting utility executives: "Every chip has to be examined, i.e., several thousand in all, 8,000 utilities, 80,000 substations . . . power is dependent on an intricate chain of millions of links that must be assessed and fixed (there are hundreds of millions of chips in utilities according to Senator Bennett), along with 800 different types of embedded controls."

The Chief Information Officer (CIO) for California Utilities says: "Situation will be somewhere between fixed and doomsday."

California's Pacific Gas & Electric had not yet assessed what chips need replacement as of August 1998.

[1]*World Magazine,* June 9, 1998, Senate committee press release.

In the *San Jose Mercury News,* a utility CIO: "Utilities rely on transportation. Fuel and banks and communications must be Y2K compliant, that's the most daunting for us."

President of Utilities Monitoring Council: "Common mode failures . . . or the coincident loss of multiple facilities could cause a cascading outage over a large area."

Electric Power Research Institute, as quoted in *Wired* magazine: "Utilities are just beginning [8/98] to look for Y2K failure points."

Y2K News: "Nine thousand small rural utilities are clueless about Y2K."

Raleigh Martin: "It takes twenty-one months to get a plant compliant, thus they would have had to start by early 1998."

Ed Yourdon: "Forty-seven percent of utilities are behind schedule."[2]

Survey by Digital Equipment Corporation in early 1998: "Two-thirds of utilities either have not started or are 'severely behind schedule.' "

U.S. News & World Report: "Because many utilities have gotten a late start, localized power outages are a threat."[3]

Energy, especially the supply of electricity, is the foundation of modern civilization. Nothing works without it.

"Will the Lights Go Out?"

I am aware that there are individuals stockpiling canned goods, buying small generators, and lining up alternative sources of power out of fear that the power will go out and stay out when the year 2000 arrives.

I don't share that view, although I must admit that fixing the Y2K problems of the energy industry is an enormous project. Rick Cowles, an electric utility expert,[4] told a congressional committee in May 1998 that there are significant technological challenges attendant to getting the energy and utility industries Y2K ready, but that what really makes the challenge formidable is a "matter of scale." What he means is that it is not difficult to see how one plant or company can become compliant, but there are thousands of companies and tens of thousands of interconnections, generating plants, and substations and hundreds of thousands of miles of power lines.

THE ENORMITY OF THE PROBLEM

The problem in attaining Y2K readiness in the energy industry is five-fold:

[2]Ed Yourdon, *Time Bomb 2000,* p. 70.
[3]*U.S. News and World Report,* June 8, 1998.
[4]Cowles has an excellent web site at *http://www.euy2k.com.*

1. The Sheer Prominence of Information Technology in Power Generation

Computer systems and embedded microprocessors operate every aspect of the industry: from transmission and distribution (the process that deals with getting electricity from the point of generation to our homes and offices) to business operations.

Energy companies use computers to exchange information among each other and to connect plants, refineries, district offices, and major administrative and operational centers. They are used to forecast how much electricity we will need for a given day, hour, and minute. Non-compliant software in a computer can adversely affect a company's back-office operations, such as financial control, human resources, purchasing, inventory, and plant maintenance. Computers are used to determine how much energy we have used, the amount of our bill, whether we have paid the bill or not, and whether to send us a shut-off notice.

Embedded systems are present at plants, pipelines, control and dispatch centers, headquarters, and other energy facilities. Finding Y2K problems in embedded systems is a difficult, time-consuming process that generally requires the physical inspection of hardware distributed well across an organization.

2. The Energy Industry's High Degree of Dependence on Other Industries, Namely Telecommunications and Transportation

Millions of pieces of vital information are passed from one place to another time and time again each day through the use of telephone and satellite communications. The lack of a dial tone will make it very difficult to have electricity. Trains and oil tankers play a vital role in the delivery of coal and oil to power-generating plants. If the computer systems that run and direct the trains don't work or provide correct information, then those plants may be unable to serve their customers.

3. The Increasing Incidence of Mergers and Acquisitions in the Energy Field and the Movement Toward Energy Deregulation

Energy companies preparing for deregulation are finding that their current software, much of it proprietary and designed in-house, is not compatible with that of their new partners. So, at the very time when these companies are forced to develop software that can talk with a new buyer or seller, they have to devote significant resources to determining whether to replace or repair their existing computer systems and making them Y2K compliant.

The authors of the magazine *Infoworld* have declared that information-systems managers should expect to see "sags, surges, brownouts, and power outages"[5] in the coming year because competition among utility providers may reduce spending on non-revenue-producing activities like maintenance, service, long-term investments, and backups. The transmission grid wasn't designed to handle the increased number of transactions that will result from the new commercial arrangements that we will see as a consequence of deregulation.

I am a big believer in electric-power deregulation. I like market free-for-all fights, as it generally means lower prices for me. But I must admit that it would have been better to wait until 2001 to start the utility deregulation.

4. Lack of Government Involvement

The government, especially government regulators who have oversight authority over various aspects of the energy industry, has been far too slow in assessing Y2K energy readiness and in demanding accurate, independently verifiable information on the Y2K readiness of industry players. The industry itself, when given the opportunity to voluntarily inform the public about its status, has been much less than forthright. Whether fearful of being subject to unwanted Y2K-related litigation or unwilling to give a commercial adversary valuable information, the utilities industry lacks the kind of cooperative communication that this problem demands.

5. The Intricacy of Power Deployment

The nation's electrical infrastructure is built like a massive spider web. It features a highly interconnected and interdependent system of power plants, utility lines, and end-users. Every electric company, even a small local power cooperative, is part of this large system. For that reason, some have argued that "the industry will succeed or fail *together* in its readiness for Y2K." [Emphasis added.][6]

For these reasons, I will say in this chapter and countless times hereafter that the complexity of the Millennium Bug challenge demands that industry participants share information with each other and the public and that they test, test, and further test their systems.

The Structure of the Electric-Utility Industry

As a first step toward understanding how the Y2K computer issues might affect the energy industry's ability to get electricity to our homes and businesses, let me briefly describe the electric-utility industry.

---

[5]*Infoworld*, January 19, 1998.

[6]North American Electric Reliability Council (NERC) Report, "Y2K Coordination Plan for the Electricity Production & Delivery Systems of North America," 6/12/98.

The North American electric-utility industry is divided into eleven major regions called Interconnections. The entire package is often referred to as the "power grid." The Western System Coordinating Council (WSCC) is the largest. It covers the western one-third of North America. The second largest, the Northeast Power Coordinating Council (NPCC), covers New York, New England, and most of Eastern Canada. The other nine councils cover the remaining regions in North America.

From these eleven divisions, the industry is divided into 150 power-control areas within the contiguous forty-eight states, six thousand power generating plants, twelve thousand major substations, half a million miles of high-voltage power lines, some 112,000 minor substations, and millions of consumers.

According to a study done by the North American Electric Reliability Council (NERC), Y2K-induced computer problems pose a direct threat to electricity transmission and distribution in four critical areas—power production, energy management, telecommunications, and protections systems. NERC represents more than three-fourths of the nation's electricity suppliers, and the large part of actual power production. It was formed in 1968 to promote the reliability of North America's power supply in the aftermath of the 1965 power blackout that affected the northeastern United States and parts of Canada.

Will the Electric Grid Fail?

Generally, a power failure within one of the Interconnections is not likely to cause cascading power failures in one or more of the other Interconnections because the Interconnections are, for the most part, independent from each other. Electricity consumers in Houston are immune from power failures that occur in Los Angeles since the two cities rely upon electricity generated from totally distinct and separate parts of the electric grid.

What happens within a specific Interconnection is somewhat different. The electric-utility system is designed so that within an Interconnection, the loss of power from one or more power-generation plants will not cause cascading outages throughout that part of the grid.

Electric-power transmission and distribution within an Interconnection *is highly interdependent.* This interdependence is the reason that we can feel confident that the lights will go on when we hit the switch. Unlike water or other raw materials, electricity cannot be stored in large quantities. It's not sitting in buckets or canisters or tanks somewhere waiting to be used. It's not produced until we need it.

When you turn on your lights, your usage of electricity is a signal to the power generator in your area that says, "Hey, go work." When you turn the lights off, a second signal is sent to the power generator that says, "You can rest."

The amount of electricity produced is subject to actual demand, and the supply and demand of electricity are kept in balance in real-time on a continuous basis. When there is a power deficit in one part of an Interconnection, the power demands of the homes and businesses in that geographic area are met by buying electricity from other suppliers within the Interconnection.

Suppose "Power Plant A" shuts down for any reason. The interconnection aspect of the grid is designed so that Power Plant A's customers will not go without power because excess power will be generated and transferred from another facility.

The interdependent nature of the electric-utility industry is not only its blessing but also its bane. Y2K-related problems may so increase the need and demand for the transfer of electric power that the transmission system can't handle it. Transition constraints will leave large numbers of customers without service. The stress to the system could also lead to a cascading outage over a large area.

Suppose now that other facilities—"Power Plants B, C, and D," all within the same Interconnection as Power Plant A—are also experiencing Y2K problems. Not only will customers who rely on Power Plants B, C, and D be without power, but there will be no excess power to transfer to Power Plant A.

Suppose further that there is a Y2K-induced computer failure that hits all of the relay controls of a certain model controller simultaneously in power plants throughout the entire grid. In that case, we could have a large number of simultaneous facility outages in Power Plants A through Z. If that happens, large segments of the power grid would be challenged as never before, and the entire grid, or a large part of it, could go black.

Even those within the industry are concerned that individual electric-utility companies will experience a Y2K-related shutdown knocking out electric service to some customers. History informs us that power outages are not all that unusual. Temporary outages of a few days to a week caused by tornadoes, hurricanes, blizzards, and other weather-related matters have been experienced by Americans from Seattle to Miami.

Commonwealth Edison is one of the nation's largest electric-utility companies. ComEd announced that it is spending $60 million to fix its Y2K problems. The company has 150 employees assigned to its Y2K team and expects to hire another 125 to find, test, and fix problems in the 15 million lines of computer code that run the ComEd network. Despite this sizable investment, Tom Wilkie, ComEd's man in charge of risk assessment, was quoted in a newspaper article as saying, "I think it is unreasonable to expect that there won't be any [Y2K-related] utility problems."

The available evidence is no more persuasive that we will be able to avoid a temporary ripple effect knocking out electricity in a wide area. Even with the industry's best-laid plans, on at least three occasions during the last thirty-five years, the industry has been unable to avoid outage blackouts over large segments of the country. The New York City incident is famous. As recently as July 3, 1996, a power outage knocked out the juice in two Canadian provinces and the western states of California, Oregon, Idaho, Utah, Wyoming, Colorado, Arizona, and Nevada.

The Millennium Bug poses a profoundly new and different threat to electricity delivery than the industry has had to deal with in the past. A hurricane might hit the coast of North Carolina, knocking out electricity service there. The Washington, D.C.–Baltimore beltway might be hit by a blizzard, knocking out service along a portion of I-95. A specific power company may experience technical problems. But we have never had a problem hit the entire country at the same time. The Millennium Bug has the potential to do just that.

The Millennium Bug forces us to ask the questions: "What if there is no surplus electricity capacity? What if the basic assumption of the industry—that excess surplus can be transferred to high-demand areas—is itself at risk?"

Even if the ComEds of the world successfully fix their own Millennium Bug problems, that by itself won't make their customers totally immune from a millennium illness. An individual electric utility company can invest tens of millions of dollars in solving its own Y2K problem, yet its customers can still be affected in a major way by a Y2K-related problem initiated in another part of the overall system.

▬▬▬▬▬▬

"Cautiously Optimistic"

I do find some comfort in the fact that in the entire history of the country we have never had a national or regional blackout that lasted more than twenty-four hours. I believe those industry experts who tell us that any Y2K-related power outages that occur after January 2000 will not last weeks or months. I think that we are looking at hours or days, except in some isolated areas.

There is also some evidence that the energy industry is making measured progress to prepare for the Year 2000. That seems to be the conclusion of the first comprehensive survey of the status of the efforts being undertaken by the electric-utility industry. The September 1998 NERC report concluded that we should be "cautiously optimistic" that the lights will stay on across the nation when the clocks inside countless computers misread the date 2000 and trip the breakers inside major power utilities. The reason for optimism: according to the report, "In an industry that meets record peak demands during heat waves and quickly restores service to millions of customers who lost power due to a hurricane or earthquake, preparing for and dealing with operating risk is an ingrained part of the business."

Are enough firms fully appreciative of the extent of the problem, and are they marshalling adequate resources to address it?

"With fifteen months to go," the NERC report noted that potential Y2K glitches "had been eliminated in 28 percent of the industry's mission-critical systems."

But it is disconcerting to note that in an industry that demands cooperation and communication from its member players, 25 percent of the two hundred bulk-power producers refused to cooperate with the NERC study. Some other electric-utility companies that did respond to the survey were later found lagging in their pace. Another group of utilities have yet to make any effort at getting the bugs out of their computer systems.

Utility companies in the last two groups, those needing to hurry up and those needing to get started, risk becoming the weak link that might jeopardize power transmission and distribution in other parts of the electric grid. The NERC report strongly urged the electricity industry to accelerate its current efforts and to test its systems for the Y2K bug and remediate its mission-critical systems—the stuff that makes the systems work. Otherwise, there might very well be "serious disruptions" in the power supply.

Are the Oil and Gas Industries Y2K Ready?

The oil and gas industries are remarkably similar to the electricity segment in that the production facilities and pipelines used for transporting and distributing oil and gas are interrelated. Both the oil and the gas industries use something called SCADA—Supervisory Control and Data Acquisition System—to manage their operations. SCADA is used to acquire information from substations and sections of pipeline, and to control the flow of fuel at remote locations by using computers linked to satellite and telephone systems. For instance, an oil producer will use SCADA to purchase distribution services based on the current volume of oil in the pipeline, check on billings, or arrange storage. Gas pipelines include compressor stations to move the gas through the lines, as well as gate stations where pressure is reduced, volumes of gas are measured, and regulators control the flow of gas into distribution lines. Stations are generally fifty to seventy-five miles apart. A Y2K interference will interrupt the flow of gas.[7]

If that's not enough, embedded chips exist in abundance throughout oil and gas properties. Embedded-chip systems, especially those in pipeline-control and terminal operations, are used to control pumping and detect leaks. Specialized computer-based technologies are used to operate oil supertankers and modern refineries. Many of the embedded chips in

---

[7]Some of this information is from a web document by Dr. Ed Yardeni, *http://www. yardeni.com/y2kbook.htm#B3,* in the section on utilities.

all of these operations are subsurface and physically difficult to access, thereby decreasing the likelihood that oil and gas operators will have sufficient time and resources to identify and correct all of their Y2K problems.[8]

The simple fact is that you now know about as much as anyone does about the progress of the oil and gas industries. There are no industry reports or government agencies that have oversight of the oil and gas industries and little evidence of any industry-wide cooperation.

Oil and gas distribution is vital to our country. Heating, transportation, national security, cars, electricity, farms, and manufacturing are dependent upon the smooth flow of oil and gas.

To not know in December of 1998 the probability of continuous smooth delivery of oil and gas is not acceptable. Congress and the president must act swiftly to correct this. Perhaps we will find out that everything is going to be fine. But if there is going to be a problem, we must be told sooner rather than later, and we need to begin to prepare contingency plans. The lack of information is simply unacceptable. Somebody in congress who has the stature to get something done needs to get royally outraged.

Will Nuclear Power Plants Be Safe and Productive?

Nuclear-power readiness is a major concern for us all. There are two principal questions relevant in any discussion of nuclear plant Y2K readiness.

First is the issue of whether domestic nuclear power plants are safe. Will they properly shut down, if that becomes necessary? Will the Year 2000 bring with it another Chernobyl? That's the last thing anybody wants.

It appears, however, that Y2K doesn't pose a significant safety threat. Most nuclear reactors are so old—there have been no new plants ordered in the last twenty years—that their plant-safety and control systems are mostly based on analog, rather than digital computer-based, technologies. In fact, a top Nuclear Regulatory Commission (NRC) official has estimated that more than 90 percent of the safety systems in nuclear plants are analog. Thus, the safety-related initiation and actuation systems don't rely on date-driven databases to perform their required functions.

The second issue relates to the effect that Y2K-safety-related or accident-related mischief could have on the nation's electricity power sup-

---

[8]For a brief analysis of the technical problems, see *http://www.house.gov/science/ hirning05-14.htm* for the testimony of Kathleen Hirning, chief information officer, Federal Energy Regulatory Commission.

ply. This question is especially important in light of the role played by the domestic nuclear-power industry. Just look at some figures.

- The 110 licensed nuclear power plants generate 22 percent of the nation's electricity.
- Three of six major regions of the country depend on nuclear power for at least one-quarter of their electricity.
- Six states—Connecticut, New Jersey, Maine, Vermont, South Carolina, and Illinois—rely on nuclear power for more than half of their electricity.
- More than eighty nuclear plants have gone on-line since 1973, and they accounted for 40 percent of the increase in U.S. electricity demand since then.[9]

There are plenty of digital systems in these nuclear power plants that must function properly so that plant operations and the supply of electricity are not disrupted. Plant operators are highly dependent on digital systems to run nuclear plant engineering, communication, and inventory-control programs.

So what's the status of the nuclear power plants? Well, again, we don't know for sure. NRC's regulatory oversight and authority extend only to safety rather than production and supply issues. And even concerning safety oversight, the NRC has been embarrassingly slow and passive about its duties. It wasn't until May 1998 that the NRC requested that plant operators describe their Y2K-readiness programs, and they aren't required to provide the agency with confirmation that their plants are Y2K ready until July 1999. If they aren't done by then, they must inform the NRC of the work that remains to be done and of the schedule for completion. The NRC plans to conduct inspections, on a sampling basis, to assess plant preparedness.

But by then, those measures may be way too little too late.

Conclusions

Here are some excerpts from a NERC report:[10]

> It is certain that not all Y2K problems have been or will be identified, fixed, and tested in the time remaining. Also, it would not be prudent to expend unlimited resources on potential problems in search of one hundred percent avoidance of component failures. . . .

[9]Ed Yardeni, "Y2K Reporter," October 13, 1997, p. 6.
[10]"Y2K Coordination Plan for the Electricity and Delivery Systems of North America," June 12, 1998.

One unprepared system has the potential to adversely impact the operation of the rest of the Interconnection. . . .

There is no doubt that cascading or even localized outages of generators and transmission facilities could have serious short- and long-term consequences. . . .

The cornerstone of the NERC Y2K plan is to coordinate industry actions in implementing a "defense-in-depth strategy" with four components:

1. Identify and fix known Y2K problems.
2. Identify worst-case conditions.
3. Prepare for the worst.
4. Operate systems in a precautionary posture during critical Y2K transition periods.

Precautionary measures may include reducing the level of planned electricity transfers between utilities, placing all available transmission facilities into service, bringing additional generating units on-line, and rearranging the generation mix to include older units with analog controls. Another example is increased staffing at control centers, substations, and generating stations during critical periods.

In commenting upon the report, Dr. Yardeni notes the following:

> Near the end of the document, NERC states, "Although the most critical period is expected to be on the dates of December 31, 1999 and January 1, 2000, configuring systems in a precautionary posture and then restoring normal conditions afterward are expected to require several weeks. *In other words, the precautions are likely to disrupt electricity service no matter what happens at the start of 2000.*" [Emphasis added.][11]

Earlier we noted that Capers Jones and Ed Yourdon both expect power outages. So does Rick Cowles.

The sense that I get from reading and talking to many experts is that we will have power losses. But not everywhere. While the power losses will not quite be random, as those utilities that have begun work early are more likely to be ready, there is no assurance that any utility or any part of the grid will escape problems. Part of the problem is that we will not have a real test of the system until we get to January 1, 2000. We can't shut down electricity for a few days around the country while we test the grid. All that the utility industry can do is to try to independently check as much as possible, be prepared for problems, and then work like mad to fix them when they crop up. The good news is that the utility industry, as much as any other, has a strong track record of keeping the power up and responding to emergencies.

---

[11]*http://www.yardeni.com/y2kbook*

Today it appears that what power problems we do experience will not be of a long duration. For most of the country, we are probably looking at hours and days, not weeks and months. We might be even more optimistic in December of 1999. The hard part is assessing what the exposure is from utilities not forthcoming with their status. Most of these are smaller utilities. We must have candid, full, and detailed disclosure from all power companies about their Y2K readiness. We must be completely briefed on their contingency plans. This disclosure must be demanded by every level of government from Washington, D.C., to the smallest town in Idaho. Information is the best antidote to panic and fear.

If we can have some realistic basis upon which to assess our preparations, we will be far better than off than we would be by trying to plan for all contingencies. If the management of a power company feels that there is a possibility of the power being off for a few days, then they should just tell us. Then we can make reasonable preparations. The American people are fully capable of understanding that this is an enormous problem and that the power companies are working hard to make sure that there are no power losses. But I doubt that we will be so understanding if we are not dealt with honestly and straightforwardly as adults. I won't be. .

Other questions for which there are no apparent answers today are "Will there be power rationing or brownouts so that we can supply those areas whose utilities are inoperable, or will utilities that are compliant move to protect themselves and their customers from failures by their competitors? Who will make these decisions?" These and other questions must be dealt with publicly. Sooner rather than later is a good rule for the disclosures.

Anything less than full, candid disclosure should meet with severe and substantial penalties, up to and including criminal charges for executives who hide embarrassing truths. Public utilities by and large benefit from monopoly positions. This favorable economic status brings with it a great deal of responsibility and the right of the public to know the details about the companies on whom their lives and livelihoods depend. This is serious. We are talking about lives that can be lost due to power failures. There is no reason that the public cannot be trusted with this information.

Later in the book, we will deal with what type of preparations you should consider because of these potential power losses.

4

Reaching Out and Touching Someone in 2000: Will We Have Dial Tone?

In the late eighties, the Federal Communications Commission decided to hold lotteries to give away licenses to operate as cellular telephone companies in particular regions of the U.S. I was lucky and participated in partnerships that won some attractive licenses. Some we sold, and some were built and later sold. In the process, I learned a great deal about the telecommunications world. I attended dozens of conferences, read scores of reports, and worked hard to try to figure out the best ways to maximize our partnership's good fortune.

I took some of the profits and traveled throughout Africa, visiting sixteen countries in search of investment opportunities and licenses. The partnerships that I put together designed systems and developed sophisticated proposals competing with or working with the major telephone companies of the world. I saw firsthand the boost that a good telecommunications infrastructure can give a country. *Without a good telecommunication system, a modern, efficient economy cannot work.*

We Take It All for Granted

Today, the telecommunications sector is, perhaps, second only to the energy and power sector, the most significant infrastructure component in the world and U.S. economies. Annual global spending on telecom services, estimated at $726 billion in 1997, is expected to grow to $1 trillion by 2001. Domestic local calling and long-distance revenues each topped $92 billion in 1997 and are hyped for much greater growth in the future. Internet retailing, which generated about $3 billion in sales in 1997, is projected to reach $16 billion by 2000. I will address this estimated growth later in the chapter.

The U.S., which has almost half of the world's computer capacity and 60 percent of its Internet assets, is the world's most advanced producer and dependent user of information and telecom technologies. Telecommunications systems deliver voice, video, and data to and from our homes and businesses through a variety of wired and wireless technologies. We use telecom services for everything: to check in with grandmother, make purchases, do our banking, order supplies and materials, and entertain ourselves. As much as anything else, these technologies have fueled the growth of our economy and brought about major improvements, conveniences, and opportunities in our daily and professional lives.

David E. Baker, who heads the Charles Schwab Washington Research Group, noted the value of the telecom industry during his testimony before a congressional committee looking into Y2K telecom readiness. Baker told the committee that:

> It is beyond question that the telecommunications capability of this country is critical to our economic health and security. Each day billions of dollars flow across state and national borders. The massive increase in electronic commerce underscores that a radical shift in how Americans conduct business will ride with the digital bits traveling through high bandwidth facilities being built throughout the world.

Everyone—whether a large corporation, small business, government entity, family, or individual—depends upon high-quality, uninterrupted telecom services.

What If There's No Dial Tone?

As a business owner I understand other owners' and managers' concerns about what might happen on New Year's Day 2000. We have to ask if we will get a dial tone when we pick up the phone. If telephone service is interrupted, how long will the interruption last? If service is disturbed, how long can our businesses operate?

William Kennard, the chairman of the Federal Communications Commission, apparently doesn't think that they could operate very long. Speaking before the Senate Committee on Commerce, Science, and Transportation, Kennard warned:

> If we have major network outages due to Year 2000, many small- and medium-sized businesses could find themselves in dire eco-

nomic straits. Many must rely on only one telecommunications carrier. So if their phone network or their date network goes out, they have to close down. And many small businesses don't have large reserves, so if the problem persists for a few days, they could be out of business.

Kennard isn't being melodramatic. Although we take making telephone calls for granted, the truth is that our telecommunications network is tremendously complicated. The network includes a complex maze operated by local and long-distance carriers, cellular networks, and satellite services. It consists of millions of interconnected parts that detect, switch, route, connect, and log literally millions of calls per minute.

There are thousands of entities that have to be readied for the next millennium. First, there are the major telecommunications carriers like the Bell Operating Companies, GTE, AT&T, MCI, and Sprint. The largest twenty phone companies provide 98 percent of U.S. phone lines. There are also fourteen hundred small- to medium-sized telephone companies that serve many rural and underserved parts of the country. Then there are the equipment manufacturers who produce the routers, switches, and other boxes that make the systems work. There are the telecommunications users, who have to insure that their own equipment—telephones, voice-mail systems, PBXs, and local-area computer networks—are all Y2K compliant. Finally, there are the global players—foreign carriers and telecom users.

All of the parts must work together. As in the case of the energy sector, which I discussed earlier, there are any number of reasons to think that curing the Millennium Bug will be a huge challenge.

- The telecommunications industry is highly complex and interconnected.
- No single entity owns or controls the network.
- Not all of the telecommunications players got started on time on Y2K preparations, especially small, rural carriers and carriers in developing countries.
- The federal government has not developed Y2K schedules and milestones for the various segments of the telecommunications industry. Even if it does, it has limited power to force the players to fix the problem.
- The ways in which the Year 2000 problem could affect telecommunications companies are unlimited. Testing all of the systems is a logistics nightmare.
- Industry players have been reluctant to share vital information because they have been afraid that it will be used later in suits against them or that it will give another company a competitive advantage.

Let's say that I want to call a client in New York from my office in Arlington, Texas. For this to happen, every part along the established telecom circuit has to work. Of course, the telephone at my desk has to be in order. After that, the Private Branch Exchange (e.g., the PBX or switchboard in my building), my local telephone company's central-office switch, the computers that connect my call to its destination, the long-distance trunk lines, the central switch in New York City, and my client's telephone all must work in a seamless flight of telephonic fancy. And there are infinite numbers of permutations and combinations of routing possibilities and service events to transit my call. If I make my call a couple minutes later, it may be routed in a wholly different manner. If anything along the way fails, my call drops.

Twice in 1998, the nation suffered telecommunications failures that affected millions of users and caused significant financial losses. On April 13, 1998, a software error in a single switch caused AT&T's data network to fail nationwide. During the twenty-four-hour outage of phone service, the carrier's corporate customers were unable to complete critical network-based business, retailers were unable to authorize credit-card payments, and financial institutions could not complete electronic transactions.

A month later, on May 19, 1998, another failure occurred. This time the Galaxy IV communications satellite spun out of control after a system failure. Again, credit-card authorizations were disrupted. The distribution of television programs and the paging services for 80 to 90 percent of all pagers in the U.S.—including mine—went on the blink.

These failures were not caused by Y2K problems. They do, however, illustrate the degree to which we depend upon reliable, interoperable, available telecommunications. It also shows how fragile that system is, when one switch or satellite can shut down entire systems. But it is also a clear demonstration that the telecommunications industry is capable of responding quickly to problems.

That's why testing will be so important. Most telecommunications companies estimate that testing comprises 50 to 70 percent of their Year 2000 efforts. AT&T's chairman and CEO Michael Armstrong estimates "60,000 years' worth of testing on systems and equipment" in the days ahead.

End users need to be concerned with testing too. Consider my call to New York. If I want to make that call on January 1, 2000, the only way to guarantee that it will go through will be to completely test the system—end to end. That means that every player from me to my client to all the manufacturers and carriers in between will need to synchronize or simulate a date change in our computer systems without interrupting our normal business. A daunting task. Short of that, we at least need to make sure that our own internal systems and those of our primary trading partners are in order. It will not do us much good, even if the telecom carriers fix all of their networks, if we cannot call out of our buildings because our internal PBX systems don't work.

A Mixed Bag

Will the telecommunications industry be ready by January 1, 2000? No one has an overall assessment of the Year 2000 risk in the telecommunications industry. Nonetheless, what we can glean from the annual reports of the major domestic telecom companies, the statements of company representatives (some verified, some not), and the buzz of activity in the industry (plus off-the-record comments from companies afraid of lawsuits) is that major U.S. telecom providers will elude lengthy Y2K disruptions and deliver dial tone with little or no interruption. The FCC's Y2K point man, Commissioner Michael Powell (the son of former Joint Chiefs of Staff chairman General Colin Powell), thinks that if we have any Y2K glitches, they will be "annoying, not disastrous." Problems will not disrupt the entire system. The situation with the small, independent, and international telephone carriers may be different.

EQUIPMENT MANUFACTURERS

Powell tells us that he has been told by the U.S. equipment manufacturers that they have already tested and fixed most of their products. Manufacturers report that most of their software and hardware products are already Year 2000 compliant and available to customers. They have targeted the first quarter of 1999 at the latest for general availability for all Year 2000–ready products. The carriers note that the manufacturers' schedules will allow them to meet their compliance deadlines.

MAJOR DOMESTIC CARRIERS

The annual reports for the major domestic telephone carriers indicate that they have been paying attention to Millennium Bug issues for two or three years and expect to direct huge sums toward addressing their Y2K concerns. For instance, AT&T expects to spend $350 million on Y2K in 1998 and is still assessing its 1999 costs. GTE expects to spend $350 million as well. SBC puts its figure at less than $250 million. U.S. West, which didn't start its Y2K work until 1997, has set a $150-million budget. Bell South thinks that it will spend somewhere between $75 million and $150 million.

In late April 1998, the FCC asked over two hundred telecom service providers and industry associations, as well as other interested organizations, to see what all this money was buying. The carriers claim that they will have completed their inventory reviews, have completed assessing the impact of the Year 2000 problem on these systems, and have set completion dates for remediation, testing, and integration by the second quarter of 1999. The claims are unverified by independent sources, but I tend to give them credence. The carriers' reluctance to expose themselves to legal problems has led them to be very careful about what they say. It stands to reason that what they do release can be backed up. With the passage of the new disclosure act by Congress, we should start to get specific information.

Well-known Y2K expert and consultant Peter de Jager, who has had direct contact with many of the larger carriers, has said in a discussion with me that these carriers are privately telling him that they are in good shape.

Major Y2K-readiness tests are already being conducted. The Telco Year 2000 Forum, an alliance of local and regional phone companies, is conducting integration testing on Year 2000 equipment and software. These tests are conducted in the phone companies' labs and assess the extent to which the individual elements, when clustered together as they would be in the real network, would work together. Tests conducted in October 1998 identified seven minor issues referred to the equipment vendors.

Another association, the Alliance for Telecommunications Industry Solution (ATIS), will conduct internetwork interoperability tests in January and February 1999. ATIS is an industry-funded organization whose mission is to advance new telecommunications technologies. The tests will duplicate the circumstances of midnight, December 31, 1999 to assess which systems will switch to the next century and which will revert to 1900. This type of cooperative industry testing is very important because it is nearly impossible to conduct interoperability and end-to-end tests on the actual public-switched telephone network. The nation's phone network has to be up and running twenty-four hours a day, seven days a week. The telephone companies cannot disconnect their network and turn the clock ahead to the year 2000 to do a test.

SMALL TO MIDSIZED CARRIERS

Families and businesses that use small to midsized and rural telephone companies have reason to be concerned. The FCC believes that many of these firms do not realize or have been slow to realize the seriousness of the Y2K problem. Other firms do not have the resources to devote full-time staff to Y2K issues. For those telcos that understand the problem and that have adequate funding, there's yet another hurdle. While they may want to test, retest, and test their systems again to get any bugs out of them, they won't be able to because of the current reluctance of many of the larger companies to share their internal test results. In fairness, the large telcos are not sharing with each other either, due to fear of liability and to competition.

Without cooperation from these large companies, the small and midsized telcos cannot perform the extensive testing necessary to insure that their customers will not be affected by Y2K failures. Frankly, this attitude on the part of large carriers must stop. There is too much at risk for the entire system for individual companies to be worried about competitive positions.

INTERNATIONAL CARRIERS

The irony is that we know more about international telecommunications companies than about U.S. carriers, largely because of two surveys done by the State Department and the UN. I find it very annoying that we can get Argentina to tell us their telecommunications status while the FCC can't get AT&T or Southwestern Bell to publicly tell us specifically how they are doing.

The surveys and other information sources tell us that making international calls may be a problem. Canada and the United Kingdom are forging ahead in their Y2K preparations. But carriers in other nations, especially in developing countries, have not taken the necessary steps to prevent Y2K system failures.

Developing nations simply may not have sufficient resources to fix the problem, especially since there is tremendous resistance in these countries to moving money from government social and welfare programs to Y2K efforts. To help, the UN is offering Year 2000–awareness courses for diplomats, and the World Bank plans to spend $30 million to educate developing nations about the problem. In Europe, telecommunication carriers and users have to juggle getting ready for the new Euro currency and for Y2K. Moreover, in Asia, the current recession may prevent adequate attention to the Y2K challenge.

The UN's director of information technology, Joyce Amenta, said in the summer of 1998 that the governments and companies in India, China, and Eastern Europe won't be ready for the computer date changeover unless they attack the problem quickly. The facts support her.

A March 1998 State Department survey of foreign carriers came to the same conclusion. The department received information from 111 countries, of which 22 percent expected to be compliant by December 1999, 29 percent stated that they were addressing Y2K but were having problems, and 26 percent were unaware of or had not begun to address the problem.

A more recent survey is of 230 telecommunications companies from around the world that responded to a Y2K questionnaire prepared by the International Telecommunications Union (ITU). They provided information updated through August 1998. ITU is the UN agency charged with assessing global telecommunications. The survey asked the telcos, among other things, to share the dates by which they anticipated completing their remediation and testing efforts.

Some of the telcos provided no information at all. Botswana, Chad, Nepal, Lesotho, Liberia, Madagascar, Malawi, Nepal, New Caledonia, and

Sri Lanka are not exactly global commercial centers. So, dead telephones in those countries might cause some distress to the locals but are unlikely to damage the global economy. Apparently, the telcos that service these countries either haven't started getting their systems ready or are so early in the process that they have no idea when they'll be finished.

(I should note that even though Sri Lanka, for instance, did not reply to the information request, Mike Fletcher, a technology consultant, reported on the Westergaard Y2K web site (*www.y2ktimebomb.com*) that in his travels he was very impressed with Sri Lanka's efforts, although he was less optimistic about the prospects of some of its neighbors. He also noted that Pakistan is having a hard time getting senior-level support for its programs. So, while failing to report is not necessarily indicative of being unaware or unprepared, it is generally not a good sign.)

But in the case of the telcos in more economically critical countries, some of the information is of dubious value at best. How is it that at least eighty companies gave the *exact same date* for completion of remediation—January 12, *1998!* That is not a typo! Supposedly they are already finished with remediating their systems. Many of them tell us that they will be testing in December 1998. Did they all get together and cheat off each other's papers? Then there are thirty or so telcos that admit that they won't finish testing until the last quarter of 1999, just days before the big event. If there's any slippage in the date or they have to fix anything after testing, they may run out of time. One thing is for certain: we cannot get an extension on the deadline.

Notice that between the State Department survey and the ITU survey, 26 percent of telephone companies that were not even aware of the problem are now telling us that they will be ready! I should also point out that some major countries such as Chile and Brazil did not report.

On the basis of these studies, I am forced to conclude that it may be next to impossible to have easy, uninterrupted telephone service in some parts of the world in 2000. Insuring that the international telecommunications system is ready for the Year 2000 is critical to the global economy. Otherwise, we may suffer serious injury to world trade.

If foreign countries can't or won't get Y2K ready on their own, we may need a more decisive strategy. Maybe Commissioner Powell can enlist his dad to lead us into battle against the Millennium Bug. He has some experience in rallying the world's leadership around a cause and defeating the enemy.

Short of that type of wartime mentality (which this problem warrants), I think that we will have serious problems communicating worldwide in the first months of 2000. There will be a huge disruption of those economies not ready, and the potential for mischief, revolution, and upheaval in countries already lacking in stability needs to be addressed.

This is one of the things that I am most worried about. I have traveled to over forty countries around the world, from the richest and most technically advanced to the poorest. I have been in Angola and Japan, Switzerland and the Congo (though it was Zaire when I was there). The one constant that seems to hold throughout the world is that *the more universal, cheap, and reliable telecommunications are, the more prosperous the country.* This is almost without exception.

If you want to destroy the productive capacity of a country, take away its telecommunications infrastructure. Our country needs the rest of the world to be as economically healthy as possible. We need to buy their goods, and we need their markets for ours. The best use of our foreign-aid money would be to help those countries that are behind to catch up.

If countries are without phones, their economies will be shattered. The resulting potential for unrest, revolution, and other political upheaval goes up dramatically. We should seriously consider as a nation the potential cost to our military budget as we try to monitor scores of potential hot spots around the globe. The loss of commerce from these countries to world trade will affect us as well.

We should consider allocating a significant budget to an emergency agency assigned the task of making sure that as many as possible of the world's telecommunications companies are working on January 1, 2000. I am quite serious about Powell or someone of his stature taking charge of this project. Short of this type of well-funded and well-organized effort, the probability of seriously disruptive problems all over the world is quite high. Even with such an effort, it is likely that there will still be problems, though they will be much less serious. We can either spend the money now, or watch as the world economy suffers and our military budget gets stretched even thinner. As the ad says, "Pay me now, or pay me later."

So, the Question Is, "Will We Have Dial Tone?"

Capers Jones says (see page 22) that 15 percent of the country will experience a three-day loss of dial tone. Based on what we know today, that is as good an estimate as any. I would further note that I think that prolonged delays of more than a few hours or days will mostly be in rural areas, based upon the reports of the difficulties some rural-area telcos may be having.

I find it highly ironic that those fleeing the cities and suburbs for rural areas may have put themselves in more jeopardy of losing dial tone and other services than if they had stayed in the service areas of the major telcos.

The record, as I mentioned earlier, of the telephone companies fixing problems quickly is good. I would expect what problems do crop up in the U.S. to be matters of hours and days, not of weeks and definitely not of months.

So, what am I going to do about the potential for having no dial tone for a few days? Well, since there is nothing I can do, I will plan to get some long-overdue filing done, read some of those important books sitting on my shelves, and maybe start my next book.

I should note that cellular phones will not necessarily experience a problem if the local carriers do, so they can serve as a limited backup for those who also have cellular service. If you have two telephone lines, and long distance is an hourly or daily imperative, you might consider having each line serviced by a different long distance company as well, in case one long distance carrier has problems.

"The King Was in His Counting House, Counting Out His Money"

In 1762, when the armies of Louis XIV approached Amsterdam, there was grave alarm. Merchants besieged the Bank, some in the suspicion that their wealth might not be there. All who sought their money were paid, and when they found this to be so, they did not want payment. As was often to be observed in the future, however desperately people want their money from a bank, when they are assured they can get it, they no longer want it.

—John Kenneth Galbraith[1]

I will admit at the outset of this chapter that my view of Y2K and financial institutions is different than that of most of my peers. But it is consistent with my view of Y2K in general.

I do not think that Y2K is a matter of survival for those who live in North America. My concern is its economic consequences.

Likewise, when I consider the effects of Y2K on banks and financial institutions, I do not think in terms of their short-term *survival*. My concern is the economic impact Y2K will have on the economy and therefore on these crucial institutions.

To put it in perspective:

I am *concerned* about the Y2K compliance of our financial institutions.

I am *worried* about the effects that Y2K will have on the solvency of our financial institutions.

I am *scared* about the possible loss of public confidence in our financial institutions.

I am going to deal with these three issues one at a time and give you straight answers about what I think you should do.

[1]*Money: Whence It Came, Where It Went,* revised edition (Houghton Mifflin, 1995).

Financial Institutions and Y2K Compliance

No industry has done more or is further along on Y2K compliance than the financial industry. There will be problems, but with proper precautions, individuals and businesses should be able to move into the next millennium with the same level of service that they currently enjoy from their financial institutions (although they may be at a *new* bank, brokerage, or other financial institution).

Even though I expect most financial institutions to be fine, that does not mean that all of them will be so. *You do not want to be in a bank or brokerage firm that is not Y2K compliant.* There are going to be banks that fail because of Y2K noncompliance. There are going to be more banks that have reduced services for the first part of 2000.

To a great extent, we are at the mercy of the utilities and phone companies. There is not a lot that we can do, other than wish them well and make some minimal preparations. You don't have the option of switching local phone or power companies.

That is not the case with banks and other financial institutions. You are in control of where you bank, which mutual funds you invest in, what brokerage firms you use, what credit cards are in your wallet, and where you borrow money.

I strongly encourage you to take action and ask some questions. You must make sure that you will have access to your money in a reasonable and timely fashion. Before I outline what you should do, though, let's look at the problems we are facing.

What Can Go Wrong?

Because of those two little digits, many of the computer systems that run our bank accounts, credit-card accounts, stocks and bonds accounts, automated teller machines, and bank vaults have the potential to generate wrong information or no information, or might be unable to make needed transactions. If we cannot write checks or transfer money, exchange financial data, and maintain accurate information, the entire community will grind quickly to a halt.

Examples of bank transactions and information that might be adversely impacted by the Millennium Bug include:

- Incorrect calculation of lending, investment, deposit, and accounting information;
- Difficulty in depositing or inability to deposit into and withdraw funds from investment, deposit, and stock accounts;

- Difficulty in making or inability to make loans, investments, deposits, and stock transactions;
- Difficulty in making or inability to make ATM or credit-card transactions; and
- Difficulty in accessing or inability to access bank facilities, for example, the bank vault, elevators, heating, communications, and security systems.

It would be easy to spend a few dozen pages detailing examples of problems that could occur. The fact is that there are hundreds of problems that can result from not being Y2K compliant. If banks are not capable of communicating with each other, their customers, and the Federal Reserve, they shortly will be out of business. If they cannot debit, credit, and maintain customer accounts, if they cannot immediately determine how much money you have in your account, and if they cannot collect on loans properly, they shortly will be out of business.

I am going to assume that you understand that if the computers at a bank or other financial institution are not working properly, you do not want to be a customer of that institution. The nature of the problem does not make any difference. Any problem should be enough to make you head for the door.

How Many Banks Are Having Problems?

I was introduced to Michael Curtiss by a close mutual friend in 1997. Michael is a consultant to the Federal Reserve (plus the equivalent of the Fed in other countries), the Treasury, and many banks (including major international banks) and banking associations on Y2K problems. He has (literally) written the book on banks and Y2K compliance. I could say a lot of very good things about him, but in short, his client list says it all. He knows about as much as anyone on the true extent of the Y2K problem and banks.

In late 1997 I did a lengthy interview with Curtiss on Y2K and banking. I will do interviews with Curtiss throughout 1999 and post them on my Millennium Wave web site (*www.2000wave.com*). He said in early 1998 that he expected that about 10 percent of the banks in this country would fail due to Y2K. Some of the failures would be from direct noncompliance, and others would come later in 2000 from loan problems. He is still holding to those numbers.

I caught up with him late in 1998, and got him to agree to a wide-ranging interview. Nearly everything that he predicted in late 1997 is coming true. We are now beginning to get some clarity about the true banking-compliance issues. Here is what he tells us:

Large Financial Institutions

The larger banks are going to be okay, although some of them will have problems with some levels of service. What he means is that the software that manages customer accounts may be fine, but the ATMs may not work. Bank tellers will be able to process your business, but the statements may not come on time.

That is because software is written in "modules." Not every part of a bank's software is going to have problems. Most of it will work. But some modules may have bugs, which will shut down that part of the bank's ability to service you. It will vary from bank to bank. Some banks may have no problems that affect you. Curtiss thinks that there is a low probability that you will not be able to access your money for as long as thirty days from a major U.S. bank. But you might have problems for a day or two, though there is not more than a 50 percent chance of a one- or two-day problem.

That means that when a problem develops, the banks will put significant resources into getting it fixed. Most software from large banks will have been tested for some considerable time in 1999, so bugs should not be pervasive and will not require a long time to fix.

Curtiss does not think that we will see any large banks fail. He thinks that there will be no banks with over $2 billion in assets that will fail due to Y2K computer problems. There are a few possible exceptions for these larger banks, and that brings us to the real problem.

Smaller Financial Institutions

Most banks under $2 billion use outside vendors or service providers for the core banking systems that run the bank. For instance, Electronic Data Systems (EDS) supplies the software that runs many of the nation's banks. If the software at EDS had a problem with Direct Deposit Accounts, then you would expect that problem to show up at every bank that uses EDS software.

There are over forty primary bank-software vendors. The Federal Reserve audits them and sends a report to each bank that uses their services. But the Fed prohibits the banks from sharing this information with anyone, including other banks!

So, if a bank has a vendor with a low rating, they cannot call their friendly competitor bank down the street and find out about the status of their vendor. While I am sure that there might be some quiet comparisons at banking conventions among trusted friends, the current rules seem designed to frustrate a bank's abilities to become compliant. Basically, the Federal Reserve is worried about lawsuits if there is a mass migration from Vendor A to Vendor B as the result of the Fed's ratings.

Curtiss estimates that about fifteen hundred of the smaller and mid-size banks will have problems with one or more vendor-provided software modules that will cause difficulties for customers for anywhere from one to ten days. About three hundred will have problems for as long as thirty days, and he thinks that these banks probably will not survive. Almost all of these problems will be vendor related. Almost all of them will affect small banks.

(My comment: Almost all of these banks will be telling their customers that they are Y2K ready, as their vendors will be telling them that they are fine, right up until the day the banks shut down.)

Many vendors simply have not properly diagnosed the extent of the problems in their systems. As we will see later, this failure is pervasive throughout the banking industry. So, many of these companies have simply not budgeted the resources to fix the problems, and are now behind the curve. That means that they are going to have to spend a great deal more money to fix their software. But some vendors do not have large enough budgets or profits to fix their software in a reasonable time period. As a consequence, some banks are telling Curtiss that they do not expect to receive Y2K-compliant software from the vendors or service providers until November 1999.

This is a potentially huge problem, because a bank must test how all the various parts of its total system work together. Curtiss is concerned that it is precisely at this point where we will see problems. He uses the analogy of an automobile-parts store. We buy batteries, tires, and engine parts from a parts store. Each supplier believes that his part works exactly as specified. But the real test is to see if you can turn on the engine and drive down the road. It is the ability of all those parts to work together that makes your automobile run smoothly.

Not getting major software revisions until November of 1999 does not leave adequate time for testing. This lack of time can only serve to increase the number of problems experienced by those banks in 2000.

Curtiss calls this the "vendor-user gap." The vendors are telling the users (banks) that everything is coming along just fine, and the banks are accepting this as fact. This is especially true for credit unions.

In his prediction that banks with over $2 billion in assets will by and large be compliant and able to do business, Curtiss does note a possible exception. There are a few banks with more than $2 billion who use outside vendors. They do have some possible exposure to any problems at their vendors. They probably have a much greater knowledge of their vendors than do small banks, and thus should be Y2K compliant as much as any large bank, but Curtiss does note the potential for problems.

Finally, he notes that in 1999 we will see a different emphasis in the regulatory environment. The Federal Reserve, the Office of the Comptroller of the Currency (OCC), the Office of Thrift Supervision, and the Federal Deposit Insurance Corporation are going to stop asking banks what their plan is and start asking what they have accomplished.

I expect that we will see the Federal Reserve and other regulators issue more warning letters and begin to step up the level of oversight.

I should note that small banks do have one major advantage over larger banks. I use a (relatively) small bank as my primary bank, precisely because I have a personal banker who has known me for many years. But I was naturally concerned about Y2K and his bank.

In talking to my banker, he assured me they were already Y2K compliant with the exception of one system which they were replacing. I asked him how this miracle happened and he told me that since his bank was small, they only used a few computer "modules" compared to the large bank he and I left a few years earlier. They recognized the problem early on and aggressively attacked the problem on their few smaller systems and are ahead of the curve as opposed to large banks with massive numbers of systems and services.

So, while I am most concerned about smaller banks, I don't think you should move to a larger bank without checking with your banker if you use a smaller bank. You may be just fine. I would ask for a letter about their compliance status. I currently intend to stay with my bank and will leave the bulk of the money I normally keep in the bank for business and personal use in my accounts.

▬▬▬▬▬▬

Weiss Research Analysis

Even by the most conservative estimates, 12 percent of U.S. commercial banks, savings banks, and S&Ls are behind schedule in their computer preparations for the changeover to the year 2000, according to a Y2K-readiness survey released in October 1998 by Weiss Ratings, Inc.

Among the fifteen hundred depository institutions participating in the survey, 127, or 8.5 percent, received "below average" Y2K grades, reflecting inadequate progress toward resolving their Y2K-related problems. An additional fifty-four institutions, or 3.6 percent, received "low" marks for slow progress.

"Based on this 12 percent finding, we conservatively project that thirteen hundred of the nation's eleven thousand banks and S&L's are behind schedule, which is of grave concern," said Weiss Ratings Chairman Martin Weiss, Ph.D.

On the other end of the spectrum, 167 institutions, or 11.1 percent, reported "high" progress in their Y2K preparations. The balance, representing 76.8 percent of respondents, indicated a level of progress deemed "average," reflecting adequate preparations at this time.

All of this has to be taken with a grain of salt. Keep in mind that the response to the survey was voluntary.

Better-prepared banks probably tend to come forward more readily. If that's true, it is quite possible that more than 12 percent of the institutions could be behind schedule in their Y2K preparations.

Forrester Research notes that companies are typically underestimating the size of their expenditures and the time that it will take to fix their software problems. In fact, 25 percent cost overruns will be common. This is borne out by the latest round of SEC filings in late November 1998. This is from an undated story on MSNBC:

> For many U.S. banks, the cost of upgrading their computers to cope with the year 2000 bug is proving to be much higher than expected. In quarterly reports filed with the Securities and Exchange Commission in recent days, many banks have disclosed that it will cost tens of millions of dollars more to fix the problem than they estimated only a few months ago.
>
> The spending increases, which aren't expected to have any immediate impact on earnings, are being reported by banks throughout the country, ranging from giant money-center institutions to tiny small-town banks.
>
> Chase Manhattan Corp., for instance, said it expects to spend about $363 million over three years, a 21% jump from its previous estimate. BankAmerica Corp., the nation's second-biggest bank in terms of assets, currently foresees a total bill of about $550 million, a 10% increase. In all, eight of the top 15 U.S. banks expect to boost spending, bringing the combined estimated cost for all 15 to $3.46 billion, up from about $3.15 billion as of June 30.
>
> Part of the reason the cost has risen, some analysts say, is that banks have underestimated the sheer size of the problem. BankAmerica, for instance, has identified nearly 24,000 separate business operations that may need to be fixed. In addition, banks not only have to reprogram their own computers, they have to make sure many of their corporate clients are addressing the problem as well.
>
> Regulators have been pressing banks for months to assess the potential credit risk of borrowers that aren't prepared. "Banks really didn't realize all the things they'd have to coordinate," said Lou Marcoccio, research director for year 2000 issues at Gartner-Group, a consulting firm in Stanford, Conn.
>
> National City Corp., based in Cleveland, blamed its 63% increase in projected year 2000 spending, which rose to about $65 million from the previous $40 million, partly on the escalating cost of outside help needed to make time-consuming fixes to its computers. "I don't think we'd be surprised if we bid up the price of contract labor," a spokesman said.

I went back to check some old reports. I found that the oldest estimates from Chase Manhattan were in the $200 million to $250 million range. Now it is $363 million. I bet that they spend $400 million before they are through, as costs just keep climbing.

Also, notice the last sentence in the MSNBC article: *" 'I don't think we'd be surprised if we bid up the price of contract labor,' a spokesman said."* That will be the understatement of the year. My concern is that these large institutions are going to bid up the prices and that small businesses and small-bank software vendors are not going to be able to pay the going price for software engineers and programmers and will not get their remediation done on time.

What to Do to Make Sure That Your Bank and Every Other Financial Institution You Do Business with Is Compliant

After I have told you all of the above, you may be wondering why I am only "concerned" about Y2K compliance at banks and other financial institutions.

The answer is simple. No one is holding a gun to my head and making me stay at a bank that is not Y2K ready! I don't have any choice about my utility and power sources, and I have few choices about my phone company. If I was stuck with no choices as to which bank I used, I would be very worried. But I can move my bank accounts with relative ease.

Take the time to make sure that your bank, mutual-fund companies, stockbroker, insurance companies, and pension-plan trustee are all compliant.

The first thing to do is simply ask the above companies about their Y2K status. Most financial institutions have had the question asked many times and have prepared materials. They should not mind answering your questions, as questions about Y2K compliance are what one would expect any reasonable person to ask of a company that has control of his or her assets.

The fact is, such a person should be asking these same questions of his or her vendors and suppliers. To not ask them would be a very bad sign.

Personally, I would like these questions answered in writing and signed by an officer of the company. I really don't want a "trust me, we are on top of this" verbal answer from the assistant vice-president for public relations.

In the following section, I give you six questions that you can ask your financial institutions. I would be grateful if you would send me a copy of their replies, or have those institutions send me a copy as well.[2] I will pass all these letters along to Weiss Research. I will tell you more about Weiss in a minute, but they are helping me evaluate for you the Y2K status of banks. Weiss will be making a list of those banks to which they give the lowest grade for compliance available to the public through their web site.

What to Ask Your Financial Institution

Question 1: Does Your Institution Have a Written Y2K Plan?

By now, every institution should have a plan for dealing with their Y2K problems, encompassing the scope of the problem and specific dates for remedying its various pieces.

Ideally, the plan should be in writing. If the institution has a written Y2K plan, ask if they will send you a copy. If they don't have a written plan, ask what preparations they are currently making in anticipation of the year 2000. If they don't have a written plan, this is a sign that they are not taking Y2K seriously.

Question 2: When Do You Anticipate Having All Mission-Critical Systems Y2K Compliant?

Since mission-critical systems are those that the institution relies on in order to continue its day-to-day operations, it is extremely important that the institution focus on these systems first. As a rule of thumb, most companies appear to be working toward a January 1, 1999 completion date for mission-critical systems, and the vast majority of the rest say that they will be done by June 30, 1999.

Remember, the earlier that the institution plans to have its mission-critical systems Y2K compliant, the more cushion it should have if the project becomes delayed, and the more time it has to test systems in conjunction with all the other systems and links in its network.

Question 3: When Do You Anticipate Having All Systems Y2K Compliant?

You don't care if their coffeepot or fax machine ever becomes Y2K compliant. You want to know when work on their non-mission-critical computer systems (those that I call *mission important*) will be completed.

---

[2]Please mail them to my newsletter publisher in Florida: Y2K ANALYST, % YEAR 2000 ALERT, P.O. Box 109665, Palm Beach Gardens, Florida 33140.

The earlier the date for having all systems Y2K compliant, including those deemed nonessential, the more likely that the institution will make a smooth transition into the year 2000.

Question 4: What Are You Doing to Ensure That Your Business Partners and Vendors Are Prepared for the Year 2000?

This could be crucial for companies relying on a business partner or vendor to provide a mission-critical service. At a very minimum, the institution should be in contact with their business partners/vendors regarding the progress of their Y2K preparations. And ideally, the institution will conduct its own testing of its significant business partners and vendors to ensure that they are Y2K ready.

If they rely upon a vendor for a mission-critical system, you want to know the name of the vendor and why the financial institution believes that the vendor will be ready. Have they seen their vendor's written plan? Will there be enough time to integrate that system into their network, or will there only be a few months for testing? Who in the financial institution is in charge of that vendor relationship? Has the vendor met all of their previous time commitments, or do they have a habit of being late? How strong is the financial balance sheet of the vendor? Do they have the financial resources to finish the project, or is their remediation effort stretching their cash reserves? If the vendor is not ready, what is the contingency plan for shifting to another vendor? What is the drop-dead date at which a decision to change vendors would be made? What are the criteria upon which that decision will be made? Will that leave enough time to actually make the transfer?

Question 5: What Is Your Contingency Plan in Case You Fall Behind in Your Preparations for the Year 2000?

Ask what steps they are taking to make sure that they will have a record of your bank account, customer accounts, investments, insurance policy, or annuity after January 1, 2000, just in case their computer systems do end up failing. It may be hard to judge the realism of the institution's response, but it's good to know that they have at least given the subject some thought.

Remember to suggest that the institution should respond to future Weiss Y2K surveys so that you will be able to more easily track its progress toward Y2K compliance. This will also help the institution by reducing the number of customers calling with Y2K questions.

Question 6 (for Banks and Lending Institutions): Have You Surveyed the Y2K-Compliance Status of Your Large Borrowers? To What Extent Have You Reviewed Their Compliance Efforts?

As I will relate in the next section, my biggest concern with banks is the strength of their customers. I expect loan losses to mount as we slip into a recession. If a bank is not surveying their large customers, not only are they ignoring Federal Reserve guidelines, they are exhibiting poor risk management.

What to Do When You Get Your Report

The first thing to do is read it. Does it make you feel comfortable? Is the language straightforward, or has it obviously been written by lawyers to say as little as possible?

Has the institution made an effort to address your concerns? Do they have a plan? If you are comfortable, then I would come back closer to the end of the year and ask the same questions. Compare the two letters. Have the dates for testing slipped? Did they make their targets for remediation? Have they assessed their vendors and major loan commitments?

There are few ways today to compare the Y2K compliance of one bank to another besides through Weiss Research. Weiss can only do this if they have a response from your institutions. Also, many banks and financial institutions will post their Y2K status on their web sites. For instance, Vanguard, the mutual-fund giant, has already done so. Of course, they are compliant and are quite willing to point that out. (An aside: I talked to the gentleman in charge of the outside firm that handled the remediation for Vanguard, and he confirmed in much more definitive language that Vanguard is Y2K ready.)

I believe that in 1999 you will see every financial institution that is Y2K ready stand up and shout about it for two reasons. One, they will see it as an accomplishment and as part of their customer assurance/communications programs, and two, they will get tired of answering the same questions from every customer and try to deal with them all at once!

Let me briefly comment on the Y2K readiness of the securities industry. From all apparent evidence, they are even further along than the banking industry. The stock and futures exchanges and the brokerage community have all begun testing not only their internal systems, but their communications interfaces as well.

While the first round of industry-wide testing was little more than the equivalent of an open-book test, it did go quite well. There is reason to believe that will continue to be the case. The SEC has been diligent in dealing with firms slow in coming up to compliance status. They are to be commended for their efforts, and other regulatory bodies should use them as a model.

Summary

Most banks and financial institutions are going to be compliant and able to do business in 2000. About 15 percent will probably experience one or more mission-critical system failures that limit service to customers for up to ten days, and about 2 to 3 percent will be out for thirty days or more. It seems likely that this latter group will be taken over by regulators. Most of them will be smaller, and the problems will most likely be vendor related.

Even if your bank has done everything possible to be Y2K compliant, it would be unrealistic to expect no problems. This is software, and software has a way of humbling the best of programmers. But today the problems that we will encounter look like they should be short-lived.

You should keep records of every transaction you do in 1999, without exception.

You should ask your financial institutions to tell you their Y2K status, and if you are not satisfied, you should change institutions. Visit my web site, and see if your institution is one of the lowest rated.

You should plan to *carefully* check every account transaction in 2000 for at least the first six months, although this is a good thing to do at any time. Not all Y2K problems will be large and obvious. The small errors will be harder to spot, and may not show up for months.

I Am Worried *About Bank Solvency*

A constant theme in this book is not the immediate problems of surviving Y2K, but rather the results from an economic downturn caused by Y2K which are going to be the far larger concern.

The same is true for banks and other financial institutions.

Banks are in the business of making loans. They are also in the business of getting those loans repaid with interest. I have sat with presidents of banks, both large and small. A year ago they would look a little oddly at you when you talked about Y2K. Now they nod in agreement. Most banks are asking hard questions of their customers. The president of a local branch of a major national bank told me that a customer's Y2K status was as important in getting a loan as any other factor, and more so in some cases! Banks are beginning to take this seriously.

The loan losses resulting from Y2K failures should not be too high if the banks really do maintain their due diligence. But I am worried about the loan losses resulting from business failures due to a recession and factors other than immediate internal Y2K compliance.

Michael Curtiss, Martin Weiss, and other longtime observers of the banking world agree with me. There are too many banks with poor financial fundamentals that will not be able to survive serious losses in their loan portfolios. Beginning in mid-2000, we are going to see hundreds of banks, again mostly small, forced into mergers or shut down. And it will be because they have made too many loans to marginal companies that have succumbed to the effects of recession.

Few depositors will lose anything, as the FDIC will cover all losses up to $100,000. But it is a hassle if your bank shuts down. You do lose access to your money for a period of time, and because there will be more banks than usual suffering through the problems of recession-induced bankruptcy, the response time will be stretched out.

There are two things that you should do. The first is to check the financial rating of your banks. There are two places where you can do this cheaply and easily. You can call Veribanc at 1-800-442-2657. They are the only group that I know of that rates credit unions as well as banks. I have done business with Veribanc. They do an excellent job and are a high-quality company. They will charge $10 for the first bank rating and $5 for each thereafter. If your bank gets a yellow rating or only a one-star/green rating, you should monitor your bank more closely and recognize that they have less of a capital cushion for dealing with Y2K disruptions and the Y2K Recession. You can also call Weiss Research at 800-871-2374 for a rating on your bank; they also will sell you a list of safe institutions in your state. If a bank gets either Veribanc's or Weiss's poor rating, then you should switch banks.

Secondly, it is always a good policy to make sure that you do not have more than $100,000 at any one bank, and it is especially true today because of Y2K. I strongly recommend that anyone with more than $100,000 at a bank consider putting the excess in a money-market fund that invests in U.S. Treasury obligations. You can put any amount in the account, and because it is backed dollar for dollar with U.S. Treasury obligations, there is no risk of loss.

Further, if you have a money-market account as one of your accounts, you have increased your chances of having a checking account that "works" in January of 2000.

In fact, there are a number of reasons, apart from Y2K, that you might consider opening a money-market account (MMA). You get:

- Higher yields (sometimes two to three times more than yields from the average personal account, with much smaller minimums required);
- Generally lower fees at MMAs (in many cases substantially lower);
- Combined checking and savings;
- Unlimited account size;
- Exemption from state and local income taxes on the interest income;
- Truly free checking (often); and
- Immediate liquidity.

The disadvantage is that there is usually a minimum amount for checks (usually $100).

Here are several Treasury-only money-market funds that I recommend:

American Century Capital Preservation Funds	800-345-2021
Fidelity Spartan U.S. Treasury MMF	800-544-8888

U.S. Global Treasury Securities Cash	800-873-8637
Vanguard U.S. Treasury Portfolio	800-662-7447
Wiess Treasury Only Money Market Fund	800-289-8100

As I mentioned earlier, the various regulatory bodies that have oversight of banks are being more aggressive about making banks ask their customers the hard questions about Y2K compliance. Ideally, banks will start looking at their loan customers' viability in a recessionary environment now, and begin to reduce their exposure to companies that may be at higher risk.

Likewise, you should examine your own situation. You should not put yourself at risk. Check out the financial stability of your bank, and open up a money-market account for part of your cash.

Why I Am Scared About Bank Confidence

Banking is the ultimate confidence game. Depositors must have absolute confidence that they can get their funds whenever they want them in order to leave them in a bank. Bank runs start when depositors begin to have worries about the ability to get their funds immediately.

First, banks typically only have a small percentage of their deposits in cash and liquid securities readily available to meet withdrawal demands. They keep an even smaller amount in the form of physical cash for depositors to withdraw (typically under 2 percent of their deposits). They have access to more cash, if necessary, through the bank's required deposits at the Federal Reserve Bank.

Secondly, banks can lend more money than they actually have in deposits. Depending upon the reserve requirements established by the Federal Reserve and the bank's lending policies, they may have five to eight times the amount or more of their liquid assets lent out to customers. Therefore, they only have to have a *fraction* of the money that they lend out as reserves.

After World War II, banks typically lent out only about 20 percent of their deposits. There was plenty of available capital, but there were not as many creditworthy borrowers. Today bank loans can approach 90 percent of deposits. This means that the money available for depositors to withdraw is close to the lowest levels in history.

By the way, when those customers to whom the banks loan money put it back into the bank, this increases the money on deposit at the bank and therefore increases the money that the bank can lend to other customers, who in turn deposit the money at the bank, and so on and so on. This is called the multiplier effect.

Fractional-reserve banking comes under a lot of criticism from various quarters and for various reasons. There are problems that stem from fractional-reserve banking, but these mostly have to do with excessive lending, insufficient reserves, money being made too cheap, or government manipulation. By and large, it has been a wonderful engine for economic growth. I am not going to go into a long explanation of the good and bad points of the system here.

Suffice it to say that anything that threatens the stability of the fractional-reserve banking system is *very bad*. I can think of nothing that would crater our financial markets more quickly than the loss of confidence in banks. And *crater* might be too soft a word. The result of the collapse of the fractional-reserve system would be a doomsday scenario.

I have a strong bias for keeping the current system afloat and working. Along with you, I have a lifestyle that is dependent upon it. *If something threatens it I get very scared.*

I think that Y2K has the potential to indirectly threaten the fractional-reserve banking system. Further, I think that the first threat directly stems from current Federal Reserve policy.

I think a change in the policy can avoid the threat.

Threat Number One

Every poll, every survey, and every report tells us that a significant number of people are planning to take some or all of their money out of their banks because of Y2K. That number could easily rise if there is a loss of confidence in the banks.

Why would people have a loss of confidence? Because they know that some banks are not going to be ready, and wonder if theirs will be.

The Federal Reserve is not telling us which banks are in trouble. They are not telling us which banks are in good shape. The Fed is a black hole of financial information. Information goes in, but it never comes out!

They do this because they are concerned about causing banks runs. That is understandable. If they were to say that "ABC Bank" is not compliant and is way behind, it would cause a loss of faith in that bank and depositors would leave, probably en masse. The Fed would seem to be responsible for the demise of the bank.

But I worry about the opposite effect. Because people (depositors) aren't sure about their bank, they simply withdraw their money. And I can't blame them. Why risk it?

A banker can tell people his bank is compliant until he is blue in the face, and that assurance could fall on deaf ears. If there is a general loss of confidence, no amount of advertising or promises will do any good. And it will take but a small number of people asking for their money to put a severe strain on the banking system.

The one thing that can avert this, in my opinion, is for the Federal

Reserve to adopt the opposite of the policy that they currently have. Sometime late in the third quarter of 1999, they need to tell us which banks are Y2K compliant and which are not. If the Fed were to certify that ABC bank is in good shape, I think that most people would relax. The Fed is the best outside, independent auditor that has the confidence of the country. While there would still be cash withdrawals for contingency-planning purposes, they would be nothing like a massive withdrawal due to lack of confidence. And the contingency cash withdrawals would soon be back in the banks after the century turns and things have settled down.

The Federal Reserve has already publicly stated that it will step in and provide whatever temporary liquidity is necessary to the system. Contingency cash withdrawals, while creating some problems the Fed would rather not deal with, are not a true threat to the system. The Fed can deal with those problems.

Large-scale withdrawals are another matter entirely. Large-scale withdrawals threaten the system. But there is no need for it to happen. All the Federal Reserve has to do is tell us which banks are okay. While some skeptics would not trust their own mother if she told them everything was fine, I believe that the vast majority of Americans will listen.

What would we lose? A few banks. But we won't risk the system.

Further, these banks will be lost because their management didn't make good decisions. It won't be the Federal Reserve's fault that they were not in compliance. The management of the bank will be responsible.

I balance the risk to the fractional-reserve banking system against a few hundred mostly small banks, and say, "Tell us." It may be a little cold-blooded, but I think that we should drive the stake through their mismanaged hearts *before* 2000 rather than *after* and risk, however remote one might feel that risk is, the collapse of Western civilization.

The Federal Reserve can even avoid most of the banking problems if they stop pussyfooting with bank vendors and service providers. If Michael Curtiss is right, and I believe that he is, then most problems that banks have will be due to service providers having noncompliant systems. The Fed audits these vendors. They know who has problems.

Why wait until one or two vendors bring down scores of banks. Why not shut down the vendor, or at least let banks know who has problems so that they can change vendors before it is too late? So what if the Federal Reserve gets sued? They will just be doing their job protecting the banks and the banking system.

I am normally for the little guy against big bad government. But there are times when I like government. I like the police catching bad guys. I like firemen making sure that we stick to safe practices. I appreciate the SEC making sure that our investment companies stick to strict standards.

And I like the Federal Reserve auditing banks and controlling bad banking practices.

The economy of the entire world depends upon the confidence of the American depositor in his or her bank. I can see no reason to risk the confidence of depositors and ultimately the financial structure of the world to protect a few vendors or banks.

There will be people who think that I am overstating the case and making a mountain out of a molehill. I don't think so, but even if I am, it is not worth the risk.

The Federal Reserve must come clean. They must tell us who the non-compliant banks are. They can wait until late in the third quarter to give those banks as much time as possible. But then they need to step in.

Federal Reserve governor Edward W. Kelley, Jr. has said, "The Fed is prepared to function as the data processing vendor of last resort for financial institutions that are unable to access their own systems." Mr. Kelley added that the Fed can also operate paper-based payment systems should there be problems with the electronic payment system. The Fed would also join other banking agencies in the takeover of any banks that become insolvent as a result of Y2K. They need to do this before the fact rather than after. By being proactive, and letting the country know about problems, the Fed will do a great deal to maintain confidence in the system. If a bank has problems that will cause it to collapse in 2000, let's go ahead and pull the trigger in 1999 and save ourselves a lot of unnecessary worry and tension.

Threat Number Two

The second threat is not a direct result of Federal Reserve policy, but the Fed, if authorized by Congress, can deal with the problem.

As I said, contingency-based cash withdrawals are not an overwhelming problem. People wanting cash or even a small cash run can be dealt with.

I am more concerned about an electronic run.

This first occurred to me when I was talking to a director of a large U.S. corporation. He told me that they have over $10 million in various banks' accounts. His board was seriously discussing withdrawing the money in late 1999 and putting it into some type of account that would not put them at risk to their banks' potential financial problems. The FDIC only covers accounts up to $100,000, and they were way beyond that limit.

Basically, he said that they were deciding that it was not worth the risk, even if it was very small, to bet their entire company on another company's software, over which they had no control. So, they were looking at alternatives, and he asked me what I thought they should do.

I discussed some alternatives with him (trusts accounts, money markets, treasuries, etc.), all of which would not be subject to the FDIC $100,000 limit.

And then it dawned on me. This gentleman's question would not be an isolated event. Boards all over America were going to be asking themselves the same question, if only because many board members serve on more than one board and if it comes up in a meeting of the board of company A, then all those directors will bring it up in the next meetings of all the other companies on whose boards they serve. And many of them will come up with the same answer my friend's company did. *Why take the risk?* We can move the money back in February or March when we know everything is working.

Think of it like this. The chances of any one building or manufacturing plant burning down is relatively nil. There are thousands of warehouses in every metropolitan area in the country. Every year a few burn down. What are the odds? One in a thousand?

And yet what board in their right mind wouldn't have fire insurance at their warehouses? And if they buy all sorts of insurance for events that are unlikely to happen, why would they risk their business on someone else's software when there is no upside, no benefit, no real reason for doing so?

While contingency-based cash withdrawals from individuals might be relative chump change, if corporate America starts a silent electronic run, that could be a *real* problem. As one banker told me, it might be hard to get all those deposits back quickly. His body language told me that he did not like that part of our conversation.

If multiplied millions that add up to billions leave the fractional-reserve system, *it could pose a serious threat to the system.* But there is an alternative.

Congress could authorize a temporary change in the structure of FDIC guarantees and Federal Reserve margin requirements. It would work like this.

On December 28, 1999, we allow banks to sweep all corporate deposits over $100,000 into a "super" account. These deposits would not be subject to loss if the bank were to fail for Y2K reasons. At some predetermined specified point in the future, after the banks have demonstrated the ability to function in a post–January 1, 2000 world, the "super" accounts would be closed and the money put back into the original accounts.

But the Federal Reserve would allow banks to count the money in the interim super accounts toward their reserve requirements.

This would kill any Y2K reason for a business to move its money out of the banks, give the banks a way to maintain deposits and control of their largest customers' accounts, and forestall any threat of a silent electronic run to the fractional-reserve system.

Congress will have to establish this authority, as it does mean that for a few weeks the FDIC and thus the U.S. government is guaranteeing all bank deposits. That is a different level of risk than is currently authorized.

But it is not significantly more than what reality presently dictates. Suppose that there were a Y2K failure of a major bank, or even two or three? Are we supposed to believe that the Federal Reserve and the U.S. government would not step in and bail out all depositors, especially if not doing so meant the bankruptcy of thousands of companies and the loss of millions of jobs? When they talk about some banks being too big to fail, it is not just idle talk. The loss of a BankAmerica, Citicorp, or Chase would so scar this country financially that it would take years to come back.

You may disagree with the whole reserve system. You might criticize the FDIC program as making it too easy for banks to loan money and creating a whole host of problems. There is some merit in the calls for reforming the system.

But now is not the time to rock the boat, when there are major Y2K leaks in the boat that need to be fixed. The entire economy of this country and therefore of the rest of the world depends on a smooth and orderly transfer of our financial institutions from this millennium to the next.

Perhaps there are other ways that these two threats can be dealt with. It would not surprise me that better minds might find superior suggestions. I hope that someone does. But these threats need to be addressed sooner rather than later. Anything that threatens our entire way of life must not be pushed aside because we are uncomfortable thinking about the threat.

I happen to believe that the Federal Reserve will deal with these and other issues as suggested above or in some better way. They will have to. The Fed is run by responsible people who take their charge seriously. In normal times, the policy of not revealing audit information is probably correct. These are not normal times. A cash and electronic run on a small percent of current deposits will put a severe strain on bank liquidity, especially since banks are near historical lows in their liquidity ratios. I do not think that it would be good if the Fed had to inject massive amounts of money into the banking system and also allow reserve margins to diminish drastically. These are options, but they are not as good as maintaining a system that has the confidence of the country's depositors.

In my opinion, the current policy of not requiring full disclosure only makes the potential situation worse.

Government:
Ready or Not?

We could have, if not the equivalent of, something that
is very much like a hurricane on the East Coast, an
earthquake in San Francisco, massive forest fires in
Montana, and flooding on the Mississippi River happening
all at once. In addition to that, we could have two or three
countries where there's civil unrest because the
government can't provide basic services. We know how to
deal with each one of those things. The question is, will
we have the capacity and the resources to deal with them
all at once. No one of them alone is necessarily
overwhelming or threatening, but the combination is
something we normally don't plan for.

—John Koskinen, assistant to the President of the United States
and Chair, President's Council on Year 2000 Conversion

It is widely assumed that the government is in worse shape
than business in preparing for Y2K. But the truth is that you can't make
such a sweeping generality. The Y2K readiness of the government is no
different than that of the business sector: *it's a mixed bag.*

Many government agencies have started late, some have made good
progress, there has been limited cooperation in a lot of areas, and the
larger actors are doing somewhat better than the smaller ones. For the
most part, the federal government is beginning to act. A lot of progress
has been made since the first questions were asked by Congress. But a lot
remains to be done.

Many of the states and a large number of municipalities are moving
uncomfortably slowly in developing a real appreciation for the fact that
they have a problem and in marshalling the resources needed to attack
it.

Those governmental bodies addressing their internal Y2K needs are
unfortunately failing to pay ample attention to data exchanges, testing,
and contingency planning even though each level of government shares
information with the other.

The Eight-Hundred-Pound Gorilla

The problem is that the government is a huge sector of our economy. Everyone in this country depends upon the computers of more than one level of government working properly.

For instance, in 1999 U.S. federal spending is expected to top $1.7 trillion—more than the combined economies of Canada, Mexico, and China. The fifty state governments now employ 4.7 million people, with education as the largest segment. The nation's eighty-seven thousand local governments operate programs that once were left to the private and charitable sectors. Combined, the federal, state, and local governments spend more taxpayer dollars, employ more government workers, and operate more government programs than at any time in American history. In all, government is responsible for more than 25 percent of the economy, directly or indirectly.

For example:

- Federal contractors market and sell billions of dollars worth of goods and services to governments each year.
- We rely upon government air-traffic controllers to guide our air travel and ensure that goods and products reach their destinations.
- Many of the elderly and the disadvantaged who become ill depend on Medicare/Medicaid. They want their fees and services to be the same as those available in the private market.
- Some family farmers look to agricultural subsidies to get them through tough times.
- Since 1935, retirees have learned to count on timely and accurate Social Security payments to help maintain their general well-being and financial security.
- Elementary and secondary-school districts and postsecondary school students have learned to depend on about 788 federal government programs in forty different federal agencies for assistance in training the next generation of American workers.
- The Veterans Administration spends nearly $50 million per year to guarantee home loans for World War I and World War II veterans.
- Many power and water systems are run by local governments. Traffic lights, police, emergency systems, and many hospitals are run by some level of government.

To make all of this happen—the buying, the selling, the billing, the paying, the counting, the tabulating, the sorting, and the myriad of other government chores—the government relies on computers. The federal government has spent billions of dollars on computers and has been using them for years, far longer than most industries. It was the government that funded the development of the first American and British computers.

Today, the federal government owns and controls the largest share of the nation's mainframe legacy programs and microchips. The government's dependency on computers is such that it cannot afford to be saddled with a Y2K bug that could affect everything from Social Security and veterans' benefits to air travel and college-tuition payments, and seriously disrupt our health, safety, and future financial security.

Washington and its counterparts at the state and local levels have had some well-publicized failures as the steward of the nation's vital assets. These past failures give me some pause as to whether the government will solve its Y2K problems. One need only look at the debacle of central-city public-housing facilities to know what I mean. But consider also that:

- In 1992, the Government Accounting Office (GAO) judged that the Federal Aviation Administration's modernization program was "well over budget and years behind schedule." In 1995 it was designated a "high-risk information technology initiative," and it was declared "high-risk" again in 1997. The current state of the computer systems at the FAA, which brings to mind the term *obsolete,* leaves few observers satisfied.
- The IRS spent over $4 billion trying to design and build a new computer system. Last year they acknowledged that they would have nothing to show for that massive amount of taxpayer money.

It is too easy to cite reference after reference of failed and late government-run computer projects. The temptation is to throw up your hands and move on. But the government sector is so huge and vital to our national well-being that we must face the problems head-on.

Office of Management and Budget Reports

One thing that the federal government is doing right and that sets it apart from industry is providing the public with information on what is happening. For this the federal government is to be congratulated. As I've said before, we simply must be given the facts so that we can plan adequately.

The problem is that what we learn is disconcerting, to say the least. Since May 1997, on a quarterly basis, the Office of Management and Budget has compiled data on the Y2K status of the various federal agencies. The OMB reports show the total number of mission-critical systems in each agency, the number and percentage of compliant systems, the official estimated cost to fix the systems, and the number of agencies in trouble.

There are at least seven thousand mission-critical computer systems in the executive branch of the federal government that are vital to everything from getting planes to fly on time to issuing monthly checks. I say seven thousand because the number changes every quarter. The number is down about 20 percent from its high in November of 1997.

I can understand that no government manager worth his salt would want his program certified noncritical. But apparently over twelve hundred were originally certified critical and now aren't. We aren't told how many new critical ones have been found over the same time.

The good news is that there has been some good progress made over

T A B L E   6 - 1 ▨

U.S. Federal Government Progress Report

Report Number and Date	Number of Mission-Critical Systems	Number of Compliant Systems	Percent Complete	Official Estimated Cost to Fix (Billion $)	Agencies in Trouble
1. May '97	7,649	1,598	21	2.8	0
2. Aug. '97	8,562	1,646	19	3.8	5
3. Nov. '97	8,589	2,296	27	3.9	7
4. Feb. '98	7,850	2,716	35	4.7	6
5. May '98	7,336	2,913	40	5	6
6. Aug. '98	7,343	3,692	50	5.4	7

Source: Office of Management and Budget

T A B L E   6 - 2 ▨

U.S. Federal Government Progress Report: Mission-Critical Repairs

Report Number and Date	Number of Mission-Critical Systems	Number Needing Repair	Percent Renovated	Percent Validated	Percent Complete
1. May '97	7,649	4,493	17	5	6
2. Aug. '97	8,562	5,332	12	5	2
3. Nov. '97	8,589	5,124	34	17	10
4. Feb. '98	7,850	4,413	46	24	19
5. May '98	7,336	4,395	55	32	27
6. Aug. '98	7,343	4,640	71	44	37

Source: Office of Management and Budget

the last year. The bad news is that there is not much time left and that there is a great deal to be done.

U.S. Federal Government Progress Report

I cannot voice my concern any better than by quoting Congressman Steve Horn, chairman of the House Subcommittee on Government Management, Information, and Technology, in the subcommittee's latest official report.

1. The Federal Government is Not on Track to Complete Necessary Year 2000 Preparations Before January 1, 2000.

The most recent data on Federal Executive branch preparations were released for the quarter ending August 15, 1998. There are approximately 7,300 mission-critical systems in the Executive branch of the Federal Government. As of August 15, only 50 percent of these systems were Year 2000 compliant. At the current rate of progress, the percentage compliant would climb only to 66 percent by March 1999, the President's deadline to fix noncompliant systems and still have enough time to test and implement the systems.

The committee is deeply concerned that approximately one-third of all Federal mission-critical systems will not be compliant by March 1999, only nine months before January 1, 2000, and only six months from the beginning of the Federal Government's new fiscal year on October 1, 1999. This is troubling in part because once these systems are "compliant," they need to be put back into operation, their compliance must be verified by an independent party, and they must be put through a rigorous end-to-end testing process that ensures coordination among multiple systems. Testing and verification can take at least nine months, and often requires even more time than that.

Several additional factors raise concerns about Federal Year 2000 preparations. One is that the focus has been almost exclusively on mission-critical systems. The problem is that mission-critical systems are only a small percentage of the total number of Federal computer systems. Many of these secondary systems are important even if not mission critical. It is unwise to ignore their Year 2000 compliance. A second concern is that many agencies are planning to replace rather than repair some of their noncompliant computer systems. This is a high-risk strategy. Experience shows that the Government does not put new computer systems in place on schedule. This time, the Executive branch faces a deadline that cannot be extended.

A crucial component of Year 2000 remediation is the exchange of data between organizations. Fixing internal systems simply is not enough. Federal agencies have data exchange partners throughout society—including other Federal agencies, state and local governments, and private and non-profit organizations. These data exchanges must be tested through cooperative effort. Current indications are that the Federal agencies lag badly in this area."[1]

The committee issues a report card for twenty-four government agencies (see Table 6-3).

Agencies that claimed that they would be finished before the March 1999 deadline earned an A. Those finishing later in 1999 received a B. My one major criticism of this report is that if you finished in 2000, you were given a C. In other words, if you turned your paper in one year late, you still passed. If you were scheduled to be finished in 2001, you were given a D. Anything after 2001 was an F.

There were seven Ds and six Fs!

The report shows that the federal government has made some progress. In November 1998 Representative Horn released the sixth federal government report card based on the data from the quarter ending August 1998. Individually, nine of the twenty-four departments and agencies are continuing to make what is deemed to be adequate progress. Among these agencies, 74 percent of mission-critical systems are now Year 2000 ready, and 89 percent of the systems being repaired have now been renovated. This progress is led by the Social Security Administration, the National Science Foundation, and the Small Business Administration, each of which garnered grades of A for their Y2K work.

Federal Computer Week reported that the Financial Management Service (FMS) in the Treasury Department brought on-line two Y2K-compliant systems for processing Social Security retirement and disability checks for 50 million beneficiaries.[2] The FMS writes most of the checks issued by the federal government. In addition, the FMS is responsible for paying veterans' benefits, sending out Internal Revenue Service refunds, and processing some federal salary and vendor payments.

The data at other departments and agencies tell a different overall story. According to Horn, in November 1998 the federal government earned a grade of D, which is an improvement from the F it earned in the previous report card. He cautioned Americans, however, about using the term *improvement* in the context of the D grade. "As a former professor," he said, "I have seen students flunk out of college by earning too many Ds. This is not a grade you take home to your parents; and it is definitely not a grade to take back to the voters and taxpayers."

[1]*http://www.house.gov/reform/gmit/y2k/y2k_report/1summary.htm.*
[2]*Federal Computer Week,* September 17, 1998.

TABLE 6-3

Year 2000 Progress Report Card

Agency	1997 Aug 15	1998 Feb 15	1998 May 15	1998 Aug 15	1998 Nov 13
Social Security Administration	A−	A	A+	A	A
National Science Foundation	B	A	A−	A	A
Small Business Administration	B	B	B	A	A
General Services Administration	B	C	A−	B+	B+
Department of Commerce	D	B	B	B	B
Environmental Protection Agency	C	B	B	B	B+
Department of Veterans Affairs	C	A	C	B−	B−
Federal Emergency Management Agency	C	D−	A−	B−	B
National Aeronautics & Space Administration	D−	D	B	C+	C+
Department of Agriculture	D−	B	D	C	C
Department of Housing & Urban Development	C	B	C	C	C
Department of the Treasury	D−	D	C	D+	C
Department of Transportation	F	F	F	D	D
Office of Personnel Management	D	B	C−	D	C−
Department of Defense	C−	F	D	D	D−
Department of Labor	C	F	C	D	C
Department of the Interior	C	C−	C−	D	B
Nuclear Regulatory Commission	D	C−	B	D	C−
Department of Health & Human Services	B−	D	F	F	F
Department of Energy	D	D−	F	F	F
Department of State	C	F	F	F	F
Department of Justice	D	C−	D	F	F
Department of Education	F	F	D	F	C−
Agency for International Development	F	D−	F	F	F
Administration Overall	—	D−	F	D	D

Source: Congressman Stephen Horn.
http://www.house.gov/reform/gmit/y2k/index.htm

Some grades are very disturbing. Eight agencies are identified as making progress, but with concerns. Seven are identified as not making adequate progress. A department that should understand the value of grades—the Department of Education—and the Department of Justice actually got worse from one grading period to the next, dropping from D to F.

The Department of Energy and the Department of Health and Human Resources, which houses the Health Care Financing Administration (HCFA), also earned Fs. HCFA administers the federal Medicare program. The Office of Management and Budget (OMB) is especially concerned that with only 14 percent of external contractor systems renovated, "At least some Medicare contractors may fail to meet the March 1999 government-wide deadline. . . ."

It may be worse than "may fail." Read what the Government Accounting Office (GAO) said in September 1998 in summarizing a report on medicare computer systems on its web site:

> The Health Care Financing Administration (HCFA) and its contractors are extremely behind schedule in repairing, testing, and implementing the mission-critical computer systems supporting Medicare. HCFA has recently begun to improve its management of Year 2000 issues, including establishing a Year 2000 organization and hiring independent contractors to oversee the work.
>
> However, because of the complexity and magnitude of the problem and HCFA's late start, the repairs lag far behind schedule. Less than one-third of Medicare's 98 mission-critical systems had been fully renovated as of June 1998, and none had been validated or implemented, according to HCFA. Compounding this difficult task is the absence of key management practices HCFA needs to adequately direct and monitor its Year 2000 project. HCFA also has not effectively managed the identification and correction of its electronic data exchanges.
>
> *Because of the magnitude of the tasks ahead and the limited time remaining, it is unlikely that all of the Medicare systems will be compliant in time to guarantee uninterrupted benefits and services into the year 2000.* [Emphasis added.][3]

The Department of Defense (DOD) earned a D. There are so many unnerving reports about the DOD that I will choose just a few. The first one is on what must be the most significant concern you should have about the Defense Department.

A report issued in November 1998 by the British American Security

---

[3]*http://www.gao.gov./monthly.list/september/sep9813.htm.* "Medicare Computer Systems: Year 2000 Challenges Put Benefits and Services in Jeopardy" (*Letter Report,* Sept. 28, 1998).

Information Council (BASIC) has brought into question government assurances that the Year 2000 problem will not disable or accidentally trigger the world's nuclear arsenal.

According to the report "The Bug in the Bomb,"[4] U.S. officials are so concerned about the possibility of launch orders being issued upon inaccurate data that they have asked Russian officials to stand "right beside" them when the year 2000 arrives.

The report notes that the complexity of the problem is exacerbated by the "launch on warning" force posture maintained by the U.S. and Russia. This policy mandates the immediate firing of weapons when enemy nuclear weapons are detected.

According to Sergev Fradkov, former–Soviet satellite control technician, "Russia is extremely vulnerable to the Year 2000 problem and an accidental launch is possible." Y2K consultant Ron Piasecki says in the report that "it is definitely in the realm of possibility for Y2K glitches to freeze or garble radar and telecommunications networks, which might lead to launch orders based upon inaccurate data."

Here is a report from an American source:

> Lt. Gen. Carleton Fulford, commander of Marine Forces Pacific, called the Year 2000 problem "the No. 1 challenge" of his command, which oversees 80,000 Marines and sailors stationed on 12 bases from Arizona to Japan, and the main "close fight we are dealing with right now. . . ."
>
> Fulford, speaking here at the Armed Forces Communication and Electronics Association's TechNet Asia-Pacific Conference and Exposition, said the problem extends far beyond ensuring that Pacific Marines fix their 26,000 computers, 150 "mission-essential" computer programs and 2,000 software programs because the Pacific Marines' systems must be able to interface with those from more than 40 allied nations.
>
> *"I'm very concerned about the fact that whatever we do in the Pacific, we must do with our allies . . . and I'm very concerned that they won't be prepared,"* Fulford said [emphasis added].[5]

The Canadians, British, and Australians are all very candid about using their military in the event of a Y2K-caused crisis or civil unrest. The quotes coming from their generals show that they are deeply concerned. The Canadians, understanding what a crisis might entail from the loss of power in Quebec last winter, are in training programs. The Royal Canadian Mounted Police have been told that there will be no vacations immediately before or for several months after January 2000.

---

[4]"The Bug in the Bomb: The Impact of the Year 2000 Problem on Nuclear Weapons" by Michael Kraig, November 1998 (BASIC Publications Research Report 98.6).

[5]*Federal Computer Week,* November 5, 1998.

Major General Edward J. Philbin, USAF (Retired), executive director of the National Guard Association, said the following in his testimony to the U.S. Senate in October of 1998 (excerpts):

> It is increasingly evident that an appreciable part of the nation's infrastructure could be adversely affected in some way, by what is commonly referred to as the Y2K problem. . . .
>
> Considering the possibilities of a large scale disruption of governmental, commercial and other routine daily activities, it is certain that the National Guard will be among the first organizations activated to assist in the revitalization of the nation's computer-dependent infrastructure. . . .
>
> The Year 2000 challenges present an emergency scenario unlike any other in our nation's history. Our technological society has grown extremely dependent upon the continuity of computer-driven systems and networks and as a consequence, the nation's vulnerability has increased appreciably. Any significant disruption of our computer-dependent infrastructure could result in a significant societal disruption. However, with the cooperative interaction of federal and state governments, the military, the private sector, and with serious advance preparation, the impact of such an event on the American people can be significantly reduced, if not totally eliminated.[6]

I must confess that the thought of someone deciding that the National Guard ought to be prepared for potential Y2K-related problems is quite comforting. I am not as worried as some are about what is politely called civil unrest. But I do want to know that if there are problems with infrastructure (electricity, phones, transportation, etc.), the Guard is ready to step in to help. The full range of contingency plans should be made soon, and then they should be made public. They should be made in concert with local civic leaders to make sure that in the event that their services are needed, there is full coordination and cooperation with local authorities.

But the main point is that the DOD is behind and is working hard to catch up and that the results of their failure could be very serious. I will address some of these concerns in the chapter on recommendations for government action.

The Department of Transportation grade includes the Federal Aviation Administration. In a previous report, Congressman Horn noted that the nation's air traffic could face serious disruptions for an extended period after December 31, 1999 if dramatic improvements are not made in the FAA's Y2K effort. As of August 1998, the FAA had renovated 59 percent of mission-critical systems, up from the 11 percent reported in May.

[6]*http://www.ngaus.org/library/philbin998.htm.*

However, with 10 percent of its systems validated and 3 percent implemented, the FAA is still significantly behind schedule.

"The agency is frighteningly behind schedule to be ready for the year 2000," according to Senator Robert Bennett, Republican of Utah, who is chairman of the Senate's Year 2000 Committee. He bases that belief on General Accounting Office reports that say it is doubtful that the FAA can make needed corrections in time.

"I wish I could say I'm confident in the claims of the FAA," Bennett says. "But given GAO's scathing reports, the FAA's assertions that it has made such tremendous progress are very questionable."[7]

Considering air travel and the Y2K status of the FAA, noted Y2K expert Ed Yardeni has concluded that "the FAA will keep the jets flying in January 2000. But I doubt that the schedules will be at 100 percent of capacity. Many flights will be canceled, especially to noncompliant airports both in the United States and abroad. My best guess is that domestic traffic will be only 75 percent of normal and that international flights could be cut by 30 percent for at least a few weeks in January."

My conversations with the personnel involved with Y2K at the Airlines Transportation Association lead me to similar conclusions. They were emphatic that the airlines would fly, but sanguinely noted that schedules could be a problem. Depending upon the level of FAA and airport readiness, instead of flights leaving major airports every minute, it may be closer to every five minutes, forcing flights to be made at very odd hours and meaning long layovers.

You will be able to get to where you want to go, but you probably won't like the schedule if the FAA is not fully operational. Remember, airlines flew prior to computers. But they didn't operate on the intense level that they do today.

THE STATES

States are involved in a wide array of concerns, including hospitals, prisons, streets and highways, public welfare, financial administration, health, natural resources, courts, social insurance administration, police, parks, and recreation and mass transit. Additionally, the states administer several important federal initiatives, such as the unemployment insurance and Medicaid programs. In the area of taxation, the federal and state governments operate separate but related systems.

It is not in the scope of this book to deal with the preparations of individual states. But I can tell you from talking with consultants and state administrators and from various reports that the level of preparation from state to state varies widely.

Some states will be ready for the century date change. Some will be

---

[7]From a web article at MSNBC

able to make the much-needed data and information exchanges. Others will have more problems, and some may (will?) have serious problems.

Many states have established web sites. If you would like to know the status of your state, I will have a link to your state's web site (if I can find one) at my web site at *http://www.2000wave.com* for updates.

THE CITIES AND TOWNS

> I'm also very concerned about small and medium-sized states, counties and cities. In fact, I think that our greatest risk is not that the infrastructure will collapse—because I don't believe it will—but that, if we can't increase the level of activity, we could see significant difficulties in a number of small and medium-sized counties and cities as well as companies.[8]
>
> —John Koskinen, assistant to the President of the United States and Chair, President's Council on Year 2000 Conversion.

The vast majority of the nation's eighty-seven thousand local governments, which administer some seventeen thousand police departments and thirty-two thousand fire departments, have done nothing to get ready for the millennium change.

The GartnerGroup tells us that 65 percent of U.S. cities and towns do not have Year 2000 projects, and midsize and smaller cities and towns are lagging far behind or have not started.[9]

Many small municipalities don't have a clue. A fall 1998 survey by Public Technology, Inc., a private consulting firm advising municipalities, found that 57 percent of respondent cities thought that they had nothing to fear. In New York, a separate survey found that 54 percent of towns, 48 percent of villages, and 26 percent of cities have not made plans for fixing the bug. Yet another survey of 402 California cities, counties, and special districts found that 25 percent have no Year 2000 action plan and 42 percent have no funds budgeted.

Never mind that without electricity jail cells won't open and close properly and elevators won't go up and down. Without telephone service, 911 calls won't go through. If we do not fix Y2K problems in their mainframe computers and software, government billing and payroll and court filing systems won't run. If we do not cure problems associated with embedded chips in the public sanitation, traffic, and water systems, those valuable government services will be at risk. Just keep in mind that in most cities even the operations of the city dump will be affected by Y2K since the electronic scales that weigh vehicles entering landfills are computer driven.

The number of local preparations that must be made is immense, to

[8]*http://www.ncs.gov/N5_HP/Customer_Service/XAffairs/SpeechService/SS98-025.htm.*
[9]*http://gartner3.gartnerweb.com/public/static/aboutgg/pressrel/testimony 1098.html.*

say the least. In appendix B is a list of actions for contingency planning that local communities need to take to prepare for January 2000. I suggest that you read through this to give yourself some idea of the depth and breadth of planning necessary. This section was prepared by Capers Jones. There are other web sites following his presentation that will provide further information. Each local community must assume responsibility for itself. If your community hasn't started yet, then you are behind. Depending upon the size of your community, you may be way behind. The best thing to do is to get started now. Don't procrastinate. Lives may depend upon how your community responds to local problems.

Contrasted with those municipalities that have done nothing are a few cities that appear to have gotten the message. Montgomery County, Maryland, is spending $35 million to upgrade more than two hundred computer systems. San Joaquin County, California, reports that it has fixed fifty computer systems containing 3,850 programs and 3.9 million lines of code. In October 1998, Lubbock, Texas, held the nation's first mock Year 2000 computer crash, complete with a power failure and prison riot. City workers improvised manual work-arounds for computer-driven government operations.

Water Treatment Facilities are in Trouble!

In researching Y2K I have literally read thousands of stories. This report which just came out prior to finishing this book is perhaps the most disturbing I have read.

A new survey by the American Water Works Association reveals some startling numbers. Remember that most "self-reported" survey results will tend to present a more optimistic picture than may actually be justified. With that in mind, read some of the results of this one (italics are my emphasis added):

- 97 percent of water treatment facilities use computers
- *36 percent have no formal plans for addressing Y2K*
- *42 percent have not even finished their Y2K assessment stage*
- *39 percent have not completed risk assessment activities* (identifying which systems are critical and which systems are not)
- Only 42 percent rated water distribution systems control as critical
- Only 36 percent rated water treatment control systems as critical
- 78 percent have not completed Year 2000 remediation efforts
- 25 percent of those who said they were finished with Y2K repairs said they didn't need to modify anything!
- 29 percent of those who haven't finished Y2K repairs are not sure when they might finish

- 74 percent have not assessed the Y2K compliance of their vendors or suppliers
- 77 percent have no contingency plans
- 79 percent have not assessed their legal liability if they should fail to deliver water

The troublesome part is that when you look at the survey you get the distinct impression that there is a lot of guessing. The lack of discernable patterns makes me nervous.

I find this report appalling. Is it only me, or does this make you angry, too? When over one-third of water utilities have no formal plan for addressing Y2K and 74 percent have not assessed their vendors, this indicates a complete lack of responsibility on the part of many of the managers of our most vital resource.

Consumer action item: I don't have to tell you how important water is. Water problems in any city or small town even for a day would be serious. I prefer a calm, reasoned approach to dealing with problems. But it is hard for me to be calm when I see numbers like those above. I would take this report and show it to your city council members. Politely but firmly ask what the status of your water source is, and request that your water district provide a written, verifiable plan to the public about their Y2K status.

I would not take no for an answer. The good news is that water delivery is not as difficult to make compliant as electric power or banks. There is no reason you should not have water IF your local utilities are not asleep at the wheel. There should be enough time for them to get compliant. I think you should check on them and *wake them up* if they are not addressing the issue.

No More Time for Lip Service

The Congressional Subcommittee on Government Management, Information and Technology chaired by Representative Stephen Horn, Republican of California, has been conducting investigations into overall federal government activity for the better part of two years now. In July 1997, the committee asked President Clinton to use the "bully pulpit" of the Oval Office to explain the Millennium Bug challenge and inspire the American people to go out and fix it. They also recommended that he appoint a Y2K czar to lead the fight.

The president has spoken with the American people on any number of issues, including his private life, in the past year. He still has not made a major address concerning this issue. A senior administration official to coordinate the national Year 2000 effort was not on board until March 1998. Finally, in October 1998, a federal council created by the president sponsored a "National Y2K Action Week" to educate small business and government. (I know: you are wondering how you missed it.)

Given the seriousness of the crisis, waiting until October of 1998 for an "Awareness Week" is just not acceptable.

It is quite clear to me that some vitally important government computer systems will simply not be prepared for January 1, 2000, putting at risk the utilities industry, the financial services sector, the telecommunications industry, certain modes of transportation, our health services, national defense, and other vital services that are all intertwined and that Americans depend upon every single day. The dollar cost to American taxpayers and business will be enormous. The personal cost to those who need these services, many of them life-sustaining, cannot be calculated.

Many of the government's mission-critical computer systems can be readied in time. But this assumes that we accelerate the pace. *We need to start treating our government Y2K-conversion and contingency plans as the technological equivalent of war.* I will address this further in chapter 17, but our political leaders must do better.

Who's Minding the Store? The Risk to American Business

In the preceding chapters, I've reviewed the Y2K readiness of the energy, telecommunications, banking, and government sectors of the economy, looking especially at what each industry has done internally to attain Y2K readiness.

Each of these sectors has a dramatic impact on the real power behind the American economic engine: our business community, from the smallest business to the largest mega-corporations like General Electric, General Motors, and Exxon. It is the ability of every business in this country to efficiently deliver products and services that makes our economy the most efficient producer of jobs and wealth in the history of the world.

Y2K is going to put this efficiency at serious risk. As we will see in the next few chapters, America will likely suffer the loss of millions of jobs. We have already seen the predictions from sober, well-respected research firms that we will lose hundreds of thousands of businesses to the effects of Y2K.

This chapter is written primarily for the business community worldwide. This book has many sobering, stomach-churning facts and predictions. My hope is that it will not scare entrepreneurs and managers into a retreat—a fall-back, batten-down-the-hatches mode—but will serve as a wake-up call to make sure that you not only survive Y2K but find ways to turn the problem to your advantage.

I want you to think through your personal situations and determine how you should respond to Y2K.

If We Do Our Parts

I don't have a crystal ball. So, a couple of years from now, when you sit down in front of the fireplace and read my forecasts with the benefit of twenty-twenty hindsight, you will find some that are dead center in the bull's-eye, and some that missed the target altogether.

All the predictions that I make are based on thorough research and the best information that we have today. But today's information will soon be history. The Y2K situation is changing weekly, even hourly. You can't rely on old data to make your decisions. You must stay continually up to date.

Forecasts of future events aren't just words. They are *themselves* events, with a real impact on the future!

Most people see forecasts as separate from the actual events. But they are not.

Forecasts of trouble, when made irresponsibly, are often self-fulfilling. They create fear and panic. They help trigger the very crisis being predicted.

But forecasts of trouble made responsibly can be self-negating. They help motivate people to take action. They soften, prevent, or even reverse the impact of the predicted events.

The mission of this book is to warn you, to stimulate action, and to help prevent the very events that I am predicting.

I see no way that the effect of Y2K will be negligible. But if we all work diligently in the remaining time, I'm hoping that the more dire predictions about the effects of Y2K will be dead wrong. If so, I will have helped to make them so. In contrast, if my predictions turn out to be right, I may get a few passing kudos for my foresight, but there will be no joy in receiving them.

In either case—whether I'm right *or* wrong—*your* mission is to look out for yourself, your family, and your business.

One man's predictions—good, bad, or indifferent—won't be worth a hill of beans if you don't act on them to protect yourself. Whether we breeze through Y2K or stumble into chaos . . . whether the economy booms or busts . . . you must take concrete steps right now.

In this chapter we are going to look at some of the biggest threats to business from Y2K, and then I am going to offer some general suggestions as to what you can do to get ready. Every business is different, but there are some things that we all can do. The more that is done prior to 2000, the better off we all will be!

The External Threat

Even if a business gets all its internal software ready, its existence can be threatened because major suppliers cannot deliver needed components for whatever products or services they offer. This is called the supply chain. Every business has one, even the smallest.

The supply chain refers to the interdependent relationship of suppliers, vendors, wholesalers, distributors, and other players linked together to produce a given product. Getting something as simple as a loaf of bread requires the interplay of dozens of actors, from the farmer through the grocery storekeeper, who are involved in the process of producing, warehousing, packaging, displaying, transporting, and selling the products. I once invested in a small chain of car washes. We bought soap, motors, chemicals, and scores of small items necessary to our operation. If we hadn't had them, we couldn't have opened for business.

This book is the product of hundreds and hundreds of companies working together. I grew up in the printing business, and owned and ran a publishing company in the late seventies and eighties. The mechanical and technical difference of how a book is published today and just fifteen years ago is night and day. I didn't realize I was in the Stone Age in 1983! But computers have changed the process dramatically, from writing and editing to printing and selling them in the bookstores! You may have bought this book on the Internet!

The ink on this page is the result of scores of businesses supplying the necessary chemicals, mixing equipment, transportation, distribution and billing software, communications, and other necessities to the ink manufacturer. Having grown up in the printing business, I can tell you that the ink on this page was specially formulated for the specific presses and climate conditions of the printer. The ink manufacturer has to know what formulations of ink thousands of companies use, and make sure they get what works best on their presses. Without computers, the process would be labor intensive and quite costly, and MUCH slower.

Likewise, the shipping, selling, inventory, paper suppliers, and editors are all part of a vast network of companies who supply some critical part of the process. It is a testimony to hard work and automation that St. Martin's Press can get this book into the bookstores only a few weeks after I write it. But to do so, every part of the hundreds of members of the supply chain has to work smoothly.

Because I have neither the time nor the space to cover every company in the supply chain of every American business, I want to look at two specific examples of the supply chain, which will let us see something of the problems business faces. First, I will take a quick look at the agriculture, food, and grocery business and share with you what I've learned about the status of their Y2K preparedness. Then I will look at the transportation industry and how it will impact our food supply.

Since other industry segments, such as retail and manufacturing, rely on ships and trains to deliver materials, supplies, and finished products, what we learn about the food-supply chain will have a direct relationship on them as well. Then we can start to assess the risks to all businesses.

Agriculture Is USDA Grade ''D''—As in D for ''danger''

Agriculture is far behind other industry sectors in attaining Y2K readiness. The GartnerGroup report, which I have mentioned before, indicates that farming and agriculture businesses will likely experience at least one mission-critical system failure due to noncompliance with Year 2000 issues. Agriculture is in the highest-risk group.

At the beginning of the food-supply chain are the 2 million farms situated in the rolling, green pastures of rural America. About 90 percent of U.S. farms are individual or family operations. At the end of the chain are 127,000 grocery stores. Supermarkets, the dominant segment of the grocery industry, represent less than 25 percent of all grocery stores but account for nearly 75 percent of total grocery sales. Since 1986, the independent supermarkets, smaller grocery stores, and mom-and-pop stores have decreased significantly in number. The number of independents and smaller grocery stores has fallen by thirty-five thousand. The principal cause of grocery-store business failure is razor-thin net-profit margins, which historically have been around 1 percent.

In the past decade or so, the food and grocery industry has followed the lead of other industry sectors in becoming dependent on computer technology. According to a 1997 survey conducted by the National Agricultural Statistics Service, 31 percent of American farmers own or lease computers, and 13 percent have Internet access. Farmers and ranchers use computers to manage the over $200 billion in cash receipts generated each year. Computers are used to buy and sell agricultural products and make trades on the commodities market. Farmers and ranchers use information technology to water fields, feed animals, and transport what they produce. Processors rely on automated systems in food preparation and packaging. Distributors, wholesalers, and retailers depend on computer-based equipment to transport, deliver, store, display, and sell food products. Today's food retailers use sophisticated point-of-sale terminals, scanning systems, credit-card operations, and electronic benefit systems that process not only food-stamp purchases but also grocery-store preferred customer selections.

One If By Land: No Trucks, No Ships, No Railcars Equals No Food

The Y2K vulnerability of agriculture is compounded by the lack of Year 2000 readiness in the transportation industry.

The average American goes to the grocery store about two times each week. Most U.S. cities have approximately seventy-two hours' worth of food within their borders. The U.S. as a whole has only a three-months' supply.[1] What's more, because grocery stores have such paper-thin profit margins, they can't afford to keep large inventories. What you see on the grocery-store shelf is what the store has. Stores get around their inventory problems by using what is called "just-in-time" (JIT) deliveries. Every day vendors bring needed inventories to restock the shelves. That's fine if there's food in the grocery store.

So what happens if there is even a limited, temporary breakdown in the food supply? The answer: there can be a demonstrable negative impact on what's on grocery-store and restaurant shelves.

> While the problems Y2K poses for the agriculture industry are similar to those facing other industries, the Y2K ramifications of the agriculture problems could have serious impact for the average consumer. In a worst-case scenario, there could even be local food shortages due to transportation problems.

Those were the words of Michael Schommer, a spokesman for the Minnesota Department of Agriculture. Here's what he meant:

▌ *Perishable Items Can't Wait to Be Delivered*

Milk, beef, and poultry are perishable items. Getting the breakfast of champions to the kitchen table is a long, intricate process. The milk for our cereal goes from the dairy farmer to the processor, who then sells it to a wholesaler. The wholesaler then sells the milk to a distributor, who sells it to the retailer. And the retailer sells it to us. A Y2K-induced computer failure affecting any link in the "farm-to-fork" food chain could slow the entire process and cause localized food shortages.

▌ *Disruptions of Just-in-Time Deliveries Mean Empty Grocery-Store Shelves and Pantries*

Bar-coded scanning devices analyze dozens of factors for every item in the store. Calculations regarding everything including usage rates, vendor information, pricing, volume discounts, minimum order quantities, credit terms, freight charges, lead time, and seasonal considerations are made each time an item is slid under the little scanner at the checkout counter. From that information, the computer system computes the optimal quantity of orders and the time to place them. And when that time arrives, the computer can place the order. Miscalculations or com-

---

[1]John Yellig, "Y2K and Agriculture: Potential Effects and Consequences." From Westergaard Year 2000 web site (*WWW.Y2KTIMEBOMB.COM/INDUSTRY/Agriculture/ agri9815.htm*), April 15, 1998.

puter failure would make it more difficult to service customer shopping needs.

It is tempting to say that this can't be that big of a problem—the grocery store could manage its inventory manually. That may be easier said than done. In their newsletter *The Millennium Bug Weekly,* Michael Hyatt and Bill Dunn argue that working around the problem manually is "a nice idea but impractical or impossible." Hyatt and Dunn suggest that:

> stores don't have the warehouse space needed to run the store manually. Even if they had the warehouse space, the storeowners don't have the huge sums of cash needed to double or triple stock levels. Manufacturers and vendors don't have the capacity to ship that much merchandise all at once. They, too, are running on "just-in-time" inventory and production systems.

In 1996 the U.S. freight-transport industry earned $425 billion for movement of domestic goods. Trucking dominated the industry. Trucking revenues for 1996 were estimated to be around $360 billion; that is, three-quarters of the total revenues within the industry. On-demand air-freight companies earned about $40 billion from domestic (and international) accounts. The railroads, small trucking, and maritime (domestic and international) businesses took in about $36 billion, $19 billion, and $6 billion, respectively. The good news is that there are no serious doubts about the trucking industry. The freight industry should be able to transport America's food supply without major interruption due largely to the fact that trucks transport 80 percent of all consumer goods.

A Delay or Failure to Deliver Valuable Hybrid Seeds Can Adversely Affect Next Year's Crop

To grow their crops, farmers use hybrid seeds, which are perishable and generally must be shipped to them. Typically, the seeds are delivered to farms in the first part of the year—in 2000 that will be exactly when transportation companies may be experiencing Millennium Bug problems. A disruption in the delivery of these seeds could dramatically impact the planting of the following year's crop, the availability of items on our grocery-store shelves, and the farmers' financial health.

And Two If By Sea: Y2K and the Shipping Industry

U.S. trade is extraordinarily dependent on maritime shipping. Throughout this book, and particularly in the international chapter, I discuss our export and import activity and the positive contribution trade makes in supporting American jobs and our quality of life. The vast majority of foreign trade comes into the country through shipping. About eighty thousand ships sail the world's waterways; 95 percent of the overseas cargo entering the U.S. comes via our ports, and over 97 percent of that comes in foreign ships.

The main problem with tankers is associated with microprocessors that control navigational, telecommunications, and alarm systems as well as real-time process controls such as engine-room and cargo-monitoring systems. Maritime-industry experts estimate that a typical tank vessel may contain between fifty and two hundred microprocessors. Eighty percent of tanker Y2K-remediation expenses have been due to fixing and replacing embedded chips.

"The reports given by oil majors Chevron and Shell in relation to their examination of their tanker fleet has shown up to 20 percent of systems to be noncompliant, with equipment built between 1987 and 1993 particularly prone to problems."[2] The U.S. Coast Guard and London's Entropy Management Ltd. reached a similar conclusion when they surveyed marine manufacturers.

The Y2K risks associated with tankers are real, although the vulnerability of tanker computer systems is difficult to discern. At this moment, information in the public domain from the marine industry is limited. So, I can't say with any certainty what the status of the maritime industry is likely to be on January 1, 2000. But we do know some things:

- In early 1997, the International Maritime Safety Agency notified all international governments that the Millennium Bug represented a threat to maritime shipping.
- Based on what we know about worldwide Y2K readiness overall, many ports around the world are probably considerably behind the U.S. and in pretty bad shape.
- Crews on the newer, computerized ships are much smaller and not as sea-experienced as those of twenty to thirty years ago. Without computers the potential for delays and accidents is much higher.

Manufacturing Was Late to the Y2K Party

Manufacturing companies were slow to wake up to the enormity of the Millennium Bug task. An April 1998 report by Forrester Research said that on average, large corporations were only 34 percent of the way through the Year 2000 job. As late as spring 1998, a majority of manufacturers had not completed the initial phase of their Year 2000 work—

[2]Paper of Vaughan Pomeroy and Alan Lough of Lloyd's Register presented to the Lisbon Meeting of the International Union of Marine Insurers, September 1998.

plant-wide assessment. The manufacturing sector faces a complex, widespread, and daunting task compounded by the sheer numbers of lines of computer code that must be fixed, the multiplicity of computer languages, and the age and size of many plants.

Since the 1970s, manufacturing has made a massive investment in computer technology. Business's investment in computers and peripheral equipment rose from $1 billion in 1978 to $132.8 billion in 1996. Computer technology is used for everything from handling back-office operations to running a factory's assembly line. No longer are tools like wrenches and winches the backbone of the manufacturing industry. Many companies spend more on their computers than they do on all other kinds of machines.

One in One Hundred Thousand: Poor Odds That Something Will Not Interrupt the Supply Chain

Just-in-time delivery makes factories vulnerable to the Millennium Bug. "Just-in-time delivery has streamlined our supply chain to make it highly sensitive to any interruption," said Ralph J. Szygenda, the chief information officer at General Motors and the person in charge of GM's Year 2000–readiness program. Added Szygenda, "Production could literally stop at our plants if suppliers' computer systems are not Year 2000 compliant."

Szygenda knows what he's talking about. General Motors just went through a strike with a major supplier that shut down GM plants and inconvenienced trading partners and customers across the country. So, we should heed his words:

> Let's say that a key sole-source supplier of brake valves shuts down as a result of a year 2000 problem. As a result, on day two, two plants that produce master brake cylinders and clutch master cylinders have to stop production because they don't have those valves. On day three, as motor vehicle assembly plants begin to run out of parts, production falls to about one-third of usual volume. By day four, all assembly plants shut down. And with no orders coming in because of shutdowns, hundreds of plants supplying parts to the assembly lines also shut down, from major engine parts to mom-and-pop subcontractors. That's the worst-case scenario—and yet it's a very real threat.[3]

That means GM has a whale of a challenge ahead. They have one hundred thousand suppliers worldwide. A problem with only one of those suppliers could temporarily stall GM production.

[3]Gene Bylinsky, "Industry Wakes Up to the Year 2000 Menace." *Fortune,* April 27, 1998, pages 163–180.

GM is not the only company worried about its suppliers and vendors. Just a few days before I completed this book, one of my associates on this project had a conversation with an executive of a factory that makes a small motor used to run the air conditioners in school buses, trams, and shuttles. The motor apparently isn't complicated, having only about a dozen parts. But each part is supplied by a different vendor. The company had already asked its suppliers to provide information on their Y2K compliancy. Some responded. Others didn't. The executive was even uncomfortable with the responses he received, because he just won't know for sure until after January 1. As the executive of a small company, he can't force his suppliers to become compliant. "It has me a little nervous," he said. This story can be repeated in a million companies throughout the world.

Part of GM's contingency plan is to put pressure on suppliers to get ready. In addition, GM is searching for alternative suppliers—just in case. But there are limits to that strategy. And it is tougher for small businesses to apply pressure than for mighty GM.

Small and Midsized Businesses Are Behind Schedule

Many of the country's 23.5 million small and medium-sized businesses are apathetic about Year 2000 compliancy. "There's a widespread consensus that they are the most at-risk population," according to Bob Cohen, a Y2K expert at the Information Technology Association of America. Last summer, I spoke with Bob at a Year 2000 conference in Los Angeles. He had just completed a study that concluded that small and midsized businesses were fairly complacent about "this Y2K stuff." While Y2K remediation and testing firms were standing ready to provide assistance, not enough businesses were calling them for help. So many small and midsized enterprises exist month-to-month, and planning for what they may consider a faraway event becomes difficult.

- A survey conducted by Arthur Andersen consultants found that more than one-third (38 percent) of small and midsized businesses with computers have not begun to address Y2K issues. In particular, smaller companies with fewer than twenty employees are even less likely to be actively addressing Y2K. More than 50 percent of small and midsized businesses addressing Y2K are looking to upgrade their computers—the most popular compliance method. Ninety-four percent of the small and medium-sized businesses in the survey now have computers, up from 79 percent in 1997. Most small and midsized businesses with computers (65 percent) use the Internet in some capacity, and one-third of all of the businesses say the Internet is the strategy that they will use to generate growth next year.

- A Gallup Poll released in November 1998 found that more than 80 percent of the country's small and medium-sized businesses are not paying attention to the Millennium Bug.
- The survey done by the National Federation of Independent Businesses cited in chapter 2 clearly demonstrated that small businesses are just not paying attention to the problem, even when they admit that Y2K could threaten the existence of their business.

A Total Disconnect

If you ask the average parent in America what he or she thinks about public education, they are quite negative. But if you ask them what they think about their children's school, they are quite positive. This is what social scientists call a disconnect: when people can't make the connection between the general problem and their personal situation. Now read this:

A survey completed by Ziff-Davis, a leading integrated media and marketing company, of 150 U.S. companies equally divided among small (less than one hundred employees), medium (one hundred to four hundred employees), and enterprise (five hundred or more employees) found business executives optimistic that they will meet their Y2K-remediation and testing milestones.

Of all the reports, studies, surveys, and stories about Y2K that I have read, this survey amazes me the most.

It boggles my mind. "I'm okay, but the rest of the world is in the toilet."

If those of you who are in business get nothing else from this book, I hope that you will come away with an understanding that this is a serious problem. The research says that there is a high potential for your software to not be ready. Your supply chains are vulnerable. A recession is going to lower your sales. Imports and exports are going to affect your business. Government services are going to be disrupted. Foreign competition is likely to force manufacturers to lower prices, which will reduce profits.

Businessmen and women must start making the connection between the effects of Y2K and their cash flows, production schedules, and profitability. Managers and owners must start thinking about the strategic implications of Y2K.

What Small Businesses Should Do in Response to Y2K

If you operate a large or midsized business, I hope that you are already well on your way to Y2K compliance. If you are not, then you should be preparing contingency plans on how to continue in business without your computers, as well as trying to fix your software and other Y2K problems.

Most small businesses, except for those with extensive proprietary software, still have time to become Y2K compliant and even Y2K ready, *if they make an all-out effort.* Here's a brief outline of the steps that you need to take.

1. The first thing that you need to do is to put someone in charge of Y2K compliance. Make sure that he or she has the support and involvement of all the rest of the employees, from the top to the bottom. All employees must know that they need to cooperate with your Y2K point person, and they need to understand the importance of the effort.

2. The first thing that your new person in charge will need to do is to conduct a thorough risk analysis and audit of all your electronic equipment; that is, all of your computers, your software, any electronic controls on production equipment, and any switches, connections, or other interfaces between your equipment.

3. After that is done, you will need to analyze your external exposure. Do you link up with outside suppliers or customers? Do you do on-line banking? What software do you use to exchange data, and who is responsible for its compliance?

4. You should check with your utilities and with your landlord, sending them requests to ascertain their Y2K preparations. Any equipment that you have that has embedded chips must be checked for Y2K compliance.

5. You should survey your main customers, distributors, and suppliers as well. Those absolutely critical to the continuance of your business should be met with face to face, and ongoing information exchanges should continue until you are comfortable with their ability to survive in 2000.

6. After you have this information, you should sit down and establish a plan for fixing your noncompliant systems. Highest priority should be given to those systems with the greatest potential for disrupting business. This decision should not be left to the computer person in your company. Your information technology staff will almost always see their department as "mission critical." The reality may well be that production equipment is the area of most exposure and should be given immediate attention. The management of a firm should make these priority decisions. You have to prioritize in terms of what is most important to the survival of the business. Ideally, you will be able to get to everything, but if you can't, then you need to make sure that you are focused on the most important items.

7. You will have to assess the size of each independent repair project,

and decide if the solution is to repair or replace the system, or substitute another method of doing the work altogether. While you are doing this, you need to assess the expertise and time availability of your staff and determine if you require third-party (outside) assistance.

8. At this point you are ready to develop a budget. If you are going to go with new software, make sure that it is certified Y2K compliant. There are inexpensive programs for checking personal computers that will also search the databases and spread sheets on your computers for date problems, and in many cases suggest a fix. You can buy these at your local software store. As new versions and programs become available constantly, I will not do a review of these programs. Currently Greenwich Mean Time, an English firm, offers excellent personal computer repair programs, and they will print out compliance certificates once your machines have passed their tests. Don't forget to make sure that your security passwords will go through the date change as well!

   If you sign contracts with software firms or for new equipment, make sure that the contract has Y2K compliance language in your favor.

9. Then you need to test the system completely. Testing it twice is even better. Don't forget to do a complete series of backups prior to December 31, 1999, and I would have a paper backup for contracts and critical files.

10. Review the status of your main suppliers. If you cannot get the comfort level that you need, begin looking early for alternative sources of supply. If you use materials or products shipped from other countries, especially Third World countries, research thoroughly the status of those countries and of your supply chain. You might consider an extra stockpile of critical material and items, especially those that you need to stay in business.

_____

Employees Could Sue Over Retirement Plan Performance

Another area that businesses need to be concerned with is the responsibility for their employee pension plans. Under the Employee Retirement Income Security Act (ERISA), it is difficult, if not impossible, for an employer to avoid fiduciary responsibility for such plans. An employer can take on this responsibility merely by choosing the type of plan, detailing its characteristics, providing employee information to those who perform administrative tasks for the plans, or providing any direction on investment of contributions.

This fiduciary responsibility can result in the employer being held personally liable for violations of the law. This responsibility extends well beyond violations due to obvious mismanagement or fraud. This personal liability can even extend to being sued for poor performance of the plan's investments.

The reason you haven't heard about this is simple—the bull market has reduced the number of poorly performing investments. Once we are in the Y2K recession, it will become more and more difficult to obtain the returns to which employees have become accustomed. Even during good times, there have been instances of legal action by the Department of Labor for poor performance. For example, a Houston firm had to pay $4.07 million for its choice of group annuity contracts to fund pension benefits. They did their homework by selecting an insurer that was rated A+ by a nationally known insurance rating firm, and by requesting bids from five different carriers. Yet, when the chosen insurance company became insolvent, the employer was held liable.

The bottom line is this: if an investment fails, the Labor Department will attempt to find someone responsible for the poor performance. And you, as an employer, may very well become the scapegoat for actions that you have little or no control over.

What can you do to prevent this from happening to you? One way to bypass many of these liability problems is to appoint a registered investment advisor to manage the retirement plan. This is different than hiring someone to take care of the administrative aspects of the plan or the use of financial planners, insurance agents, or stockbrokers to help manage the investments. Even making someone a co-fiduciary doesn't stop an employer from being responsible for damages—instead it could make you responsible not only for your own actions, but the co-fiduciary's actions, as well.

There is a special report called "Fiduciary Liability for Plan Sponsors" that explains the problems that employers face on this issue, and details how to appoint a registered investment advisor to delegate some of this responsibility (and reduce your liability). It can be obtained free of charge from ProFutures Capital Management by calling 1-800-348-3601.

Thinking Strategically

While this may sound a little cold-blooded, there are going to be opportunities for businesses that have their Y2K act together.

If in the process of becoming compliant, you realize that your industry is more exposed than most realize, you might want to start thinking about how you would exploit a competitor's delivery problems. Will you have the necessary excess capacity should opportunities arise? Will you be able to get the materials that you need? Can you get lines of credit authorized in advance if your competitors have problems and you have the opportunity to buy them and increase your market share?

What about your suppliers? Have you wanted to control more of your supply chain? You may be able to pick up companies that produce your needed materials for pennies on the dollar. Is now an opportunity to buy or replace some of your distributors?

You may not feel comfortable thinking along these lines. But I would caution you that your competitors may not have the same qualms. You need to think through all the ramifications of Y2K for the economy and on your business. It just might be that Y2K will be a blessing in disguise for you.

How Will Your Business Deal with a Recession?

After you have your software compliant, after you have thoroughly assessed your suppliers and customers, after you have thought through the strategic implications of Y2K:

You have to plan to deal with the Y2K Recession.

Chapter 9 is going to show you why there will be a recession. There will be a great deal of Y2K-remediation work accomplished in 1999, and perhaps it will only be a small and short recession, but today it appears that we will be facing the worst recession in post–World War II history. Whether you run a business or are responsible for your family's income, you need to understand why we are facing this recession, and then begin to think about how you will make sure that you and your dependents will survive and prosper during the Y2K Recession.

Around the World in Two Thousand Years

Sitting in the departure lounge in the Denver airport, waiting for a late flight, I struck up a conversation about Y2K with two consultants from a major accounting firm. They were on their way back from Asia, where they had been consulting with some of their firm's major clients.

They related how difficult it was to get their clients concerned about the Year 2000 problem. The financial problems of the various countries were one reason. In addition, the Asian executives politely pointed out to them that it was not the year 2000. It was the year 2541!

Most of the world will not be celebrating the advent of a new millennium later this year. For most of the world, it is 2541 (Buddhist) or 2048 (Buddhist) or 1914 (Hindu) or 4396 (Chinese). Different countries and religions have different calendars.

In those countries, the computers often have been programmed to work according to the local calendars. As these consultants related to me, the underlying code is still based on the Gregorian calendar, so the executives are not aware they have a "2000 problem." Convincing them about the problem was the consultants' first task. They frankly admitted that they were not successful in doing so.

As we are going to see, the consultants are not alone. The rest of the world, with few exceptions, is in much worse shape than we are. Given what you have learned in the last few chapters, that fact should give you serious cause for concern.

Even if one conceded that every computer and chip in the U.S. could be fixed on time, the impact from the international problem alone is enough to trigger a recession.

If the World Doesn't Cure the Y2K Flu . . .

Given the importance of trade to both the world and U.S. economies, if world trade declines, if major world players and our principal trading partners are forced to decrease their purchases and investments worldwide and in the U.S. because their governments and firms are not Y2K ready, *our farmers, workers, and businesses will suffer too.*

During the nineties, American families and businesses have seen very good economic times. The U.S. is now in its seventh consecutive year of continuous economic expansion. Since 1990, our economy has grown 17 percent, adding more than $1 trillion to the gross national product (GNP). Over 14 million net new jobs have been created in the U.S. since 1992. The average American pocketbook has increased by over $3,700. The dollar has been strong, inflation low. In fact, in 1997, inflation and unemployment were at their lowest levels in twenty-four years. We continue to be extremely attractive to foreign direct investments. From 1990 to 1996 the cumulative direct-investment position of foreign firms in the U.S. increased by 60 percent to $630 billion.[1]

International trade was responsible for much of that success.

International trade accounts for about one-third of our national wealth and for over one-third of the average U.S. national income of $19,700 per person. In 1997, our exports and imports accounted for about 14 percent of total world trade. Today, we are the world's largest exporter of goods and services. More than 12 million Americans depend on export jobs that pay between 12.5 percent and 18 percent more, on average, than nonexport jobs.[2]

. . . the Global and U.S. Economies Will Suffer

Given the interdependence of the world's economies and the potential for cross-border disruptions from Y2K failures, we must not view Millennium Bug readiness as a parochial, national concern. It's a global one.

We know how delicate global trade is and what can happen to U.S. trade when other countries experience problems. California is the country's number-one exporter to Asia. California alone accounts for more than one-fourth of all U.S. exports to that region. When the region caught the "Asian flu," Golden State workers saw their sales to Asia fall 11 percent from the first quarter of 1997 to the same period in 1998. The

---

[1]The Heritage Foundation, "Issues '98': The Candidate's Briefing Book," *International Trade,* p. 3.

[2]The Heritage Foundation, "Issues '98': The Candidate's Briefing Book," *International Trade,* p. 3.

same thing happened to Iowa farmers and Nebraska leather producers, who saw their sales to Asia fall 27 percent and 15 percent respectively during the same period. In other states, other workers experienced similar losses.

But it is not just export sales that we depend on for our standard of living.

Companies that rely on imports for their livelihood could face severe problems. It takes anywhere from ten to fourteen companies and agencies (such as shipping companies, banking and credit facilities, insurers, and government agencies) to cooperate in delivering a product from a factory in country A to a destination in country B. If any one of them has a problem, the whole process is slowed down while somebody tries to sort out the problem and solve it.

Industry and manufacturing in the U.S. are highly dependent upon international resources. While most of us have the perception that the U.S. has abundant resources and could operate independently of the rest of the world, the actual facts are more sobering.

Table 8-1 is cited from the U.S. Geological Survey. This table talks about strategic minerals. If I had the space, I could show charts demonstrating dependence upon various countries for manufacturing equipment, machine tools, and supplies. We import over 50 percent of our oil.

TABLE 8-1

Percent Imported	Various Minerals	Used in
100%	Arsenic	Wood preservatives, glass manufacturing, agricultural, chemicals
100%	Bauxite & Alumina	Aluminum production, abrasives, chemicals, refractories
100%	Columbium	Steelmaking, superalloys
100%	Graphite	Refractories, brake linings, lubricants, foundry dressings
100%	Manganese	Steelmaking
100%	Mica, Sheet	Electronics & electrical equipment
100%	Strontium	Television picture tubes, ferrite magnets, pyrotechnics
100%	Thallium	Superconductor materials, electronics, alloys, glass
100%	Thorium	Ceramics, carbon arc lamps, alloys, welding electrodes
99%	Flourspar	Hydrofluoric acid, aluminum fluoride, steelmaking
80%	Tin, Tungsten, Cobalt, Tantalum, Chromium	Various products

And there are numerous minerals and chemicals of which we import more than 50 percent of our consumption. In short, the manufacturing and business capacity of this country is *highly* sensitive to imports and the ability to efficiently move materials and products.

In a few more pages, and in chapter 9, I'll talk about the level of preparedness in different countries. The countries from which we import most of the items in Table 8-1 are almost universally in the worst categories. Some of these countries are going to be in very bad shape.

I have traveled to over forty countries, and know firsthand that many Third World countries have poor infrastructure. Yet they somehow manage to export the materials we need. Some people suggest that because these countries are used to power or phone outages, they will be able to continue exporting.

But most of those who suggest this possibility have never been involved in shipping products internationally, let alone from Third World countries. Most countries have a great deal of government involvement in the export and import of products, far beyond what we are used to in the U.S. As we will see, because of Y2K, government services are going to be nonexistent in many of these countries. Are entrepreneurial people going to figure out how to get products moved? Yes, of course. They will need our dollars, and we will need their products. But it is *not* going to be business as usual.

These difficulties may be compounded, as international telecommunications services are likely to be severely impacted in some countries. The State Department released a survey in March of 1998 of the Y2K preparedness of the telecommunications companies in 113 countries. Twenty-six percent were either unaware of or had not yet begun to address the problem, and another 29 percent admitted that they were having problems becoming compliant and declined to project that they would be ready by December 1999. British Telecom has already said that they expect problems in Africa and are working on the situation. As we get closer to 2000, more announcements of this type will certainly be made.

Will companies take steps to insure their supply lines? You would think so. Will there be disruptions in spite of the best-laid plans? It seems likely that there will be. The more companies that begin to develop contingency plans, the less overall effect there will be on the world economy. But as of this date, there are indications that world trade will be impacted, perhaps severely, by the Y2K problem.

How Bad Is the International Problem?

Capers Jones's authoritative report "The Global Impact of the Year 2000 Software Problem" has noted that about 78 percent of all code is located outside the United States.[3] The amount of work to be done in Japan is about 47 percent of the work to be done in the U.S., and Germany has about 28 percent relative to us. But these two major trading partners are much further behind than we are. The situation is such that credit-rating agencies are downgrading the credit worthiness of some Japanese banks. Japanese banks that are comparable in size to our largest U.S. banks are spending a few paltry tens of millions of dollars on Y2K work, compared to U.S. banks, which are spending hundreds of millions of dollars. These Japanese banks clearly have not gotten the picture. These same banks provide many of our trading partners in Asia with credit.

About 80,000 ships sail the world's waters at one time or another. Risks of collisions from a faulty navigational system to cargo delivery problems are just two possibilities facing maritime shippers as the millennium approaches. You would think with millions at stake and the possibility of losing lives, the maritime shipping industry would be hot on the heels of the millennium bug. In a recent survey, the U.S. Coast Guard surveyed marine manufacturers and discovered 20 percent of the embedded chips tested were non-Y2K compliant. This information is prompting the Coast Guard to weigh heavily the possibility of including Y2K compliance as part of its safety checklist.[4]

GartnerGroup Releases International Study

As I was about to complete this book, the GartnerGroup gave to the Senate a comprehensive report on global Year 2000 readiness.[5] The report confirms my position that the Millennium Bug is a major global challenge that will lead to a worldwide recession—an illness a lot deeper and wider than the "Asian flu" that we still haven't shaken. The Gartner-Group is a worldwide business and information-technology advisory company that provides research and advice in more than eighty areas, including technology.

I am going to comment on this report extensively. I could cite numerous other sources that give evidence supporting this material, but frankly this is the most credible and comprehensive international survey that I have found, and I think that it stands on its own merits. Any conclusions that I draw from the facts in the report are my own and should not be assumed to be those of the GartnerGroup report or its authors.

Lou Marcoccio of GartnerGroup testified before the U.S. Senate. I

---

[3]This can be computed from the data in Table 20, pages 50–51, *ftp://ftp.spr.com/articles/y2k52.pdf.*

[4]*http://marketspace.altavista.digital.com/WebPort/English/I-School.asp?ArticleId=541.*

[5]*http://gartner3.gartnerweb.com/public/static/aboutgg/pressrel/testimony1098.html#top.*

found his comments and the report itself extremely compelling. The report conclusively illustrates that global economic good times and American prosperity are seriously threatened by the general lack of Y2K readiness among many members of the global economic community, and especially among several of our most important international trading partners.

I draw my own conclusions concerning export-related job losses and the actual dollar effects on the economy in detail in chapter 9, but for now let's look at the basics of what Marcoccio revealed to the Senate.

Y2K Readiness Differs by Company Size, Industry Sector, and Country

The GartnerGroup looked at the Y2K readiness of fifteen thousand companies in eighty-seven countries. For research purposes, the firms were equally divided into three groups based on company size—small (under 2,000 employees), medium (2,000 to 20,000 employees) and large (over 20,000 employees)—and by industry sector. Research data were gathered by a variety of methods, including client interviews, surveys, consortia groups, user companies, equipment manufacturers, consulting firms, and law firms.

Small Companies Have Not Started Y2K Efforts

The GartnerGroup found that the Year 2000 status of companies and government entities differs depending on size, industry, and country, and provided detailed confirmation of some of what we already knew. *A sizable percentage of companies and governments, 23 percent in fact, have not started any Y2K effort.* Not surprisingly, the vast majority of these firms are small companies. Eighty-three percent of companies and governments that had not begun Y2K efforts were firms with fewer than two thousand employees. Small companies have fewer resources and less flexibility to address this issue and are more reliant on outside vendors than internal IT teams to fix their Y2K problems. The GartnerGroup makes a fairly distressing prediction about the future Y2K efforts in small firms: *by January 2000, nearly 20 percent of companies and governments still will not have started,* with small companies mostly comprising this group.

As we have discussed elsewhere, large companies are the farthest ahead. They began earlier for a number of reasons. They have much greater financial and technical resources to devote to Y2K efforts than do small firms. As of the third quarter of 1998, large companies had completed remediation of 20 to 80 percent of their internal systems, and 30 to 50 percent had started significant levels of testing. They are now focusing on contingency planning and assessing business-dependency risks, while continuing to fix their internal systems and beginning to test.

Worldwide, 30 to 50 Percent of Companies and Agencies Will Experience a Failure

What is the likelihood, cost, and length of a Y2K mission-critical failure?

The GartnerGroup defines a "failure" as an interruption to a business operation, a business dependency that cannot be provided or delivered as required, or inaccuracy of data or customer transaction. "Mission critical" is defined as any business dependency that, if it were to fail, would cause any of the following:

- A shutdown of business, production, or product-delivery operations.
- Health hazard to individuals.
- Considerable revenue loss.
- Significant litigation expense or loss.
- Significant loss of customers or revenue.

The GartnerGroup predicts that anywhere from 30 to 50 percent of all companies and government agencies worldwide will experience at least one mission-critical system failure. Ten percent of the failures will last three days or longer at a cost ranging from a low of $20,000 to a high of $3.5 million.

How big a company or agency is indicates whether or not it is likely to experience a mission-critical failure.

- Fifty to 60 percent of small companies and agencies will have at least one failure.
- Forty to 50 percent of midsized companies and agencies will have at least one failure.
- Ten to 20 percent of large companies and agencies will have at least one failure.

Worldwide, 50 Percent of Important Industry Sectors Will Experience a Failure

Some industry sectors are doing better than others at getting ready for the next millennium. At one extreme, worldwide insurance, banking, and investment services have been working on the Millennium Bug problem longer than other industry sectors and enjoy a lead in getting ready. Government, as we know, is lagging far behind.

Overall, the GartnerGroup analyzed and predicted the risk of a mission-critical failure of twenty-seven industry sectors. After grouping the sectors into four categories, they made the following findings:

- Category 1—Fifteen percent of insurance, investment services, banking, pharmaceutical, and computer manufacturing companies will experience at least one mission-critical system failure.
- Category 2—Thirty-three percent of heavy equipment, aerospace, medical equipment, software, semiconductor, telecom, retail, discrete manufacturing, publishing, biotechnology, and consulting companies will experience at least one mission-critical system failure.
- Category 3—Fifty percent of chemical processing, transportation, power, natural gas, water, oil, law practice, medical practice, and construction companies will experience at least one mission-critical system failure.
- Category 4—Sixty-six percent of education, health care, government agencies, farming and agriculture, food processing, and city and town municipal service entities will experience at least one mission-critical system failure.

Countries Already Plagued with Financial Woes Are Farther Behind . . .

How well are individual countries doing?

The GartnerGroup ranked countries into four categories according to the level of risk of a mission-critical failure and the predicted percentage of companies within the country that would experience a failure. Countries were placed in four status groups depending upon the percentage of companies within the country that would likely experience a failure.

- Status Group 1—Fifteen percent of the companies will likely experience a failure.
- Status Group 2—Thirty-three percent of the companies will likely experience a failure.
- Status Group 3—Fifty percent of the companies will likely experience a failure.
- Status Group 4—Sixty-six percent of the companies will likely experience a failure.

In chapter 9 we will list each country in each category, but for now we will look at just a few highlights.

In the majority of countries—sixty out of eighty-seven—more than 50 percent of firms and government agencies will experience a mission-critical failure, according to the GartnerGroup. The prospect of walking down any Main Street in Egypt, Germany, Japan, Kenya, or Congo, to name a few of the countries in this category, and finding every other front door locked and the business temporarily shut down is very disconcerting.

You will note that some of the countries currently being hit the hardest with financial problems, sharp increases in inflation, limited monetary reserves, and high unemployment—Argentina, Japan, Malaysia,

Indonesia, and Russia—are some of the same countries the farthest behind in Y2K compliance. The GartnerGroup has determined that it takes approximately thirty months for a midsized company to get to the point where it has completed compliance efforts on at least 80 percent of its mission-critical items. If that's the case, for those companies and government agencies that are so far behind in getting ready, there's no way to meet the Year 2000 deadline.

▌ . . . And Will Suffer the Most Widespread and Severe Disruptions

The GartnerGroup sought to determine the distribution and severity that Y2K failures will have on eleven different infrastructures in each of the eighty-seven countries.

- Will there be interruptions of telephone service, natural gas operations, air transportation, and government services?
- Will there be shortages of power, oil, water, and food?
- Will there be bank interruptions and/or panic?
- Will there be general unrest?
- Will there be interruptions to imports and/or exports?

If there is some impact, will the incidence of the Y2K failure be distributed in an isolated, moderate, or widespread fashion across the country? Will the severity of the Y2K failure be minor, moderate, or severe?

The GartnerGroup concluded that the distribution and severity of a Y2K failure in:

- Status 1 countries are likely to be "isolated and minor."
- Status 2 countries are likely to be the same as in Status 1 countries, except that the distribution and severity of power loss and natural-gas interruptions in those countries are expected to be "moderate" rather than "minor."
- Status 3 countries will increase, generally, and there are likely to be more "moderate and minor" problems in the areas of power loss, telephone operations, and air transportation.
- Status 4 countries are expected to be much worse than the other countries. The impact of a Y2K failure on power, telephone, and air transportation is likely to be "widespread and moderate," while the impact on natural-gas and food supply will be "isolated and severe."

Government operations in every country are expected to be adversely affected, especially those in Status 4 countries. Additionally, every country is expected to suffer an adverse impact on import and export activity.

From what we know from the GartnerGroup report and data from the International Trade Administration (ITA) at the U.S. Department of Commerce, we can see how vulnerable are the global and U.S. economies to the Millennium Bug and why I firmly believe that recession will greet the Year 2000.

Figures from ITA indicate that our leading trading partners are Canada and Japan, which account for one-third of all of our exports and imports. Mexico and China, respectively, are now our third-largest and fourth-largest trading partners, and together they account for about 13 percent of total U.S. trade.

The GartnerGroup assigned to Japan and China, our second and fourth most significant trading partners, Y2K status scores of 3 and 4, meaning that *between 50 percent and 66 percent, respectively, of the companies in each country will experience at least one mission-critical failure.* They can't engage in international trade without compliant electricity, phone service, financial institutions, and transportation.

Even if the U.S. and nearly every other country were 100 percent Y2K compliant, losing our ability to substantially trade with two of our major global trading partners would by itself result in a global recession. The money and jobs supported by trade with Japan and China are tremendous. Over 60 percent of U.S. exports to Japan are manufactured goods, and Japan's purchases of these goods support nearly 1 million American manufacturing jobs. Two-way merchandise trade between the U.S. and Japan totaled $187 billion in 1997. U.S. exports to China have nearly quadrupled in the past decade. Exports grew 7 percent in 1997 alone, while imports from China climbed 21 percent.

Trade with Japan and China is so important to our economy that the Clinton administration has negotiated no less than thirty-three trade agreements with the Japanese to promote sales of American automobiles, financial services, telecommunications, and medical technology and granted Most Favored Nation status to the Chinese (despite their dubious record on human rights).

Nonetheless, it's so bad in China that they are barely in the middle of drawing up plans to start to work on Y2K. The most populous country in the world hasn't even started fixing their code and chips! A dearth of technical know-how, questionable financial commitment, and a short time line strongly suggest that they won't nearly be finished by 2000. Their situation is compounded by the unknown factor of stolen software. The Chinese (how do we say this delicately?) have never been picky about things like U.S. copyrights, license agreements, and patents. No one knows how much software is being used in China without the benefit of the support of the original software developer. That means that they have no documentation, maybe have no source code, and certainly have no expertise to help them in fixing any problems.

Zhang Qi, the Information Ministry official in charge of the problem, was quoted by the Xinhua News Agency as saying that if those deficiencies aren't corrected soon, "This task cannot be completed."[6]

[6]*AOL News,* October 19, 1998.

China has some 9 million computers, and many of them, particularly in big state industry, will be at risk once the clock ushers in the year 2000. "They're not interested in it, not yet," said Jim King, vice president of sales and marketing for Dell Computer (China) Co. Ltd., when asked if Chinese customers had shown concern about the problem. "So far it is not a focus."[7]

To try to finish work on time, China has set up a central command body and "ordered" ministries to draft plans for industries under their supervision. But that approach demonstrates a complete misunderstanding of the nature of Y2K preparedness. You can't just compress the Y2K repair time line to any degree necessary to make it fit the time remaining.

Besides Japan and China, we have other trading partners with Y2K problems.

There are thirty-one countries—including nine of our top fifty trading partners—rated by the GartnerGroup in the lowest Y2K status group. Also in this group are member countries of the Asian trading bloc. U.S. two-way trade in merchandise goods with Asia was over $738 billion in 1997, or nearly 47.5 percent of total U.S. two-way merchandise trade worldwide. Merchandise exports to Asia support 2.5 million American jobs.

Combined, these thirty-one countries purchased over $127 billion in American products in 1997, for 15 percent of our total exports. They sold us some $64 billion of imports, accounting for 9 percent of our imports. If they have Y2K disruptions, and it's certain that they will, it will be very difficult for some of these countries—like Russia, Thailand, and the Philippines—to produce and deliver the products that our factories depend on and to have sufficient money to make the purchases that support so many American jobs.

I've tried to be brief but persuasive here. While I've only discussed our trading relationship with countries in the GartnerGroup's fourth category, companies and government agencies in the other groups also have problems. Those failures, too, will negatively impact global trade. But I am, and by now I trust that you are persuaded that firms in the countries discussed above will experience Y2K failures that will spread widely throughout those countries, impacting a number of industries and adversely affecting trade with the U.S. and the rest of the world.

[7]Reuters newswire, August 21, 1998.

The Y2K Recession

Despite the first eight chapters of this book, I believe myself to be an optimist. Where others see problems, I look for opportunities. I believe that we will get a significant portion of the Y2K problem solved in 1999. There are companies and individuals that will be written up as heroes because of their efforts.

Writing in late December of 1998, I believe that the large majority of companies will survive. Most of them will be Y2K compliant by the end of 1999. I think that the electric grid will be back to normal within a short time after the turn of the century, and that most areas of America will not experience a problem. The banking and finance system will be working, with some minor hassles. The phones will work, although we may see some problems early in 2000.

But I am also a realist. The data that we are looking at today says that not everything will get done on time. There will be disruptions. If we do not get a Herculean effort from industry and government, the problems could compound. If government does not act to pass needed legislation, and if the Federal Reserve does not step in to allay banking and credit fears, as well as deal with a deflationary environment, the situation could become much worse than it has to be.

(In chapter 16, I will tell you about the "Things That Go Bump in the Night." These are the potential problems that make me lose sleep. There is no reason for them to happen, but I can't categorically rule them out.)

For eight chapters we have looked at the problems. I have tried to be as sanguine as I can be. In this chapter I am going to tell you why I think that the cumulative effect of these problems will be a full-blown recession. I think that it will be worse than the 1973 to 1974 recession caused by the Arab oil embargo and inflation.

You probably remember the gasoline shortages in the early 1970s. For about a year and a half, we all sat in long lines at the gas stations because of the Arab oil embargo. I believe that the Y2K problem is going to create similar shortages and delays and disruptions, but across many different industries.

The recession in 1973 and 1974 was due to an artificial disruption in the oil supply and an increasingly inflationary environment. The Y2K Recession will be due to a disruption in the *information supply* and an increasingly *deflationary* environment.

The primary difference between these crises is that the first recession was prolonged because OPEC did not drop oil prices. It was in their best interest to hold the world hostage. So, it was many years before the world's economies and markets recovered.

The Y2K Crisis is different. There is no special-interest group that wants to maintain a problem with computers as OPEC did with oil prices. It is in everyone's best interest to get these problems solved as quickly as possible. So, while I see no way to avoid a recession, I think that if the governments of the world do not make the problem worse with trade wars and bad economic policies, we could begin to rebound within a year and see the markets recover within a few years.

Also, let me remind you of the obvious: *this is just a recession. We survived the recession of 1973 and 1974, and we will survive the coming recession as well.* It does not have to be devastating for you if you prepare for it. For those who refuse to prepare, it will create significant difficulties. For many, it will actually be a time of both personal and financial growth. I hope that this book will convince you to act.

Setting the Stage

Before we look into the specific reasons why Y2K will trigger a recession, we need to examine the current economic and political climate. There are three areas to consider:

- The end of inflation and the beginning of deflation.
- The growing world recession.
- The fragile nature of the world political climate.

THE END OF INFLATION AND THE BEGINNING OF DEFLATION

As the saying goes, every general is always fighting the last war. We assume that the strategies and tactics that worked in the last war will work in the coming wars—and they often do. But then a new weapon is developed, or the enemy adopts a new strategy, and everything changes. Generally, this is a prescription for disaster for the generals, as they (and we) are not ready to deal with the new set of problems.

For a long time now—almost sixty years—investors in the U.S. (and most of the world) have been dealing with inflation. Recently, inflation has slowed down significantly. Economists and analysts have been using the term *disinflation*. By that they mean a period when there is still inflation but the rate of inflation is dropping.

I think that we will soon find out this is the last war. We are about to enter a period of deflation. By that I mean a period in which prices in general drop and interest rates get very low. If I am right, the investment strategies that have worked for the last sixty years will need to be changed to reflect the new economic realities. (I am not suggesting that inflation is gone forever. Economies run in cycles, and as long as tax-and-spend governments are around, we will have inflationary periods.)

Deflation is not some new beast. There have been some significant periods of deflation in the U.S. Some of the most prosperous times in our history have been deflationary. The last period of deflation was in the 1920s and 1930s. Misguided government policies turned it into the bad type of deflation, and the result was the crash of 1929 and the Depression. Good deflation produces a period of economic growth and lowering prices. Bad deflation hurts growth, costs jobs, and destroys investment values.

For instance, between 1869 and 1898 we experienced deflation and abundant growth. (See Table 9-1.)

During this time of excellent growth, the overall Wholesale Price Index dropped 49.7 percent between 1870 and 1896! That means that the price for bread, transportation, and clothes dropped by almost 50 percent. Wouldn't that be great news for someone living on a fixed retirement income! And this occurred while the economy grew at a rate of over 4 percent and consumption (what we actually bought) grew at almost 5 percent *per year!* That means lifestyles improved dramatically over that period.

T A B L E   9 - 1

U.S. Economic Growth 1869–98[1] (Average Annual Growth Rates)

Population %	GNP %	GNP (per capita) %	Consumption %	Consumption per Full Consumer %
2.17	4.32	2.11	4.75	2.33

[1]*Deflation* by Gary Shilling, Lakeview Publishing Company, New Jersey, p. 263.

Of course, farmers who did not figure out how to be more productive were hurt, as were businesses who could not compete by becoming more productive. There were losers. But there have been big losers in infla- tionary times, too. Inflation hurts those on fixed incomes, mostly retirees and businesses who can't raise prices as fast as costs rise.

I do not pretend that deflation is a prescription for an economic nir- vana. However, if someone gave me the power to take either the numbers in the above table for the next thirty years or what will really happen, I wouldn't hesitate. I would say "book 'em" as fast as I could.

In an ideal world, deflation should be the norm. In theory, over time competitive businesses should become more productive and more able to produce more products for less cost. Prices gradually drop, and we all get more bang for our buck. In fact, you can have a comfortable growth rate and rising real wages (as demonstrated above) when there is a proper level of deflation. There is nothing wrong with that.

An exaggerated example of price deflation is the computer. We have all been witness to the extraordinary drop in computer prices and the tremendous growth in productivity of computers over the last two dec- ades. In constant dollar terms the prices of many commodities have actu- ally dropped due to increases in productivity. The lowering of real prices in commodities is not always apparent, because they have been masked by the rise in prices due to inflation. But the lower prices are there, and they are real. If you factor out inflation, almost all prices of basic com- modities and consumer items have dropped over the last thirty years. And while computer companies gripe about market pressures and lower profit margins, their stocks have been the darlings of Wall Street. We should all have such problems!

I recently read a headline in *USA Today* that fifteen years ago would have been impossible. Major automobile manufacturers announced *price cuts of 5 percent* for some types of cars. I felt I was living in the age of miracles.

Alan Greenspan's nagging concern about inflation aside, the reality is that inflation is not showing any signs of rising. Inflation is currently only 1.5 percent and dropping. If you subtract the widely acknowledged 1 percent overstatement of inflation built into the measuring system, then inflation is less than 1 percent. If you have ever analyzed how the Federal Reserve actually tracks inflation, you realize how easy it is for that number to move up or down in any given period. But what is important is the overall trend, and it is definitely going down.

I know that the thought of deflation is scary to a lot of readers. We viscerally associate deflation with the stories that our parents and grand- parents told us of the Depression. But we have learned to live with the demon of inflation. We know that it does bad things, yet we have figured out how to live with it.

Inflation erodes the value of savings. Unless you take above-market risks, it has been difficult to have your savings grow in buying power after taxes and inflation. But in a deflationary environment, if you save a dollar, in ten years you have more than a dollar's worth of buying power, and even though interest rates are low, you are farther ahead in actual buying power terms than you would be in inflationary times.

Stocks do not have to grow at 15 percent annually to keep up with inflation. Investments don't need to compound at extraordinary rates for you to be able to retire with dignity. As we will see, even though the rules are going to change, *if you adapt,* you will be better off in ten years than you are today, assuming that we see inflation disappear. If you don't adapt, you will lose.

What is causing this trend from disinflation into deflation? Long-time market analyst Gary Shilling has written a very clear, often-compelling book called simply *Deflation.* Along with over 250 charts and tables, Shilling presents one of the best overall explanations of deflation that I have ever read, and I think that every investor should read it.

Shilling lists fourteen reasons why deflation is in our near future. Some of these have been written about by numerous commentators, and others are original with him. He has not mentioned the Y2K problem, which I think is inherently deflationary in many of its aspects. Y2K will give us another three reasons to anticipate deflation. As we proceed through this chapter, I'll explain why.

Shilling's fourteen deflationary forces (and my comments in parentheses) are:

1. The end of the Cold War led to global cuts in defense spending. (Shilling sees government spending, especially deficit spending, as one of the chief causes of inflation. In particular, defense spending is inflationary because it uses assets and produces no physical goods in return. Defense spending as a percentage of GNP has dropped dramatically all over the world.)
2. Major-country government spending and deficits are shrinking.
3. Central banks continue to fight the last war—inflation. (As long as central banks are focused on keeping inflation from rearing its head, they are actually pursuing the policies that will lead us to a deflationary environment. This is not altogether bad as long as they wake up soon and realize that they are fighting the wrong battle.)
4. The increasing number of people retiring in G-7 countries (the seven major economic powers) will lead to reduced benefits and slower growth in incomes and spending.
5. Restructuring of business continues in English-speaking lands and will spread (which helps to lower prices).
6. Technology cuts costs and promotes productivity.
7. Information via the Internet increases competition (and thus lowers prices).

8. Mass distribution to consumers reduces costs and prices.
9. Ongoing deregulation cuts prices.
10. Global sourcing of goods and services curtails costs.
11. The spread of market economies increases global supply.
12. The dollar will continue to strengthen (thus making imports cheaper and causing price cuts and thus lower profits for domestic companies due to foreign price competition).
13. Asian financial and economic problems will intensify global glut and reduce worldwide prices.
14. U.S. consumers will switch from borrowing and spending to saving.

You could write a chapter on each of these topics. In fact, Shilling has. But for our purposes, it is sufficient to realize that we are rapidly approaching a period of actual deflation. In and of itself, this would mean that we would need to change our investment styles and expectations. But when we add the Y2K Crisis into the picture, it is even more important that you make a decision in the near future to take action to insure the safety of your investments.

The Growing World Recession

In October of 1997, the U.S. stock market dropped 11.15 percent over four days as investors reacted in panic to the crisis in Asia. As it began to look like we would avoid any real problems stemming from Asia, the market went on to new highs. But the markets were prescient in 1997. The Asian crisis has begun to have an effect on the U.S. and the rest of the world. Look at Table 9-2.

Asia is clearly in a recession and could easily slip into a depression. Japan is already in a depression. Latin America, especially Brazil, is be-

TABLE 9 - 2 ▨▨▨▨▨▨▨▨▨▨▨▨▨▨▨▨▨▨▨▨▨▨▨▨▨▨▨▨▨▨

World Index Market Declines

Country	Index	Market High	Market Low	Time Period	% Decline
Brazil	SENN	47,500	15,900	6 months	−67%
Russia	RTS	506	65	1 year	−87%
South Korea	KOSPI	1,074	297	4 years	−72%
Australia	AS30	2,880	2,325	3 months	−19%
Japan	NKY	38,916	13,406	9 years	−66%
Thailand	SET	1,690	210	4 years	−88%
South Africa	JOHMKT	8,350	4,750	6 months	−43%

coming a real problem. The rest of the Third World is either slowing down or on the ropes.

How did we get into this predicament? There are a lot of reasons, but I see two main culprits: government and corruption.

It seems that governments worldwide have a difficult time leaving the markets alone. They either print too much money, overregulate, or force money into nonproductive or overbuilt sectors. And when you compound this problem with the greed displayed by leaders all over Asia and the emerging world to fatten their own pocketbooks at the expense of investors and taxpayers, it is a prescription for the disaster that we are seeing unfold.

Government corruption exists almost everywhere. Most of the time it is petty stuff and doesn't affect the overall economy significantly. But in a lot of emerging and Third World countries, the leaders don't stop at petty corruption. They begin to view it as a right of personal privilege to raid the public coffers for loans, special deals, kickbacks, and bribes and sometimes commit outright theft. It usually starts out small at the beginning of a cycle, and then over time they get more arrogant and greedy. They are like the thieves that killed the golden goose. Only it is usually the "little people" who get killed. The fat cats simply move their money to Switzerland and live on the Riviera.

But whatever the reason, we are staring a growing world recession in the face. This global recession is on the brink of becoming a depression, and in many countries it already is one. Since we depend upon exports to the rest of the world for 12 percent of our GDP, this is a serious development.

There are two countries that we need to pay particular attention to: Japan and Brazil.

Japan is a prime example of government being the problem. While there appears to be some corruption in Japan, it doesn't seem to be of the type that makes an impact on the national economy. The problem there is the government willingly propping up failing banks and businesses and encouraging disastrous lending policies.

As usual in these situations, things seem to work for a while. Remember when we read article after article about Fortress Japan? About how its markets were different and price-to-earnings ratios of eighty were justifiable? And Tokyo really *was* more valuable than all of California?

Japan's stock market is now down almost 60 percent from its high, and going lower. Interest rates are $1/4$ percent, and Japan's economy is growing more slowly than you would expect given those lower rates. In fact, Japan is experiencing negative growth, deflation, and what many observers call a depression.

Japan is trying to sort out its problems. Basically, its banks are in deep trouble. They have massive amounts of bad loans. Merrill Lynch analyst

Jeff Bahrenburg estimates that bad bank debts could be up to 15 percent of the entire GDP for Japan. The Bank for International Settlements reports that as of 1997 Japan has outstanding loans to Asian countries of $123 billion.

The Bank Credit Analyst, one of the most respected financial analysis firms in the world, had this to say about Japan in their October 1998 newsletter:

> Perhaps the biggest reason for concern in global outlook is that Japan remains trapped in debt deflation. There cannot be any economic recovery before the bank crisis is resolved and the progress on that front remains hamstrung by political infighting. The longer a solution is delayed, the bigger the problem becomes. Some estimates place bad debts at more than 20% of GDP, but the truth is nobody seems to know just how bad the position is. Kenichi Ohmae of McKinsey Japan has noted that "we have about $100 billion set aside for rescuing all financial institutions. I think that one bank could use up all of that." Ohmae, who is not prone to taking extremist views, believes that $2 trillion (40% of GDP) might ultimately be needed to deal with the banking problem.

The list of problems could go on and on. The reality is that Japan is going to have worsening problems as 42 percent of its exports go to Asia and sales drop monthly. The restructuring of their banking system is going to mean lots of bankruptcies, as banks will stop lending to companies incapable of survival without continuous supplies of new debt, which of course will not be repaid.

Japan is the engine for Asia and for much of the world. And they are not going to be running on all cylinders anytime soon.

Let me quote again from the same issue of *The Bank Credit Analyst* newsletter:

> A major global slowdown appears inevitable during the next year (1999). Even if the Asian economies are close to bottoming, a sharp rebound seems implausible given the collapse in confidence and shattered financial systems. Meanwhile, in its desperate attempt to avoid a currency devaluation, Brazil has all but guaranteed it will have a recession by pushing interest rates up to crippling levels and by promising major fiscal restraint after the coming elections. A recession in Brazil will drag down growth in other Latin America countries.

In the middle of October 1998, I spoke at the largest hedge-fund conference in the world. If you asked the hedge-fund managers—who trade vast amounts of currencies and world equities—which they thought was the bigger problem, Brazil or Y2K, it would not be even close. Brazil would win hands down.

I heard numerous comments from managers seriously worried about Brazil. Several predicted Brazil would melt down, even in the face of the news that the International Monetary Fund was going to inject massive amounts of new monies.

The concern in financial circles is that if Brazil's currency is devalued, it will send a shock wave throughout the world system that will trigger another round of stock-market crashes, as well as potential defaults and more debt restructuring (similar to the problems stemming from the Russian debt default).

World Political Climate

The list of countries unstable or on the verge of internal chaos is growing every month. The list of countries destabilizing the world, such as Iran, Iraq, North Korea, and Bosnia, is growing. The list of countries capable of responding to a world political crisis is not growing. There is serious concern about the ability of the U.S. to lead if there is a major crisis.

When you talk to businessmen from other parts of the world, you find that their worry is real. They cannot figure out why we are worried about stains on blue dresses when there is a global recession dragging down the world economy. The confidence in Clinton and the U.S. is dropping, and concerns that rogue states might use this perceived weakness as an opportunity for aggression are increasing.

While things are not *bad* yet, conditions are not improving. If the U.S. slips into a severe recession in 2000, much of the rest of the world will almost surely go into a depression. With many countries far behind in their Y2K remediation efforts, the potential for international instability is increasing.

Why There Will Be a Y2K Recession

This environment, precarious as it is, does not in and of itself mean that there will be a recession. The U.S. economy is amazingly strong and resilient. While the developing global recession will surely slow our economy down, there is no reason to think that it will lead to more than a mild recession in the U.S.

But this economic situation reminds me of Joe Frazier when he was the World Heavyweight Boxing champion. Frazier was right-handed, and he could kill you with a powerhouse right. You had to watch for it. So he would set you up with his right jab, and then while you were focusing on his right hand—POW! Out of nowhere would come a murderous left hook. You only saw it coming when you watched the tapes back in the dressing room, after you woke up.

Y2K is going to be like Smoking Joe's left hook. It is going to hit us seemingly from out of nowhere. Most of the economists will never see it coming, and will even deny that it exists. As I discussed earlier, it just makes no sense to the average person. Our faith in technology is so strong that we simply cannot perceive that such a simple-sounding problem won't be fixed. It is only as you begin to thoroughly investigate it that you begin to understand its complexity and depth.

My analysis and conclusions are dependent upon the analyses of others. But the facts, statistics, and predictions on which I base my analysis are from the leading software and technological research firms in the world.

Those who disagree with me must do one of two things:

1. They must show me a world-class software or technological research firm whose data contradict everyone else's; or
2. They must challenge my economic reasoning based upon the data we do have.

I do not think that they will find the former. I have looked. It is not out there. To sit by and say Capers Jones or GartnerGroup or Rubin or Yourdon or Yardeni or Forrester Research or Triaxsys are wrong without backing it up with research is not acceptable. There is nothing more frustrating than some armchair quarterback telling me that there can't be a problem without having one ounce of data. All that they have is their hope or some anecdotal story that has no relevance to the problem.

These people are whistling past the graveyard. They are a larger part of the problem than those who see the end of Western civilization.

Now, challenging my financial interpretation of the data is another thing altogether. I expect such challenges. I hope that someone can prove me wrong. I hope that the actual outcome shows me wrong.

But I expect that the challenges based upon my interpretation will be those of degree and not direction. By that I mean that someone may think that there will be greater or lesser unemployment or more or fewer changes in the tax receipts, but they will agree that the data suggest that Y2K will affect these numbers negatively.

What are the cumulative effects of tens of thousands of companies going bankrupt because hundreds of thousands of programs, embedded chips, and computer-controlled machines are not working properly and have to be fixed? What is the cumulative effect of a month or more of basic-system problems and failures? What is the cumulative effect of government services being slowed down or nonexistent for a period of time?

And even if we could get everything in the United States ready by January 1, 2000, what would be the effect of all the problems that the rest of the world will be having?

I can see no other alternative than that it will have a major impact on productivity. I can see no other alternative than that it will have a major impact on profits. I can see no other alternative than that it will have a depressing effect upon prices. Consumer confidence will go down and we will buy less.

All these cumulative effects will bring about a recession. A recession is, by definition, a retreat from growth in the economy. It is not just a slowing down, but an actual contraction. The economy gets smaller. Stock prices go down—usually by quite a lot!

The question is how deep will the recession be, and how long will it last? To answer it, we must look at what will be the causes of the Y2K Recession, and how quickly these causes can be fixed.

There are three basic problems that convince me we are going to have a recession:

1. Job losses and bankruptcies stemming directly from Y2K-related problems.
2. Job losses from lowered exports due to the seeming lack of international preparations for the Y2K problems.
3. Reduced productivity due to computer programs and equipment not working.

After we explore these problems in detail, we will look at the "soft" secondary problems that cannot be quantified but will nonetheless have significant impacts upon the economy: reduced U.S. corporate profits due to lower-priced foreign goods and the possible increase in demand for temporary employment.

The Effect of Job Losses on the Economy

The data that we look at today tell us that there is going to be a large number of business casualties. Depending upon which research forecasts you want to accept, there could be 200,000 or more small and medium-sized businesses that fail because of Y2K, and even some Fortune 1000 companies.

I find few consultants, researchers, or analysts really knowledgeable about the actual Y2K problem who are pushing the panic button. There are some, but they are not the majority. But almost universally, there is deep concern and an assumption that there will be both business and service failures. The number of problems varies by industry and the person being interviewed, but I find very few who see no or only minor problems who actually have a professional background in information technology (IT) and the industry in question.

There is a general prediction from industry observers that there will be numerous business failures across multiple industry lines.

I quoted the following projections from Capers Jones in chapter 2. Let me repeat them here in Table 9-3. (Remember, these are updated projections provided to me by Jones and therefore different than those that you may have seen quoted elsewhere.)

What Does This Mean?

Let's try to get some perspective on this. We need to try and develop an understanding of how significant the loss of 3 million jobs might be. To do this, we need to look at the size of the economy as a whole.

The Bureau of Labor projects that there will be 137,581,000 jobs available in 1999. These jobs will produce $7.7 trillion in gross domestic product (GDP).[2] The GDP is the total of all economic activity in the country. That means that for each job available the government projects that approximately $55,950 will be added to the national GDP. In 1996 the number per job was $52,850. This also means that the government expects each worker on average is going to produce about 5.9 percent more goods and services in 1999 than he or she did in 1996.

Because the Y2K Crisis will affect the entire economy and not just one sector, I make the assumption that the loss of one job lowers the projected GDP by $55,950. That means that the loss of 1 million jobs will mean the loss of $56 billion dollars of GDP.

If one assumes current levels of productivity, Table 9-4 shows the drop in GDP at various job-loss levels. I am going to take Capers Jones's projection as a midrange number, increase it by 50 percent and also decrease it by 50 percent to give us a fairly wide range of job losses. Let's

TABLE 9 - 3

Business Size by Employees	No. of Businesses in Category	Bankruptcies	Job Loss
1	5,000,000	300,000	300,000
2–10	1,000,000	50,000	200,000
11–100	350,000	17,500	525,000
101–1,000	75,000	3,000	900,000
1,001–10,000	10,000	300	1,050,000
10,001–100,000	1,000	1	25,000
>100,000	25	0	0
Totals	**6,436,025**	**370,801**	**3,000,000**

[2]Congressional Budget Office estimate based on 1992 constant dollars.

look at how much these levels of job losses would decrease the gross domestic product.

T A B L E   9 - 4

Job-loss level	1,500,000	3,000,000	4,500,000
Loss of GDP	1.09%	2.18%	3.27%

The projection of job losses at 3 million is certainly reasonable from a lay perspective. These numbers are from the loss of a relatively small number in terms of percentage of businesses. Let's remember these facts:

1. The NFIB survey told us that over 1 million small businesses are planning no Y2K-compliance efforts, yet admit that they have exposure to the problem.
2. Many midsized companies have waited well past the date for an orderly remediation of the software. The past record of actual on-time software projects shows us that many of these companies will not be ready, no matter how hard they try.
3. A small but significant percentage of small and midsized firms are living "paycheck to paycheck" and cannot suffer a serious cut in sales for a period of two to three months. Due to budgetary pressures, many of these companies were late in starting what Y2K efforts they have made.

I suspect that not all of these jobs will be permanently lost. Some of these companies or their assets will be bought or merged. I suspect that companies who are compliant and viable, with large cash positions and ready lines of credit, will be ready to move swiftly to take over failing companies. Therefore, layoffs might not occur or might be temporary.

I would also suspect that the larger the company, the more attractive it will be to competitors and thus the less likely it will be to pass from existence, although the shareholders will not be pleased with the results of their holdings.

However, Jones's estimates do not include the number of people who will lose their jobs due to downsizing, temporary layoffs, companies having to cut overhead to survive because they are doing less business, and other factors. Over the course of the first six months of 2000, we could easily see many more companies suffer losses and a large number of jobs lost.

The additional losses among small businesses stemming directly from a recession could be significant. The economy has been growing at record levels and corporate downsizing has given many middle-management types the "opportunity" to start their own businesses. It is not surprising, therefore, that we are seeing record numbers of business start-ups.

Michael Gerber, author of *The E-Myth,* tells us that 80 percent of businesses fail in the first five years, and another 80 percent of the remaining companies fail in the *next five years*. There are a variety of reasons for this high number of failures, and if you run a small business, I commend Gerber's book to you. But one of the main problems of small businesses everywhere is undercapitalization.

Businesses operating close to their money's edge will have a lot more problems during the Y2K Recession. Most small businesses are service businesses or cater to larger businesses, which will be having problems of their own. During recessions, one thing that always happens is that accounts receivables start growing and checks seem to take longer and longer to arrive in the mailbox, even from normally solid companies and individuals.

In summary, these job losses will stem directly from the procrastination of businesses and governments in dealing with the Y2K problem. We know that too many businesses have started too late. We know that many software projects are finished way behind schedule, and a significant number are either dramatically behind schedule or canceled. It is quite reasonable to assume that many companies will simply cease to exist because they will not be able to deliver services, account for costs or inventory, keep track of invoices, or produce products. And when the companies file for bankruptcy, their employees will lose their jobs.

But the United States is in better shape than any other country in the world. If we can expect this level of job losses, what is happening in the rest of the world, and how will that affect jobs in the U.S.?

To estimate the potential impact, we need to do a little math. Those of you who love tables and graphs will enjoy this next section. I would urge those of you who normally skip over them to take your time and think through these tables with me. It is important for you to get a sense of the size of the problem so that you can later make informed decisions about what to do for your family and with your money.

Job Losses from Decreased Exports

Of all the studies that I have seen done on the Y2K problem, the one prepared by Lou Marcoccio of the GartnerGroup for his U.S. Senate testimony is the most disturbing to me. Gartner surveyed fifteen thousand companies in eighty-seven countries worldwide on their Y2K preparations. It is the most thorough and comprehensive report to date on the world situation.

Gartner rates each country on its Y2K vulnerability. It then divides the world into four categories. Status 1 is the best level, and Status 4 is the worst, in terms of what Gartner predicts will happen due to the Y2K Crisis.

Before we look at which countries are in which categories, let's look at what Gartner thinks will happen to those countries in a particular category. Table 9-5 projects potential problems for each of the four categories on a scale of 1 to 10. 1 is no impact, and 10 is widespread and severe.

For instance, as I read this table, a designation of 4 means that Gartner expects the possible failure effects to be isolated but severe; a 6 means that the effects would be moderately present throughout the country and moderate in impact.

A few things leap out at you. The levels of government-service interruptions are signficant even in the best of countries. Of equal note is the impact on exports and imports in all categories.

Status 4 countries earn 9 in electric-power disruptions, telephone-operations disruptions, and air-transportation interruptions, and 10 in government-service failures. Bank interruptions will be moderately widespread and moderate in impact, as will oil shortages. If one lived in these countries, there would be ample reason to believe in a doomsday scenario. Fifty percent of the world's population lives in Status 4.

Status 3 is better off, but people in these countries will not have a walk in the park. Power and telephone losses earn a 5, meaning Gartner expects them to be moderately widespread but minor in severity. Some government services are severely impacted. Air transportation is given a rating of 6. Thirty-one percent of the world's population lives in Status 3 countries.

I was quite surprised as I looked down the list to see that some of the world's major countries fall into Status 3 and 4. I began to wonder how Y2K would affect our exports to these countries. The following tables show the countries in each category. I have also included the export and import numbers[3] from each of the countries as well as the population figures. The export figures here are the numbers for the goods portion of exports only and not for services. Take a minute, and look through this list. Then we are going to try and estimate the potential effect of decreased sales or exports of our goods and services to these countries.

Status Group 4 includes China, Indonesia, the Philippines, and Russia. Status Group 3 includes Japan, Germany, Malaysia, and Venezuela.

If we are going to have a recession in the U.S., even a mild one, then it stands to reason that the rest of the world is going to be worse off than we are. We will see our exports to those countries decrease, and therefore will see a reduction in GDP and an increase in unemployment.

There is broad agreement that the Y2K crisis is going to reduce our exports. There is no consensus on how large that reduction will be. Since there is no way to predict exactly what effect Y2K will have on exports,

---

[3]Export and import numbers are from the International Trade Administration of the Department of Commerce.

T A B L E   9 - 5

Infrastructure Predictions: Distribution & Severity
(Q3 September 1998)

Possible Failure Effects	One	Two	Three	Four
Power loss/brownouts	2	3	5	9
Telephone operation interrupted	2	2	5	9
Natural gas interruptions	2	3	3	4
Air transportation interrupted	3	3	6	9
Oil shortage	3	3	4	6
Certain foods—shortage	2	2	3	4
Water shortage or interruptions	2	2	3	3
Government services interrupted	6	6	7	10
Bank interruptions or panics	2	2	3	6
Unrest	2	2	3	6
Interruptions to imports/exports	4	4	4	7

1 No Impact		6 Moderate & Moderate
2 Isolated & Minor		7 Moderate & Severe
3 Isolated & Moderate		8 Widespread & Minor
4 Isolated & Severe		9 Widespread & Moderate
5 Moderate & Minor		10 Widespread & Severe

Distribution & Severity Scale Key

T A B L E   9 - 6

Status One	Population	Imports*	Exports*
Australia	18,613,087	$ 4,602	$ 12,063
Belgium	10,714,922	8,151	14,132
Bermuda	62,009	30	338
Canada	30,675,398	168,201	151,767
Denmark	5,333,617	2,138	1,757
Holland	15,731,112	7,293	19,827
Ireland	3,619,480	5,867	4,642
Israel	5,643,966	7,326	5,995
Switzerland	7,260,357	8,405	8,307
Sweden	8,886,738	7,299	3,314
UK	58,970,119	32,659	36,425
USA	270,311,758	—	—
Total	435,822,563	$251,971	$258,567
Percentages:	**8%**	**30%**	**39%**

*Figures in Millions

TABLE 9 - 7

Status Two	Population	1997 Imports*	1997 Exports*
Brazil	169,806,557	$ 9,626	$ 15,915
Chile	14,787,781	2,293	4,368
Finland	5,149,242	2,392	1,741
France	58,804,944	20,636	15,965
Hungary	10,208,127	1,079	486
Italy	56,782,748	19,408	8,995
Mexico	98,552,776	85,938	71,388
New Zealand	3,625,388	1,579	1,962
Norway	4,419,955	3,752	1,721
Peru	26,111,110	1,772	1,953
Portugal	9,927,556	1,138	954
Singapore	3,490,356	20,075	17,696
South Korea	46,416,796	23,173	25,046
Spain	39,133,996	4,606	5,539
Taiwan	21,908,135	32,629	20,366
Total	569,125,467	$230,096	$194,095
Percentages:	**11%**	**27%**	**29%**

*Figures in Millions

TABLE 9 - 8

Status Three	Population	1997 Imports*	1997 Exports*
Argentina	36,265,463	$ 2,228	$ 5,810
Armenia	3,421,775	6	62
Austria	8,133,611	2,368	2,075
Bulgaria	8,240,426	171	110
Columbia	38,850,949	4,737	5,197
Czech Republic	10,286,470	610	590
Germany	82,079,454	43,122	24,458
Guatemala	12,007,580	1,990	1,730
India	984,003,683	7,322	3,608
Japan	125,931,533	121,663	65,549
Jordan	4,434,978	25	403
Kuwait	1,913,285	1,816	1,390
Malaysia	20,932,901	18,027	10,780
North Korea	21,234,387	—	2
Poland	38,606,922	696	1,170
Saudi Arabia	20,785,955	9,365	8,438
South Africa	42,834,520	2,510	2,997
Sri Lanka	18,933,558	1,620	155
Turkey	64,566,511	2,121	3,540

United Arab Emirates	2,303,088	920	2,607
Venezuela	22,803,409	13,477	6,602
Yugoslavia	22,544,572	525	437
Total	1,591,115,030	$235,319	$147,710
Percentages:	**31%**	**28%**	**22%**

*Figures in Millions

T A B L E   9 - 9

Status Four	Population	1997 Imports	1997 Exports
Afghanistan	24,792,375	$ 10	$ 12
Bahrain	616,342	116	406
Bangladesh	127,567,002	1,679	259
Cambodia	11,339,562	103	19
Chad	7,359,512	3	3
China/Hong Kong	1,243,621,623	72,846	27,979
Costa Rica	3,604,642	2,323	2,024
Ecuador	12,336,572	2,055	1,526
Egypt	66,050,004	658	3,835
El Salvador	5,752,067	1,346	1,400
Ethiopia	58,390,351	71	138
Fiji	802,611	4	6
Indonesia	212,941,810	9,188	4,522
Kenya	28,337,071	114	225
Laos	5,260,842	14	3
Lithuania	3,600,158	80	87
Morocco	29,114,497	296	435
Mozambique	18,641,469	31	46
Nepal	23,698,421	114	27
Nigeria	110,532,242	6,349	813
Pakistan	135,135,195	1,442	1,240
Philippines	77,725,862	10,445	7,417
Romania	22,395,848	400	258
Russia	146,861,022	4,319	3,365
Somalia	6,841,695	—	3
Sudan	33,550,552	12	36
Thailand	60,037,366	12,602	7,349
Uruguay	3,284,841	229	548
Vietnam	76,236,259	389	287
Democratic Republic of the Congo (Zaire)	49,000,511	282	38
Zimbabwe	11,044,147	140	82
Total	2,616,472,471	$127,660	$ 64,388
Percentages:	**50%**	**15%**	**10%**

we need to look at a range of possible effects. In an effort to give us some broad parameters, I have constructed the following scenarios. Let's look at what might result from either a mild or a serious global recession.

In Table 9-10, we show how a decline in exports in each of the four categories would decrease total U.S. exports. I assume that there will be a greater decrease in exports as we go to progressively worse categories. I have shown three separate levels of declines in both the mild and serious global recessions.

Even the smallest imaginable impact of Y2K puts over 1 million people out of work and reduces our GDP by almost 1 percent. And that figure assumes that our exports to countries in very grim condition for a period of time are only reduced by 12.5 percent and that exports to Status 3 countries are reduced by only 10 percent.[4]

To put this in perspective, if you can believe the anecdotal stories in the business press, the current Asian meltdown has certainly reduced exports to those affected countries by more than 10 percent, although there are no hard figures yet available. Y2K could do at least as much harm in countries where it has only a moderate impact. Gartner does not tell us what a 7 means in terms of exports to those countries in actual percentages, but with no government services and widespread power and

T A B L E   9 - 1 0

	Mild Global Slowdown % Decline in Exports			Serious Global Slowdown % Decline in Exports		
	Minor	Moderate	Major	Minor	Moderate	Major
Category One	5.00%	7.50%	10.00%	10.00%	15.00%	20.00%
Category Two	7.50%	11.00%	15.00%	15.00%	22.00%	30.00%
Category Three	10.00%	15.00%	20.00%	20.00%	30.00%	40.00%
Category Four	12.50%	20.00%	25.00%	25.00%	40.00%	50.00%
Net Reduction to Total Exports:	7.57%	11.40%	15.13%	15.13%	22.80%	30.27%
Reduction in GDP	0.91%	1.37%	1.82%	1.82%	2.74%	3.64%
#'s of Jobs Lost	1,252,000	1,886,000	2,504,000	2,504,000	3,772,000	5,008,000

[4]Just for the record, we were not able to get country by country *service* exports. The ITA has scores of charts and graphs available of almost everything you could imagine. When their representative was told those numbers were absent, which he confirmed, he simply said he didn't know why, and didn't know where to find them. Your government at work. We did take the total number for all U.S. service exports and assumed that service exports broke down roughly the same as goods exports by category, so the above numbers also include a decline in service exports. My personal guess, however, is that service exports will decline more than goods exports. Accounting, consulting, insurance, and similar areas will not be deemed as important as food, machinery, and hard goods in countries experiencing a serious recession.

telephone outages, it certainly does not seem outrageous or overly pessimistic to suggest at least a 20 percent curtailment for a year or more. This is especially true in countries where the government is highly involved in approving all exports and imports.

Here is what GartnerGroup Director Lou Marcoccio says in the Senate testimony:

> Even if we were to miraculously fix every one of these domestic issues and make certain all U.S. companies and government agencies will get themselves Year 2000 compliant before 2000, the absolute largest risk to the U.S. and to U.S. citizens is the impact from companies and governments outside the U.S. Far too many companies and governments that are critical to our continued strong economy, and are providers of key resources, are more than 30 months behind private industry in the U.S. Since it takes an average of 30 months for a midsize company to achieve compliance of their most critical systems, many of these lagging foreign companies and governments simply will not have enough time to get their systems fixed before 2000. Failures will lead to a negative impact on our economy and on availability of critical resources. We'll see significant impact from failures in these regions, including economic, sociopolitical, investment shifts, market changes, critical resources, national security, and defaults on federal loans.[5]

The Combined Effects of Business Failures and Export Reductions

Let's first look at the combined effects of both direct job losses and export-related losses in a mild global recession. Tables 9-11 and 9-12 show what I consider to be a best-case scenario, in which unemployment would only rise to a little over 7 percent and GDP would only drop by 2 percent. A more significant slowdown would mean 10 percent unemployment and a decline of 5 percent in GDP. To put this in context, the 1973 to 1974 oil crisis recession involved a GDP drop of 3.7 percent.

In a more serious global recession, we could see the unemployment rate between 8 percent and 12 percent, and GDP drops of almost 3 percent to 7 percent, as Tables 9-13 and 9-14 indicate.

Before I get to which of the above scenarios is likely and why, we need to discuss the next major contributing factor to a recession: productivity losses.

[5]Testimony before the Senate Special Committee on the Year 2000 Technology Problem, Oct. 7, 1998.

TABLE 9-11

Mild Global Slowdown—Unemployment

	Number of Jobs Lost		
Jobs Lost Due To:	Minor	Moderate	Major
Decline in Exports	1,252,000	1,886,000	2,504,000
Y2K Related Layoffs	1,500,000	3,000,000	4,500,000
Total Job Losses	2,752,000	4,886,000	7,004,000
Unemployment Rate	7.17%	8.73%	10.28%

TABLE 9-12

Mild Global Slowdown—Decline in GDP

	Reduction in GDP		
GDP Loss Due To:	Minor	Moderate	Major
Decline in Exports	0.91%	1.37%	1.82%
Y2K Related Layoffs	1.09%	2.18%	3.27%
Total Decline in GDP	2.00%	3.55%	5.09%

TABLE 9-13

Serious Global Slowdown—Unemployment

	Number of Jobs Lost		
Jobs Lost Due To:	Minor	Moderate	Major
Decline in Exports	2,504,000	3,772,000	5,008,000
Y2K Related Layoffs	1,500,000	3,000,000	4,500,000
Total Job Losses	4,004,000	6,772,000	9,508,000
Unemployment Rate	8.16%	10.21%	12.23%

Productivity Losses

The GartnerGroup says that in the U.S. 15 percent of companies and government agencies will experience a mission-critical system failure (see

T A B L E   9 - 1 4 ▓▓▓▓▓▓▓▓▓▓▓▓▓▓▓▓▓▓▓▓▓▓▓▓▓▓▓▓▓▓▓

Serious Global Slowdown—Decline in GDP

	Reduction in GDP		
GDP Loss Due To:	*Minor*	*Moderate*	*Major*
Decline in Exports	1.82%	2.74%	3.64%
Internal Y2K Issues	1.09%	2.18%	3.27%
Total Decline in GDP	2.91%	4.92%	6.91%

section on country status of U.S. versus all other countries), and that 10 percent of failures will last three days or longer. The cost of recovering from a single failure after it occurs will range from $20,000 to $3.5 million.[6]

Throughout this book, we have talked about "mission-critical software." By that we have meant software absolutely necessary to allow a company to stay alive by supplying a product to a customer and getting paid for it. But what about the software that is not mission critical? Presumably it was written for some productivity-enhancing purpose. Let's call this software *mission important.*

Let's optimistically assume that 90 percent of the mission-critical software in this country will be ready for 2000. The lion's share of our corporate energy has been spent on getting the most-critical software done. The later a company gets into the process, the less of the merely "important" software will get fixed. But we know that many companies started late in the process. *That means that a significant portion of merely* mission-important *software will not be ready.*

There is a great deal of difference in definition from company to company about the difference between critical and merely important. No one knows how much of this second class of software—the mission important—will not be ready and how important it really is. For instance, several government agencies first classified a number of programs as mission critical. When they realized that they could not get them all remediated in time, someone decided that a number of these programs were no longer mission critical.

Beginning in 2000, a number of employees in businesses all over the world are going to become familiar with pencils and yellow pads. They are going to have to figure out how to do the important things without their "mission-important" software. Is it keeping track of inventory? Customer orders? Billing? Payroll? It largely depends on what someone

[6]Gartner Senate testimony, *http://gartner3.gartnerweb.com/public/state/aboutgg/pressrel/ testimony1098.html#top.*

in a particular company decided was critical to company survival and what was "merely" important.

Between mission-critical failures, scrambling to meet missed software deadlines, random infrastructure problems (power and phones), failed government services, supplier failures, international import and export hassles, increased personal difficulties, and many other problems, how much productivity will we lose? One percent? Two percent? Five percent?

Obviously, there is no way to know exactly how much. But for some period of time, a significant number of people will be less productive. To get a serious hit to the GDP, we do not have to be dramatically less productive. What if, on average, the nation went back to the productivity levels of 1998, 1997, or 1996? This was just a few years ago. In percentages it wasn't huge.

But just so that we don't go overboard and appear completely negative, let's assume that all the mission-important software is up and operating by the summer of 2000. That means that we will be back to full 1999 productivity levels in the summer of 2000. (So, for our calculations, we are going to *cut in half* the productivity losses and their effect on GDP levels in 2000.)

Tables 9-15 and 9-16 show us the effect on GDP of going back to productivity levels of only a few years ago for both a mild and serious global slowdown. In these tables, we are assuming that we have job losses due to Y2K problems and export reductions, so we are looking at productivity losses on the *remaining workforce* and the effects on GDP. The percentage figures show the drop in GDP at different job-loss levels and different productivity levels.

The bad news is that the above reductions in GDP would be at least partially in addition to those from job losses and export reductions.

Before we begin to try and sort through this, let's look at a few other factors that are difficult, if not impossible, to quantify.

T A B L E   9 - 1 5

Decline in GDP Due to Productivity Loss—Mild

| Reduction in Productivity to: | Mild Global Slowdown | | |
	1998 Levels	*1997 Levels*	*1996 Levels*
Job Losses			
Low	2.43%	3.51%	4.71%
Mid	3.98%	5.04%	6.22%
High	5.51%	6.55%	7.72%

TABLE 9-16 ▬▬▬▬▬▬▬▬▬▬▬▬

Decline in GDP Due to Productivity Loss—Serious

	Serious Global Slowdown		
Reduction in Productivity to:	1998 Levels	1997 Levels	1996 Levels
Job Losses			
Low	3.34%	4.41%	5.60%
Mid	5.34%	6.39%	7.55%
High	7.32%	8.35%	9.49%

Price Competition from Foreign Companies

When it comes to bad news, I am from the tell-it-to-me-straight-and-tell-it-to-me-quick school. Then let's figure out what to do. It probably seems like there is no end to the problems that Y2K may be bringing our way, but if we are going to be realistic, we need to address them.

Not immediately, but beginning sometime later in 2000, it is quite possible that our domestic corporations will begin to see much more serious price competition from foreign competitors than what they have seen in the past. In the first few months, the data suggest that foreign companies are going to have far more serious problems than our U.S. companies. But as they get back on-line, or get bought out by major international corporations that have managed to survive and thrive, they are going to start looking for markets in which they can sell their goods.

Current world deflationary pressures are largely due to too much producing capacity. The world has built more steel mills and factories to produce more goods than we can buy, anticipating a growth in consumer spending, especially from Third World countries such as China and India. Even in a global recession, this productive capacity is not going to disappear. Much of it will doubtless be bought by financially stronger companies. There is no reason to think that supplies of goods and services will dry up, although we can anticipate that there will be some periodic and short-lived shortages in products that are only produced from a few, mostly Third World countries in Status Group 4.

How much pressure will a glut of foreign goods put on the ability of U.S. companies to set prices? How much will profits be hurt?

The good news is that if foreign prices are lower, then they are lower across the board. The materials that we buy internationally to produce our products will be cheaper and therefore will allow us to produce at lower costs.

How much will we be able to increase market share as a result of lower costs? How much will profits be helped?

In a conversation that I had about these questions with economist Gary Shilling, he (correctly, I think) pointed out that if foreign countries are really having Y2K problems, our market share might actually increase, as foreign production could go down for a period of time.

Will the dollar become the de facto world currency if Japan has trouble coming out of its own depression? Will the new liberal governments in Europe drag the new Euro down as they cater to their labor allies in a time of global recession?

How strong can the dollar get? Will there be a new Bretton Woods Agreement to try and stabilize world currencies?

There are a lot of questions and not a lot of answers. We simply do not know how bad the rest of the world will be. Based upon what we do know, it is not a bright scenario.

About all that can be said is that some companies will lose and some companies will win. Because I have a basic trust in the marketplace, I tend to think that most of this will sort itself out over time. As long as governments worldwide do not do something drastic (see the chapter entitled "Things That Go Bump in the Night"), the overall effects of the above should be relatively marginal. Of course, if you are working for a company that must compete with lower-priced foreign goods, what is a marginal problem for me is a much more serious problem for you.

There is no way to predict what effect the above concerns may have on the economy. As I said, there are possible scenarios in which it could actually be beneficial for some period of time. We will have to wait and see what happens. But knowing that it has the potential to be quite a volatile period, we can make some decisions about what to do with our investments, as we will see in later chapters.

Employment Gains

There is one unknown factor that could temporarily offset the loss of jobs: people who will be hired as temporary employees by companies who need to throw bodies at the Y2K problem.

For example, let's say that the accounting department of a large company experiences a major computer glitch. The chief financial officer walks into the office of the chief information officer and asks, "How long will we be down?" The CIO tells him that he has to get in line behind the customer-service manager, the marketing manager, and a host of smaller managers, each with some bug that desperately needs to be fixed *today.*

At the quickly convened emergency meeting, the senior staff learns that there are not enough programming staff to fix the problems in less than six weeks, and there are no outside programmers available for less than $200 an hour, even if you could find one and train him quickly.

So, priorities are fought over, and accounting loses, primarily because they can do things manually for a period of time by hiring temporary bookkeepers and accountants. Budgets get blown, profits get shot to hell, but the company gets the work out. Employees get paid. Customers get billed, checks get deposited, and eventually everything gets put into the computers, and things return to normal.

For a brief period, employment at the company actually increased! Even if it eventually is forced to reduce its workforce due to the recession, the initial impact was an increase in employment.

What if management says, "We have enough inventory of product A, so let's just close the plant for three weeks while we work on other problems."

The fact is, you can think of so many "what ifs" that you soon come to realize that there is almost no way to project what will happen to employment in the beginning of 2000.

But whatever the outcome, companies will not be more efficient during this period.

Just because a business fails does not mean that the demand for its products goes away. There will be some companies that dramatically increase market share during this period, and thereby increase their employment rolls. But the period will be marked by what economists call *displacement*. That means, among other things, that jobs disappear in one locale or business and reappear in another. The same people don't necessarily keep the job, especially if there is a long distance between the locales.

If you are the one losing your job, *displacement* is a nice word for serious problems. The old joke goes that a recession is when your neighbor loses his job and a depression is when you lose yours.

Today we don't see losing a job as a huge problem. In fact, the number-one problem for many employers is finding employees. For most of you, if you lose your job today, you can find another job fairly quickly. It might not be as good as your old job, but there is work available.

In a recession that is not the case. New jobs come from a growing economy and growing businesses. But in 2000, businesses will not be growing. There will not be a new job created somewhere every minute. The probability is that we will be losing jobs at a fast rate after the early part of 2000.

Which Scenario Seems Most Likely Now

In trying to determine the probable impact of the Y2K Crisis on GDP, unemployment, and the economy, we have to keep in mind the following thoughts:

1. Even though nearly every company will be telling us that they expect to be ready, forty years of software-productivity research tell us that a significant number won't be. Many of those companies will desperately be trying to get ready, and may even get close, but they are going to experience problems. Remember, the information-technology people telling you that they will be ready on time are the same people who have been telling you for forty years that they will make the deadline, but they only do so 50 percent or less of the time.

2. We must remember the "Kenya factor" (chapter 1). That is where management asks how much time is available for a project and then decides that the project will be done in that amount of time—never mind the reality. Many of the companies in the U.S. and elsewhere in the world have simply started too late. Despite good intentions and aggressive efforts, they are not going to be ready.

3. There is a small but significant number of companies who simply do not have the cash reserves to go for three to four months with reduced sales or no profits due to Y2K-related problems. Because they have less cash, these are the very companies that have waited the longest to start programs and are therefore the most at risk. It may be that more companies are lost due to lack of capital and staying power than due to a direct inability to service customers. By that, I mean that their problems could be fixed and they would survive if they simply had the capital to last until they had full, efficient productive capacity back on-line.

4. Research firms are telling us 98 percent or more of large companies will survive and 95 percent or more of small and midsized companies will survive. But, as we have shown above, even a small percentage of companies with problems will cause a serious rise in unemployment.

5. The rest of the world is in serious, potentially disastrous shape. Our exports will take a hit. There is no way that the *average* U.S. worker will be as productive in the first half of 2000 as he or she was in 1999. Admittedly, for many workers there will be no loss at all, but for some workers the loss will be significant. Even a small loss in total productivity will have serious effects upon GDP and profits.

6. We are already in a period of very low inflation. We may be close to deflation as we enter 2000.

7. The world economy may already be in a recession before 2000, and the U.S. almost certainly will be experiencing low growth if not a mild recession in 1999.

8. Government services will be disrupted.

9. There will be a significant number of companies that have mission-critical systems fail, and the cost of repairing them and the resulting lost revenue will impact profits and growth.

10. Given the current lip-service leadership from government officials, from the office of the president through state governors on down, and the perception on the part of a majority of Americans that this is not a big problem, I do not expect major national efforts to address all aspects of the Y2K problem to begin before the second quarter of 1999. It will not happen at all unless there is a groundswell of public opinion demanding action, or unless major government figures (besides the few congressmen and senators who are doing their best to let the public know the extent of the problem) stop waiting for opinion polls to tell them what to do and *lead*.

Putting all these factors together, I think that we are facing a recession that will be the worst in postwar history. It is likely that we will see 10 percent unemployment and a GDP reduction of 5 percent. If we put more energy into fixing the problem here and abroad, it will be less severe. If we continue on as we are today, it will be worse. I am assuming that Congress, the Federal Reserve, and our business and government leaders are going to become more aggressive in dealing with this problem. If nothing happens, I expect things to be worse. I have had talks with some government leaders. Many of them recognize the seriousness of the problem. I think that they will act.

We must begin to treat this problem as the technological equivalent of war. It is not too late to soften the impact of the recession. Even if we cannot get everything fixed on time, the sooner problems are fixed, the sooner the recovery will begin.

Let me once again quote Dr. Ed Yardeni.

> How much might the U.S. price deflator fall in 2000? Conceivably, prices might drop 5% in a deflation scenario. If real GDP drops as much, then a 10% decline in nominal GDP would amount to a loss of nearly $1 trillion. Is this a worst-case scenario? Maybe, maybe not. By the way, this $1 trillion potential loss estimate is just for the U.S., and before litigation fees and damages, which may also exceed $1 trillion.
>
> Stock investors might lose at least $1 trillion if stock prices drop as they do in every recession. The Dow Jones Industrial Average peaked at 1051.7 on January 11, 1973. It plunged 45% to a trough of 577.6 on December 6, 1974. The bear market lasted 23 months. A similar drop in the Dow from the July 17, 1998 record peak of 9337.97, would put it at 5150.[7]

So, what can we expect? Obviously, we can expect the stock markets to drop. There will be increased volatility in every market, with lots of opportunities for profits and losses.

---

[7]This quote is in chapter 1 of Yardeni's excellent web-book at *http://www.yardeni.com/y2kbook.html*.

Government revenues will be hit. Income tax receipts could be down at least 5 percent (there will be 5 percent fewer people working), Social Security receipts will be down by at least 5 percent, there will be less capital gains and less corporate profit, and therefore the revenues from corporate taxes will not be as high. More people will "retire" sooner and go on Social Security. More people will apply for welfare benefits.

I went to the web site of the Congressional Budget Office (*www.cbo.gov*) and pulled down a spreadsheet on income and expenditure projections for 2000. If you drop individual taxes, Social Security, excise taxes, and miscellaneous revenues by 5 percent, customs duties by 15 percent, and corporate taxes by 20 percent, you find that total revenue drops in 2000 by 7 percent. Am I being overly pessimistic? Maybe, maybe not. I am assuming personal income taxes will be down 5 percent, but that is not even taking into account the drop in capital gains taxes that are included in that figure and which makes up a significant portion of that number.

If you increase food stamps by 5 percent and Social Security and Medicare by 3 percent and don't even bother increasing anything else, including earned income credits, expenses increase by 1 percent.

The bottom line number goes from a surplus of $81 billion to a *deficit* of $68 billion. They would have to hold the line on spending (difficult) and only have a mild recession to come close to keeping the balanced budget (doubtful).

Goodbye surplus, hello deficits.

For states, cities, and school districts, as there will be less GDP and employment, sales tax revenues will go down. In a recession, real estate values will drop, and so will property tax revenues.

Businesses will need to start planning for a recession. That may not necessarily mean, however, that businesses should pull back and wait for things to get better. For some businesses, this will be a time to increase market share by taking advantage of competitor problems, or by buying competitors who are not Y2K ready. *Remember, if we only lose 5 percent of GDP that means that there is still about $7 trillion dollars waiting to be spent somewhere on something.*

While the analogy is simple, relate this recession to our personal income. If our income dropped 5 or 10 percent, most of us could survive. We would simply cut back on some expenses, change our lifestyles, and try to figure out how to get our income back up. Only a few who were stretched too thin would not be able to make it without filing for bankruptcy.

Our national income is going to drop 5 percent. As a nation, we are going to have to spend less for a period of time until we can figure out how to make more money. We are going to have to change some of our habits. For most of us, it is not going to mean a radical change in lifestyle. For the 5 percent or more who become unemployed, it will make a huge difference. For companies unprepared to deal with a recession, it will be a big problem. But most companies will react quickly and survive quite well.

Companies and individuals who do not take protective action will face big problems and suffer serious consequences.

Where are the major economists who saw the Asian crisis or the Russian debt default before it happened? There were a few signs, but these events caught the markets mainly by surprise.

The Y2K Recession does not have to take you by surprise. You have time to take action. In the next chapters, we are going to see what you should do to protect your family, your community, and your investments.

An Important Introduction to the Chapters on Investing Your Money

The Y2K Recession is coming. As we will see in the next few chapters, if you are going to protect your investment gains made in the eighties and nineties—if you want to have your investment portfolio grow during the Y2K Recession—*you are going to have to adopt a new investment strategy designed to take advantage of a recession.*

In the next chapters, I am going to tell you how stocks, bonds, gold, real estate, mutual funds, and collectibles should fare in the Y2K Recession. I am going to show you specific strategies that will not only help you weather the coming storm but will allow you to prosper in the face of it.

Before we examine what type of investment strategy is appropriate for you before and during the Y2K Recession, I want to briefly discuss my basic investment principles and biases. You need to understand my basic approach to investing and then decide if it agrees with your personal beliefs.

1. *Successful investing is primarily about quantifying and controlling risk.* Before I invest my hard-earned money, I want to know everything I can about the inherent risk in an investment (and every investment has risks). After I have analyzed the risk, then I want to know what the potential return is from the investment. With these two numbers, I can determine what type of risk I am taking for the size of the potential reward.
2. *If I cannot quantify the risk, it is very doubtful I will make the investment.* That is particularly true as the Y2K Recession approaches. Some investments that have been touted as "rock-solid" are going to become quicksand.

3. The greater the risk, the smaller the percentage of my portfolio I will allocate to any one investment.

4. I believe in getting counsel from professional investment advisors. I think it is important to have someone you trust talk with you from time to time and discuss your investment strategies. Notice I used the plural when I said get counsel from advisors. I like to get advice from more than one source. Investment newsletters and publications, books like this and other media qualify as a source of ideas. But ultimately you need to take responsibility for your investment strategy.

5. It is important you that have an investment strategy. You need to set goals and have a realistic plan to achieve those goals.

6. The riskier the investment, the more counsel and help I think you should have to analyze the investment. Ninety percent of amateur commodity investors lose money. Eighty percent of new businesses fail within five years. Most of our poor investments are based upon emotions like greed or excitement. We get a hot tip or a "hunch" and don't thoroughly investigate it. *The best way to save money is to not lose it.*

7. I like to know if the people with whom I am investing have their own money in the investment. The old joke goes something like this: when I met Bob he had the experience and I had the money; Now I have the experience and he has the money. There are exceptions to this rule, of course, but they should be well thought out exceptions.

8. I prefer to let professionals manage the bulk of my money. After I have decided what portion of my portfolio to allocate to a particular area, I like to find professionals with proven, long-term track records to manage that allocation. These professionals can be investment advisors, mutual and hedge-fund managers, a trusted broker, or you can follow the advice of investment newsletter writers whom you read and trust.

   Professionals beat amateurs not only in sports but in investments and in almost every area of life. You should consider yourself to be the general of your investment strategy, deploying your assets among your "troops." Trying to become an expert in every area of investing is just not practical if you already have a full-time job. Also, I cannot emphasize the importance of a long-term track record. Even if the investments are relatively "safe," I prefer to have experience on my side.

9. The corollary to number eight is that for those areas of your portfolio for which you do assume active, direct investment responsibility, you need to become a professional in that area. There is a high correlation between the success of individual investors and the knowledge they have about an investment.

Most of my personal investment portfolio I allocate to managers and funds according to my overall goals and strategies. I directly invest only in areas where I consider myself somewhat knowledgeable.

10. My father told me a thousand times, "You never go broke taking a profit." Don't be greedy. Don't try to milk an investment for every penny of profit. Never be afraid of taking profits. I believe we are entering a period of great uncertainty and think it is time we take the profits we have made during the last bull market off the table.

11. You should diversify your portfolio, and the bulk of your assets should be in less risky investments. Because of my belief that we are facing a recession, I am not going to recommend a large number of investments. In a bear market, our choices are much more limited than when we are in a bull market. But even then, it is important to diversify.

12. Never get into a gunfight with Wyatt Earp, never bet on three-card monte on the streets of Manhattan, and never buy stocks from a broker or salesman who calls you on the phone with a hot tip. All three are guaranteed losers.

In the next three chapters I am going to talk about investments. If after you have read these chapters, you understand why I make the choices and suggestions I do, then I have accomplished my goal. You may not agree, but I hope you follow my reasoning.

If for some reason I have not made the logic for a particular investment perfectly clear, *then do not make the investment.* Do not invest simply on my suggestions if you do not understand why you are doing so, and understand the risks involved. Before you invest in any recommended investment, you should read the prospectus and disclosure documents thoroughly. I also suggest that you make it a general rule to seek independent counsel on every investment you make.

The strategies outlined in chapters 10 through 14 are based upon my personal interpretation of the research you have read in the previous chapters. I believe that we will have a Y2K Recession, that we are entering a deflationary period, and that interest rates are going down. If these events do not happen, it is possible that my suggestions could either lose money or keep you out of investments that go higher, and thus potentially cost you profits. In every case I try to analyze the risk involved and tell you both the upside as well as the downside.

I am an outspoken advocate for full disclosure on everything involving investments. Let me tell you about my personal businesses and investments that are pertinent to this book. I have been in the investment business in one form or another for many years. It is how I make my living and how I will continue to make my living after this book goes out of print.

For many years I have been a consultant to various investment funds, but I do not mention any of the funds to which I am a consultant in this book. Also, I am a partner in a firm, ProFutures Fund Management, which manages privately offered hedge funds. Because these funds are available only to accredited investors and must be offered on a private basis, I do not mention them in this book.

I am also a partner in an investment advisory firm called ProFutures Capital Management. This firm recommends professional investment advisors employing a variety of strategies to interested investors and receives a fee from the recommended investment advisor for doing so. In the following chapters, I mention investment advisors with whom the firm has representative business relationships. If you were to invest with these advisors, it would ultimately benefit me personally. You need to understand this is a serious potential conflict of interest. While it is not always the case, it is best to assume there is some level of a conflict of interest when I mention anything connected with ProFutures and its related companies.

In every case, I offer alternatives to these advisors or show you where to go to find you own advisors, if you should so choose. There is no one right way or wrong way to implement the advice I offer for dealing with the Y2K Recession. Some of you will prefer to implement the suggested strategies directly. There is nothing wrong with this. There are also those who would prefer an investment advisor to implement the strategies for them. While I am comfortable with my recommendations, I am under no illusions that these are the only choices. I tell you ways to find your own different advisors, should you so choose. Before you make any investment, read the offering material very carefully. If you make an investment, do so because you feel it is the correct choice for you and not merely my suggestion.

After wrestling with this obvious conflict of interest, I decided that it would be wrong to write a book and leave out what I personally feel are appropriate potential investment decisions. I mention these advisors because in my personal judgment they typify the type of strategy I think is appropriate for dealing with the Y2K Recession.

You should also know that I have money invested with these and other advisors and managers and that I also follow my own advice on other investments I recommend. However, I do not invest in any recommended fund in which I might benefit by your investment. As an example, my recommendation of a particular mutual fund or gold, for instance, is not going to affect the price of that product. Likewise, if I recommend an advisor, I do not get special treatment or reduced fees. My money is treated just like any other account.

I also publish an investment newsletter called *Year 2000 Alert*, in which I give more specific and timely advice. If you are interested in receiving this letter, the contact information is in appendix A. While it should be obvious, if you subscribe to this newsletter, I will benefit financially.

Finally, the ideas and suggestions in this book are my responsibility. Neither my book publisher nor my newsletter publisher nor any of the firms mentioned in this book nor my business associates nor the managers of funds to which I consult are in any way responsible for the content of this book. It is quite possible that the research firms that have provided the material upon which my analysis is based would not agree with my interpretation or conclusions.

I have tried to seek an appropriate balance between the doomsdayers on one hand and the Pollyannas on the other. You need to weigh the evidence I have presented. Ultimately, you must make your own decision on where you stand on the issues surrounding Y2K, and invest and prepare accordingly.

This book was finished in late January 1999. Considering the massive amounts of information we will have thrust upon us in the next year, it is possible my views could change, and with it my suggested investment strategies. If I change any fundamental advice or have a major change in the approach to Y2K preparedness offered in this book, either positive or negative, I will publish it in my newsletter and on my web site. I urge you to check my web site regularly (*www.2000wave.com*).

Taking Stock

As I travel around the country, speaking at conferences or talking to friends, I find that the questions uppermost in people's minds are "What do I do with my stocks and mutual funds? Should I sell, or should I hold? How can I protect my investments? How can I make money if there is a recession?"

There is no one right answer because everyone's situation is different. Some of us have our money in pension plans with limited choices. You may be young and just starting to build your nest egg or older and already retired. But the key factor to remember is that we are going to have a recession. In every recession in history stock markets go down, sometimes dramatically. Just as a rising tide lifts all ships, it is difficult for a ship to rise as the tide lowers. The bull market has helped all stocks, but a bear market will hurt even the best of stocks. That does not mean there will not be opportunities to make money in the coming recession. There are some very exciting possibilities, as we will see.

At the end of this chapter I am going to suggest some alternatives for you to consider. Don't skip to the end of the chapter. It is very important that you understand exactly why I am making these suggestions. As a premise for this chapter, I will tell you that you are responsible for your own investment decisions. When you buy or sell any investment, you need to know why you're doing it. Investing simply because someone else told you to do it is a prescription for disaster.

It is important for you to have a goal for your investments. Is your goal to have a comfortable retirement or a larger home, or to leave an inheritance for your children? Whatever your goal, you need to have a plan, preferably written, that will allow you to achieve it. And while it is okay to modify that plan as new opportunities come along, in general you should stick with it.

The large majority of Americans who have a plan simply assume that if they save money and invest it in the stock market, they will reach their goal. I cannot tell you how many times I have talked with people who simply assumed that if they saved money and "bought on the dips," the market would eventually go up, and everything would work out. It seems that the younger the person is, the more prevalent that attitude.

For the last sixteen years this type of buy-and-hold approach has been successful precisely because we've been in the greatest bull market in history. It will not be successful over the next two years.

You need to seriously consider whether the Y2K Recession should alter your investment strategies. You should not have to change your goals, but if your plan assumes that the current bull market will continue with only a minor or brief disruption, then you will be putting your goal in serious jeopardy.

Buy-and-Hold or Buy-and-Fold?

For sixteen years, buy-and-hold has been a good strategy, primarily because it worked. Buy-and-hold will continue to be a good strategy until it stops working, and then it won't be.

Now, that seems obvious, but to listen to the majority of brokerage- and investment-advisor communities you would think that buy-and-hold is the only investment strategy a *serious* investor should employ. They are wrong, wrong, WRONG! You are going to read very few investment advisors who will tell you in clear, unambiguous terms to get out before the market drops. But after it does, most of them will say that they told you to get out and direct you to the third paragraph on page five of their newsletter as "proof" that they said the markets could be a problem.

Buy-and-hold works until there is a recession. *And yes,* I know that the market has always eventually come back and made new highs, but do you want to suffer through 50 percent or more of unnecessary losses and wait years or more to make new highs? If you had bought the S&P 500 in 1968, you would have waited fourteen years until 1982 just to break even. Do you really want to wait that long?

Unless you have a high tolerance for pain and a long time until retirement, I don't think so!

During a recession the stock market always goes down. It has never gone up during a recession. Never. Not once. And in the preceding chapter, I hope that I convinced you that we are looking at a recession, and possibly a severe one.

First, let's look at two measures of how far the markets could go down. The first is a simple table (Table 10-1) of how much the stock market has fallen in past bear markets. Notice how long it has taken to recover.

If you invested in February of 1966, sixteen years later you would be roughly where you had started, but you would have gone through the worst inflationary period in this century. In real terms you would have lost over 50 percent of your money! In 1981, buy-and-hold was a tough sell.

But most brokers working today don't remember 1981 or 1973, let alone 1966. Their experience has been of one long boom interrupted by quick corrections and a very mild recession. Unless your memory is long, most of you don't remember a serious recession. I was a working student in 1973, and the fact that we were in a recession didn't really register.

The 1987 "crash" was not a recession. It was a correction by the market of an extremely overbought condition and was made worse by com-

T A B L E   1 0 - 1

Bull-Bear Market Cycles in the United States, 1901–1997

Market Top	Market Bottom	Index High	Index Low	Bull % Increase	Bear % Decline
July 1990	October 1990	369.78	294.51	67.14	20.36
August 1987	December 1987	337.89	221.24	233.09	34.52
November 1980	August 1982	140.52	101.44	61.70	27.81
December 1976	March 1978	107.48	86.9	72.58	19.15
January 1973	October 1974	119.87	62.28	73.00	48.04
November 1968	May 1970	108.37	69.29	48.05	36.06
February 1966	October 1966	94.06	73.2	79.78	22.18
December 1961	June 1962	72.64	52.32	86.35	27.97
August 1956	October 1957	49.74	38.98	267.08	21.63
May 1946	June 1949	19.25	13.55	157.70	29.61
November 1938	April 1942	13.79	7.47	62.24	45.83
March 1937	March 1938	18.68	8.5	131.76	54.50
July 1933	March 1935	12.2	8.06	120.61	33.93
September 1932	February 1933	9.06	5.53	105.91	38.96
September 1929	June 1932	31.86	4.4	393.95	86.19
July 1919	August 1921	9.51	6.45	39.85	32.18
November 1916	December 1917	10.21	6.8	38.91	33.40
December 1909	December 1914	10.3	7.35	64.80	28.64
September 1906	November 1907	10.03	6.25	60.22	37.69
June 1901	October 1903	8.05	6.26	111.29	22.24

Source: Global Financial Data

puter selling. The market clearly corrected too far on the downside, and it was not long before it went on to new highs. In 1990 we had a mild recession, and the market did go down, but not a lot, and it then continued its relentless charge. In the fall of 1997—and again in the summer of 1998—we had another "correction" stemming from fears over the Asian economic problem, but the market quickly recovered and went on to new highs.

So, our three most recent corrections were all short-lived, and all resulted in new highs. Like Pavlov's dogs responding to the dinner bell, the stock market is training us by Pavlovian methods to "stay the course." (I can never write those words without thinking of Dana Carvey's impression of George Bush saying, "Stay the course—a thousand points of light"! I can almost hear your broker and mutual-fund manager saying the same thing, trying to calm you down as your funds go lower and lower.)

As I write this in January 1999, is it possible that the markets will go on to even more new highs before the onslaught of the Y2K Recession? Sure it is! I rather doubt it, but it is possible. Some of the strategies that I am going to share with you later actually take into account that possibility.

Let's look at a very reliable indicator of stock valuation: *price/earnings ratio* (P/E). For those unfamiliar with the term, price-to-earnings ratio is figured by dividing the price of a share of stock by the per-share earnings of the company. As you would expect, the more money that a company makes, or that investors think it will make in the future, the higher value the stock will be. At some point, though, the price of the stock gets so high that it does not seem a good buy in terms of its future earnings potential relative to its price.

In a bull market, stock prices go up, and therefore the P/E ratio goes up. In the current bull market, which was accompanied by a growing economy, higher profits due to corporate restructuring, and a growing optimism, P/E ratios went to all-time highs. If stocks return to their historical (and normal) P/E range of fourteen to seventeen, you will be looking at a stock market decline of approximately 50 percent!

How Low Can It Go?

The answer is that nobody knows, and if anyone tells you that they do, ask to see his or her investment track record. I doubt that it will confirm their prophet (or profit!) status.

But today it does not matter how low it will go. We can begin to ask that question in the middle of 2000. Today all we need to concentrate on is that the direction or trend when the recession becomes clearly visible will be down.

G R A P H   1 0 - 1 ▓▓▓▓▓▓▓▓▓▓▓▓▓▓▓▓▓▓▓▓▓▓▓▓▓▓▓▓▓▓▓▓

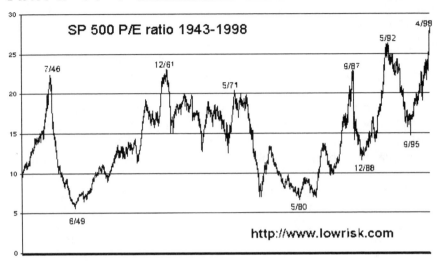

Source: LowRisk.Com

If the market behaves at all as it did in the past, we should expect the lowest points to be reached *before* we know the full extent to which the Y2K Recession has damaged the economy. I expect the market to drop significantly before January 1, 2000 and on into the first part of 2000. If the first few weeks and months are chaotic, with very little good news, then the market could drop further. Then, as we get a handle on the problem after the first months of 2000 and begin to get some good news, we could see a market rebound.

At that point we will have to deal with earnings reports from the first quarter. If earnings are down, as I expect they will be, we will probably see another downward movement. And it could continue down or sideways until we begin to see reasons for a turnaround in the economy. Typically, the market will recognize that turnaround before the statistics show up, so we could see the market rising in the face of what still seems to be a recession.

Why is this? It goes back to P/E ratios. Investors buy a stock because they think that the company is going to grow. And one of the ways that we measure growth is earnings growth. What happens is that some investors who are contrarians (meaning that they prefer to buy when everyone else is selling) look for buying opportunities. But they don't necessarily buy just because a stock or the market is down.

They look for signs that indicate an upward movement in the future. These signs are generally called *leading indicators* because they are guides to what is likely to happen in the future.

The index of leading economic indicators (LEI) is a composite of the following eleven leading indicators:

1. Average workweek (manufacturing).
2. Initial unemployment claims.
3. New orders for consumer goods.
4. Vendor performance.
5. Plant and equipment orders.
6. Building permits.
7. Change in unfilled durable orders.
8. Sensitive material prices.
9. Stock prices (S&P 500).
10. Real M2.
11. Index of consumer expectations.

Now, these statistical tools are probably not at the top of your must-read list. There are other, more commonly used statistics that can warn you about impending stock market trouble or opportunity.

I would recommend that you pay particular attention to the NYSE Advance/Decline Line, New Highs/New Lows, Volume, and, of course, any signs of serious stock market weakness. A good, free web site to help you sift through all these esoteric indicators is the Daily Rocket (*www. dailyrocket.com/markcom/*).

I expect that these leading indicators will give us a signal that it is time to begin to move back into the market. With luck, it won't be too far into 2000. But that timing will all depend upon how much software is fixed before 2000 and how severe the problems are overseas. But remember it will take at least several years *or longer* for the market to return to 1998 highs. It will not go back up as fast as it went down. When it does resume its upward course, you will once again have the opportunity to make exciting returns from stocks. We will get the opportunity to invest and watch the Dow go from 5,000 to 10,000 all over again. If it were to take even five years that would be an annual growth rate of over 15 percent per year which is good in any time period.

So today, what should we do? My advice is simple. If you believe that we are going to experience a recession, you should sell your stocks and equity mutual funds, unless you have a compelling reason to hold onto them. If you are reading this and the markets are at a cyclical low and you feel you just *have* to wait until it goes higher, then consider selling 10 percent to 20 percent of your holdings every week until you are out of the market. The advantage of selling gradually is that if the market goes back up, you will capture some of the gains, and if it continues down, you will not lose as much as you would have if you had held on waiting for the rise.

But My Broker Says to Hold On—the Dawn Is Coming

Let's look at some of the reasons that you will be given to not sell.

a. Buy-and-hold has proven itself the best system. Nobody can time the market successfully.

This is patently wrong. There are in fact numerous investment firms that have timing systems, from simple to complex, that have beaten the market over many years. But you don't hear about these firms.

In the first place, when a mutual-fund manager tells you to invest for the long term, what he is really saying is "Don't take your money out of my fund. My income is derived from the amount of money I have under management, and I don't want my income to go down."

I know that that sounds harsh, and a lot of managers will have much-better and nobler-sounding reasons, but that is the bottom line. For the life of me, I can't understand why anyone would want to hold an equity (stock) mutual fund that is by law invested in a large number of stocks when the broad market is moving down.

Further, while fund managers may talk buy-and-hold, their investment pattern is anything but! The vast majority of mutual-fund managers turn over their portfolios many times during the course of an investment cycle. They only hold a stock as long as they think that it is going up. If they have reason to believe that a stock may go down, then they sell it. But if the broad market in stocks goes down, they want you to ride it out with *them.*

There are a few funds that may do well in this market, and I will mention them later, but they are the exception. Look at Table 10-1 again, which shows the losses for the twenty bear markets in this century. (This table does not include the market losses of 20 percent or more in late 1998.)

The *average* loss is 35.04 percent!

The only way that you can argue with that column is to assert that there is not going to be a recession or that it is not going to be deep. Period. There is no other argument.

In 1987 the average growth-oriented mutual fund lost 29 percent, and the average aggressive-growth mutual fund lost 39 percent. The Y2K Recession is going to look like the 1972 to 1974 bear-market recession, rather than the relatively painless bear markets that we experienced in 1987 and 1990.

In the environment that we are in, the first concern that you should have is the return *of* your money, not the return *on* your money. The winners in a recession are those investors who have the most money at the end of the recession. *It is difficult to do this if your investment is dropping by an average of 35 percent.*

You want investments that will, at a minimum, preserve your capital, and that have the potential to make it grow without appreciable downside risk.

But What About My Favorite Stock?

There will be a few stocks that will go up during the recession. There will be some stocks that will get so beat up during the early part of the recession that they will be hard to resist at discounted prices.

There *will* be some opportunities. Companies that deal with distressed debt, some technology-oriented companies, and companies that will actually profit from a recession but whose stocks will get dragged down initially from the overall weight of the market come to mind as possible winners.

But these will be exceptions. It will take hard work and some luck to find them. The vast majority of stocks will go down, and many significantly, during a recession. If your favorite stock is selling at an all-time high P/E, it is a candidate for selling. If it is susceptible to a recession, then it should be sold. Even companies with the potential to do well in a recession should probably be sold until we are well into the recession.

Further, going back to the last chapter, the projections are for a small, but significant, number of large and midsized companies to go belly up. We have no way of knowing today which companies will do so. In 1999 every CEO in America will tell you that they are going to make it. In July of 2000 we will know who did.

Understand, it will not just be the Y2K compliance of a company that will determine its long-term viability. There are the added complications of their customers and suppliers, their banking lines and credit exposure, the nature of their business, and other factors. We will lose a significant number of companies from the secondary or ripple effects of the Y2K problem.

So, before you decide to hold a stock, you need to *know that you know,* as the preacher says. Murphy's Law says that the stock that you have had in the family forever is the one that will be vulnerable. It might even be one of the 5 to 7 percent that will disappear, and then you will lose everything. I have a hard time finding a stock so exciting today that I want to own it in the face of a recession, especially when we do not know how severe the recession will be, or what will be the real effects of the Millennium Bug on any particular company.

b. I will have to pay too much in capital-gains taxes if I sell.

This one is quick and easy. Which would you rather do: pay a 20 percent capital-gains tax that you are going to have to pay sometime anyway, or watch your assets drop by 40 percent?

Let's assume that you have done well and have significant profits. Also, we will assume that the capital-gains tax rate is the maximum at 20 percent. (The new rates are too complicated to figure, and somehow *my* investments never qualify for the Republican-sponsored tax reductions, so I will assume that you are in the same situation.) Table 10-2 below shows how you would have done if you sold and paid the taxes versus letting your investment drop 40 percent or more.

T A B L E   1 0 - 2

Investment	Gain %	Left After Tax	After 40% Drop	After 50% Drop
$1,000	50%	$900	$600	$500
$1,000	75%	$850	$600	$500
$1,000	90%	$820	$600	$500

Even if you have an investment that has gone up ten times, you are much better off by selling now. And this strategy does not even take into account the return that you will make on your money by investing it in instruments that will rise by 10 to 30 percent or more as the markets drop. Conservatively invested, you could have as much money after eighteen months as you had before paying the taxes. If you are still in love with the stock you sold, then buy it back, and get twice as much!

c. But my stock/mutual fund/etc. is already down 20 percent, and I want to wait until it goes back up.

I repeat, this is a recession. It is not going to go back up for a long time. Until then, it is going to go down more. Sell it now, unless you have a *very* good reason to believe that it will go back up. (And a very good reason is not the manager telling you the market is turning around!)

d. My favorite analyst, friend, or stock market guru tells me that we are not going to have a recession. This is just a correction and any day now we will see new highs.

I guess that the best way to deal with this objection is to look at why someone would think there is not a bear market and a recession in our future. Abby Cohen of Goldman Sachs is one of the most influential bull-market proponents on Wall Street. *Fortune* magazine listed her reasons for being in denial about a recession and a bear market.

This is important, so I am going to quote the article point by point and then respond.[1]

Worried about the problems overseas? What for? They're nothing new. Cohen argues that the 1990s have never featured consistent global growth. Back in 1994, Mexico and parts of Latin America went into a spiral of recession and devaluation, yet that didn't stop the bull.

[1] *Fortune*, Sept. 9, 1998, article by Nelson Schwarz: "Counterpoint: The Bull Lives!" You can access this article by going to *www.pathfinder.com/fortune/1998/980928/mrk7.html*.

She's right, there has not been consistent global growth, but in the past there was *overall* growth. If some economies were not doing well, many others were doing spectacularly. But now we are experiencing consistent global recession. Region after region is in the midst of a serious slowdown or outright recession, and some are in depression. Further, in this bull-market cycle, the Asian tigers were a significant source of growth. Europe was generally improving as well. But now, Asia and most of the Third World are experiencing significant losses. Russia is a basket case. Latin America is crumbling, led by Brazil. Growth forecasts for Europe are anything but robust and are being revised downward. U.S. growth will likewise slow down in 1999. Where is the engine to pull the world into another long-term bull market? There is simply no valid comparison between any period for the last twenty years and the current world situation.

And the problems in Japan? That economy has been in recession . . . all through the '90s. Japan's domestic weakness failed to prevent GE, Microsoft, Merck, and a host of other companies from doing just fine.

Granted, but the problems in Japan are getting worse, not better. Let me make two points.

First, I remember reading—when the Nikkei Index (the measure of the Japanese stock market) was approaching forty thousand—that *Japan was different*. The Japanese invested for the long term and did not care that P/E ratios were ridiculously high by Western standards. The bull market in Japan wouldn't fail because the Japanese were investors by nature and there would always be plenty of buying. Now, all this is history.

Bottom line: *a trend is a trend until it isn't*. Trends change. Situations change. To suggest that something will remain true just because it has been true in the past is a grave mistake.

Second, the banking situation in Japan is deteriorating rapidly, and by the time you read this, it may be approaching a crisis.

Some of us in Texas remember what happened when banks lent money on shaky collateral, mostly real estate and oil at high prices. You got a 1986 S&L crisis that the rest of the nation had to bail out, and Texas went through a very serious recession. At the bottom, homes were being auctioned off in Houston, and the winners were using credit cards to buy them, they were so cheap.

Japanese banks have loaned enormous amounts of money on unbelievably inflated real-estate and stock prices. At one time Tokyo was worth more than all of California if you could believe the real-estate prices. But in the United States, we did not hide the problems under a rug. They were addressed, and quickly. It cost a lot of taxpayer money, and many investors and businesses were wiped out, but life went on and we recovered.

In Japan, the opposite is true. The government has done everything it can to postpone the day of reckoning, hoping for a return of boom times. But recession has given way to depression, and boom times are nowhere in sight. The day of reckoning for Japanese banks is fast approaching. The consequences will be enormous. And this time, the rest of Asia will be dragged further down as well.

While Japan alone may not drag down Merck or IBM, a global recession is very likely to deeply affect them.

The *Fortune* article continued:

> Then there's deflation, to which bears ascribe a kryptonitelike power. In fact, it's another case of been there, done that. "Tech companies have been dealing with falling prices for 20 years," Cohen notes. What about deflation leading to a replay of the 1930s? The problem then wasn't falling commodity prices, Cohen points out; it was shrinking incomes. And when you adjust for inflation, Cohen says, incomes are growing faster today than they have in years.

I fail to see the relevance of tech companies and falling prices to this discussion, but it makes a nice sound bite. The prices for computers are falling because of improvements in technology and increased productivity—which are good things! The main reason for the coming deflation is oversupply, which is a bad thing. It is not shrinking incomes. As we enter into recession, and especially after January of 2000, there is going to be growing unemployment, and that is when we will see shrinking incomes.

There is no reason the economy cannot grow in a period of deflation, as long as it is mild. Inflation in the range of 1 percent is not a problem either. It is when we start moving far away from equilibrium that we have problems. But I think that stocks will not be judged and priced the same way under deflation as they have been under an inflationary environment. And that means a serious correction as we adjust our valuation criteria.

So What Do I Do With My Money?

I hope I have convinced you that now is not the time to be invested in stocks or mutual funds where the only way you can make money is if the market goes up. If I have, you will be selling your stocks and closing out your mutual funds. But where do you put your money?

There is not, unfortunately, an easy answer. It depends upon how much you have, how old you are, what your earning power is, whether your money is tied up in an IRA or pension plan, how much debt you have, how secure your job or business is, and when you will need to access your money. You also have to decide how much risk you want to take and how aggressive you want to be.

In later chapters we will deal with bonds and other alternatives to stocks. But right now, let's examine how we can make money in a falling stock market.

Seven Bear Market Funds

There are over 3,364 stock mutual funds in existence today. I know of seven funds that are designed to make money in a bear market. And you can divide those seven bear market funds into two categories—those that *will* make money and those that *should* make money in a bear market. As we will see, there is a huge difference between *will* and *should.*

The practical difference is that half of these bear funds are passive index funds and the other half are actively managed funds. (I will explain the difference as we go along.) The index funds, which have a negative correlation to the S&P 500, are designed to automatically increase in value during bear markets. The actively managed funds should, but aren't guaranteed, to go up in value during bear markets.

(I will be using the terms *long* and *short* throughout this chapter. By "long" I mean an investment strategy that makes money when the market goes up. By "short" I mean an investment strategy that makes money when the market goes down. Obviously, to make money in a bear market, you must use some kind of short investment strategy.)

But What If You're Wrong?
Some Bear Funds Hold Up Better in Bull Markets.

Anytime you make an investment you should also consider the consequences of being wrong. In the case of bear market funds, being wrong means that the stock market advances. As you know, the stock market can go to ridiculous extremes between greed and fear. That means you need to be aware of how much money you may lose if this overextended market continues to advance even further before encountering the Y2K Recession. If you decide to "go short" the market too early, the losses could be painful. As they say, timing is everything.

Again, the distinction is pretty straightforward. The passively managed bear market index funds will lose the most money in bull markets. By definition, these index funds will have to inversely mirror the S&P 500. If the market advances, you lose. Some of the actively managed bear market funds, however, have shown a reasonable tendency overall (with the notable exception of last October and November) to protect their shareholders from large losses during periods of advancing stock prices. The portfolio managers take active steps to minimize the cost of being wrong.

The passively managed index funds mentioned below are primarily used by market timers and investors who are convinced the market is going down. I am not suggesting that you take a significant portion of your money and invest in one of these funds in a buy-and-hold manner. After we talk about these funds, then I am going to suggest ways you can use them to your advantage.

Funds That Will Make Money in a Bear Market

PASSIVELY MANAGED INDEX FUNDS

You are probably familiar with index funds. When most people think of index funds, however, they think of funds that replicate the performance of the S&P 500, like the Vanguard Index 500 (VFINX) fund.

These S&P 500 index funds are very simple. If the S&P 500 rises by 10 percent, then an S&P 500 index fund is designed to rise by approximately 10 percent, less management fees and expenses. The bottom line is that these funds are designed to move in the same direction and by the same amount as the S&P 500. These funds would have a beta of 1.0 (a way of measuring stock market volatility), meaning that they have a perfect correlation with the S&P. 500.

But there is a group of three S&P 500 index funds that work very, very differently. Instead of moving in unison with the S&P 500, these bear market index funds move in *inverse correlation* with the S&P 500. In beta terms, these funds would have a beta of *negative* -1.0. That means that if the S&P 500 goes down by 10 percent, these funds would go up by 10 percent.

The concept is really quite simple. These bear market index funds will do the opposite of what the stock market does. They will be very profitable funds during bear markets.

The Rydex Ursa Fund

The Ursa Fund is part of the Rydex family of funds. Rydex has designed a family of funds primarily for market timers. And the Ursa Fund (*ursa* is Latin for *bear*) is designed to go up when the market goes down. Basically, if the market goes DOWN 1 percent, then Ursa should go UP 1 percent. And of course, the reverse is true. If the market goes UP 1 percent, then Ursa should go DOWN 1 percent.

The fund has a very reliable history of actually doing what they set out to do. You can get a prospectus by calling 800-820-0888 or reach them through their web site at *www.rydexfunds.com.* The minimum investment is quite high, though—$25,000.

The other interesting feature of the Rydex fund family is that they are specifically designed to accommodate market timers, which means you may buy and sell as frequently as you wish. Try this at other fund families and see how long it takes to get a "Dear John" letter. Rydex, however, will let you trade to your heart's content. Rydex has another fund called the Nova Fund. Nova is designed to have a beta of 1.5, or to go up 15 percent when the market goes up 10 percent. Of course, that means it is also designed to go down 15 percent when the market goes down 10 percent.

Many market timers, both professionals and individuals, use Rydex Nova and Ursa to time the markets, moving between the funds as their systems dictate.

If you use a Registered Investment Advisor to manage or time your account for you, the minimum may be as low as $15,000. I will talk more about professional market timers in a minute.

▌ *ProFunds Ultra Bear*

This fund is very similar to Rydex Ursa with one substantial difference— this fund has a beta of negative -2.0. That means that this fund will advance twice as much as Rydex Ursa in bear markets. For example, Pro-Funds Ultra Bear would advance by 20 percent if the S&P 500 went down by 10 percent.

This fund pays off twice as much as Rydex Ursa in bear markets, but loses twice as bad during bull markets. That means this fund is primarily suitable for aggressive investors who want to make a high-risk, one-way bet on falling stock prices.

The minimum investment is a little lower at $15,000. Call 888-776-3637 for information or see their web site at *www.profunds.com.*

This fund is not for the faint of heart. I would only recommend it for very experienced, aggressive investors who understand the risks. It is not unusual to see upward moves of 10–15 percent or more even in a long-term bear market. That means you could lose 20–30 percent in a very short time period!

▌ *Potomac US Short*

The underlying investment strategy at this fund is the same as the first two. That really isn't a surprise because the founders of this fund family originally worked for Rydex. The same is true of the ProFunds group. This fund's objective is the same as Rydex Ursa. It attempts to produce a beta of negative -1.0 and move in perfect inverse direction of the S&P 500.

This fund has the lowest minimum of the group at only $10,000. This appeals to investors with small accounts who do not wish to commit a larger dollar amount to this contrarian strategy. Call 800-851-0511.

If you are going to invest at least $25,000, though, I would probably go with Rydex.

FUNDS THAT SHOULD MAKE MONEY IN A BEAR MARKET

Actively Managed Funds

Actively managed funds are very different from passively managed index funds. With active management, you are hiring professional money managers to pick the stocks that they feel have the highest likelihood to produce the largest gains. In the case of bear market funds, the portfolio managers will try to "short" those stocks considered the most overpriced and most likely to go down in value. At the same time, they may go "long" on those stocks that have high potential for appreciation, most often contrarian industries such as precious metals, utilities, and natural resources. The end result is that the success of these funds is dependent upon the stock selection ability (both long and short) of the portfolio managers.

The Prudent Bear Fund

This fund, managed by David Tice, will short stocks that it feels are overvalued and be long in stocks that are undervalued. The fund will always have a combination of long and short positions. Of course, the success of the fund depends upon Tice's skill at identifying thoroughbreds (good stocks) and mutts (bad stocks).

The different thing about this fund is the great flexibility to change the ratio of longs versus shorts. When the stock market is humming along and doing well, Tice may reduce the proportion of the portfolio devoted to shorts to as low as 30 percent. During periods of market turmoil or when Tice feels the market is vulnerable to a decline, the allocation to shorts may go as high as 90 percent.

The most recent bear market is a good example. Since the stock market peak on July 17 through the middle of October, 1998, the S&P 500 lost about 20 percent. Prudent Bear gained an impressive 70 percent during that time. Not only did Tice deftly increase the proportion devoted to shorts, he also correctly shorted the right stocks.

But as the market rebounded in October and into December the Prudent Bear Fund gave back all those gains and went to new lows. The obvious bias of the fund is short, and whatever timing system Tice is using is clearly telling him to maintain his short positions. This fund is only appropriate for aggressive investors who don't have faint hearts and who want a more actively managed portfolio than a bear market index fund. But this fund is volatile. During bear markets it is not uncommon to have large gains, and past performance says this fund will have large losses during major rallies and bull markets. That being said, if Tice sticks with his system, he should do well in 1999 and 2000 as we move into the Y2K Recession. The minimum investment is $2,000 and you may call 888-778-2327 for more information.

Not all that glitters . . .

There are two other funds designed to make money in a bear market. However, they have not performed as well. But it is likely that you will hear about them in any article about bear market funds. I am not recommending them.

We need to see much better performance from them before we invest money with them. They are the Robertson Stephens Contrarian Fund and the Crabbe Huson Special Fund.

These funds are not alone in their problems. In fact, there are many privately offered funds called hedge funds, composed primarily of wealthy investors, which lost 50 percent or more in September and October of 1998. Many of the hardest hit were so-called *market neutral* funds, which use sophisticated investment strategies to supposedly neutralize the volatility of the markets and allow them to prosper in almost any conditions. The conditions they would have problems in were supposedly very unlikely. Except that late last year, those very unlikely conditions occurred and investors in these funds took a bath. Other funds also had problems for a variety of reasons.

Every fund has a story or a reason for being. Sometimes the story is very compelling. Many of the funds hit the hardest last fall had long profitable track records and prestigious, even Nobel prize–winning names associated with them. The fall of 1998 is precisely the reason that when you read the words, "Past performance is not indicative of future results" you should take them *very* seriously.

Finally, there is one fund called the Year 2000 Fund offered by The Homestate Group. The fund attempts to invest in stocks that will benefit from the Year 2000 problem and can go up to 30 percent short. Since its inception in April of 1998 it has not performed well enough to garner my interest. It lost 37 percent from July to the market bottom in October, almost twice the S&P loss and did not recover those losses as the market rebounded to new highs. I am generally in favor of only investing in funds (with some exceptions) that have a minimum three-year track record, and this fund needs to show me more reason to invest. I mention it because you will be reading about it a lot in Year 2000 investment articles.

A Spider That Won't Scare You

There is another type of investment that has the potential for bear market profits. They are called "Spiders" but stand for S&P Depository Receipts (SPDRS). Spiders are essentially the same as an S&P 500 index fund. Just like the Vanguard Index 500 fund, Spiders will mirror the performance of the S&P 500.

Unlike the Vanguard Index 500, which will only make money if the S&P 500 advances, Spiders can make money in both directions—up or down. How? You may either be long or short the S&P 500 via Spiders.

Spiders are listed on the American Stock Exchange, which means they trade just like stocks. Just like a stock, you can either be long or short. Instead of buying Rydex Ursa, you could sell Spiders short and protect yourself during the Y2K Recession.

It gets a little technical, but Spiders are essentially the same as closed-end mutual funds but *never* trade at either a discount or a premium. This accurate tracking of the S&P 500 is why you can rely on Spiders to make money during bear markets (assuming that you are short).

There are several differences that Spiders have when compared to the bear market mutual funds, like Rydex Ursa. Unlike mutual funds that are priced only once a day at the closing, Spiders trade continuously during the day. That gives you extra flexibility to move when your system says the time is right, and not just at the close of the market.

Spiders are specifically exempted from the "down tick" rule, which states that you cannot short a stock unless the last trade was up. During market crashes, this "down tick" exemption may be the best way you can short the S&P 500 during a market meltdown.

Spiders have low internal management fees of only 0.18 percent, which is even cheaper than the Vanguard Index 500.

WHAT ABOUT DISADVANTAGES?

1. You will have to pay a brokerage commission to buy or sell a Spider. That would have been an important negative a few years ago, but in

this day and age of deep discount brokers, commissions are much lower. You can now trade over the Internet for as low as $8.
2. You cannot reinvest your dividends. All dividends are paid out in cash, which is something that you need to keep in mind about short sales. When you short a stock, including Spiders, *you have to pay* the dividends to the brokerage house. That isn't a large factor with Spiders because the S&P 500 dividend yield is now a paltry 1.5 percent a year.

If you would like more information about Spiders, call the American Stock Exchange at 800-843-2639.

"LEAPS" into the Year 2000

This next section deals with an investment for more aggressive investors who have some money with which they can afford to be speculative. This type of strategy is only for a small portion of your portfolio and should only be attempted if you thoroughly understand the nature of options. That being said, let's look at one excellent way to profit from the Y2K Recession.

If you want to protect your portfolio, or aim for a speculative profit, December 2000 LEAPS puts (long-term put options) are one of my favorites. Unlike heavily leveraged futures and because it is an option, you can never lose more than you invest. You also have a good opportunity to take advantage of any major market decline between now and expiration of the option in December of 2000.

Long-term Equity AnticiPation Securities, more commonly referred to as LEAPS, are options that give the right to buy (call) or sell (put) shares of a stock or underlying index, on or before a given expiration date. The uniqueness of LEAPS resides in their expiration date that can be up to three years in the future, unlike most options that have expiration dates of just a few months. This provides a longer time frame for the price of the stock or index to move toward your objective.

In simple terms, if I want to bet on a decline, I buy a LEAPS put option. The person selling me the option agrees to pay me a specific price (called the *strike price*) for a share of stock in the future. I am hoping that the price of the stock will go down so he will have to pay me a higher price for the stock than the market value. If the price goes down, I could do one of two things: (1) go into the open market and buy the stock and then exercise my option and make him pay me the higher agreed-upon strike price, or (2) sell the option on the options market as the value of the option itself will have increased.

However, if the price of the stock (or index) goes up, I lose the money I paid for the option.

A LEAPS option is a way of making a long-term bet on the direction of a stock or market index. When you buy an option, you are buying a specific amount of time in which an event could occur. The longer the time frame, the more expensive the option. That also means that if you buy an option, it will go down in value the closer you get to the expiration date.

For instance, I have said that I think the stock market could drop by 50 percent or more between now and the end of 2000. It is also possible the market will be rebounding by the end of 2000. But I have no idea when the bottom will occur. I also have no idea how high the market might go in 1999. I could buy a LEAPS put option today with a strike price of 1000 (as the S&P is around 1200) that would require the seller to buy my S&P Index option at 1000. If the S&P dropped to 600, I would make a tidy profit, as we will see.

But what if my timing is not perfect and the S&P (for some reason we cannot predict today) goes to 1300 or even 1400 in the middle of 1999 before it starts to go down? My option is not as valuable as the distance will lose value as time goes by and as the market level moves further away from the strike price. But the beauty of LEAPS is that I am not making a short-term wager. I currently have my sights on what the market will do in the middle of 2000.

If I were a time traveler and knew exactly when the market was going to make its high between now and the end of 2000, I would buy futures on stock indexes at very high leverage. But history is riddled with the bodies of investors who thought they knew when the market was at an all-time high and made highly leveraged bets on their belief. Remember, every time you think the market is at an all-time high and decide to short, there is another investor who thinks the opposite and will go long.

I don't want any reader to decide to get very brave after reading this book and to start trading stock index futures in his personal account as a way to make money on the stock market decline. That is a market for professionals. With futures, you can easily lose more than you invest. Even if you are right about the long-term direction of the market, a short-term spike can wipe you out.

LEAPS are excellent option strategies that find the happy medium between aggressive, short-term option trading and an outright purchase of the stock or index futures contract. It can be much more profitable to use the short-term trading strategies if a stock or index is expected to move soon. If, however, the time horizon calls for a longer holding period, and you want a leveraged way to play a stock or index without committing a lot of money, LEAPS may offer the most profitable strategy.

Index LEAPS Strategy

An index LEAP strategy does not have to be complicated in order for you to profit from the Y2K Recession. Although you may be knowledgeable about sophisticated financial strategies such as covered LEAPS, zero-collars, and straddles, a strategy that will maximize profitability requires an understanding of the basics.

While there are LEAPS for individual stocks, I encourage you to pursue a more diversified approach and concentrate on stock index LEAPS. Index LEAPS options are based on the average price of a specific group of stocks. Some stocks will do worse than others will and some stocks will do better. In general, I expect the larger stocks to do better than the smaller stocks in the Y2K Recession. (By doing better I mean they will go down less.) The problem with individual stock options is that most of the ones available are for very large companies. They will probably not go down as much as the index average does. Plus, Murphy's Law says you might pick the one company whose management figures out how to grow in a recession. I think it makes much more sense to bet on the direction of the market in general.

The index I like best is the Reduced Value S&P 500 Cash Index. Other options on the full index come in very large denominations. For many people, it's too much to spend on just one investment. That is why I recommend instead the Reduced Value LEAPS, which represent one-tenth of the full contract, allowing the investor to control their market exposure in smaller increments. For example, if the S&P 500 Index's value is 1200, the one-tenth value of S&P 500 Index LEAPS would be based on an underlying index value of 120, representing an underlying value of $12,000 (120 × 100). Investors can utilize these Index LEAPS to tailor their positions in the market to reflect their market expectations and investment philosophies.

I like these for Reduced Value LEAPS for three reasons:

1. Liquidity—they are among the most widely traded LEAPS available.
2. Diversity—the broad range of companies represented by the S&P 500 index.
3. Profitability—profit potential compared to other index LEAPS.

Yes, smaller cap stocks are going to be hit harder than the large companies in the Y2K Recession. This might imply buying options on the Russell 2000. Right now, however, the Russell 2000 is already down 20 percent, even as the larger indexes like the S&P and the Dow are making new highs. Therefore, at this juncture, I think the S&P 500 will fall further than the Russell, in terms of percentage.

The S&P 100 and the Dow should do better than the S&P 500, because larger companies are better prepared for the year 2000 and have more capital to survive any problems.

I do not know when you will be reading this book. If you are reading this book late in 1999 and the market has already dropped significantly this LEAPS strategy may not be appropriate. If you are reading this then and the S&P 500 is still above 1000, then this is an excellent strategy. If the S&P 500 is around 800, it will depend upon how much the options cost. You will need to consult with a professional or go to my newsletter web site for my thoughts at that time.

But today, the market is providing an opportunity to buy LEAPS puts at what I consider bargain prices. The S&P 500 is at 1200. In the Y2K Recession, if we see typical recession declines, the index could easily drop to 600 or below. (In the Reduced Value S&P Index, the equivalent drop would be from 121 to 60.)

The higher the market is when you buy, the more you will make when it drops. If you are considering LEAPS as a hedge or an investment strategy, you want to buy as early in 1999 as possible to consider taking full advantage of LEAPS. The general rule of thumb would be not to spend all your money at one time. Allocate an amount you feel comfortable with. Then, start buying LEAPS in stages over a period of a few weeks. Since I cannot know the market conditions when you read this, you will need to adjust your strategy from the one I outline below. I cannot give actual strike prices in a book when these markets are subject to change.

Focus on the December 2000 Reduced Value S&P 90, or 100 puts. Puts with higher strike prices are too expensive, and the lower strike price puts do not give me as much cushion as I want in case the recession is not as bad as I think it will be. Meanwhile, buying LEAPS puts that end in 1999 or June 2000 or may not give you the full time advantage you want. That's why I've chosen these.

If your broker doesn't know much about them or can't find them on his screen, don't let that frustrate you. They are available, and they are easy to buy. Each broker's symbols may differ but the exchange symbol for the December 90 put is LSZ XR. The exchange symbol for the December 100 is LSZ XT. (If your broker is using Bloomberg, tell him to look up LSZ + XR and LSZ + XT.)

What kind of profit potential do LEAPS have? This explanation is going to get a little technical. If you are not considering LEAPS you might skip over it. But do not skip this and call your broker. Never buy any investment unless you thoroughly understand the investment!

If you look in the *Wall Street Journal* on the options page you can find the S&P LEAPS contracts. Remember, since this is the Reduced Value LEAPS, everything is getting divided by 10. Just as an illustration (this is not an actual recommendation, because conditions will change by the time you read this!), if you want to buy a December 2000 put option with a strike price of 100 it will say Dec 00 100p in the column giving the LEAPS price. The date means the contract expires in December of 2000, the strike price is 100, and the "p" means it is a put. After the 100p there will be a number that is the cost of the option. To get what you actually pay you must multiply that number by 100. Today, the price in the *Jour-*

nal is 8 so that means the cost to buy the December 2000 option is $800 ($8 × 100).

An investor concerned about a possible market decline during the next two years, could decide to buy Index LEAPS puts to benefit from the potential decline. The investor purchases four of the LSZ LEAPS for $3,200 ($8 × 100 × 4). The puts will become profitable when the LSZ Index drops below the break-even point of 92 (the strike price less the cost of the puts or 100−8). The investor's risk or maximum loss from this strategy is equal to the total cost of the options or $3,200. The following are possible outcomes at expiration:

Index above the strike price
If the S&P Index goes up or stays above 1000 at expiration (which means the LSZ Index would stay above 100), the Index LEAPS puts would generally expire worthless and the investor would incur a maximum loss equal to the total premium paid.

Essentially, the person who sold us the put option said he would pay us if the S&P Index went below 1000. The S&P Index has to go below 1000 before he pays us anything. The index has to go below 920 for this option to break even.

Index below the break-even point
If the LSZ Index declines in value to 60 at expiration in December 2000 (which means the S&P dropped to 600), a 50 percent drop in the market, and the put holder exercises the puts, the holder will receive $4,000 (the strike price less the current LSZ Index value × 100) per contract.

The investor paid $3200 for the four options but would receive back $16,000. The put holder would realize a profit of $3,200 per contract (40 less the $8 premium paid × 100) per contract or a total profit of $12,800 ($3200 × 100 × 4). That's a total return of 400 percent, minus commissions.

Index between the strike price and the break-even point
If the LSZ Index is valued at 95 at expiration December 2000, the put would be worth $500 (the strike price less the current value of the LSZ Index × 100) per contract or a total of $2,000 for the four. However, this amount is less than the amount originally paid for the puts. Therefore, the investor's total loss is equal to $1,200 plus some commissions ($3,200−$2,000). If the holder does not exercise or sell the put, the holder will lose the initial investment of $3,000.

Technically, a LEAPS option is a European-style option and that means it can only be exercised on the day the option expires. This would be the Thursday before the third Friday of December 2000. But you can sell the option itself at any time. It has its own price. I expect that we will want to sell our LEAPS option long before December of 2000, sometime in the third quarter of 2000.

Buying LEAPS is an aggressive strategy. It is the most aggressive strategy I will discuss. If you decide to use this strategy, remember the following three points.

1. Time is a factor. The S&P 500 LEAPS expires in December of 2000. That means that the stock market needs to decline before then for you to make money. If for some reason we can't foresee today, the stock market does not crash until 2001, you are too early and your options will expire worthless. However, all the Y2K problems should have asserted themselves well before December of 2000.
2. LEAPS are a wasting asset. When you buy an option or a LEAP, you are essentially buying time. LEAPS will automatically lose some of their value the closer you get to the expiration date. That is why I believe LEAPS are so much better than traditional options for this purpose—you have a lot more time for your position to work itself out.
3. You can lose 100 percent of your investment. If the crash doesn't happen and the stock market stays flat or goes up, your LEAPS will expire worthless. That means that you will lose every penny that you invested in these. The good side though is that, unlike the futures market, your risk is limited because you cannot lose more than you invest.

If you would like more information about LEAPS, you should visit the Chicago Board Options Exchange web site (*www.cboe.com/products/leaps.htm*) or call 1-800-OPTIONS. I will also be updating information on LEAPS in my newsletter and on the newsletter web site, *www.2000alert.com*.

Where to Get Help with Your Mutual Funds

If you are going to manage your own mutual fund portfolio, as I have said repeatedly, you need to take an active role. That means keeping informed about the markets and your mutual funds.

Let me recommend several sources of information, some free and some subscription, that I like for mutual fund information. You should know my bias here, though.

There are LOTS of mutual fund newsletters and services. Some of them are written by good friends I know personally or have worked with over the years. But most have a bull market bias. By and large, they are in the market all the time, waiting for the next wave up.

It should be obvious by now I don't recommend that strategy to you. So the services below are market timing services. They are designed to take you out of the market if their systems indicate that is the correct strategy.

Fabian Premium Investment Resource is the former *Telephone Switch* newsletter. Doug Fabian runs the operation. They have a very simple premise. They use a thirty-nine-week moving average with a few twists to time domestic, international, Asian, and gold stock funds. A thirty-nine-week moving average is the average price of the stock or mutual fund over the last thirty-nine weeks. In Fabian's case, if the current price of the mutual fund is above the average, they are "in" or invested in mutual funds. If the current price is below the average they are out of the market. They are always either in or out and they are very disciplined. By disciplined I mean they do not second-guess the system. They do exactly what the system says to do. The newsletter is $99. They have a fax service for $149 that will fax you if there is a buy or sell signal. To subscribe, call 800-950-8765.

One of the beauties of Fabian's system is its simplicity. Complex is not necessarily better. You can substantially duplicate the work that Fabian does at a free web site, Big Charts (*www.bigcharts.com*). Hit the big red button that says "interactive charts," click on the indicator button and choose SMA (smoothed moving average) as the indicator. Type in the symbol for any fund or index for which you wish to see a graph of the moving average. Enter 195 (days) which corresponds with Fabian's thirty-nine-week moving average and hit the "draw chart" button. However, Fabian also offers a lot of value by suggesting funds and giving you other information.

Fabian's system is designed to keep you from the major market drops. However, it is not unusual to experience drops of 10 percent or more. But if you use a shorter moving average to get you out of the market quicker, you also sacrifice upside potential. Through testing and a long history of actual performance the thirty-nine-week average was chosen as producing the best upside results while reducing the market downside.

If you want to time your own funds, I would suggest your either subscribe to Fabian or be very disciplined about checking the web site regularly, if not daily, and then following whatever system you choose.

Monocle For Mutual Funds is a mutual fund analytical and timing software program. If you have a computer and enjoy the process of managing your own money, you will need a powerful software program to help you to deftly move in and out of the stock market. Monocle is an excellent and easy-to-use software program that I highly recommend. You don't have to be a computer genius to use it, and it will help you make the right decisions.

The software is $299 (one-time charge) and there is an annual datafeed charge of $240 a year. Included in that price is a one hour one-on-one telephone tutorial to help you master the program. Several of the money managers I respect the most use and swear by Monocle, so I highly recommend it. Call 800-251-3863 for information.

If you want to track your stocks or mutual fund portfolio for free you can go to *www.ProFutures.com* and click on "investment tools." You can get immediate access to all the latest information on stocks, mutual funds, market indices, financial news and more. You can even track stocks and mutual funds in your own portfolio.

Timing Mutual Funds and the Stock Market

If you believe all the cocktail party chatter, you would think everyone is making lots of money with their investments. You may even feel left out, wondering why you can't seem to get the kind of results others like to talk about. Talking about making money is easy. Actually doing it is very difficult.

For a long time, I have been a believer in market timing. There are basically two ways to do it. *Asset allocators* attempt to move between different types of stocks or mutual funds. *Market timers* simply move in and out of the market, trying to be in the market when it is going up and out when it is going down.

I am also a believer in letting professionals do this work for you. Individual investors in general (and you may be the exception) do not do well at timing and choosing their own funds.

Two reports have come out in the past few years detailing about how spectacularly *unsuccessful* investors are in their mutual fund investing. Dalbar Associates, a widely respected research firm in Boston, studied the returns of various asset classes from 1984–1995, but with a twist. They weighted the returns by cash flows and retention rates, trying to get a picture of how the *average* investor actually did, considering when they invested and how long they stayed in.

The Dalbar study clearly shows that what you see in mutual fund performance history often is NOT representative of what most investors actually got. People tended to buy funds after they went up and then sold them after they went down. Please understand that these people would have done very well if they had bought at the beginning of the period and held on. There was obviously a major bull market going on. But the Dalbar study shows that this is not what most investors experienced. They kept looking for the end of the rainbow in the latest hot fund.

Dalbar has conducted the study for several different time periods, and the results are basically the same. The funds do much better than the investors. It would seem like this would be an object lesson for buy-and-hold, but it isn't.

What it shows us is that many investors either don't have the stomach for large losses and/or are always in search of a better performing fund. But as I have discussed above, a buy-and-hold strategy is not necessarily the answer, and certainly not with the prospect of a major reces-

GRAPH 10-2 ▬▬▬▬▬▬▬▬▬▬▬▬▬▬▬▬▬▬▬▬▬▬

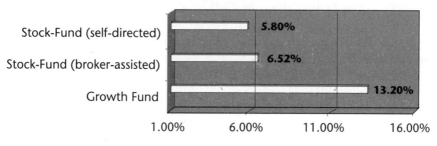

How Much Did the Average Mutual Fund Investor Make?
1984 -1995

	Average Annual Return
Stock-Fund (self-directed)	5.80%
Stock-Fund (broker-assisted)	6.52%
Growth Fund	13.20%

1.00%   6.00%   11.00%   16.00%

Growth Fund	13.20%
Stock-Fund (broker-assisted)	6.52%
Stock-Fund (self-directed)	5.80%

sion in our future. The answer is either to find a system that has been successful and be very disciplined with it or to find professional managers who have a demonstrated ability to deliver returns more closely resembling the actual returns of the market. It would be even better to find investment advisors who had superior returns and also reduced the overall market risk.

There are over 20,000 investment advisors registered with the SEC. I am aware of a few hundred who are active asset allocators or market timers. If you conduct a search, I think you should have one major bias. You must look for managers who would be willing to get out of the market if the economic climate warranted exiting. You might be surprised, but that narrows the number of advisors considerably. Most advisors think the essence of investing is to buy good stocks and stick with them through thick and thin, no matter how thin it gets. But then, most advisors have begun their practice since 1982, and a considerable number of them were not even in businesses in 1987.

To make a long story short, if you conduct a search for advisors, you will find some who beat the S&P 500 index but did so taking the big risks, or managers who reduced the risk but made less than the S&P. But finding managers who could do both is quite difficult. Indeed, less than 2 percent of the managers that I am aware of fit this bill!

The rationales for using a manager are simple. While it should be obvious, the top professionals beat amateurs 99 percent of the time. If your track record is better than the top 10 percent of professionals, then you either spend a lot of time studying the markets (in which case you might consider becoming a professional—if you are good it can be a nice living!) or you are extremely lucky (in which case you should be in Vegas!).

Further, most of us don't have the time or natural inclination to manage money. The Dalbar study and others consistently demonstrate that fact. I don't like mowing my yard. I could do it, but I would rather have someone else, who likes doing it and does it better than I can, handle that task for me.

If you want to find your own manager, you can do one of two things. You can call local financial advisors in your area from the telephone book and interview them. I have to say, though, that this can be very random. It is doubtful they have spent the time or money on a serious search, and most of what they will have are buy-and-hold types. You can try this approach, but I wouldn't recommend it.

A better approach would be to subscribe to The *MoniResearch Newsletter*, which is an advisor search service and publication written by Steve Shellans in Portland, Oregon. MoniResearch is the only service that I know of that tracks, evaluates, and ranks market timers. The research is exhaustive, accurate, and thorough and will help you narrow your search down to a manageable list of superior money managers. The cost of the service is $149 per year. He will also conduct personal searches for individuals, although the price is considerably more. Call 800-615-6664 (for more contact information see appendix A).

What should you look for when seeking an investment advisor?

First and foremost you want to see a long-term track record. I want at least five years' experience directly managing money and preferably longer.[2] All managers will have years where they do well and some where they don't do well. I want to see the average for their system and that is why we need to see some time. I want to know how they did in the 1987 and 1990 and 1998 market drops. Overall, I want my manager to have equaled or outperformed the S&P and to have done so with less overall volatility. This narrows the field considerably.

Secondly, I want their track record independently verified. I prefer to look at random accounts and check those accounts against the track record to see if there is consistency. I realize that most advisors are not going to allow smaller investors to do this (as it would take up all their time) but they should have some independent verification. It is too easy for a manager to "cook the books," showing you only the best accounts or a "simulated" or "model" account using only his best trades. I want to see what happened to a real live account for whom the advisor has managed money. I want to know what is likely to happen to my money if I give it to him.

---

[2]The only exception would be investment services that have a *real-time* management system that they have sold. That means they have been in the business of selling signals or issuing advice and have established a track record that is independently verifiable. This does not include hypothetical or back-tested systems.

You should check out his accounting and back-office systems. If he does not have adequate office help, it is possible you will have accounting nightmares. Do his statements go out on time? Do you get your year-end tax reports on time?

The investment advisor has to file forms with the Securities and Exchange Commission. Ask the advisor for his Form ADV, Part II. This should include all the relevant information about his fees and expenses as well as discuss any problems in his past that are relevant.

Most advisors will tell you the general theory about their trading system. Look at their track record and see if it seems consistent with the trading system. If the performance is poor or flat when the market is going up or something doesn't seem right, ask the advisor about those periods. Don't be afraid to ask hard questions. If there are problems in the Form ADV, ask about them. You are thinking about giving your hard-earned money to this person and you deserve to know all the facts.

Ask the advisor if they have changed their system, and if they have, what type of changes were they and when did they make them? It is not infrequent that an advisor will change systems in the middle of his career. As far as I am concerned, that means he is starting over. I will call on him after he has built a new track record in a few years.

Always ask them if they have ever made an investment decision contrary to their system. In the business, this is called overriding the system. If they have, this is a huge red flag. It almost always is a prescription for problems, if not disaster. Maybe they had a reason and can convince you they were right. In sixteen years I have only heard one good excuse that I accepted.

The simple reality is that you are *not* buying the nice person you are talking with, although we all prefer to deal with people who are pleasant to be with. You *are* buying the trading system. The performance record was based upon their system. If from time to time they emotionally override the system then you really have no track record that is useful, because they could do anything in the future.

This was hammered home to me on the last day of the editing of this book. I have been looking for some time at a particular investment advisor. His performance record goes back to 1974. It is one of the best timing systems I have ever seen. It is an unusual situation, and I won't go into detail here. But the point is that in 1998, after twenty-four years, the gentleman overrode his system. He was afraid to go back into the markets when his system said to, and his clients missed a great upward move. His signal was dead on the money. I talked to him from his home in Israel and you could hear the chagrin in his voice.

And that brings me to the last point. Every investment prospectus always has the legend, *past performance is not necessarily indicative of future results*. Truer words have never been spoken. And while I have made a big deal about track records above, and will continue to, do not invest your money and then forget about it based upon past records. Continue to monitor the managers or mutual funds or stock and see if something changes that raises a warning flag.

If I had money invested with the advisor I just mentioned, I would withdraw it after he overrode his system, unless I got a blood oath from him to never, ever do it again. I might give him one more (and only one more) chance because he has been so successful in the past. If his override decision has been the right one, I would have withdrawn it even faster because he would then be even more tempted in the future to override his system.

I hope you understand that choosing an investment advisor is serious business. Surveys tell us that the number one reason people choose an investment advisor is because they like them. This is clearly not a good enough reason. Do not pick one from the Yellow Pages or just because he is in your local service club. Choose an investment advisor because he is good at what he does.

I would like to bring to your attention three investment advisors I am familiar with and who are particularly suited for Y2K investing. These firms are represented by ProFutures Capital Management (PCM). Please remember that I am a partner in PCM. There is no extra charge or fee involved. The fees for these managers are the same whether you go to them directly or through an intermediary service such as PCM. Typically, managers are not set up to handle numerous phone calls and often elect to use outside firms like DCM to represent them.

Cooper Linse Hallman (CLH) is one of the most interesting financial timing companies I have ever seen. When I first met Don Linse at an industry conference and he told me their methodology, I simply walked away. I was convinced that no one could do what they said they could do. But then I saw their track record, and decided that CLH warranted a further look. I went to Illinois to meet with CLH in their offices and randomly check customer accounts to verify their track record and trading practices.

Basically, every day the market is open they go to their computers at 2:45 P.M., crunch a lot of numbers and decide whether to be in or out of the market based on their system. Checking the markets every day is not unusual, but the amount of times they trade in one year is. It is not unusual for them to make 30–40 trades in any one year! Their record is remarkable. There have averaged 16.0 percent for the last eight years, and the worst losing period they have ever had is 3.2 percent. I know of no other investment advisor that approaches their risk to reward ratio.

CLH will go short when their system gives them a short signal, and so there is the potential for some bear market profits, although in this bull market they have not gone short often.

CLH is for investors who are worried about capital preservation first. I don't think they will capture the full move of a bear market by going short. But their record says they will also not have large losses. In the past, they have avoided large losing periods.

You might consider them for that portion of your assets that you want to allocate to equities but want to feel very secure about. Just as bull markets don't go straight up, bear markets don't go straight down. The nice thing about CLH is that when there are upward moves, they have the potential to capture some of the upside.

I can't make a stronger recommendation. I really like Don Linse and Tom Hallman. I have watched them worry over a 50 basis point loss, when most managers wouldn't even blink. They worry about your money like it was the last dollar in the world. That is the type of attitude I want in someone handling my money.

By the way, they use a large trust company to hold your account over which they have trading discretion. Your money is in a separate account that you can always access if need be. You get prompt, once-a-month reporting, and can always call to inquire about your account. To find out more about CLH, call ProFutures Capital Management at 800-348-3601 and ask for a complete information packet on CLH.

Hampton Advisors, Inc. is based in New York City. After learning of them and studying their materials and asking scores of questions, I went to New York to do the normal due diligence, checking of track records, etc.

The two brothers who are partners in Hampton, Charles and Gary Mizrahi, greeted us. Charles is the trading partner and Gary handles customer service and administration. They started in the business handling family money, and that still makes up a significant portion of their business. Charles started trading S&P futures as a floor trader and eventually developed a market timing system that he uses for mutual funds.

(A personal note on the Brothers Mizrahi: I will never forget when we first met. They took this Texan to lunch on Forty-third Street in Manhattan at a Kosher Iranian restaurant where we ate vegetarian. Is this a great country or what? You can find anything in New York.)

These are two of the nicest guys you will ever do business with. They have true old-country character in their bones. And they have a keen sense for the markets. They have also been in the business long enough that they have experienced all types of markets conditions. Sometimes those markets conditions mean that they have "drawdowns" or losing periods.

All advisors have losing periods. The important things to learn about an advisor's losing period is how long they lasted, how much is lost, and how they responded to the losses. I have watched Charles go through losing periods, and he always sticks to his system. After observing scores of traders, and talking with numerous industry analysts, there is one thing that stands out. It is almost always fatal to start overriding your system. I like that Charles sticks to his guns.

Basically, Hampton has ten indicators they follow. When so many indicators are "up," they are long the market. When only a few indicators are up, they are either neutral or short. Over the years, since 1982, they have developed a very serious track record, averaging 18.2 percent with a worst-case losing period of only 9.1 percent. They were up over 53 percent for 1998.

Their system, unlike CLH's, will go short with more frequency and they tend to stay in longer. Partly because of that, they are more volatile, but over time, they have produced excellent overall returns.

Hampton is appropriate for a more aggressive investor. While they have been successful in the past, let me stress they will have losing periods. Even so, I have a significant portion of my personal investment money with them. I know I will sometimes have to go through a losing period, but so far, their system has performed above my expectations.

To find out more about Hampton, call ProFutures Capital Management at 800-348-3601 and ask for a complete information packet.

Harvest Advisors Inc. Tony Sagami is a longtime friend. I first met him about ten years ago when he was the operations manager of a successful money management firm. We have eaten a lot of sushi together. Since then, Tony started Harvest Advisors, and began to manage money on his own. I have learned a great deal from Tony. I have followed his system for some time now, and although the track record of his new firm is shorter than either CLH or Hampton, I think he is going to be one of the shining lights in our industry.

What makes him unique is that he designed the systems for Manhattan Analytics, a mutual fund research and software development firm of which he is a co-owner. This software allows you to apply sophisticated quantitative analysis and powerful computer technology to the investment process.

If you like to manage your own funds, you can purchase the software from Manhattan Analytics. Go to *www.manhattanlink.com* for a free demo and more information. This is a very useful and powerful tool for serious investors. Tony also edits an excellent newsletter, *The Mutual Fund Alert* (see appendix A). His advice has been on target and he is very good at explaining difficult concepts. In addition to his twelve monthly issues, he also sends out *flash alerts* with advice and signal changes.

He has done quite well in both the upside and downside of the recent markets. Call 800-553-8969 for more information.

I should mention one more advisor and that is Rich Paul at *Potomac Fund Management, Inc.* He has averaged 19.6 percent over nineteen years, and his longterm record is a little more volatile than Hampton's, with a worst losing period of 16.3 percent. But he did over 57 percent for 1998. In recent years, he is arguably the best of the advisors I have mentioned as his volatility has decreased. For those of you who want to diversify among several money managers, he is an excellent addition. You can get information on Potomac by calling ProFutures Capital Management at 800-348-3601.

Some of you are asking, "Since the market is going down, why doesn't John just tell me to buy the Rydex Ursa or ProFunds Ultra Bear funds and be done with it?"

Because the statistics show that the best market timers will outperform buy-and-hold fund managers. I simply do not want to be in a buy-and-hold position with the extreme volatility I think we are going to have in the stock markets in 1999 and 2000. And that buy-and-hold goes for short positions as well, no matter how convinced I am of the future Y2K Recession. I know that markets go up and down and that investors just don't want to sit through 20 percent or more losses. I know that I do not know the future.

Let me be very clear about what I think you should do. You should sell all, or as much as you can (and then hedge the rest) of your stocks and equity mutual funds now. If you want to have the potential to make money from the bear market, and you want to manage your own money, you should choose a market timing system (such as Fabian's or Sagami's) and then follow it religiously. If you do not want to take the time to diligently follow the markets but you want the potential to make money in a bear market, then find a competent investment advisor who is a market timer, either through your own search efforts or through Moni-Research or check out the timers I have mentioned here.

I don't think you should stay in the stock market and try to get just a little more upside. I don't think you should invest on emotion, moving in and out of the markets based upon the last tip whispered in your ear. Get a plan. Get a system or an advisor and stick to it. That is the best advice I can give you.

Making sure your investments survive and prosper during the Y2K Recession is not impossible. It is very important that you do not get overwhelmed and do nothing. Just as bad as doing nothing is deciding to do something and then procrastinating. It will take careful planning, adept timing, and knowledge. You will need to devote enough time to familiarize yourself with the problem, plot out your plan of action, and know when to act.

If you have comments that are generic, you can e-mail them to me at *John@2000wave.com.* I or my staff will forward them to someone who can help you, if at all possible.

The Revenge of the Nerds: Bonds Will Glitter

I am more concerned about the return *of* my principal than the return *on* my principal.

—Will Rogers

The conventional wisdom is that bonds are boring, safe investments for investors and managers who want to reduce risk. Bonds are the things that brokers put into their "widows and orphans" portfolios. As we will see, the Y2K Recession takes bonds from boring to glamorous!

Basically, a bond is a loan from one party to another, whether the borrower is a government, a business, or an individual. The actual risk of the bond is if whoever borrows the money will have the ability to repay.

There are many types of bonds: federal, state, city, mortgage or collateral backed, corporate, junk, and government-agency backed, among others. And they all pay different levels of interest. In general, the higher the interest rate, the higher the risk.

I am not going to go into great detail making the case for bonds. The argument is pretty straightforward, especially if you agree that there is a recession coming. I want you, however, to get a basic understanding of the case for bonds at this time.

Interest rates usually drop in recessions, and I know of no one who thinks that this time they will do otherwise. The one real exception was the 1973 to 1974 recession. But if you remember, *that was in an inflationary period*. Do you remember the gas-station lines and President Nixon's wage and price controls? It was the rising rates, along with the increase in oil prices, that caused that recession. The more typical pattern is for rates to go lower as the economy softens because there is less demand for loans. As we are in a deflationary period, it would be very unusual for rates to go up.

As you might expect, businesses are not too interested in expanding or starting new ventures during recessions. This absence of loan demand is one of the primary reasons that interest rates decline during recessions.

Graph 11-1 shows the rise and fall of the value of bonds. Notice that bonds have bull and bear markets just like stocks, and that the swings are just as large.

A Lesson on Bond Values

For those of you who have never thought about the value of a bond, let me quickly explain. Let's say that you loan me $1,000 at 10 percent for thirty years to buy a house. As in a normal mortgage, I agree to pay you interest plus some principal every year. Interest the first year will be $100. After one year, you need your $1,000 for another venture, so you decide to sell my loan to someone else. If interest rates are the same, then you can sell the loan for the face value, or the amount of principal left on the bond.

But let's say that interest rates have gone to 12 percent. That means that someone would want $120 in interest for a $1,000 loan. My loan is only paying you $100, so you have to "discount" the loan, or sell it for less than $1,000. The amount that you sell it for depends on current rates, the amount of time before the bond comes to maturity (or is paid off), how good my credit is, and a few other factors. Basically, your loan has gone down in value.

GRAPH 11-1

Change in Value of Thirty-Year Treasury Bond

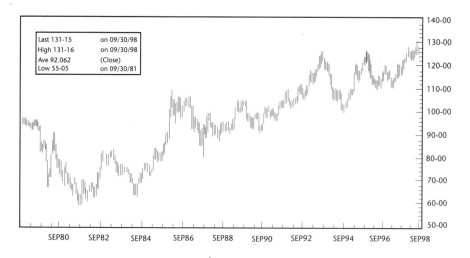

Last 131-15	on 09/30/98
High 131-16	on 09/30/98
Ave 92.062	(Close)
Low 55-05	on 09/30/81

Source: Bloomberg Business News

What if interest rates went to 8 percent? That means that someone would only be expecting to get $80 in interest. You have a loan that is paying $100, so you can actually sell my loan for more than $1,000!

Bond values and interest rates are just like playground teeter-totters. If interest rates rise, the value of your bond goes down. Conversely, if interest declines, the value of your bond goes up.

Look at Table 11-1. It shows how much a drop or rise in thirty-year bond yields will affect the underlying value of your investment. Notice that if rates fall from 5 percent to 4 percent, then your thirty-year bond is worth 16.62 percent more. That is quite a lot of growth in value, thank you. Of course, that cuts both ways. If interest rates go from 5 percent to 6 percent, you would *lose* 13.84 percent of your "safe" investment!

Final lessons before we get into the nitty-gritty: the shorter the length of the loan or bond, the less the movement of interest rates affects the value. Conversely, the longer the term, the greater the volatility of the bond.

Additionally, you get a higher interest rate for loaning your money for longer periods of times, but the risk is higher. (As an historical note, whenever short-term interest rates have gone higher than long-term rates, we have always had a recession follow soon. This is known as an *inverted yield curve.* It will not be unusual if we see an inverted yield curve soon.)

Which Bonds Should You Invest In?

I think that you should have a significant percentage of your money in bonds at this time. In the past, I have not been a huge fan of bonds, because there were other places I at least thought (and usually did) make more money. But times are changing. Today, I think that most investors should have a significant portion of their money in bonds.

There is one prime reason for this: *safety* and return of principal! We are going to be in the Y2K Recession. The bulk of our money needs to be

T A B L E   1 1 - 1

Interest Rate	10 Year Government Bonds		30 Year Government Bonds		27 Year Zero Coupon Bonds	
	Incremental	Cumulative	Incremental	Cumulative	Incremental	Cumulative
5.00%	0	0	0	0	0	0
4.50%	3.67	3.67	8.08	8.08	14.02	15.43
4.00%	3.75	7.42	8.54	16.62	13.95	27.97
3.50%	3.85	11.27	9.09	25.71	14.29	42.26
3.00%	3.92	15.19	9.64	35.35	14.80	57.06

Source: Central Plains Advisors

safely invested. Now is not the time to take big risks with core capital. We want to preserve as much capital as we can so that we will be able to participate in the next bull market. So, in choosing which types of bonds to invest in we should have risk uppermost in mind. Why get out of stocks if they are too risky, only to get into certain types of bond investments that are also risky?

What percentage you invest in bonds depends upon your age, how much money you have, what your goals are, and other considerations. We will go over these topics in chapter 13. But for now, let's look at what type of bonds we should buy and where we should do it.

I am probably going to make a few bond salesmen angry, but my view of bonds today is that many of them are neither safe nor appropriate for widows and orphans. As I have said, bonds are no less volatile than stocks, and you can lose money on bonds, even on U.S. government–backed bonds.

That said, I think that certain types of bonds and bond investments are excellent places for our money during the Y2K Recession. You should have a higher percentage of your money in bonds than would have been appropriate in the past. If you will monitor your bond investments, then I think that you not only can collect interest, but also watch your money grow from the increasing value of the underlying bond. And when we decide that the market is ready for the Y2K bounce, we can move back into stocks and equities.

But notice that I said that not all types of bonds are appropriate investments for the Y2K Recession. My first rule in investing in bonds is safety. I want to have as much money as possible when the recession is over. Then it will be time to take some extra risk, when we have the wind at our backs. Now, I just want to worry about the return of my capital, not the return on it (to paraphrase Will Rogers). Let's look at what I would avoid first, and why.

Forget Junk Bonds

The "high-yield" world is more risky to begin with, and in a recession could be a land-mine field. Companies that issue junk bonds are like individuals with questionable credit—they pay more because they aren't as likely to repay the loan. In Wall Street lingo, junk bonds are issues by companies with less than investment-grade credit. These are usually small to midsized companies, some of them start-ups, and while some are good companies with great futures, some are not.

Let's go back to one of my previous points. According to a number of researchers, we could lose as many as two thousand midsized companies. The logical progression is that we could also see a lot of other companies become very sick and require a lot of hard medicine in order to survive.

For the average investor, I can see no point in investing in junk bonds over the next two years just to chase a few extra percentage points of yield. And that means junk bond or "high-yield" funds as well. Even though a high-yield bond mutual fund will lower your risk by investing in many different types of bonds from different types of companies, too many bankruptcies in a bond fund's portfolio will take away any of the extra interest you might otherwise have obtained from the fund.

The historical default rates for junk bonds in the last twenty years are about 2 percent. Keep in mind that we have been in the greatest bull market in history and that defaults have been kept under control. I am confident that this default rate will soar during recessionary times.

But junk bonds can get killed during seemingly good times too. According to Manhattan Analytics, the average junk bond fund lost 16.58 percent of its value in just the three months from July to October of 1998. Just imagine how hard junk bonds could get hammered during a severe recession.

I freely acknowledge that one or two junk bond mutual fund managers might do very well since they control the assets in their funds, and through either luck or skill pick the right bonds. But Y2K is going to hit companies from somewhere off the financial predictions charts. There is just no way today to reliably assess the full exposure of a company when you include as part of the problem its customer and vendor base. The best that we can do is to rely upon the press releases of the company. I am sure that most of them will be accurate. But which ones? We will read about one analyst after another telling us that there was just no way that he could have known about XYZ company's Y2K problems. We will see a lot of excuses. I do not want to be near ground zero if (when) the junk bond market implodes in a flight to safety. It is not worth the risk for a few points of yield, and I suggest that you stay clear as well.

▌ *But What About High-Quality Corporate Bonds?*

By high quality, I mean AAA-rated mega-businesses like Citigroup, Exxon, and IBM. You can make a case for these if you are talking about short-to-mid-term duration bonds. By that I mean bonds that mature in five to ten years. You are not going to get a lot of capital gains appreciation (growth in the value of bonds, as we discussed earlier) as interest rates move down, but you will get less than $1/2$ of 1 percent more interest than a U.S. guaranteed bond offers.

Think about that. A rock-solid corporate bond pays you only slightly more than $1/2$ of 1 percent more than a comparable U.S. government guaranteed bond. In my opinion, that is hardly worth the extra risk, especially as it pertains to liquidity.

Liquidity is an underappreciated but critical factor in bond investment. Liquidity refers to your ability to find a ready buyer. There are billions of dollars of U.S. government bonds traded each day, but there is only a tiny fraction of that trading volume for even the most credit-worthy of corporate borrowers. What that means is that you will have more problems finding a ready buyer for corporate bonds, especially when times get tough.

That is the whole premise of owning bonds during the Y2K Recession. Times will get tough, and our financial markets have a history of cracking under stress. And guess who gets hurt during these times of stress? The sellers of anything less than the most liquid, most frequently traded investments—U.S. government bonds.

This gets a little technical, but there is a "spread" between the bid and ask price of a bond. This spread is essentially your transaction cost—somewhat like an auto dealer's markup. The spread between the bid and ask price of U.S. government bonds is small and will probably always be small. However, the spread between the bid and ask price of corporate bonds is much wider and could widen enough to accommodate a Mack truck during a recession. What this means to you is that just at the time you want to sell, Wall Street will be squeezing you with a low-ball offer.

Further, there is a liquidity problem for a lot of bonds other than U.S. treasuries: they are easy to buy but can be hard to sell. If you are buying individual bonds you could easily pay a markup of 3 to 5 percent! While this seems outrageous, it is often the case. Bonds that sell in amounts ("lots") of less than $1 million are deemed a "broken lot," and dealers hit you with deeper discounts to sell them. Trying to reach for that extra interest can easily cost you whatever extra interest you might gain if you have to sell before the maturity date of the bond.

My point is that the upside of high-quality corporate bonds over U.S. government bonds doesn't even come close to compensating you for the additional risk that you are taking.

And that isn't the worst of it. Some research organizations are telling us that we could lose anywhere up to fifteen (and maybe more) Fortune 1000 companies, depending upon how pessimistic they are on the day they do their analysis. In a recessionary environment, many of these large companies will have some problems, even if they don't go bankrupt.

What happens then? Bond-analysis companies like Moody's or Standard and Poor's decide these companies' debt quality is not as good as it used to be, and so "downgrade" their bonds. For instance, the grade on a bond could go from AAA to merely A. That does not mean Moody's thinks that you won't get paid. If they put an A on "paper," as a bond is called, it means that they think that it is quite good. AAA just means that they think it is better.

So, companies with AAA ratings pay less interest than companies with A ratings. If you hold a bond and its rating goes down, the underlying value of the bond goes down as well when you try to sell it.

And guess what? The major bond buyers of the world with their huge inventories of bonds know about these rating changes long before the guy on the street or your broker. They will act before you get a chance to sell, further eroding the value of your bond.

This is going to be a recession. Bond ratings are going to go down for a lot of companies. I don't want to be in the bond ratings guessing game. I think that the small advantage you get with corporate bonds *could* be eaten up by a few failures, downgrades, and the lack of liquidity. If the recession is milder than I think it will be, you are going to make about 1 percent less on your bond investments if you stay away from corporate bonds. If it is worse, then you will send me a nice Christmas e-mail in 2000. I want to sleep during this recession without having to worry about all the bad news from companies whose bonds I might hold individually or in some fund.

Finally, if interest rates go lower, then you will see corporations recall your bonds because they can get better rates elsewhere. So, those high-yielding bonds that you thought you had for the next ten years will evaporate as rates go down and your corporate bonds get called. It's a kind of heads-they-win, tails-you-lose investment.

Municipal Bonds Are Generally Not on My Investment List

I am not a fan of tax exempt or municipal bonds either, for a variety of reasons. And I can hear screams coming from some of my readers. I can see some possibilities for exceptions, but first hear me out.

In the first place, the research tells us that the least prepared government organizations are the cities. While I believe most cities will be just fine, thank you, why would I want a fund with bonds from a lot of cities that the fund managers buy almost willy-nilly based on a rating from a bond-rating company? And these ratings agencies have not yet begun to figure Y2K into their numbers. Further, Capers Jones predicts that 350 cities will file for bankruptcy protection.

In a recession, there will be fewer sales, so the sales tax receipts that a city receives are going to go down. In a recession, housing and business real estate values will go down, and therefore so will property tax receipts. There will be less construction, therefore fewer permits and permit taxes, and generally less of everything that has to do with receipts.

Of course, there will be more problems, and you can bet it will cost money to solve them. Please send me all the notices of police and firemen offering to cut their salaries because tax receipts are down. In fact, they will argue that times are worse, and that we need their services more than during better times. Education, teacher salaries, and school costs are not going to be cut as substantially as income will decline in school districts, causing more budget pressures.

In short, a lot of towns are going to have problems. A lot of school districts are going to have problems. These are governments, and they will try to raise taxes or will be forced to cut costs, so I think most (99 percent) will pay, but bond ratings could (will probably) get downgraded.

For that small group of people who are in the 40 percent tax bracket and have enough savings to live off the interest from municipal bonds (we should all have this problem), there might be an argument for tax-exempt bonds. But I think I would stick with bond funds that only invest in bonds issued by states, so as to minimize the problem of downgrading. Also, since many states have a state income tax, and many of them tax incomes from the bonds of other states, you would need to find a bond fund that only invests in bonds issued from within your state.

The logical conclusion is that you should stick with municipal bonds that are either general obligation bonds (G.O.s) or insured bonds. A local financial planner or broker can probably steer you to a fund like that.

Other drawbacks to municipal bonds are the wide spreads and markup costs. Municipal bonds typically have the widest spreads of all bonds. This is not a problem if you hold to maturity, but if you have to sell, you can take a serious haircut of 3 to 5 percent or more.

Finally, I do not like to invest solely on the basis of tax considerations. Congress has a nasty habit of changing the rules, and a lot of people have had their investment heads handed to them when the rules changed. Let me talk briefly about one such risk to tax-exempt bonds.

I have talked with senior members of the House Ways and Means Committee and their staffs. They think that it is possible that we are going to have some problems with income tax collection. The IRS has serious computer and organizational problems, and not just Y2K-related ones. It goes much deeper. There is a growing risk that we will not be able to collect income taxes on a fair and equitable basis because the computer systems simply are not up to the task.

There is some sentiment among members of Congress in favor of radically overhauling the tax system. But simply going to a flat tax won't fix the computer problems of the IRS. The computer problem is not in figuring out what percentage to charge you, but how much actual income you earned.

I sometimes file over fifty pages of income-tax forms and documents. It takes only a few lines to figure out how much tax I owe, but all the rest are devoted to trying to determine how much income I made or lost. That is where the real problems are.

This you can count on: Congress will collect taxes! If things get worse at the IRS, you could see a move toward a national sales tax, if for no other reason than that it is one of the only viable tax-collection methods. It is simple, easily collectible, and for those of us who care about such things, will be a huge boost to the economy. If we ever go to a national sales tax, I think that we will see a growth period after Y2K as strong as any we have witnessed in history!

But a sales tax will kill the tax-exempt bond market. Tax-exempt bonds get a lot of value imputed to them because of the tax-free nature of the income. Without the tax savings, municipal bonds would drop in value 40 percent overnight. The only problem is, the drop in value would happen long before the actual changeover because the market will start marking the bond values down—way down—the minute it looks like we could seriously go to a national sales tax.

There is not a huge risk of this scenario, but some chance of it does exist, and you should be aware of it if you want to invest in tax-exempt bonds.

The Bonds to Buy

Very simply, I want to own U.S. government direct obligations. I do not expect to maintain that attitude for more than a year or two, but right now risks are something that I want to take very judiciously.

We have the opportunity to make 15 percent capital gains (or more) over the course of the Y2K Recession, plus interest, while investing in U.S. government backed obligations. In a recession, I would submit that is a pretty good return!

Remember that the value of bonds goes up as interest rates go down. That is what we want to try and do with our bond investing.

How low can rates go? In Japan, official rates are $1/4$ of 1 percent! Interest rates, based on market costs on some government obligations, are actually negative in Japan. People are actually paying to own the bonds! Economists Dr. Gary Shilling and Dr. Ed Yardeni both tell us that rates could go to 3 percent in late 2000. Bond-timing expert Don Peters of Central Plains Advisors has 3.5 percent as his target by the end of 2000. (He actually lowered his target as I was finishing this book.) The well-respected Bank Credit Analyst talked about a 3.5 percent Federal Reserve funds rate in 1999 in their November 1998 newsleter. In October, they said there was no reason to think that government bond rates would not go down to 4.5 percent, and they clearly made the point that 4.5 percent was with an inflation rate of 1 to 2 percent. If there is a recession and deflation, the implication is that rates could go lower—much lower.

I think you can make a case for two separate categories of bond investing. The first is simply to preserve capital. The second is to recognize that as rates move down, there is the potential for very high returns.

I'm a Chicken—How About a Safe Money Fund?

The first category is for people who simply do not want to worry about the direction of interest rates. As emphatic as I have been about rates going down, I acknowledge that there are events that could make rates go up. I don't think that they will happen, but it is possible. If you are not willing to monitor the interest rate markets or have someone do it for you, then you might consider simply investing in a government-only money-market fund.

You won't get rich in a money fund, but your money will be safe, and you will earn interest. Not much, mind you, because I believe that interest rates will go lower. But sitting in cash while the rest of the world loses their shorts is not a bad experience.

Not just any money fund, though. I encourage you to invest in a government-only money fund, but not all government funds are the same.

There are two types of government money funds—U.S. Treasury–only and government-agency funds. The difference is that the full faith and credit of the U.S. government do not back some government agency obligations. When the Y2K trouble hits the fan, the only type of debt obligations that you will want to own are those unconditionally backed by the full faith and credit of the government.

There are only four obligations that are full faith and credit obligations: U.S. Treasuries, Federal Farm Credit Bank, Student Loan Marketing Association, and the Federal Home Loan Bank. Besides being supersafe, the other benefit of these full faith and credit obligations is that the interest is exempt from state and local income taxes. Your interest earnings will be taxable on the federal level, but not at the state level.

I like U.S. Global Government Savings Fund (800-US-FUNDS) the best. It deals exclusively in U.S. treasuries and the four other full-faith and credit government-agency obligations and historically has been one of the highest-yielding money funds in its class. It also offers free checking with $500 minimum.

Those of you who insist on U.S. Treasury obligations only should instead consider the Vanguard Treasury Money Market Portfolio (800-662-2739). It will have a slightly lower yield than the U.S. Global fund, but it will provide extra protection for those of you who are extremely cautious.

Another excellent U.S. Treasury money market fund with full checkwriting capabilities and lots of other consumer friendly features is the Weiss Treasury-Only Money Market Fund. The fund has a low $1,000 minimum and you can write checks on the account as long as they are over $50, which is quite low for a money market fund. Call 800-289-8100 for a prospectus and more information.

Any of these funds will accomplish the task of preserving your money. The companies have also stated that they are currently Y2K compliant.

Making Money in Bonds—Another Way to Skin the Bear-Market Cat

I am not going to go for simple capital preservation with my money. There is an opportunity to use bonds to grow your investment capital. If interest rates indeed go lower, bond investors will make money and lots of it. If shorting the stock market makes you nervous, you should instead consider taking a substantial position in bonds.

Not any bonds—just U.S. government bonds. Why? All bonds have "call provisions," which means that the issuer may prepay them ahead of time. You and I do essentially the same thing with our home mortgages. If interest rates decline, we refinance our mortgage, and swap the old higher rates for a new lower rate. All bond issuers do the same thing, except one—the United States government.

That is why I strongly believe that the best way to profit from declining interest rates is with long-term U.S. government bond funds. That doesn't mean Ginnie Maes. Their bonds can be called. You want to invest in a bond fund that *only* invests in U.S. Treasury bonds.

And when it comes to bond funds, expense ratios are extremely important. Stock funds are different—a good portfolio manager can pay for himself many times over through savvy stock selection. But a portfolio manager's contribution is less significant for bond funds. That is why you need to choose the bond funds with the lowest expense ratios.

The Vanguard family of funds is known for rock-bottom expense ratios and has long been the industry leader. If you want low expenses, Vanguard is your fund family. The fund I recommend is the Vanguard Fixed Income U.S. Treasury Fund. This fund only invests in Treasury securities and will do extremely well if interest rates decline.

Those of you who are confident that interest rates will go lower may want to instead consider American Century Target Maturity Trust 2025 Portfolio (the former Benham family of funds). This portfolio exclusively invests in zero-coupon Treasury bonds that mature in the year 2025. Although this is a bond fund, it offers all the profit potential (and risk) of many stock funds. Declining interest rates can produce eye-popping profits in excess of 20 to 30 percent in a short period of time. If interest rates decline from 5 percent to 3 percent, you would make 57 percent just in capital gains!

The concept is quite simple—if interest rates rise, the investor loses. If, however, interest rates do indeed decline to 3 or 4 percent, investors in this fund will make substantial gains that will make them think that they own a high-powered stock fund. Call 800-345-2021 for more information.

So, What Could Go Wrong?

Now, if interest rates were simply going to 4 percent or even to 3 percent, it would be a no-brainer. Just load up in one of the above funds and sit back and enjoy the ride. Of course, nothing is ever that easy. There are some things that worry me about a simple buy-and-hold bond strategy.

As I mentioned earlier, I am concerned about what will happen if there is a silent run on bank deposits due to concern about the availability and safety of the money deposited in an individual bank. While I am hopeful that Congress and the Federal Reserve will act to reassure the public that their banks are safe, as of December 1998 there is no such move underway, nor is any such move being talked about in any public manner.

As a reminder of the problem, if enough money were withdrawn from demand deposits in the banks of our country, it could create a serious problem for the banks in regard to their reserve requirements. They would have to either call loans, raise more capital money, or attract more deposits, or the Fed Reserve would have to lower reserve requirements. My concern is not about individuals wanting a little extra deposit, but about businesses deciding to not have more than $100,000 in any given bank and putting the rest in money-market accounts "just for a while" till things settle out. I have talked to officers of certain major U.S. corporations who are seriously considering doing just that. And they are talking about tens of millions, not a few thousand here and there.

One of the logical things for a bank to do to offset these problems would be to try to get more deposits. This is not just a matter of offering bigger and better microwaves; it would very likely involve raising interest rates. Interest rates could spike quickly for Certificates of Deposit (CDs) as banks scramble to compete with one another for scarce depositors. That would create a completely new set of problems, but we are talking about bonds in this chapter.

Would people decide to take the potentially much higher rates from CDs? I don't know. Maybe. Would this take money from Treasury bond funds? Maybe. Would there be a flight to quality and would government rates drop even lower? Maybe. Could government rates rise as bank rates rise? Maybe. Will the Federal Reserve change reserve requirements or unleash a flood of liquidity? Maybe.

I could ask a dozen other questions, and the answer would always be "maybe." It is anybody's guess. We have never seen similar circumstances in any history that I have read; we are in totally uncharted waters. Frankly, if anyone could do the right thing and calm the markets, it is probably Alan Greenspan. I have never met the gentleman, and probably never will, but I have tremendous respect for and confidence in him.

While we are speculating about what else could make interest rates go up instead of down, let's think about all the foreign holdings of U.S. debt. If foreign governments and businesses decide that they need money in their own currency and began to sell back their U.S. debt, we could see a rise in interest rates. Some very smart people think that this is quite possible. I don't, because I think that even if there are some countries and businesses that decide to sell dollars, there will be even more foreign money looking for the safe haven of U.S. Treasuries.

Neither of these scenarios is likely. The point is that they COULD happen. And if you are invested in the bond funds above and get your monthly statement and you are down 10 percent and then another 10 percent the next month, you are not going to be happy. You will be tempted to sell because of the very real pain of being down 20 percent or more. And even though you know that whatever is driving the rates up is (probably) a short-term event and that long-term rates are headed down, you will want to sell.

So, if you decide to put your money in the bond funds above (or any bond fund), then you need to pay attention to the bond market! You don't want to get blindsided and make an emo... decision based on a big drop in your assets. But you also don't want to watch the market drop out from under you.

What can you look for besides the obvious trends of interest rates? In the past, it has been typically bearish for bonds if the Dow Jones Utility Average goes down; if the Journal of Commerce Index goes up; if the Commodity Research Bureau (CRB) Index goes up; or if growth in the monetary base goes up.

Just to complicate things more, these indicators are what has worked in the past. The CRB Index may no longer be reliable as we move from inflation to deflation.

As for the last indicator, we have seen huge growth in the monetary base lately and no indication of inflation or of rising rates. I think that we can assume that the Federal Reserve's lowering of rates is a sign that it is more worried about deflation, a softening economy, and currency problems than about inflation. Further, we are experiencing a significant lowering of the inflation rate in the face of a rapid rise in the money supply.

This is a major departure from the past and makes me suspect that a number of indicators that have been reliable in the past may no longer be useful in a deflationary environment. Japan, for instance, has $1/4$ percent interest rates and is trying its best to increase its money supply. It has been like pushing on a string due to their deflationary economy and embattled banking environment.

Another publication that always keeps a close watch on interest rates is Martin Weiss's *Safe Money Report* (800-236-0407, $96 per year). I will also be watching rates closely in my newsletter, *Year 2000 Alert*, which is also published by Weiss Research and can be reached at the same number.

If you have Internet access and enjoy surfing the web, a great site for bond-timing information is Paul Merriman's *www.fundadvice.com.* Paul, a well-respected and nationally known market timer, provides his buy-and-sell recommendations for free. And free is a very good price.

No matter what your investments, you need to stay on top of them day-to-day if you are taking responsibility for them. To simply invest and then let the market "do its magic" only works in bull markets. It has been easy the last sixteen years to buy and hold, invest and forget. The last half of 1998 has shown us that this is not always wise. And I can almost guarantee that the next eighteen months will show the same.

Bond-Timing Help

I have already told you that my inclination is to hire a good manager for my basic investments and concentrate on a few areas where I can make a real difference and enjoy in-depth study. I consider bonds to be the most basic of investments. But like everything else in life, to be really good in something takes a lot of work and time. Investing in bonds is no different.

I would like to introduce you to one of the premier bond timers in the country. This firm will manage your bond portfolio (for a fee, of course). The results that they have achieved over twenty-three years is nothing short of extraordinary.

The point of hiring someone else to decide which bond funds to be in and when to be in them is simple. The statistics tell us that professionals will beat amateurs over time. But frankly, the statistics tell us that many professionals don't do all that well. It is hard to find bond timers who add enough value to a bond portfolio to justify their expenses.

I am a big believer in the principle of knowing as much as possible about what you are investing in. However, I think that most people would rather research something more exciting than bonds. My target for a return in my bond portfolio is about 15 percent a year for the next few years, given my view of where interest rates are going. I would rather use what research time I have to devote to investments that offer more potential or to spending time with my family and friends or to improving my golf game.

If you want to conduct your own search for a professional bond timer, you can start with Steve Schellans's excellent MoniResearch newsletter mentioned in chapter 10 (see appendix A) or meet with a local financial planner whom you trust and ask him or her to make a recommendation.

Then I suggest that you compare whatever firm you find to Central Plains Advisors and make your own choice.

Central Plains Advisors

One of the problems in finding a good bond timer for individuals is that if a bond timer gets really good, his account minimums go way up, and he or she starts handling only *really* big accounts. From the perspective of the manager, this makes sense.

Another reason is that bond managers generally target for an average performance. They buy a portfolio of bonds across the yield curve. This has the effect of smoothing out the down markets, but it also smooths out the upside performance. As noted above, if all you want is a basket of bonds with different maturity times, then buy the appropriate fund from the Vanguard family.

But if you want performance and are willing to take a little volatility, then let me introduce you to Don Peters of Central Plains Advisors in Wichita, Kansas, far from the machinations of Wall Street. Don Peters likes it that way, too. After over thirty-five years managing bond portfolios for large institutions, he believes that he and his clients are far better off avoiding the "conventional" approaches to bond investing, which usually lead to mediocre results. He lived through the 1973 to 1974 bear market, which most of today's portfolio managers know about only from history books. The lessons of that experience led him to a far better way to invest in bonds.

Don Peters spent twenty-three years in the trust department of the largest bank in Kansas, managing over $1 billion in bond portfolios for the bank's biggest customers, including large pension plans. Matthew Peters, Don's son and comanager, is an experienced investor in his own right, with ten years as a fixed-income portfolio manager at Boatman's Trust Company in St. Louis. Don eventually formed his own firm, Central Plains Advisors, and has continued his successful career.

Bonds are often thought of as "safe" investments to buy and hold. This may have been true back in the 1950s, but it is hardly so today. By some measures, bonds are even riskier than stocks. In fact, there have been more bear markets in bonds than in stocks. The total decline in these bond bear markets was more than that in stock bear markets, and the length of these bond bear markets was over twice as long. For these reasons, Peters rejects the passive approach to bond management, which simply holds a group of bonds in whatever maturities match the investor's objectives. Instead, he practices an "active duration" style, which seeks to anticipate changes in interest rates and swap in and out of government bonds as interest rates move up or down. Unlike most managers, he is less concerned with the yield of the bonds than with their potential for capital appreciation—or loss.

After years of looking at track records, I have never seen one as consistently good as Don Peters's. I am going to start with his record because I want you to understand why you should pay attention to what he says, even if you manage your own bond portfolios.

The table below is from a study done by Callan & Associates, an old, well-known, and respected investment-rating agency. In this study, they rated bond managers. The database that they used contained 1,137 funds or managers.

TABLE   1 1 - 2

Performance	3 yrs.	5 yrs.	7 yrs.	10 yrs.	23 yrs.
Top 10%	13.1%	9.8%	11.1%	10.9%	11.1%
Median	10.2%	7.5%	8.8%	9.3%	10.1%
Bottom 10%	7.7%	6.1%	7.1%	7.8%	9.1%
Central Plains	**21.9%**	**18.8%**	**18.1%**	**16.0%**	**14.5%**

In each of the time periods, except for the seven-year period, Don was in the top 1 percent of managers. He "slipped" to 3 percent in the seven-year performance.

Don Peters's performance record goes back to 1975. This includes accounts that he managed for his bank, and others he has handled since he became independent. For comparison, we can look at the Lehman Brothers Government/Corporate Bond Index, which represents the passive style that Peters rejects. As the graph shows, Peters has handily beaten that benchmark over many years. In fact, the record is even quite competitive with the stock market as measured by the S&P 500. This is an amazing accomplishment for a bond manager.

G R A P H   1 1 - 2

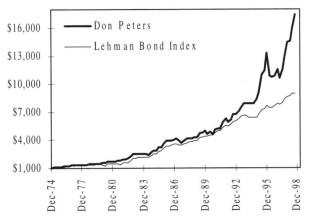

That kind of success doesn't come without risk, of course. There have been times when Peters has been wrong about interest rates. For example, in 1996 he had a 17.5 percent loss in the first quarter. Of course, this followed an almost 60 percent gain in 1995, so if you were there for both years you still did quite well. He contends that his forecasts are fundamentally right, but the markets sometimes dwell more on perceptions than on reality. Eventually reality catches up, of course, but it can take awhile. Investors need to be patient and give Peters time to recover from such periods.

Peters's record is a performance that a lot of stock fund managers would like to have. And he did it with less volatility than most stock funds. So, how did he do it? What is his secret?

Central Plains follows five basic principles in their investments. First, they use their own analysis to anticipate movements in interest rates. Peters is a student of the "Austrian" school of free market economics (as I am, in case you are wondering), and believes that this gives him a unique edge in understanding why markets behave as they do. He rejects the Keynesian model that Wall Street firms usually follow.

Second, Central Plains always manages for total return. In other words, they want not only interest payments, but capital gains on the bonds they purchase. They also seek to avoid capital losses. Third, they never take credit risk. This means buying only U.S. government bonds. They never use corporate, municipal, or junk bonds or bond funds. This doesn't mean there is no risk, of course; if the interest rate forecast is wrong, they can still lose money. But they won't lose money because an issuer went bankrupt.

Fourth, they never use derivatives, and they make sure that the bond mutual funds that they buy don't do so, either. Fifth, they use technical-analysis tools during times when their fundamental interest-rate forecasts are in conflict with market perceptions.

For institutional clients ($5 million or more) Central Plains uses these principles to buy a portfolio of U.S. government bonds. Small investors can take better advantage of the Central Plains program through their mutual fund program. For the small investor, dedicated no-load mutual funds are a superior management approach to buying individual issues. The investor opens a custodial account at a trust company, and Central Plains then takes discretion over that account to buy and sell various bond mutual funds according to their forecasts. Currently they focus mostly on the American Century (formerly Benham) group of funds.

To learn more about Don Peters and Central Plains Advisors, you can call ProFutures at 800-348-3601 and ask for information on his firm. The minimum account is just $25,000, which allows this exceptional manager to be available to most of you.

But whatever course of action you decide to take, my point is that you should consider a commitment to bonds. I expect bonds to be one of the big winners during the Y2K Crisis.

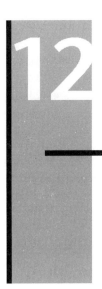

An Alternative Investment Lifestyle

Life is more than food and drink, and there are more investments than stocks and bonds. Everything is affected by a recession, whether for the better or for the worse. In this chapter we are briefly going to look at other investment areas.

The first two are gold and real estate. Investing in these areas is like investing in stocks or bonds: it is largely a directional play. By that I mean that the value of the asset (gold, a mine, a house, or an office building) must by and large go up in order for you to have a profit. In the case of gold, during the Y2K Recession the directional move will probably not be significant, and in the case of real estate, the move will probably be down.

We will then move on to two types of specialty funds: commodity funds and hedge funds. These funds typically (though not always) have the potential to make money in any type of market. For those of you who are aggressive investors, they can be a very profitable portion of your portfolio. And finally, we will briefly touch on collectibles.

All That Glitters

Few things stir the imagination as does gold. It seems to be deeply imprinted into the psyche of the human race. There are times when I really wonder about this. Gold is, after all, simply a soft metal with few practical purposes. There are many metals rarer and more costly. There are many metals with more practical uses. But for some reason, for thousands of years gold has been the one constant of commerce. Gold from Solomon's fabled mines is probably still being used today.

I know all the usual answers about why. Back in the eighties, I wrote a newsletter on gold stocks. We concentrated mostly on developing and junior mining companies. I read a great deal about gold, visited mines, attended mining conferences, and thoroughly enjoyed the experience. I have invested in many mining stocks. During that time I saw the gold and mining stock market from the inside. Gold has been good to me. I will tell you a few of the things I learned, and how I feel about gold today.

In the first place, I divide gold into two piles: *insurance gold* and *investment gold*. I feel strongly about insurance gold. I think that everyone should own some gold. I am buying a little more insurance gold as I write this book in late 1998, and will probably buy some more next year as well.

Now, the gold I am buying is not an investment. I do not intend to sell it. Ever. If you are buying something with no intention of selling, it is not an investment.

My fondest dream is that I will give it to my grandchildren (assuming that one of my seven children actually has some kids) and that *they* will give it to *their* grandchildren. If that happens, it means that nothing disastrous has happened in my life, or theirs, to force me to part with my gold.

Understand, I am not buying gold as a hedge against inflation. I think that there are better hedges if we are just talking about "normal" inflation. I own gold as a hedge against the unknown, improbable event.

I read a lot of history. Most of the time the world rocks along just fine. But then, out of the blue, something comes along and upsets the apple cart. War, famine, invasion, disease, weather patterns, gunpowder—the usual litany of culprits. It is precisely because everything is going along so well that most people are unprepared. And 99 percent of the time the unprepared have nothing to worry about. For most of the world the next day is much like the last. It is that 1 percent of the time when life deals you a terrible blow that makes you glad you have insurance.

I have life insurance. I sincerely hope that my great-grandchildren reap the benefits. But I still pay the premiums every year, even though the doctor and my genes tell me that I will live into my nineties. I buy health insurance, and usually my only visit to the doctor is for my annual allergy shot. But I still buy it.

I also think that you should buy gold. I don't think that your insurance gold should be 20 percent of your net worth, but you should have some. The right amount is whatever you feel comfortable with.

My theory is that if there is really a crisis or disaster, then a little gold will go a long way.

So, when you ask me if you should buy some investment gold because of the Y2K Recession, the answer is no. But if you ask me if you should buy some insurance gold, the answer is definitely yes. If you need the possibility of a serious problem stemming from the Y2K Crisis to give you a reason for buying gold, then that is fine.

Do I expect to have to spend my gold because of Y2K and its effects? No, I don't. I don't think that we are going to see the end of Western civilization because of Y2K. But can I imagine some things that are highly unlikely that would be disastrous? Sure, we all can. I do not live my life worrying about these events. I refuse to. But my reading of history says that it is precisely when no one is expecting it that a crisis strikes. That is why it is a crisis.

I am responsible for seven kids. So I buy a little insurance.

Those of you worried about the Y2K problem bringing down civilization should buy your gold in smaller-size coins and buy some junk silver.

I buy one-ounce gold coins. I buy the coins with the cheapest premiums possible. I think that in a crisis scenario, if people really want gold, they will not care whose picture is on the coin. Lately, though, American Eagles have been the same price as other gold coins. If that is the case when you are buying gold, you should choose American Eagles.

To give you an idea of the relative cost of buying gold coins, I pulled the following prices from the MSNBC world gold prices web site at *www. msnbc.com/modules/commerce/gold2.asp.* Gold was roughly $296 that day (prices vary slightly from the morning to the afternoon and according to the dealer). Notice that the smaller sizes of gold cost more per ounce.

TABLE 12-1

Coin	Price
American eagle, 1 troy oz.	$315.06
American eagle, .50 troy oz.	$164.88
American eagle, .25 troy oz.	$ 87.29
American eagle, .10 troy oz.	$ 38.86
Aus. 100 crown, .9802 troy oz.	$300.14
Maple Leaf, 1 troy oz.	$315.36
Mex. 50 peso, 1.2 troy oz.	$370.89
China panda 1992, 1 troy oz.	$319.00
Krugerrand, 1 troy oz.	$309.00

As a study for this chapter, I called four companies that sell gold on the same day as the above-posted prices. Here are the results and the phone numbers and addresses for the companies. Interestingly, the prices from the dealers were slightly lower than the posted internet prices. My staff and I checked that for several days, and it seemed to hold true.

TABLE 12-2

Company	1 oz. Amer. Eagle	1/10 oz.
Jefferson Coin (800) 987-2646	307	34
Dallas Gold & Silver (972) 484-3662	311.10	36
Republic National Bank of New York (212) 525-6338	310 (one) price drops $4 per coin after 50	38
David Hall North American Trading (800) 359-4255	306	33

You should always call for quotes from several sources, but I would make one of those sources Van Simmons at David Hall North American Trading. Simmons seems to consistently sell gold for less. (I have no business connections with David Hall.)

Investment Gold

As of this month, November 1998, I am not buying investment gold. Here's why.

1. Gold is languishing at around $300. It runs up to $300 and then seems to get kicked back down. If there was ever a scenario in which gold should go up, it should be now. Where are all the millions of Asians who are supposed to buy gold in times of crisis? There is certainly a crisis yet the price goes nowhere.
2. Every time that the price of gold moves up, it seems like some national government somewhere decides to sell. National banks still have enormous stores, and they seem intent on selling a lot of gold.
3. We are getting ready to experience deflation. The theory is that the price of gold should actually go down in a deflationary world.
4. I view investment gold as a speculation. I would rather take that portion of my money allocated to speculative investments and put it in strategies that will short the market. I think the risk-to-reward ratio is much higher for shorting the market. Even if gold went up to $500, that is only a 66 percent profit. If the market drops 40 percent, I can make a lot more. I think that it is much more likely that the market will drop 40 percent than that gold will go to $500.

That said, I think that it is quite possible that we will see a spike in gold prices in late 1999 as there will be a flight to all kinds of quality.

How much will it spike? I don't have the foggiest idea, and neither does anyone else.

I can't argue with people who want to buy some more gold today as extra insurance with the intention of selling it in 2000 and not caring if they make a profit or not. I think that it is likely that they won't. If there is a spike in the price of gold due to Y2K concerns, then when everything settles down and the Y2K Recession starts to kick in, I would expect the price to drop back down. That is what experience tells us will happen in a deflationary recession.

I should admit, being an ex–gold bug, that I will probably buy a call option or two on gold just for old times' sake. I know, I would probably make more money on LEAPS, but I still like to follow gold prices.

Gold Stocks

Now, gold stocks and all the related mining stocks are something else entirely. If gold prices were to move up only 10 percent, correctly chosen gold stocks could jump enormously. Gold stocks give you some real leverage if you want to play in the gold-stock world.

I think that it is entirely possible for gold prices to move up 10 percent or 20 percent and make some gold stocks double, or triple, or more. This is because if gold were to rise by, say, $40, then companies that are gold producers would be big winners.

Here's why. If a company is mining gold and its costs are $280 an ounce to get the gold out of the ground, it is only making $20 an ounce if gold sells for $300. But if gold sells for $340, then the company makes $60 an ounce; that is, three times what it makes at $300 gold. That is a 200 percent profit increase on just a 13 percent rise in gold price. There are many mining companies that have a cost of gold production very close to $300 per ounce. Many mines in South Africa are losing money at $300 for gold. A small move in gold can make huge differences in the profitability of a company.

But notice that I said *correctly chosen gold stocks*. There's the catch. There are lots of gold companies and promoters more interested in mining your money than in mining gold. They take advantage of our human fascination with gold to separate us from our hard-earned cash.

The gold-mining investment world is a small, incestuous one. The entire amount of gold in the world is less than the market cap of Exxon or GE. All the market caps of all the gold companies in the world combined amount to less than $30 billion.

The gold-investment world is full of sharks, con artists, promoters, and thieves. Like professional gamblers, they love rookies—fresh meat for the taking!

The gold-mining world also has some of the nicest, most honest people whom you will ever meet. There are some genuine businessmen and engineers who simply live for the thrill of extracting gold or other metals from the ground. Sometimes you can just decide to invest in people rather than a particular stock. There are some mining-company managers who are winners no matter where they go. They will figure out how to get *something* profitable out of the ground. There are lots of examples, but I think that Ross Beatty of Pan American Gold is a prime example. I have followed his career for years. People who have invested in his projects long-term have always been happy.

The only way to invest in the gold world is to have a reliable guide who knows the good guys from the bad guys, as well as the companies that really have minable gold or serious prospects.

I have said that the only way to invest is to either become very informed about an investment area, or to let a professional do if for you. That goes *triple* for the gold-stock market! If you decide to use gold stocks as a way to profit from the Y2K Recession, it will do you no good to invest in the wrong stocks. You can't rely on most of the information or promotions that you get in the mail on gold stocks. Much of the so-called independent analysis isn't independent and is financed by the companies themselves.

This is not a market in which to invest a few thousand dollars on a hot tip. You have better odds in Vegas. If you want to invest in gold stocks, then you need to become very knowledgeable. You need to find some reliable gold-stock newsletters and brokers, attend gold conferences, and get a real feel for the gold-mining world *before* you ever invest a penny! This is not a world for rookies or amateurs. If you are going to do it, then be serious about it.

Subscribe to Bob Bishop's *Gold Mining Stock Report.* Bob is one of the most knowledgeable analysts in the mining world. I would not consider investing in gold stocks without a subscription to Bob's newsletter. To subscribe or get more information, call 800-759-7677.

Depending upon your desire to subscribe to newsletters, you might consider Adrian Day's *Investment Analyst.* Adrian talks about more than gold stocks, but he does devote a considerable amount of attention to them. He is also conscientious about his work, and puts in long hours looking for investment opportunities. I like reading Adrian every month, and find him informative and thought-provoking. To subscribe or get more information, call 410-234-0691.

Before we leave the precious metals, I am sure some of you are wondering what I think about silver. I think the market is telling us silver has lost its luster as a monetary equivalent. But it is a rare and valuable metal, and has many industrial uses. The savviest investor in the history of the world, Warren Buffet, has reportedly bought about 20 percent of the world's supply.

I don't think silver is going to move up any more than gold will because of the Y2K Recession. But there is one silver investment that might. Bags of junk silver coins ($1,000 face value in pre-1965 U.S. silver coins: dimes, quarters, halves, and dollars) sell for a premium over the actual value of their silver content. Last year bags sold for about $3,500. Today the price is close to $5,000 and supplies are dwindling. There are a number of Y2K survivalist types who have recommended the purchase of bags of junk silver. I have talked to coin dealers around the country and they agree with me. I think there can be no other conclusion than that Y2K is moving people to buy one or two bags of coins as a hedge "just in case" the doomsday crowd is right. If bags of silver have not moved over about $6,200 by the time you have read this, you might buy one or two and sell them late in 1999 for a profit. I don't think there is going to be much downside from this price and I think you could make a tidy profit. If you really want to keep some junk silver, buy twice as much as you need below $6,200 and sell half and let the market pay for some of your silver. And who knows, maybe Buffet knows something that we don't and the price of silver goes up and we make even more. Call the same sources for silver bags as for gold coins mentioned a few pages earlier. Once again, I would check any price against the price from Van Simmons at David Hall.

Where Do I Buy?

If I decide to invest in gold stocks, I will do what I did about ten years ago, when I sold my gold-stock newsletter. I called Rick Rule of Global Resource Investment in Carlsbad, California (1-800-477-RULE), and opened an account. Rick's advice made me a lot of money. He didn't lose too much when the markets were lousy, and he made a lot when they were good.

Rick is a very knowledgeable analyst. He also knows where most of the rocks are in the mining world, and has turned a lot of them over. He is the source of a lot of the information on mining stocks that you find in investment newsletters. Because he is a large player in the mining world, he has access to a wealth of information.

Rick's business has now gotten larger, and he is often out of the office researching and doing analysis on mining and resource stocks. When you call, ask for Rick or Paul Van Eeden.

Global Resource Investment is an excellent choice for the execution of your gold stock orders. When it comes to trading mining stocks, all brokers are not the same. There are huge differences among firms, not only in the amounts of commission they charge, but in the actual execution prices that they get. It is important to get a firm that focuses on gold stocks and understands the market to do your actual stock transactions.

Also, as a client you get access to the research of Rick and his team. Don't underestimate the value of having a seasoned mining-stock professional on your gold stock mining team.

If you are going to invest in gold stocks, either get serious about it and spend the time needed to become very familiar with the markets, or let a professional help you. Or don't do it at all.

Real Estate

In a recession, real estate values generally go down. Home values do too. I see no reason why real estate should fare any better during the Y2K Recession.

First, if you don't own investment real estate now, then the simple advice is to not buy any. Wait a few years until the bottom of the recession. If this recession is like past ones, we should be able to buy income-producing real estate at very good prices. I doubt that we will ever again see the massive amount of cheap real estate that was available during the S&L crisis, but there should be some very good bargains available in the Y2K Recession for investors who like real estate.

I watched one friend after another buy cheap Texas real estate at the bottom of the market in the late eighties. They made a killing. This scenario could be played out again during the Y2K Recession, but all over the country and not just in isolated regions.

But what if you own investment real estate today? If you can sell at a good price, and you are not in love with your real estate, then you should consider selling. You should especially do so if you are heavily leveraged and could not service your debt if you lost some tenants or had to lower your rents.

Now, the good news is that interest rates should be much lower in a few years, so you may be able to refinance your debt and get more cash flow out of your property, provided you have sustainable cash flow from your commercial property. If you have stable long-term tenants with locked-in contracts, you might actually be in very good shape as your costs (interest) go down and your income remains steady.

But if you are highly leveraged and your tenants can move or if their contracts are coming up soon, you need to sit down with your accountants and run the numbers.

If you are not heavily leveraged, have adequate capital to withstand a recession, and really want to own the real estate you have in five or ten years (because of its location or other investment potential), then just shut your eyes to the price appraisals for a few years.

What you don't want is to be in a position in which you are forced to sell in 2000 at the bottom of the market. If that is a real possibility because of your specific circumstances, then you should consider selling now.

What About Your Home?

This is a tricky question. There is no right, one-size-fits-all answer. It makes me more uncomfortable to write these few paragraphs than it did to write any of the sections before them. Americans have an emotional bond with their homes, and touching that nerve is dangerous. You need to think carefully about what follows before you decide to do (or not to do) anything.

In general, if you want to live in your home in five years, I don't think that you should sell. Even though your house price *might* go down some over five years, so will your mortgage rates. You will have the same home you have now, but be paying less for it!

If mortgage rates drop 2 percent from where they were when you refinanced last year (you did refinance, didn't you?), you will save about $160 per month for every $100,000 of loan value when you refinance in mid-to-late 2000. That is, if rates drop.

If you are one of the millions of homeowners who see their homes as *investments,* then you have a different question. Unless you have some very desirable location or unusual circumstance, your home value is likely to go down over the next few years if we have a recession. If you are planning on selling your home in a few years and "moving up," then you should consider selling now, renting for a year or two, then buying when values and rates are lower.

But there are a lot of factors to consider, such as the tax deductibility of your interest, how much equity you have, and the availability in your area of desirable or livable rental property at reasonable prices.

If your home is an investment and you sell now, your real risk is that for some reason housing prices go up. That would be odd in a recession, but no one knows the future perfectly. The odds are that prices will go down. In some areas, depending on the local economy, prices may drop significantly.

If you are in an area where foreign competition could cause a significant number of layoffs, selling a home may be a problem during the Y2K Recession. If you suspect that your job or income is in jeopardy and you could not make payments for an extended period of time, then you should consider selling now.

Finally, don't panic and sell just because some investment writer (me or anyone else) is telling you that your house's value is likely to drop. Sit down with your advisors and family and think through your circumstances. The reality may be that you don't care if your home is worth 20 percent or any amount less for a few years. You aren't selling anyway, so it may not make a difference. If you are in your dream home, then forget about it, and worry about something else.

Commodities

Many commodity prices are the cheapest in a decade and, in some cases, in a generation. As a result, a lot of people are looking to get into these markets. However, it is important to understand that commodity prices are falling for one reason—*deflation*. So, before you decide to invest in some market because it looks cheap today, read the pitfalls below!

It seems that almost every week I get a direct-mail piece touting some incredible new futures or options-trading system guaranteed to make me 100 percent or more on my money. All I have to do is send $95 or $149 to this genius who wants to share with me his simple, time-tested formula for minting money.

I cannot tell you how angry this makes me. Most of these people are frauds! The best professional commodity trading advisors (CTAs) make millions of dollars a year. I mean real millions, not just your garden-variety million here and million there. None of them, not one—I repeat—not one, even approaches the track records that you have the opportunity to buy in your mail every week from the guy who just wants to share his system with the public, as a way of giving back something because he is so grateful for his success.

If these systems were even remotely as good as these guys say, they could sell them for millions of dollars, not $149. In fact, they wouldn't sell them at all. They would manage other people's money and make gazillions.

Commodity-industry executives have admitted for years that at least two-thirds of all individual investors lose money in futures. Actually, the real number is probably a lot higher! In fact, one senior executive of one of the largest brokerage houses in the country once told a private group of industry insiders that fully 95 percent of his firm's clients lost money!

When you look at the track records of the professional commodity advisors who make their livings every day in these markets, you realize how hard it is to win. It is not uncommon for even the best traders to have losing rates of 20 to 30 to 40 percent or more. The commodities futures markets are not for those with weak stomachs.

Do *not* attempt to trade futures on your own. I cannot make it any clearer than that. *You will lose money.* The worst thing that can happen is that you will make money on your first few trades and decide to get serious about the commodity markets.

And don't let some broker whom you have never met talk you into a sure-to-win, always-been-in-the-money trade on heating oil or soybeans. Think about it. If the trader were that good, he would be managing big money and wouldn't have time to call you.

So Why Even Write About It?

While investing in commodities or futures on your own is a recipe for disaster, there are some reasonable ways to participate in these markets. More so than in *any* other area, if you want to invest in the commodity markets, you need to find successful professionals to do it for you. I have been involved in the futures markets for over a decade, and I know a little of what I am talking about!

The professional traders you want to seek out in this world are known as commodity trading advisors. These people are registered as such with the Commodities Futures Trading Commission (CFTC) and meet strict guidelines for reporting their performances (unlike most promoters in the mail). Unfortunately, the best CTAs require large minimum investments. In fact, some of the very best no longer take any new accounts, regardless of how large. So, most of us have to look at commodity or "futures funds" as a good place to start.

Most futures funds are formed as limited partnerships. Most of them are private and available only to wealthy individuals or accredited investors (more on that later), but some are "public" in that they have filed the required documents to send an offering memorandum to the general public. Even then, the states usually require a minimum net worth of some amount for participation in the fund, though in most cases it is not especially high.

You won't read about futures funds in ads in *Forbes* or *Barrons*. That is because these funds are under dramatically different advertisement and marketing rules than mutual funds. To get a prospectus you have to find out about the fund (usually from an investment newsletter or through a broker) and call and request more information.

Getting information on futures funds is not easy. If you call Dean Witter, they will only show you the material on their funds. You won't get information from them on Merrill Lynch's funds. The same goes for most other major investment houses. Further, it is very expensive to keep public commodity funds "open" because of all the legal and regulatory fees. It is quite common for a firm to form a fund, open it for a period of time, then close it, often forever.

Talking about futures funds is like talking about mutual funds because there are so many types of mutual funds. There are many different types and flavors of futures funds as well. But futures funds have one thing in common: in general, they have the potential to make money in a bear market. Some will do quite well.

One newsletter that covers the commodity trading advisor and futures-fund world is *Managed Account Reports,* published in New York. You can reach them at 212-213-6202. The cost is a bit pricey at $425 per year. You can get their excellent MAR *Performance & Evaluation Directory* for $295, which gives you the performance results and contact names of a number of funds and CTAs. Their web site is *www.marhedge.com.*

I could mention the names of a few funds, but there is the real possibility that they will be closed by the time you read this. Most major brokerage firms sponsor futures funds of their own, or have access to funds.

Investing in S&P Futures

For the aggressive investor, there is one CTA that I want to recommend. I mentioned the mutual-fund timing program of Hampton Advisors earlier, in the chapter on stocks. They are also CTAs and trade S&P futures for individual clients and funds. Their track record is nothing short of outstanding.

TABLE 12-3

1995 (July through December)	−1.29%
1996 (12 months)	36.48%
1997 (12 months)	41.91%
1998 (Through mid-December)	97.90%

Hampton Advisors basically uses the same system for its mutual-fund timing program as it does for its S&P futures programs. The difference in performance is due primarily to the increase in leverage possible with futures and secondarily to the ability to make investing decisions at any time of day rather than only at the close of day, as is the case with mutual funds.

Hampton uses a maximum leverage of three times in its futures program. That means that if the S&P index goes up 1 percent, Hampton's program will either go up or down approximately 3 percent (if at the maximum leverage), depending upon whether they are on the "right side of the trade." Depending upon how strong their signals are, they can be (a) long one, two, or three times leverage; (b) in a money-market fund; or (c) short three times leverage.

While these numbers are excellent, I must emphasize that this is for aggressive money. You can see how volatile they are by looking at the graph. They have had losing months of 10 percent or more on several occasions, and one month the losses were close to 20 percent. Of course, they have had four times as many winning months of 10 percent or

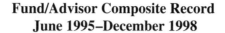

CHART 12-1

Fund/Advisor Composite Record
June 1995–December 1998

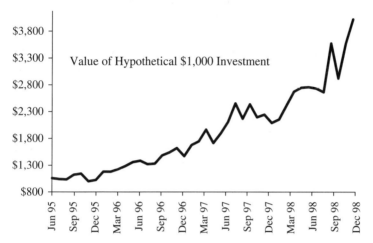

Value of Hypothetical $1,000 Investment

more, and in August 1998, when the market was plunging, they were up 36.62 percent.

The reason for this volatility is that their system is *anticipatory*. That means that it is designed to tell them in which direction the market is expected to go. One of the traits of their system is that sometimes it has been early about market moves. While this means that they are positioned correctly when the market does turn, it also may mean that they may be early.

The important thing is that Hampton's founder, Charles Mizrahi, has stuck with his system every time. As I mentioned previously, a huge warning sign is an advisor who overrides his or her system.

The normal minimum for a managed account is $500,000. But there are ways to access Hampton's services for much less money. You can call ProFutures at 1-800-348-3601 and ask for information on Hampton Investors.

Privately Offered Funds and Hedge Funds: The Secrets of the Superwealthy

My contention throughout this book is that the Y2K Recession is going to involve a huge transfer of wealth to those who grasp the reality of the crisis from those who stay in denial. While the latter group is still the vast majority of investors, it will grow smaller as we near the next century.

Let me go out on a limb here and make a startling prediction: the rich are going to get richer.

I can hear you muttering now, "Real bold, John; tell us something that we don't know." Okay, I will. I will tell you why many are going to get richer and what some of you can do to get richer along with them. First of all, it is not because they are any smarter than you or have better connections or are members of the right country club.

It is because the government has set up the rules of the game to the advantage of the wealthy in the name of protecting the "little people." But many of you reading this book can take advantage of the same opportunities as the wealthy. You just have to know the right code words.

Two of the code words are *accredited investor.* By official government rules, for investment purposes an accredited investor is someone who has a net worth of $1 million or more, *or* makes $200,000 or more per year in the immediately preceding two years.

If you are an accredited investor, you can go behind "door number three" and see what investment funds the rich get to invest in. The interesting book *The Millionaire Next Door* tells us that there are approximately 3 million millionaires in the U.S. There are also a lot of future millionaires who make $200,000 per year. Private funds are generally limited to a small number of accredited investors.

The hard part is getting information about private funds, because by law they cannot be advertised. If I told you about specific privately offered funds in this book, then you could not invest in them, according to the rules, because mentioning them in this book could be considered advertising, which is prohibited. However, it is in this little-known world of privately offered funds that many sophisticated investors put serious money.

In general, these private funds are often lumped together in a class of funds called *hedge funds.*

About the only time that you hear about a hedge fund is when there are problems. And then all hedge funds get lumped together in a series of poorly researched stories by writers who have limited experience with hedge funds and no background in the evaluation of sophisticated financial strategies.

The truth is that there are about four thousand hedge funds (plus thousands more offshore for the *very* wealthy and sophisticated). They come in all flavors and sizes. Some funds are highly leveraged, ultrarisky, volatile gambles on a particular market. Others are quite low risk and designed to yield a particular percentage return for a defined risk. Some are designed to yield 8 percent with no losing months. Some are designed to yield 50 percent with losing periods of 50 percent.

There are convertible funds, arbitrage funds, leveraged index funds, private-placement funds, venture-capital funds, and long-short strategy funds. In fact, there are probably several funds for just about any strategy that you can imagine.

In many cases, hedge funds do better than mutual funds when compared apples to apples. (If they didn't, the sophisticated investor would not invest in them.) There are several reasons for this. Hedge funds typically charge a management fee plus what is known as an "incentive fee." This fee means that the manager gets a portion of the profits that he makes for you in addition to the fee for managing the fund. The more the fund makes for you, the more the manager makes. The opposite is also true.

As you can imagine, managers who demonstrate the ability to generate profits prefer to do it in a hedge fund rather than in a mutual fund. They make a lot more money in the private hedge fund from the same amount of managed money.

Plus, the mutual fund managers are relatively limited by legal statute in their investment strategies. In a private offering, each fund gives prospective investors a private offering memorandum. This POM states what strategies a manager will use and may limit what they can do. But since the POM is drawn up by the manager, in effect the only limit to the management of a hedge fund is his or her imagination and management ability. So, over time, the better managers tend to form hedge funds. Many move offshore, where only rich and/or sophisticated investors can access them.

Statistically, only a small percentage of the readers of this book will be accredited investors, so I don't want to spend a lot more time on the subject. But I think that it is important for those of you who are accredited investors to learn more about the world of private investing.

To help you, I have created a web site called *www.accreditedinvestor. com.* There are articles that will help you "learn the ropes." I list as many of the conferences and seminars geared for accredited investors as I can find. I give you links to sites that will help you research hedge funds. I list other publications in which you can find more information.

If you don't have a computer (though you should get one), write my office and tell us you are an accredited investor, and I will send you my report on hedge funds and other materials from time to time. The address is in the back of the book.

That this two-tiered investment system still exists in modern times is due to large donations and well-funded lobbyists. I am not happy about this system, and think Congress should change the laws. They hurt all investors and damage the economy. I discuss this problem in detail at *www.accreditedinvestor.com.*

Collectibles

Don't we all wish that we had kept the baseball cards that we so cavalierly traded as kids and that our mothers then threw away? Ever wish you had kept that Barbie doll in its original box? Or your metal lunch box?

I think that everybody has a weakness for some type of collectible item. One of my business partners collects the most beautiful rocks. I have some friends who spend long hours fondling coins. I have other friends who collect wine.

And from time to time, the values of these items go up. Sometimes they go up a lot. But I don't think that they are investments that you want in a recession. If you see your collectibles primarily as an investment, then you should think about selling. You will probably be able to buy many of them back at much better prices in a few years.

But most of us kid ourselves about our collections being investments. As I said, it is not an investment if it is not for sale. For example, you can't buy the letters from John Wayne to my dad hanging over my desk. And the autographed game jersey from Nolan Ryan—forget it! And don't ask for my first-edition octavo King James Bible, or my original front page of Luther's reply to Pope Leo X (though I have some pages from the same pamphlet I might trade for another historical item).

The point is that we should collect things because we enjoy them. I don't care if the price drops 50 percent or 80 percent. I will enjoy them just as much because they evoke a feeling in me, and let me touch a piece of history meaningful to me.

Collectibles only have value because somebody else wants them at some price. And in a recession fewer people have money to buy what is obviously an extra. Don't expect your favorite widget to be able to hedge you against a recession. The market for collectibles is always thin, and will get thinner in 2000.

The good news is that we will be able to get more collectibles for our dollars. I have always wanted a collection of autographs of those Texans who helped to found the Republic of Texas. Maybe they will become cheap this time around, and I will be able to afford a few. If you have the collection bug, just sit still (if you can), and you should be able to get some bargains in a few years.

One last thought. Don't collect things just because they are expensive and want to show them off. When the value drops, what will you have?

In forty years, I will look at Nolan's jersey, and remember watching him pitch with my kids and friends. That is truly priceless. You can keep your Picassos.

Where Do You Invest Your Money?

The previous chapters might have been a bit overwhelming in that I mentioned so many funds and investments. What most people really want to know is what should *they* do? The answer is that there is no way that I can give specific advice in a book, as everyone's situation is different. But what I can do is to tell you what I am doing with my money and give you some general ideas for different income and net-worth categories, plus try to sum up an overall philosophy.

The Basics

In a few paragraphs this is what I am saying:

If you want to hold stocks and equity mutual funds, realize that you could lose 50 percent or more and that it might take years to recover. *Buy-and-hold strategies are going to cost you.* You want to have a larger portion than usual of your net worth in government bonds. You should avoid any bond not backed by the full faith and credit of the U.S. government.

If you want exposure to the stock market it should be with either:

1. Professional asset managers who specifically have successful long-term records of timing the market.
2. The view to making money from "shorting" the market so that you can make money as the market goes down.
3. Managing your own selection of funds using a time-tested, proven market timing program.

Gold beyond an insurance portfolio is fine if you want to spend time getting to know the gold stock market, but physical gold will probably not be a huge winner over the long term. If you want to be aggressive, I think that there are better alternatives than gold. Real estate is where you want to be at the bottom of the market, but not now. Look at refinancing your home and loans as interest rates go lower. Certain types of commodity or futures funds should do well. And higher–net-worth investors should consider the advantages that a few specific hedge funds will bring them.

Simple enough? The truth is that during a recession our choices are much more limited because most investments have to go higher in value in order to make a profit. During a recession, most investments do not increase in value. In fact, they do just the opposite.

I should point out once again that just as important as making it through the Y2K Recession is being ready to take advantage of the Y2K bounce when it starts. The portfolios below are for getting us through. These will change when the Y2K Recession draws to a close.

Sample Portfolios

I am going to structure a few sample portfolios at different net-worth levels. These are for illustrative purposes only and not to be confused with anything approaching a rigid view. The only thing that I am fairly rigid about is not to be long in the stock market. So, use these as a guide, and tailor them to your own needs and purposes.

As I am constructing these portfolios, I am imagining a couple in their forties with 2.3 kids (I have figured out where the .3 kids come from; they are teenagers who only use about .3 of their brains), who live in a house with a mortgage, and who must work to make a living.

If you are older, then you should be more conservative, as presumably you will be needing your money for retirement sooner. If you are younger, you can be more aggressive because you have more time to recover from mistakes.

As general advice to every size investor, you should get out of debt, especially if your job is one that might be vulnerable to a recession. I am assuming my imaginary couple has no debt other than their mortgage and maybe a car payment. Further, when I talk about net worth, I am *not* including home equity.

How do you calculate your net worth when trying to decide what category you are in? It can be tricky. For instance, many business owners have a large net worth, but not a lot of money that they can invest because they have to keep much of their net worth available for business emergencies. Further, many of us (myself included) invest in private businesses that are good ventures but that tie up our capital for extended periods of time. So your net worth, for instance, may be much higher than the amount of money you actually have to "invest."

If you have a high net worth and are confident that your illiquid investments are safe for the long term, then you might want to be more aggressive than I suggest. If you are concerned about the viability of your investments, then you should be correspondingly more conservative. If in doubt, it is always safer to take the conservative view.

I would strongly urge you to get an advisor whom you trust and who also considers Y2K a problem before you make radical changes. Asking your broker whether you should take money from accounts that he manages is not going to get you the most neutral advice, especially if he thinks Y2K is not an investment concern. I know that there are many fine brokers and advisors who can help you allocate your resources. You might have them read this book and then sit down with them and go over your portfolio in the light of it. They will probably have other ideas. Then you will be able to make your own decision in the light of multiple counsels.

Finally, many of the investments and investment advisors I suggest in the portfolios have the potential to do well in any type of market. These managers have the flexibility to go long or short. That is the reason I emphasize using professional managers and market timers. As explained earlier, using professional managers is my personal bias. If I am right in predicting a recession, then the funds and investments I have suggested should do fine, but you need to take an active role in frequently monitoring your investment portfolio. If you want to be more conservative, then I suggest that you consider one of the managers whom I recommend or find your own. For those of you who have skipped to this section, let me repeat that I am an affiliate of a firm that represents some of these money managers. You can do your own search, or consult with your local planner or counsel. I do not want you to feel that I think that these are the only good market timers and managers in the country. I think that you should seriously consider professional management. Professional managers beat amateurs.

I am not going to take up any more space describing the investments, managers, and newsletters mentioned below. They have all been covered in the previous chapters. (Please note that the addresses and phone numbers of the funds and managers that I recommend below are in the preceding chapters or appendix A.)

Net Worth of $10,000 to $50,000

The first thing that I would tell you is that it is important to protect your nest egg. I would choose one of the bond funds from chapter 11 and put

50 percent of your money in it, and put another 30 percent in a shorter-term bond fund in the same fund group. The rest should be in government money markets for emergency use. This is not the time in the investment cycle for you to be getting aggressive. Wait a few years, and then let's move back into the market. Although most money managers have higher minimum investments than you can make, Central Plains Advisors for bond timing will take accounts of $25,000, and Cooper Linse Hallman (CLH) for equity-fund timing will take accounts of $10,000 if you will mention that you read about them in this book.

If you don't use a manager or you don't subscribe to one of the investment newsletters that I mentioned in the bond chapter to help you keep track of the interest rate markets, then I would suggest going to my web site on *at least* a weekly basis and checking for any major change in direction. I don't want you to be in a long bond fund in case interest rates move up for some reason that cannot be predicted today.

Net Worth of $50,000

Again, I don't think that you should be getting too aggressive. I think that at least 50 percent should go into long-term bond funds. I think CLH (mentioned above) is appropriate if you want some exposure to equities. If you want to manage your own money, consider subscribing to an investment-advisory service like Doug Fabian or Tony Sagami. If you are closer to $100,000, and you are younger and want to get aggressive with 2 to 3 percent of your money, buy a few LEAPS if the Dow has not already dropped below 7500 by the time that you read this.

Net Worth of $100,000

At this level you have more options. I would still put 50 percent or more into long bonds. Personally, I would put my bond money with Central Plains (minimum investment $25,000), but if you are going to watch your funds carefully, then one of the bond funds that I mentioned will be fine.

For your equity money consider a conservative timer like CLH, although allocating more money to bonds is certainly a reasonable strategy. If you want to manage your own money, consider following a newsletter advisory service like Fabian or Sagami.

If you are younger or more aggressive, consider Hampton Investors managed accounts. Also, consider a small amount (1 to 2 percent) in LEAPS for very aggressive investors. If you are older or more conservative, increase your bond exposure, but use funds with shorter-term duration.

You won't get much in the way of capital gains, but the risk factor resulting from a rising interest-rate market will be considerably reduced.

If you are going to watch the markets and have a system or advisor to follow, you might consider a small allocation to a Rydex Ursa–type fund. (Do not buy and hold the Ursa fund! This fund is only appropriate for timing programs, and you need to either follow someone's proven system or let a professional do it for you!) The higher your net worth in this category, the more you might want to look at Hampton as a manager for a portion of your assets as well. (Remember, they time the markets using Ursa and Nova in the Rydex family.)

Net Worth of $250,000

Again, 50 percent or more into bonds, but I would seriously consider using Central Plains Advisors for a significant portion of that. You can split your equity money between CLH and Hampton, or follow Fabian or Sagami. I would put your 10 percent aggressive money into the Hampton Investors managed accounts and consider a small amount in LEAPS.

Net Worth of $500,000

The strategy is the same as that for the $250,000 group, except that if you are younger or more comfortable with being aggressive, you might put up to 20 percent into aggressive investments.

Net Worth of $1 Million+

Depending upon your aggressiveness and your age, you should still be weighting a considerable portion of your portfolio to long-term bonds. Your advisors will have access to good bond managers, although I would compare their records to that of Central Plains. You should seriously consider Hampton Investors for your aggressive portfolio.

Not only can you invest in the bond and short-equity funds mentioned above, as well as have access to a number of good advisors, but you can begin to look seriously at hedge funds that have strategies designed to take advantage of bear and/or volatile markets. Sit down with your financial advisors, and ask them if they can direct you to appropriate hedge funds, or visit my web site for accredited investors (see appendix A for details) for more information about hedge funds in general. There are more opportunities that may be appropriate for you than just the ones mentioned in the stock section in chapter 10.

Pension and Profit-Sharing Plans

I am frequently asked about pension and profit-sharing plans. The problem is that the available funds for investment are quite limited and most are equity funds. Sadly, there is not a lot that you can do until the middle of 2000. I would move your funds into the longest-term government bond fund available.

I recently met with a friend who had concerns about her 401K plan. Her only choices were a midterm corporate-bond fund and a variety of equity funds, along with a government money-market fund. Not a lot of choices, and none of them what I would like. I suggested she do two things. Move her money into the money-market fund, and ask her employer to find a better plan sponsor with more fund choices.

As I mentioned at length in chapter 7, I think that employers are going to face legal action for their fiduciary liability over these pension and profit-sharing plans when they drop 50 percent or more and the beneficiary is ready to retire and then can't afford to. If you are an employer, it is important that you read this section. You may be exposed to a risk that you don't even know is there.

What Am I Doing with My Money?

I must admit that in the past I have been more aggressive than I would counsel someone else in my position to be. But I believe that there will be a Y2K Recession and am taking my own advice and reducing my risk and exposure to the market.

I have several illiquid investments in good companies that, coincidentally, look like they will be able to be cashed out soon, but probably not before this book goes to press. I intend to sell these positions if at all possible. At that point I will have no real estate or stock market holdings of any kind, other than my home or indirectly through a hedge fund or managed accounts.

I am going to invest in government bonds. I have to admit, it won't be 50 percent, but I intend to send a good portion of my net worth to Central Plains. (I am more aggressive than I would counsel anyone else to be, but analyzing investments and assessing risk is my business. I do it daily. I would not hesitate to pull money out of an investment if conditions changed.)

There have been few times in my life when I thought bonds would significantly outperform stocks or other portions of my portfolio. If bonds move into the forecast range of those whose opinion I hold most highly, it is entirely possible to see gains and interest of over 30 percent.

I think that that is a pretty good return for any period and excellent for a recession.

For the aggressive portion of my portfolio, I have money with Hampton Investors, and I will buy some LEAPS, but Hampton is my primary aggressive investment.

I have a significant portion of my portfolio in hedge funds, and will also place some funds with CLH. I will keep a decent portion in short-term Treasury-only funds so that I will have money to invest in other opportunities that develop over the year.

I am buying some more gold, but it is not a significant portion of my net worth.

I know that I have probably sparked more questions than I have answered. While I can't answer any and all questions, I will be answering general questions at my web site, and you are invited to send general questions there.

Preparing Your Home and Community: Plan for the Worst, and Hope for the Best

By now you have gotten the message that I don't think that Y2K means that you should sell your home, move to the country, and buy guns, gold, and lots of stored foods. Yet there are groups of people moving to survival minifortresses all over the country.

I agree with them that this will be a crisis. But there is little reason to think that this will be a *survival* crisis in the United States. It is going to create more economic hardship than did the oil crisis of 1973. But from what we currently know about the problem, I think that we will have major hassles that will last for a few weeks, rather than major breakdowns that will last for months.

I believe that as a country, as businesses, and as individuals we will do what we have to do to get through this event. Because of the short amount of time left, much of what we do will be with chewing gum and bailing wire. The crisis won't be pretty, it won't be elegant, and it won't be economically profitable. We will lose productivity and see profits erode, but we will muddle through.

But just because I am an "optimist" doesn't mean that I don't see a potential for serious disruptions in our infrastructure. I do, and we need to prepare for them. But there are many things that we can do short of moving to the country and building survival retreats.

I have seven children. I am responsible for making sure that they are warm, fed, clothed, and in a healthy environment. For me to ignore the very real potential for power failures and other disruptions and to make no preparations based upon what I know today would mean that I am not taking my responsibility as a father seriously. I can't say it more plainly or strongly.

I think of my Y2K preparations as insurance. I never complain about not using my health or life or car insurance. I hope that I don't have to use any of my Y2K "insurance." But it will be there if I need it.

What kind of insurance do you need? It is impossible to know. I intend to have more than I *think* I need. Today I am going to make the following assumption, after reading and talking with numerous experts and getting an average estimate of the problem.

The estimate that keeps coming up is that we will have about one week of serious problems. That means that I am going to prepare for about two weeks. And by serious I mean no electricity, water, or basic phone service.

Now, if Capers Jones is right in his estimate, and he seems to be near the consensus, about 15 percent of the country will experience five days of no power and three days of no phone service. *That means that most of us will not have a problem at all from a power standpoint.*

But I think that we have to operate under the assumption that Murphy's Law will be working in full force. *If something can go wrong, it will go wrong.* And the corollary is that the less we are prepared for an event, the more likely it is to happen. As the father of seven children, I feel compelled to assume that I will be in that 15 percent, even though it is likely that I won't be because I am in Texas (see chapter 3).

Further, if an average of 15 percent of the country is down for five days, then some parts of the country will be down for more days and some will be down for fewer. So I will plan for almost three times the expected period; that is, for two weeks. If I lived in the country, I might plan for a longer period unless my local electrical provider had a good reputation for managing problems and fixing them quickly, and it was completely open about its Y2K remediation process.

I have talked with many friends around the country about this scenario. Some of my Midwest friends point out that it is not unusual for them to be without electricity for a few days. Other friends from various parts of the country remember a particular occasion when their power was off for a day or more. Interestingly, they routinely take the actions that I talk about below.

The outlook for problems with our electric supply has the potential for change, good *or* bad, as we move toward the end of 1999. It will bear close monitoring. I will be updating my web site as to what changes I see, if any, in the outlook for our power. I would encourage you to check for any updates, especially during the summer of 1999. If you don't have a computer, go to your local library, or get a friend to call up the web page and print it out for you.

So, exactly what are we talking about in way of preparing our homes and families? Let's first discuss what we are not talking about.

There is no need to worry about your household electrical appliances, despite some early assertions that these devices will cease working. Your dishwashers, coffee makers, and microwaves will be okay. Many of these devices have chips in them, but their date and time functions are not calendar sensitive. The manufacturers of these products have all begun to issue statements on the compliance of their products on their web sites.

Your home air conditioners and climate controls will work, according to Emerson, Honeywell, and Carrier. Window units will also do just fine. Even the devices that keep track of time tend to do it on a weekly basis. Some large office systems may need to be checked. Home security systems will be fine, although some office systems will need repair or replacement. Of course, most security systems are dependent upon phone lines.

Your automobiles will be fine. The Big Three Detroit companies have all issued statements that even their most sophisticated cars are compliant. Toyota will send you a letter saying that they are compliant.

Fax machines manufactured during the 1990s will generally be fine. It is reported that older machines made by NEC and Panasonic may have clocks that malfunction or require resetting. Refrigerators and freezers will be fine, as will stoves, say Kenmore, Kitchen Aid, Magic Chef, and The American Home Appliance Manufacturers.

Most pagers will work, except that certain Motorola pagers will require upgrades. There is not a lot of information available, however, about the actual paging companies themselves. (Murphy's Law strikes again: yes, my Pagenet pager is manufactured by Motorola. It will probably be fine, but I will need to check it out sometime this year or buy a new one. Hello, Pagenet? Can you tell me if you are going to be ready?)

New models of video recorders will be fine, although some older models *may* require manual setting to 2000. Get the kid who figured out the VCR to do it for you. Camcorders made since 1990 should be fine and operate without complications. If you are still using a camcorder device made before 1990, it will work even if the clock used to record the date malfunctions.

Timex and Casio tell us that our digital watches will be okay. Ordinary telephones will work just fine, although office phones set with clocks may require an upgrade. If you have a much older system, as I did, it is almost impossible to get someone to tell you if your system will work. My staff finally found an excuse to get me to buy a new system.

For most of us, the only real Y2K appliance problem we will face around the home will be with our personal computers. Home PCs are not difficult to fix. An inexpensive software package can tell you what your problem is and what to do about it. Advice for fixing PCs is in appendix C.

Y2K Home Insurance

Actually, preparing to live without electricity or water for a few days is not all that difficult, expensive, or time-consuming. If you begin now, you should be ready in plenty of time.

First, let me say that this is not a book on survival preparedness. I am going to recommend some books, videos, and web sites for greater detail than I am going to give here. But I want to give you a feel for what you are going to have to do, and some specifics about things that you need to think about and act on.

If Murphy's Law strikes and I am in that 15 percent of the country that has longer-term (five-day) problems, then my goal will be to simply get through that period. I am not trying to figure out how to maintain a lifestyle designed around the loss of power. I think that I can live just fine without electricity for a few days. I am not saying that I will like it, but I can make do.

Much of what I am saying makes sense for any time. You never know when the power is going to go off. It happens—seemingly randomly—for an extended period somewhere in the country every year. So it makes sense to have a few weeks' worth of food and supplies as a simple precaution against such a random event. Just ask the people in Montreal, Quebec. Remember the winter of 1998?

What will we need? Water, food, ways to keep warm in colder climates, ways to cook our food, extra medicine, and so on.

WATER

Most of us could survive for quite some time without food, but water is essential. Fortunately, storing water is quite simple. The specialists say that you need about one gallon per person per day. You can buy it in one- to five-gallon containers from grocery stores or water companies.

Or, if you are like me and the thought of spending money on water cuts against your grain, you can bottle your own. Simply clean and save your two-liter soft drink bottles (not plastic milk bottles for longer periods of time—they deteriorate), and in December fill them with water, put a little nonscented Clorox bleach in them, and store them someplace cool and dark.

You will want water for your toilets so you can "store" water in late

December in large containers (such as large plastic trash cans) outside the house or in a kids' pool or your pool. Most toilets use only a few gallons of water, and toilets don't need electricity to operate. Also, many neighborhoods have someone with a large pool. Work out a deal with them to "borrow" ten to fifteen gallons a day for your toilet use. Creek water, rainwater, or whatever is fine for toilets. (We are not drinking it.)

In an extended crisis, you can always boil water—over a fire, if need be. Plus, there are simple filtration systems that can purify small amounts of water.

When it is obvious that the "crisis" is over, and you want to redeem some of your storage space, be sure to recycle the plastic containers.

FOOD

I must confess that I have problems with the normal survival food-storage programs. It is not that I disagree with somebody buying this type of food; I just don't like the food.

I think that you should have about two weeks' worth of food on hand in any event, so I will actually have about a month's supply. I don't like to grocery shop, so I sometimes buy large quantities anyway. I intend to buy the kinds of food that I would normally buy and eat. For example, I like pastas. Dry pasta stores for a long time. Ditto for spaghetti sauces in large jars. My kids eat large amounts of Campbell's chicken noodle soup. (I guess they have a salt deficiency.)

I will go to Sam's sometime in the third quarter and buy several cases of food that I know I will use in any event. In my case, it seems that I host a few fund-raising events every political season. The beginning of 2000 is the height of fund-raising, so I can tell you now that some of the events will be chili dinners with ranch-style beans. In the event that we actually have to use this food, my family may not get the variety they are used to, but they will eat. And I won't be stuck with massive amounts of food that I won't use.

Sit down and talk with your family about this. Make a list of what you know you want anyway. What you buy will depend upon your personal tastes. I suggest reading Karen Anderson's suggestions on food and other items on her useful web site *(www.Y2kwomen.com)* for some practical ideas.

Don't forget that if there is no power, it will be difficult for grocery stores to operate. So buy extra quantities of what personal items you normally need. Don't forget to buy paper plates, cups, and disposable dinnerware, as well as extra bathroom items such as toilet paper, deodorant, and toothpaste. These will not go out of date.

By the way, I would not wait until the last minute. I think that it is quite possible that everyone will decide en masse that they will buy a little extra "just in case." It is not that you won't be able to buy something; it is just that you might not have the selection you want (unless you are a fan of lima beans).

Let me make one more suggestion. After January, when the threat of power loss is lower, you might take some of the excess food that you bought to your local food bank. The Y2K Recession is going to put a lot of people out of work and therefore a lot of strain on the food supplies of the local food charities.

POWER

You will want some way to cook food and read at night. If you have a gas grill or portable stove, just have some extra fuel handy. Many gas grills now have burners attached to them, or you can buy them separately. In a pinch, you can cook on your barbecue grill, using charcoal, or in your fireplace, using wood. It will be no different than what you would do if you were camping, although you will not want to use your good cooking utensils. So, unless you have some old pots and pans, go to the thrift store and buy some.

Obviously, you can buy flashlights or other lights that can run on batteries, and for most of us that would be fine. Coleman Lanterns are quite handy as well, though harder to read by. If you have some medical need that requires you to have electrical power, then you should have an appropriate-sized generator.

Also, a lot of guys (including me) are like Tim the Toolman. We buy a garage full of tools just because someday we *might* need them. I can understand why someone might want to buy a small gas-powered electrical generator completely apart from Y2K reasons. If you are going to do that, then make sure it is powerful enough to run your refrigerator and freezer. You might want to go in with several neighbors to buy one and then take turns keeping your freezers running. But be very careful how you store gas. It would be sad to blow your house up while trying to protect yourself from a potential problem.

The power went out in Montreal last year for eight weeks in the dead of winter, and they have *real* winters up there. Peter de Jager reports that twenty-two people died as a result of the power outage, but not as a result of freezing. They died from sleeping in the same room with their gas generators.

HEAT

January 1 is in the dead of winter. Especially if you live in a place where it gets bitterly cold, you need to have an alternate form of heat. Fireplaces and wood stoves would be appropriate in such climates in any event.

These are nonelectrical devices, but don't wait until December 1999 to buy a cord of wood.

Sleeping bags are cheap, efficient, and useful for many purposes besides a crisis. Ski clothes are very warm but can be expensive if you don't use them a lot. Consider going to the thrift store to buy used ski clothes, assuming that you need warmer clothes and would rather invest in bond funds than ski clothes.

ALTERNATIVE HOUSING

If you are really worried about a more severe survival problem, but don't want to move or buy a second home in the country, here is a simple alternative.

I have friends all over the country whom I would dearly love to spend a week with. And I would love it if they could come spend a week with me. We keep talking about getting together for a vacation or a weekend, but time slips by, and we never seem to make plans.

Here's what you can do. Simply agree to open your home to some friends if their power goes out and it looks likely that it will be out for some time, and they can do the same for you. You might do this with several friends to have a backup.

The friends need to be far enough away that they are not served by the same power company, but close enough to drive to. It would be best if they were on a different part of the power grid. Check before you leave to make sure that gas is available along the route, or store some gas in a five-gallon safety-rated container (or in a number of them). Remember, gas will only keep for about a year.

Bring your food, sleeping bags, and a good attitude, and enjoy the time with your friends. If you have seven kids, you get to find out who your real friends are, or at least who the crazy ones are.

COMMUNICATIONS

If the local phone lines go down, communication will be a problem. In many cases, cell phones will work even if the local lines won't. As long as the long distance provider you use still works, you should be able to make calls into areas where the local phones are working or to other cell phone users.

A strategy for small businesses: Most businesses have multiple lines. Get a second long distance provider on one. Make sure that it is a different prime-service provider. Many long-distance companies are simply resellers of one major or prime carrier like AT&T, Sprint, or MCI; it will do you no good to have two long-distance companies if they both are ultimately using the same system. While these major providers should not be down for long, if they do have problems, it is a big hassle to be unable to do business for even an hour, let alone days. This "insurance" doesn't cost much extra, if anything, and is not a bad idea even for normal times.

MEDICINE

Obviously, if you can avoid being in the hospital during the first few months of 2000, then you should do so. If you know that you have surgery coming up, try to schedule it sooner. But most of us cannot anticipate when we will have health problems.

While hospitals are late in addressing their Y2K problems, the latest news says that there are not as many medical devices at risk due to embedded chips as was once thought. Most hospitals are beginning to share information and are working aggressively to be ready with their critical health-care systems. I think that the main worry about being in a hospital in early 2000 will come from the environment outside of the hospital—especially from such areas as telephones and transportation. I will keep you updated on my web site.

As a reasonable precaution, I would have several months' supply of any medicine that you regularly take on hand before the end of the year. Don't forget that if you are on a medical reimbursement plan, many insurance providers will need to be contacted for approval prior to a doctor making a multiple-month prescription.

CASH AND BANKING

It is a good rule of thumb to make and keep copies of the documents of all your financial transactions—not only bank statements, deposits, and checks, but investment-brokerage accounts, mutual-fund statements, insurance records, and credit-card statements. This is important under any circumstances. Make a backup of your computer records, and store it away from your computer.

If the computer that holds the data from one of the above types of account goes down, remember that the companies are not going to lose access to their backup records. The numbers are in the computer somewhere, and they will do whatever it takes to get access to those numbers as quickly as possible.

I am far more worried about a computer program that seemingly chugs right along and debits my account an extra $417 for no reason. I am not worried about it charging my account $417,000, because the money isn't there. But it could get $417. You need to check your statements much more carefully than usual during the first half of 2000.

This advice is not only for banks. Any computer program can make mistakes if there is a bug in it. There will be a lot of bugs in software in 2000. We will hear stories in which some company gets five hundred boxes of nuts and bolts instead of five. That is, of course, unless they desperately need five hundred boxes to get a job out tomorrow, and then they will get five. The first few months of 2000 are going to be frustrating. We have come to rely so heavily upon computers to do the detail work for us. Because there will be so many seemingly random bugs, many of which may not show up for months, we all will have to pay much closer attention to details than we have done in the recent past.

Nearly every place where I speak I am asked if I am going to get any extra cash or take my money out of the banking system.

Yes, I am going to take out some cash. Not because I think that my bank will not be compliant, but because of the *possibility* that the ATMs may be down due to electrical, telephone, or computer failure. I want enough cash to get me and my business through a few weeks. As soon as I see the ATMs and my bank working again, the extra cash will go right back in. I don't like to have large amounts of cash stashed.

How much is enough? That figure varies from family to family. I will probably need more than a single person with no dependents. If for some reason you cannot write a check due to a bank problem, it is unlikely that your utilities are going to be turned off or your phone will be disconnected. I believe that most businesses will be as lenient as possible.

But the grocery store may not want a check on a bank that is down for more than a day. If there is a power failure, credit cards won't work. You won't need a full month's paycheck, because the mortgage company is not going to take your home if you don't bring them cash as long as you can demonstrate that your bank is down. For that matter, you can write the mortgage company, utilities, and other obligations a check, and they can cash it when the bank gets back on-line.

Your bank will want to work with you. It will desperately need you to stay as a customer, so it is going to do everything in its power to help you get through any problems. Call me naïve, but I believe that most businesses know that if they anger their customers, they will vote with their feet by switching to a business that treats its customers right.

If you get written verification by the end of summer in 1999 that your bank is compliant, then you should be fine. If you cannot get written verification that satisfies you, then I would change banks. It is as simple as that.

Am I going to take my money out of my bank? I see no reason to as of today. My bank is currently compliant. I have extra working capital in money-market funds if something unexpected happens. If your bank is compliant, then the only other issue you should really consider is its solvency. If there is a problem, you do not want more than $100,000 in any one bank, or you really want to know and trust your bank. But that is just prudent business at any time.

Finally, when you are taking that extra cash back to the bank, consider donating 10 percent of what you thought was emergency cash to the food bank or Red Cross.

KNOW YOUR NEIGHBORS

Many of us do not know the people who live around us. Our "neighbors" have become the people we work and associate with. They may be in the same town or across the country. In a mobile society, our relationships are no longer limited to those within proximity of our home.

We all bemoan that fact and have a nostalgic longing for the days when people knew their neighbors. The Y2K Crisis is a good opportunity to get to know your neighbors. Most of them may not be ready to talk about the problem in the beginning of January 1999, but I think that their awareness level will change by the summer. The fact that you are reading this book means that you are probably one of the more aware individuals in your neighborhood.

Invite your neighbors over to your home, and start discussion groups about what you can do in your neighborhood in case of a Y2K problem. Are you in a high-crime area, or near one? If that concerns you and your neighbors, then you should discuss what to do about that as a local community. Frankly, if there is a problem, you don't want to be the only one in the neighborhood with water and food. Part of your own strategic plan should be to make sure that your neighbors are self-sufficient and prepared.

Loan them this book, or better yet, get them to buy a copy, or give them one as a way to introduce them to the problem. We are all in this together, and if there *is* a problem, you will be in it with your neighbors. It is better to get to know them now rather than in the middle of a crisis.

YOUR COMMUNITY

The GartnerGroup says that 66 percent of local communities will have at least one mission-critical system failure. Capers Jones says 90 percent of local communities are not expected to be completely ready in time. The readiness of state and federal agencies varies tremendously.

What will be the response of your city if there is a power failure? What if a government agency cannot deliver critical services to the elderly, sick, or poor, or to children or the homeless? Who is going to be there in your town to make sure that the people least able to take care of themselves are okay?

The problems of getting a community organized are multiple, as community organizer Ian Wells *(www.lowellonline.org/BnA/Y2K)* of Lowell, Massachusetts, notes. There is little middle ground in the Y2K world. The extremists seem to validate the public perception that Y2K is too extreme to be real. Many view the problem as being on someone else's computer, so no one "owns" the problem. Further, the problem is so large and unusual that paralysis results.

But the reality of the problem is somewhere between the ideas of the survivalists and of those in denial or despair. In order to organize a community you have to create a sense of urgency without being extreme. You have to occupy the middle ground and get your community to join you.

Without being preachy, I must say that each community is responsible for itself. The quality of life in your community is dependent upon you and your neighbors developing a contingency plan to take responsibility for your own backyard.

I have mentioned the city of Lubbock elsewhere in the book. Here is an example of a city preparing for problems. *If* they happen to experience them, they will be ready. I hope that every community will emulate their positive, forward looking programs.

There are a number of excellent resources to help your community get organized. Ian Wells's site mentioned above is one.

I have reproduced in appendix B a month-by-month list of measures that a community should consider taking. This list was prepared by Capers Jones and is printed with his permission. The reason that I include it in this book is that I think that you should see what many cities will be doing. Is your city one of them? I urge you to look at this list, copy it, and share it with your city leaders. It is available along with more commentary at *www.angelfire.com/mn/inforest/capersj989. html*.

Here are descriptions of some other excellent sites.

The Cassandra Project web site is excellent for community planning (as well as personal planning). This is *www.millennia-bcs.com/casframe. htm*.

The Napa Valley site has an excellent community as well as family preparation site: *www.y2knapa.com/*.

Karen Anderson's informative site written for women: *www.Y2Kwomen. com/*.

There are two other resources that I should bring to your attention. Mike Hyatt has written a provocative book called *The Millennium Bug*. Those wanting to explore a more pessimistic viewpoint than mine will find it interesting. (See appendix A.)

Edward and Jennifer Yourdon have produced a videotape on personal preparation for the crisis. Ed Yourdon is the dean of software teachers, having written or published over fifty books. He is the author of *Time Bomb 2000* (see the minireview in appendix A) along with his daughter Jennifer, a first-rate thinker in her own right. You can find out where to purchase the video at *www.yourdon.com*.

Don't Procrastinate

The point is to think creatively. You don't have to prepare to survive the next two years in chaos, but you should have a contingency plan that addresses the possibility of a few weeks' loss of basic services.

Beyond that, consider getting involved in your community preparations. Don't wait for someone else to call the first meeting to order, but be active in urging your community leaders to consider preparing an active contingency plan.

What I Think Is Going to Happen

The question that I hear more than any other is "What is going to happen?" None of us likes uncertainty very much. We don't like it at all when our families and economic futures are concerned. Because there is so much misinformation about the Millennium Bug and because the gulf between the various schools of thought is so wide, the level of uncertainty about this issue is as high as any I have encountered in my adult life.

In this chapter I'll give you my best guess as to what lies in the future. If we were sitting around a table, discussing this topic over dinner and a good bottle of wine, I would tell you what I am going to write now. But I would make you understand that this is a guess based upon what we know in January of 1999, also that I am allowed to change my mind as time goes on, and I would want your blood oath that you won't remind me that I wrote this unless, of course, I am dead solid on target.

I am doing this so that you can plan your own preparations. But your plan should have some off-ramps as things change and new facts come to light. With luck, there will be good news.

To give you a way to keep up on any changes in my thinking, I am going to post any changes to this "preview of coming attractions" on my web site. When you go there (www.2000wave.com), you will see an icon that will tell you whether I am more optimistic or pessimistic and by how much, and whether I have made any changes in my scenario outlined below.

And again, just for the record, I sincerely hope and pray that the negative projections that I make prove totally unfounded.

Things That We Can Be Pretty Sure About

There are some things that I think we can be sure about, and we need to keep these in perspective as we talk mostly about the negative aspects of Y2K.

Business will not stop. AT&T will buy another cable company and make plans to compete with the Bells. Bill Gates will drag his lawsuit into the next millennium and buy more companies. Companies will still make plans for the future, and new companies will be started that will become the next Microsoft or Intel or Dell. No serious businessman is going to dig a hole and crawl into it over Y2K, although it seems that a lot of survivalists plan to do just that. You can bet that corporate boardrooms all over America will be trying to figure out how to make money out of this, and many of them will. More than 90 percent of businesses will develop Y2K contingency plans, and will come out on the other side of the recession in good shape.

Life will go on. We will buy gas, cars, groceries, go on vacations, go to the movies, and spend time with family and friends. We will go to church and date, marry, divorce, and have kids. One-tenth of 1 percent of us will move to the country and become survivalists, and the media will spend 50 percent of its Y2K airtime talking to that tiny number. The rest of us will pay attention to the crisis and prepare our families as best we can.

With this in mind, let's look at my best guess as to what will happen quarter by quarter.

First Quarter, 1999

Ian Hayes of Triaxsys points out in an interview on my web site, "In January of 1999 we will get our first real glimpse of how good or how bad things are." (By the time you read this book, we will be *well* into the first quarter. It will be interesting to see how well my prophet robes will fit.)

Forty-four percent of the Fortune 500 companies surveyed by Dr. Howard Rubin in a third-quarter, 1998 survey said that they had already experienced a disruption or financial miscalculation caused by a Y2K failure. Ninety-five percent of those respondees expected to have some Y2K-related failures in 1999.

The question that Hayes posed was not whether there would be lots of problems but how severe they would be and how long it would take to get them fixed. This first quarter will be our first real bellwether of the extent of the problems we face.

I expect there to be a few spectacular failures, on the order of last year's paging-satellite problem. Everyone will know about them and they will be news for a few weeks. The media will play up these failures. But more importantly, these events will give us a glimpse of the problems that we will probably be facing one year later. I can almost guarantee that whatever happens in January 1999 will be trumped in spades in 2000.

What you will want to watch is how widespread the problems are and how long it takes to fix them. Every Y2K analyst in the world will be watching, and the Internet will be dancing with stories. Unless there are serious and widespread problems, which I doubt, we will need to wait until February or March 1999 to evaluate what really happened. I will post my analysis on my web site as we go through this period.

I think that the stock market will still be fixated on Asia and South America, currency problems, and global recession. Perversely, since bull markets climb a wall of worry, we may see some new highs. I don't see any end to the stock market volatility that we are now experiencing. Most mainstream economists will still be ignoring the Y2K Crisis as a significant economic factor.

Watch for Congress to discuss legislation that will require full disclosure from public companies and government agencies and for Congress to give indemnification (reduced legal liability) for those disclosures. The real issue will be whether or not the trial-lawyers union can persuade the president to veto the indemnification parts of the bill. My hope is that they won't be able to. Indemnification is the right thing to do, and there will be a growing awareness of the seriousness of the problem by late in the first quarter of 1999. We are going to have enough problems without the trial lawyers of America costing us an extra trillion dollars.

Another debate will be over banking. Will the Federal Reserve come clean, or will Congress require them to do so, on which banks are Y2K ready? Those large banks that are ready will say that they have no problem with the concept. See which banks fight this tooth and nail. My suggestion is to take your money out of those banks and put it in other banks. Either the banks that fight the requirement are in trouble and don't want you to know, or they have management that has its head in the sand. Either way, vote with your feet.

The media will be looking for any Y2K story. Editors and producers will be wanting the spectacular story, so I expect that most of the press will be negative. There will be lots of books out on the subject, and the survivalists will be out in full force with a sense of apocalyptic fervor not seen for, well, a millennium. ·

I am concerned that the fringe elements of this debate will be so shrill that the entire subject could lose credibility in the eyes of many. They will consign it to the same category as UFOs and conspiracy movements.

Things to do:

1. Put your investment strategy in motion. Get together with your financial advisors. Call the funds and managers suggested in this book.

Don't procrastinate. I suggest that you start getting out of the stock market if you have not done so already, and that you decide what bond strategy you want to implement. If you are going to take any of my aggressive suggestions, now is the time to start.

2. Decide what your family survival strategy will be. Don't put it off. You must begin to gather some items this quarter (see chapter 14), and plan what further items you will purchase and when.

3. Contact your community leaders (city council, pastors, etc.), and see who is organizing your community contingency plans. Call them, and see what you can do. If no one is planning, then you need to be the catalyst. Read appendix B about community efforts.

4. If you don't have a computer and Internet access, get them. Not only can you stay updated through my web site, but there are other excellent sites as well to keep you informed, help you with buying decisions, and help you in your community-wide efforts.

5. There is a coupon in the back of this book for a discount on my monthly newsletter, *Year 2000 Alert,* from Weiss Publishing, if you want more specific investment information from me.

Second Quarter, 1999

Do not expect any major corporation to announce that it is in trouble. But expect many corporations to trumpet their Y2K readiness in ads, web sites, and public forums. Those corporations that say nothing or little will be conspicuous by their silence. The general public will still not have a clue.

I expect a trickle of ads from companies about their Y2K status, and it will grow into a river. It would not surprise me to see little buttons touting Y2K compliance showing up in the corners of ads. Some of the buttons will have the same real-world meaning as "low fat" does on cartons of ice cream.

We may begin to see the first real movement by major Wall Street figures and analysts to join Dr. Yardeni in his assessment of the seriousness of the Y2K problem. When analysts begin to talk with information technology staff and to see the triage and contingency projects move from the coffee rooms in the computer departments to the executive suites, they will start to take notice.

Unless we see a lot of Y2K related failures in the first quarter of 1999, I don't think that we will see much Y2K effect on the stock market yet. I don't think that we will be at new highs by the end of the quarter, but most analysts will still be telling us that the worst is behind us (meaning Asia et al. and the global recession) and that now is a great time to buy. And it may be—for S&P LEAPS!

More of the same will come from corporate America. The disclosures will still be "happy face." But watch as the number of merger talks and buyouts begins to increase. You might see some deals done at what look like *very good prices*. No one will mention Y2K as a reason. The buzz formula will be: "This was a strategic acquisition to take us into the next millennium." The *real reason* will be that one of the parties was not Y2K compliant, and had to sell in order to insure some value for their shareholders.

We will start to see some positive reports on Y2K compliance. Industry boards will begin to trumpet how they are cooperating and how everything is working. And for the most part, it will be true. If we get a true indemnification bill, I expect the Bell companies to disclose their Y2K status (if not their compliance), as will many other large public monopolies.

Corporations will begin to rethink their supply chains and purchasing programs. There will be big winners and losers, as corporations decide to simplify and go with proven suppliers that can demonstrate Y2K readiness. *I think that this is going to be a very big trend.*

If you are a CEO or major department head, you will be telling your staff to @#$$# well make sure that the companies that they purchase critical parts and supplies from are in good shape. It will become a "your-job-is-on-the-line" issue. Buyers and managers are not going to feel like risking *their* jobs just to make some salesman happy. CEOs are not going to willingly risk their companies and their big paychecks. This is going to be a serious business issue.

Some of the winners in the Y2K software company world will be companies who verify Y2K compliance. They are going to be a boom industry. I am not sure what they will do in the summer of 2000, so I don't think that I would buy stock in one of them. But if I could invest in one privately to get the profits that they will make in the next nine months, I would be tempted. Some of them are going to clean up.

I do not know when we will know fully who wins and who loses, but the facts will start to show up this second quarter.

We will see a movement by various state legislatures to require full disclosure from public entities in their states. The laws will vary, but the main purpose will be to calm the public over Y2K. Further, I think that state legislatures will begin to put some teeth into these laws, especially for government-granted monopolies like utilities and communications. I think that we will see most states pass legislation that will indemnify state and local governments from Y2K litigation.

More than 95 percent of the disclosures will be good (what would you expect?). Remember, computer professionals are outrageous optimists. They nearly always tell you that the project will get done on time. And the CEOs will believe them, and tell us that they have everything under control. Most will be proven right. But compliance won't be more than

95 percent. Fifty percent of computer projects are delivered late, but you can bet that 100 percent of the CEOs were told when the projects started that they would be on time. The computer professionals will by and large not start to panic until the third quarter.

We will begin to see an upsurge in Y2K-related lawsuits, as companies are forced to spend millions to upgrade software that they feel should have been compliant to begin with.

A good trend will be the large scale contingency planning by communities all over America. Watch for churches and businesses to join with local governments to begin to decide how to deal with potential problems. The local media will be brought into the project. They will be doing continual updates on the local preparations. The emphasis in most of these projects will be twofold. There will be an effort to calm the public, and there will be genuine development of programs to deal with potential local crises.

More and more cities will begin to emulate Lubbock, Texas, and go through Y2K emergency systems preparations and simulations. Lubbock has led the nation in this effort, and the people there are to be commended!

I think that we will hear the slogan "Plan for the worst and hope for the best" so many times that it will drive us nuts, but that will be exactly what we should do.

Y2K rural retreats and survival communities will begin to spread. The number of apocalyptic books will increase exponentially, each trying to outdo the other in its doomsday scenario. I wish that I could buy electric generator futures. Just remember, a lot of this will be simple overreaction and pessimism.

The stock market may start feeling some Y2K selling as the negative publicity begins to have a cumulative effect. As the market moves up and down, each succeeding high will be lower than the last. We will be dealing with the effects of a global recession, and more and more investors are going to be looking to step aside until there is more certainty about what will happen. Plus, the roller-coaster ride will continue, and it will start to wear psychologically on investors.

Things to do:

1. Make sure that your investment plans are in place.
2. Certain survival-type items may be getting scarce, so check your list, and if you know what you are going to buy, then do so. If you are going to buy generators, for instance, now may be your last chance to get an order and hope to have delivery. Check my web site for the latest status of power and telecommunications systems.
3. Make sure that your community has contingency-planning programs well under way. Get involved.

Third Quarter, 1999

The media are going to be the real news in this quarter. We will see almost daily Y2K updates on topics ranging from local community preparedness programs to the status of local businesses. The talk shows will be full of Y2K stories, and most of the news will still be around the pessimistic point of view, although there will be a considerable effort on behalf of community and business leaders to put forth positive news as well.

This "disconnect" (the substantial difference between the messages of the various groups) is going to make most people nervous. You will be wondering whom to believe and whether you should trust anyone. And actually it will be impossible to "prove" the positive points. A Y2K compliant business or community will be able to say that it is until they are blue in the face, and some people simply will not believe them. Because the only way to absolutely prove it to die-hard skeptics will be to wait until January 2000.

Most large corporations will have their publicity machines in full gear telling us that they are okay. And most of them will be. But companies whose stock is down, and there will be a lot of them, are going to be telling us that now is the time to buy.

I think that we will begin to see the effects of the Y2K Crisis on the markets this quarter. It may happen earlier, but this quarter it will kick in much more aggressively as the news from around the world gets worse. S&P LEAPS bought early in the year will start to look really good. Long bonds will look excellent as interest rates begin to slip toward 4 percent. Commodity-fund investments will be doing well, as volatility will be increasing.

I think that there will be a massive movement from around the world into U.S. bonds. The grim reality of the foreign Y2K situation will begin to dawn, and the smart money will seek safe havens. It will not be that smart-money investors don't trust European governments or the new European Monetary Unit (EMU) so much as that they will also be looking for capital safety. Europe is highly dependent upon exports, and the export market in 2000 will be looking weak. European markets have the real potential to crash as the EMU collapses.

All this money moving to the U.S. will make one country after another slap on currency controls, further destabilizing local markets and making it more difficult for us to sell our products. It will not surprise me to see some outright defaults on debt. Look for the Presidential administration to make repeated requests for large sums of money for the International Monetary Fund. If not before this time, we will then see real efforts to have another Bretton Woods–type conference to stabilize the world's currencies.

There will be a lot of activity in the merger-and-acquisition field. Again, no one will say publicly that it was done for Y2K reasons. But rumors will surface. Companies that have their Y2K act together and cash and credit lines will be sitting pretty. The questions that they will have to determine will be:

1. Do we let our non-Y2K-compliant competitors get into 2000 before we buy them so that they are on the ropes and we get them cheap?
2. Are our competitors more valuable to us alive than dead, so we buy them today at a higher price, but we get a real company and maybe just enough time to convert their noncompliant systems to our compliant ones?
3. Do we just let them die and try to get their customers?
4. What are the other compliant companies in the industry doing? Are they looking as well? And is someone bigger looking at us to take us over because we have our act together?

When a company looks at a potential acquisition, they will go in and investigate with due diligence. They will attempt to get a handle on the computer systems and production readiness of the target acquisition.

And in this case, those companies that realize that they are not going to make it will be in very poor bargaining positions. The best that they can do will be to try and salvage as much as possible for their shareholders and employees.

There will have been some great opportunities for shorting companies, but most of them will be long gone by now. You should only consider shorting individual stocks if you have some experience in this arena. There will be companies that are known problems but are still basically sound. You could short them and then find that a white knight arrives and watch your short position get very ugly very quickly. Shorting is for large, sophisticated investors who can take multiple positions knowing that if one or two go bad, then the others likely won't. They expect to lose on a few of their positions. If you only have one or two positions, you could get clobbered. And the potential loss for a short position is unlimited.

Corporations are going to be demanding more and more detailed reports from their suppliers. Expect to see hundreds of thousands of web sites from companies and governments detailing their Y2K readiness and/or contingency plans.

As fiscal year 2000 begins for a lot of corporations, we will read about more problems emerging. Many government entities and corporations begin their fiscal year 2000 in October. And of course, we will see the dreaded date September 9, 1999, which I predict will be more or less a nonevent, although if there are any spectacular failures the media will hype them heavily.

A survey done in October of 1998 by Dr. Howard Rubin showed that corporations did not rank the Year 2000 issue in their top five concerns. By this quarter it will start showing up in their list of concerns, although it may be expressed as a concern over loss of trading partners, a worsening economic environment, and other potential sources of difficulty. Corporate leaders will still be reluctant to admit that *they* have a problem or concern.

Salaries for computer programmers will reach the stratosphere. Remediation budgets will be blown out of the water. We will see signing bonuses approach six figures for some specialized programmers and services as deadlines make management panic. What will an extra $100,000 for a programmer matter when compared to a malfunctioning program that produces or controls $50 million in revenue?

Of course, that programmer will be leaving either some other company in the lurch or, more likely, a government entity. Government programmers will be leaving in droves all through the year, and this trend will increase as we get into this quarter. Corporations will cancel vacation and holidays and demand overtime from their information technology (IT) workers for the rest of the year leading up to January and for the first few months afterward.

Lots of software will just begin testing in this period, and this is when the panic in many boardrooms will begin, as executives learn just how much work remains to be done and how much money remains to be spent.

The global recession will hurt the profits of many companies, and the stock market will take more hits and become even more volatile.

Triage and contingency plans will become a topic in more and more corporate press releases.

Now, it gets tricky. I *think* that the Federal Reserve will tell us which banks are Y2K compliant and which are not sometime late in this quarter. They should do it earlier. But in any event, I think that people will start withdrawing money from the banks. I expect that most will only withdraw a month or two of cash reserves, but depositors will worry about the availability of cash if they wait till December.

If the Federal Reserve does not tell us the Y2K status of the banking institutions in this country, I expect to see people closing accounts and either keeping the cash or moving it to a bank that they feel confident in. You will see major advertising by banks and S&Ls about their Y2K status. But if there are still 5 percent of banks on the Federal Reserve's noncompliant list, there will be doubt among consumers.

There will not be one bank that will publicly say that it is not going to be able to tell you how much money is in your account in January 2000. But since the world will know that 5 percent (or whatever the number) are lying, the question will become, is my bank lying to me? I would not be surprised if those banks that have good ratings *somehow* let it be known what their ratings are and damn the consequences if they see their customers getting nervous. This will be tricky, as it is now illegal for a bank to reveal its Y2K ratings. (My banker will not tell me their Fed rating. But he did say no one has a higher rating.) This is one of those items where we have to say, "Stay tuned."

Watch for money-center banks to form an alliance that only admits banks, both nationally and internationally, that can prove that they are Y2K compliant. They will begin to build a fire wall around themselves so that their major customers will have enough confidence to leave their money in the bank. If a bank cannot get into the alliance, it will have problems holding customers. Its only defense will be either to release the Federal Reserve rating (if it is good) or to sell to another bank on terms less than advantageous to their shareholders.

I actually expect the number of banks with real problems to be small; most of them will be smaller banks with inadequate capital that could not afford to begin repairs in time. Most of these will be forced by the Federal Reserve to merge with compliant, healthy banks. I honestly believe that the government and business leaders of this country understand how vital confidence in the banking system is to our entire way of life and will pull out the stops if they think that our confidence in the system is in danger.

That doesn't mean that people won't take a little cash out as a precaution, but there is a big difference between taking a little cash out and taking it all out.

Things to do:

1. As I mentioned in the previous chapter, I intend to withdraw *some* cash from my bank account. Not a lot, but enough to last for a month on the assumption that my credit cards, ATM cards, and other resources might not be available due to power glitches, telecommunications problems, and other difficulties. I will not be taking anywhere close to all my money out of my bank and money market funds and putting it into cash under my mattress.

   If you are going to get cash, then begin to do so now.
2. If you are managing you own bond portfolio, watch interest rates closely. Strange things *could* (not *will*) be happening as money is withdrawn from banks at the same time that more foreign money comes in to our government debt market.
3. I would start buying my food items late in the quarter. But monitor supplies. I doubt that there will be shortages, especially this early , but you should watch, just in case.
4. Visit my web site and other links that I provide more often, as there will be more news.

Fourth Quarter, 1999

By now, nearly all of America will know that *millennium* is spelled with two *n's*.

By this time we should have a real idea of what we are facing. I will be posting on my web site my overall observations and what I am hearing from my travels and from Y2K experts with a greater frequency, as we will be getting much more information. I *hope* that things will be better than the data presently indicates. But I have to temper my optimism with the data we are looking at. So, forging ahead:

Work will be moving at a feverish pace to fix programs and get testing done. Programmers and technicians will be working long hours, seven days a week. Talk about being in a fishbowl! Mostly these experts toil in obscurity, but now the CEO will be coming down to the office, looking over their shoulders and getting daily updates. Successful changeovers to Y2K-ready programs will be celebrated with the vigor usually reserved for World Series victories.

The bond market will be booming as more and more money is thrown at government bonds from both here and around the world. There is going to be a lot of nervousness in the markets, and only the most stalwart (or risk-prone?) investors or those afraid to do anything (deer-in-the-headlight syndrome) will be hanging around. International stocks will be in the toilet. Bonds of Third World countries will be selling at discounts, or not selling at all.

The stock market will be down and on its way further down. The talking heads on the business-news shows will be talking about real values and bear markets. Mutual-fund managers will be talking about real values and why you should invest now. The Federal Reserve will continue to lower rates. Earnings reports and estimates are going to be lower, and it will be very interesting to see what analysts decide to project for 2000 earnings.

There will start to be some stocks that will be very tempting according to current P/E ratios, but for the most part I suggest that you resist. There will be exceptions, though. Companies that have a "franchise" name or market dominance and that are known to be compliant may be buys, but the price will have to be so good that we don't care if it drops. There won't be many. Frankly, there may very well be more good opportunities overseas for the "steal deal" than at home.

Watch large investors and savvy international hedge funds buy whole companies for fractions of their book values, using borrowed money at very low rates. The rich are going to get much richer. This quarter is when we will see the beginnings of the transfer of wealth from unprepared and weak hands to prepared and strong ones.

But most of the large money will still be on the sidelines, although

Warren Buffett may not be able to resist a major deal here or there. Investors like him, with really long-term profiles and huge hoards of cash, may find some companies so cheap that they will feel that they have to step in, even if it is early.

But remember, the world won't come to a halt. We will still buy food, clothes, and Christmas presents. I wonder, in fact, if we won't have a very good consumer Christmas season as people decide to have one last good party. It is too early to predict the mood of the country.

Year-end sales will also be helped as almost everyone buys a few extra weeks' worth of groceries, batteries, and candles, some extra propane for the outdoor grill, water, gas cans, and other useful items. If you are going to do this, don't wait until the last few weeks of December. Ziff-Davis is the largest publisher of computer magazines. They surveyed over sixty-three hundred of their on-line subscribers, most of whom were programmers or are involved in the information industry. *Over 55 percent said that they were going to purchase extra supplies and food, and 45 percent said that they were going to purchase extra fuel, although less than 7 percent said that they believed in a doomsday scenario.* And what is the software and techie group surveyed by Ziff-Davis group going to do? *Over 61 percent said that they were planning to take some of their money out, and 24 percent said that they were going to take 90 percent or more out of their accounts!*

If we are going to see a spike up in certificate of deposit (CD) rates, it will start to show up now. People are going to be asking their neighbors and friends if they are taking money out. Unless there is a huge change in public sentiment between now and then, the answer is going to be yes. I think that people will be watching their information technology friends for a lead. There are always a few people in every group that people listen to. Those trendsetters will have great influence.

If this is true, there is going to be a need for a great deal of cash. As noted elsewhere, there is about $3,500 to $4,000 of available cash for each family in the country. That is a lot, but it doesn't take too much demand to put a strain on the system.

Bank lending is going to go down as lending criteria get tighter and banks have less money to loan, because all the money leaving them will force them to raise cash for reserve requirements. The Federal Reserve will be watching this situation closely. We will know that it is bad if the Fed responds by temporarily lowering reserves requirements or with some similar measure. It is at this time that we will all be thankful that Alan Greenspan is Fed chairman. There will be no right decision, but he will probably make the best one. Lots of people will be earnestly praying that he does, especially bank chairmen.

The irony is that lending rates will be dropping. Companies with good credit, good business plans, and proof of Y2K compliance will be getting money at bargain rates. You will be tempted to refinance your home. I will be telling you to wait, but check my web site in November 1999.

Millennium fever will hit. The media will be talking about the stories of the twentieth century; books will come out making all sorts of predictions about the next century. Some of them will be good. Most of them will be garbage as publishers look for anything with *Millennium* in the title. Again, check my web site for my reading recommendations. (Of course, when I come out with *The Millennium Wave*, it will be one of my recommended millennium books!)

Community contingency plans will be in high gear by this time, and for the most part people will be working together, although the media will try to find the critics and give them the same status as those actually in there doing something.

This will be a special time, and I hope that Y2K worries do not overtake the joy and wonder of being alive at the arrival of a new millennium. I plan to spend some time taking stock of my life and of the future. I think that it is important to remember that the reason that we have a millennium is that a child was born two thousand years ago. We need to put our concerns about Y2K in that perspective, and as we approach the new millennium, we should think about what really matters: our relationships with God, our family, and our friends. Those of us who live in this great country, and benefit from the sacrifices so many have made to achieve a level of prosperity and freedom envied by the world, should pause to be grateful. All the rest is window dressing.

▬▬▬▬▬

First Quarter, 2000

One of the standard pieces of wisdom in the investment business is to buy on the rumor and sell on the reality.

I expect that the first few weeks of January will not be as bad as we thought they would be. Partially that is because we will be expecting it to be pretty bad and partly because the infrastructure, utilities, telephones, and banks by and large will work.

There will be random power outages, phone disruptions, and bank hassles, but they will mostly be short-lived, except maybe in the rural areas to which the survivalists have moved. They will probably need their generators.

Most of us will be wondering what to do with a case of green beans and a three-year supply of candles. Maybe it would be a good idea to donate the excess food to food banks and homeless shelters, whose supplies will be depleted because of the holiday season. Their services may be in great demand over the next year, and so it would not hurt to help these worthy charities stock up in advance.

The media stories for the first few weeks will be about the major disruptions in power, phones, and so on. But by the third week of January, those difficulties will mostly be over, except in the isolated rural areas, and even most of those will have figured out some way to get things back to normal.

I think that the operative term for this period will be *muddle through*. When everyone realizes that his or her worst fears have not come to pass and life goes on, the country will breathe a huge sigh of relief. When the hassles come, they will be so much smaller than what we all feared that everyone will have a remarkably good attitude about all the hassles that we do have.

Now, before you call me a Pollyanna, I will say that this period will be like the Christmas spirit. It will be nice while it is there, but it won't last long. I expect it to be pretty much gone by the end of the quarter as patience wears thin with those who have not fixed their problems within a few months. Even Job griped a little after his afflictions went on and on.

This is when we will see the payoff for all the time spent developing community contingency plans. Those communities that have prepared will find that their efforts have made their cities or towns much nicer and better places to live. The needs will vary from community to community and from state to state. I hope that you will have been part of the effort in your community. You will feel better about yourself and your community if you have participated. You will have made new friends and have realized that we are all in this together. For many of you, this will be one of the best times of your life, as you will feel the true joy of having been of service to others.

So much for the good news. At the same time that most of us are getting back to normal, we will also realize that government services have become a real problem. There will be a total breakdown in some agencies, and contingency plans will be put into place. These will more or less deliver services, but they will be spotty, and there will be problems as people fall through the cracks. Without community efforts to make sure that those least capable of dealing with the problems are taken care of, there will be a disaster. It will take weeks and months, sometimes many months, for some of these agencies to dig out from underneath the burden of having to revert to paper. There will be ample opportunity for fraud and just as much opportunity to miss those who are legitimately eligible. The cost overruns will be staggering in some agencies, but emergency appropriations will be made.

Today it looks like the airlines will be ready, and the Federal Aviation Administration tells us they will be, although the congressional oversight committee is still giving them a grade of D. The problem is that some of our major airports are just now beginning to figure out to what extent they have a problem. It is scary to think that O'Hare and Atlanta haven't completed an assessment as I write this.

Any organization that has not completed an assessment cannot really tell you that they will be okay. If they do, they are obviously only *hoping* that they will be, because they have no basis for their optimism. I want to know how many chips they have to replace and how many function points of code they have to fix before I attach any credence to their happy-face press releases.

Internationally, as we have pointed out elsewhere, it is dicey whether we will be able to fly "over the pond." Many countries will not have their air traffic control systems fixed.

I intend to be within driving distance of where I want to spend the first two weeks of the year. If you do go overseas, make sure that it is to someplace where you would want to be stuck for a few weeks or longer and with someone you want to be stuck with. With the right person and the right place, this could be a bonus, but most of us will not be stuck in Tahiti alone with our soul mate for a few extra days as things sort themselves out.

Traffic overseas will be slower as flights revert to 1950s technology (yellow pads and radio), but we will not forget how to fly. I just want someone else to be first. I am perfectly willing to be third, but then I have flown Air Zambia, so my judgment about airline safety may be questionable.

Trains will get where they are going, maybe more slowly than usual. Everything will slow down for a while as we all take extra precautions and/or experience delays in getting information. I don't expect this period to be long—weeks instead of months in this country, although it may be months or even quarters in some countries overseas.

It would not be a total surprise to see the market rebound at this point. The perennial bull pundits will be looking for good news and will tell us that the worst is behind us and that now is the time to buy. They will point to the Fortune 500 companies as examples of business as usual, and for the most part they will be right about those companies. Just because there may be a momentary rebound does not mean we are out of the woods yet.

This is where it will get tricky for long-term market timing. The major infrastructure will be working, but what about everything else?

It is not the Fortune 500 that worry me. The thirty thousand companies who employ between one thousand and ten thousand workers are my biggest concern. And getting data on them is going to be a lot more difficult.

I expect to see slowdowns, disruptions, and outright failures. The questions are "How fast can they fix their problems? Do they have enough cash to hold on until they do? Will their customers wait around?"

Just as in football, it is the middle of the line that makes or breaks a team. It is not the spectacular part, or the one that gets all the glory, but without the middle of the line working properly, everything else breaks down.

Similarly, in our economy, it is the middle that is the key. Middle-size businesses are the engines for new jobs. They provide a great deal of the innovation and creativity in our country. And they employ a significant number of people.

Today, the data seem to suggest that there will be lots of problems in this group, for all the reasons cited in previous chapters. The large majority of these companies will be fine as far as their software and equipment are concerned, but a significant percentage won't be. And a significant percentage of those in trouble will either have insufficient cash to get them through several months of slowdown or no product availability.

Many companies will figure out ways to produce their product or service in spite of software problems in key systems, but the loss of productivity will send them over the edge. Again, it is not necessarily the direct effects of Y2K that will ruin a company; it could be the indirect ones.

Just as there are many households in America living from paycheck to paycheck, there are many companies making it from month to month or quarter to quarter. If there is a significant slowdown in cash flow, they will be on the ropes.

We will want to pay close attention to the statistics on late payments. How many bills are thirty to sixty to ninety days past due? How is overall cash flow? And is cash flowing, or is it taking longer and longer for businesses to get their money? Will businesses start to offer significant discounts for early payment? Will cash flow worries begin to dominate management time, to the detriment of production concerns?

We won't know the answers in the first month or two of this quarter. The statistics will take a long time to work themselves into the hands of those who collect and disseminate them. There will be lots of "real-time" surveys conducted on an industry by industry basis, but it may be hard to get a clear picture until March or April.

Compounding this situation will be the loss of productivity that businesses experience because their employees are having to deal with personal and family problems. Family members who get government services, especially those connected to federal bureaucracies, may be in doubt. It is likely that Medicare, Medicaid, food stamps, and other programs in some states will not be working properly, if at all. Somebody will have to take responsibility for those parents and families in need. Even if employees are on the job, if their minds are somewhere else, they are less productive.

And then we will begin to feel the effects from the loss of exports, which will mean the beginning of the real Y2K Recession. The first few months' effects in the U.S. will pass relatively quickly. For some of us two months will go by r-e-e-a-a-l-l-y fast. Things may seem okay, but factory orders for goods, especially those for delivery overseas, will slow down.

Raw materials that we need for production will take longer to get here and will cost more in transportation, although that cost may be offset by the increase in the value of our dollar against that of other currencies, and the willingness of those selling to us to do whatever it takes to get hard currency. It will be the delay, rather than the cost, that will be the problem.

Goods and services from developing countries that compete with those manufactured in the U.S. will be cheaper, forcing us to either lower profits or cut costs or do both. In many cases these options will not be possible unless labor costs go down.

Management will look at costs and have to make hard decisions. I am close friends with the majority owners of a small ($70-million) company that produces U.S. consumer products sold in Wal-Mart, Sears, Target, and similar stores. A few years ago, they were faced with a similar problem. They could either go out of business, or ship their production offshore. There was no other choice. It was move or die.

They moved. The unfortunate thing was that because of this move the U.S. lost seven hundred jobs to Asia, mostly to China. But consumers now pay less for these products than they did three years ago, and, when the price is adjusted for inflation, less than they did twenty years ago. And the company survived.

The situation will be even more stark in 2000. Competition will be tough, but now a company will be able to go overseas and buy facilities at a fraction of the cost that they paid in the past. They will get favorable tax treatment from foreign governments eager for any investment and jobs. The world, and especially Asia, overbuilt capacity in the late nineties because money was easy and times were good. Now times will not be so good. There will be empty plants, many of them quite modern, for the taking.

U.S. managers will be faced with the same choice that my friends had—to either go out of business, or move production offshore. Either all their employees lose, or some of them do. It is a Hobson's choice, and one that I am glad that I will not have to face.

The decision for this choice will start to be made this quarter, but the real effects won't be felt until the third quarter, as it is not usually possible to switch overnight. But it will begin here as a trickle and could turn into a stream.

So, the market could move up because the Y2K Recession effects are underneath the radar screen. Could the Dow move up 10 to 15 percent or more in a short time in January? Absolutely, and depending on how positive the news is, maybe more.

But after this sigh of relief, and a bit of euphoria, reality could come back to bite us. Will I be tempted to sell my S&P LEAPS early on if things look good? Yes, of course—with the thought that I can always buy back if things turn out the way that I think they will. But it will mean close, almost daily monitoring. That is why I will stick with my money held by managers and let them watch their markets for me while I concentrate on the areas where I can add the most value.

An interesting thing is going to happen in January. Bank deposits are going to go up dramatically. All of us with a little extra cash will either spend it or put it back in the banks as soon as we see that we can write checks and that the ATMs work. No one wants to keep a lot of cash on hand. That is why we use banks now. Interest rates will come down at the banks and might temporarily rise on government bonds as money is moved back into the banking system and stocks.

But any rise will be short-lived. Rates will be down at the end of 2000 from where they started, unless foreign buying of bonds pushed them into the 3.5 percent range, which is hard to imagine. By the end of 2000 I think that we will see rates in this range, and I expect the Federal Reserve to lower rates again during the year. Deflation will clearly be the order of the day, and the Fed will not want us to get into a situation like the one the Japanese got into when they waited too late to stimulate the economy and ended up in a deflationary depression.

February 29 (leap day) will roll around and be a big yawn, at least as compared to January 1. Lots of one-day hassles, but work-arounds will abound. Watch some companies declare that February 29 does not exist and go on. It won't be elegant, but we will muddle through. (Remember, years that can be divided by 100 are not leap years. That is, unless they can be divided by 400. The year 2000 is a leap year. But many programmers forgot the divide-by-400 rule, so a significant number of programs do not know that there is a February 29, 2000).

Politics as Unusual

Why would I jump off and talk about politics in a book on Y2K and investing? Because the outcome of this next election cycle will have huge repercussions on our economy and our investment future.

This may be one of the more interesting political seasons in recent memory. We will be campaigning and holding primaries as we turn over the clock. Much of the country will be sorting through lots of Y2K-caused hassles, and some politicians will want us to focus our attention on them.

The major effects of the recession won't start to be felt until the primary is all over but for the shouting. But I think that the recession will be in full swing when the fall campaign begins. The economy will be at the center of the debate, and various candidates will be pushing the "America First" hot button as U.S. jobs are lost to overseas competition (which of course is always unfair) and to the conspiracy in which Big Business takes *our* jobs and gives them to Third World workers.

We will analyze the importance of this race to our economy in the third-quarter comments.

Life in general will go on. Cokie Roberts and Sam Donaldson will still show up on Sunday morning. We will go to church and to the movies and on vacations and watch TV and visit with friends and enjoy life as much as we can. The survivalists will come out of their bunkers and try to figure out what to do with five hundred pounds of flour and beans and a retreat home that no one wants.

Things to do:

1. Donate your extra food to your local food bank.
2. Don't rush back into the market until we see what the toll from overseas is going to be.
3. Keep a larger-than-normal defensive position in government bonds.

Second Quarter, 2000

This will be the quarter during which we get the worst economic news. Most of the companies that are going to go out of business will do so now. I think that we will lose more businesses because of the ripple effects of Y2K than because of the actual failure of their software. Weak businesses fail in weak economies. I think that unemployment will reach levels not seen in twenty-five years. Welfare rolls will expand dramatically, and government budgets at all levels will get hammered.

The stock market will get ugly as corporate earnings take hit after hit. Only a small fraction of companies will make the analyst's projections from a year earlier. By the end of the quarter there will be blood in the streets.

The smart (big) money will form private pools to buy private placements in companies that are basically sound but that need cash to make it through the next year. Instead of venture capital, this will be "vulture capital." These investors will get unbelievably favorable terms and will make huge returns. Their target returns in these private placements will be five to ten times on their investment or more.

What better way to participate in the coming boom? Instead of investing in risky start-ups, investors will be able to get proven products and technologies at a fraction of what it would take to build the companies again. Much of the smartest money will go into these winners so that they can buy their competitors or overseas production lines or a whole list of potential resources that will make them more competitive.

It is much like those investors who bought real estate in Texas at the bottom of the market in the late eighties. They bought buildings at a fraction of what it would have cost to replace them. When the inevitable boom came, many of them got enough in two or three years to pay for the whole building or apartment complex or rental property.

This time it won't be just property, although in some areas of the country it will be. The really smart money will be looking to pick up good companies on the cheap. It will not only be investors. Companies that have their act together and good credit lines will be on the prowl. Investment bankers will be going crazy to get business and will be putting together pools of capital for major companies to have at their disposal.

This is where those of you who have done your homework on hedge funds and kept your powder dry will clean up. You will get to step right in along with large investors and see these outsized, once-in-a-lifetime returns.

Money will be cheap. The Federal Reserve will have its fund rates down to at least 3.5 percent and maybe lower. Long-term bonds will be getting close to a fifty-year low. And mortgage rates will be moving toward the 5 percent range. I will refinance at what may be the lowest rates we will see for the *next* fifty years. If someone wants to loan me money for thirty years at 5 percent, I will feel obligated to help him or her out and take the money.

Banks will be hemorrhaging. Personal and business bankruptcies and slow payments will be at an all-time high. Banks will have money, but not enough creditworthy borrowers, so CD rates will drop through the floor as banks will not need more money and will have trouble making a profit on what they do have.

Brokerage firms will be suffering through even more massive layoffs. Wall Street will be in a depression as investors simply stay away waiting for the dust to settle. If for some odd reason you want that Upper East Side penthouse, now will be a good time to buy. Mutual fund companies will also be devastated as funds under management in equity funds dwindle to less than half of their market highs. This will be due partially to the market losing 40 to 50 percent from the highs and partially to withdrawals. Since mutual fund companies make money directly in proportion to the money they manage, this will be a serious problem. And the money that they make from bond and money-market funds will be much less percentage-wise than what they will make in equity funds.

New car sales will be in a slump, though not disastrous, as low rates and incentives make it cheaper in some cases to buy a new car than to keep the old one. But these incentive programs will be a big hit to earnings, and auto stocks will feel the heat of investor expectations being unfulfilled.

Airlines will feel the pressure as business and pleasure travel falls off significantly, especially high-revenue and profitable international travel.

Travel agencies and the corresponding travel-tourist industry will be hurting as foreign tourism in the U.S. falls way down and we travel less.

If you were ever going to plan that once-in-a-lifetime vacation, this might be the summer. You will get incredible deals at some of the greatest resorts in the world. Your dollar will go further than it has in the last few decades, especially in places where the economies are really hurting and they want dollars badly: Bali, Fiji, some parts of Latin America, and especially Africa. Start planning now, and buy next year. But as I will mention later on, you will have to pay serious attention to the possiblity of civil unrest in many Third World countries.

Third Quarter, 2000

The bleeding will start to slow down. Most of the really bad news will have happened. Most companies fated to die will have done so, and the rest will have figured out how to survive. The international markets will start to come around as companies have their Y2K problems fixed.

We will get a few positive signs. Wholesale orders will start to pick up. Stock prices will firm, and some stocks will begin to have nice recoveries. More jobs will be created than lost, and unemployment will reach its peak and begin to drop.

I think that this will be the time to take profits on your S&P puts. We could be up four to five times or more on them if the market goes to five thousand or less—a normal recession bear market. I think that many of the market timers will begin to see their systems turn long-term bullish. Our bonds will be up 15 to 20 to 25 percent or more (depending upon when you bought them).

It will be time to get out of our bear-market defensive funds and into those funds and stocks poised for growth and a new bull market. But just as this market was not a one-way down market, the new bull will not go up without corrections, especially in this early stage. Remember, bull markets climb walls of worry. In this initial stage, there will still be a lot of worry.

There will be some serious international problems. The usual droughts and weather disasters will seem worse because there will be less international aid for relief. There will be revolutions as the economic plight in many nations results in unrest and the leaders are blamed for not fixing the problems.

To compound this unrest, these international problems will be happening in the middle of a presidential campaign with a lame-duck and probably weakened president. This will be one of the most serious times that the world has faced in fifty years. We will need statesmen. It will be interesting to see if some can step up to the plate. The old saying is that it is difficult times that allow or require ordinary men to step up and become visionary leaders. If there is ever again a time when we will need visionary world leaders, it will be this time.

The election rhetoric will hinge on the economy. There will be lots of blame and name calling, and I expect a nastier-than-usual campaign period.

The topic will be whether or not the U.S. should tighten trade controls and raise tariffs to protect American jobs. The turnaround will not be fully evident even though better numbers will be showing up. Clinton and many Democrats are supporters of free trade, as are many Republicans, but there is a significant movement in both parties that would support trade controls. The temptation will be for both sides to succumb to the siren call of the demagogue who blames our problems on those "foreigners who aren't being fair."

I should point out that this will not be just a U.S. problem. It does not take a whole lot of clairvoyance to imagine the French leading a European effort to raise trade barriers and close their markets to our products, especially food products. Government leaders around the world will be under pressure from local labor leaders to "protect" jobs at home by raising tariffs.

This will be one of the most dangerous periods for world trade and free markets. Trade wars are the one thing that could turn what should be a short recession into a world depression that could be deep and long. Tragically, it will hurt the rest of the world more than us, but it will hurt us deeply nonetheless. It will be cold comfort to know that other countries are worse off when we are mired in a depression made by government interference in the marketplace, even if we did not fire the first shots in the trade war.

I am all for hard negotiating to make sure that there is free trade that is really free. I don't think that we should roll over and let our markets be destroyed by unfair trade practices. But the specter of another Smoot-Hawley Act, which was a main contributor to the world depression of the thirties and led to World War II, haunts me. (See the second part of chapter 16, "Things That Go Bump in the Night," for more thoughts on this.)

I don't believe that this will happen. I expect cool heads to prevail. But an international trade war has more potential than any other event for upsetting the recovery.

I think that this will be the quarter when I become a raging bull. I will change the name of my newsletter from *Year 2000 Alert* to *The Millennium Wave* as we go from worrying about the Y2K Recession to trying to figure out how to participate in the Millennium Boom. (See chapter 18.) It will be several years until we return to the 1999 highs, but I intend to enjoy the slow ride up.

Things to do:

1. It will be time to begin to lighten up your position in bonds and to slowly increase your exposure to equities. If you bought LEAPS, it will probably be time to take your profits.

Fourth Quarter, 2000

The crystal ball is beginning to get *really* cloudy.

The recovery will continue apace, although I rather doubt that the market will go up as fast as it went down. I think that it will be several years before we see ten thousand on the Dow. But the market should be starting to trend up. If there are no major interruptions from around the world, then we should see the basis forming for a long period of prosperity. By interruptions, I mean major wars—either trade wars or hot wars. There will always be places where tensions erupt into fighting. The trick will be to isolate them so that they do not have a major effect on the world economy.

Bonds and interest rates should stay steady for some time, although rates may head back up as we get into the later stages of the bull market and the Federal Reserve starts worrying about overheating. But that is many years off. I actually hope that we will see a long period of very mild deflation. That means that prices will go lower, our retiring baby boomers on fixed incomes will not have to worry about inflation, and the economy will have good growth. It is way too early to even guess if that will happen, but if the governments of the world don't screw it up, that is what should happen.

I won't even hazard a guess as to where the markets will end the year. As long as they end *up* we should be happy, no matter what the level.

2001

We will begin the new year with a new president. With luck, we will get a statesman who can lead the world out of its problems. If we really want to stimulate the economy, we will pass a tax cut quickly.

Maybe we will have learned that waiting until the last minute to fix a major problem is not wise. Maybe we will decide to fix Social Security and Medicare before they become an actuarial nightmare for our kids (not to mention for those of us who plan to live to a ripe old age). There is potential here for a more severe problem than Y2K. It would be nice if we could bite the bullet and act now.

We will celebrate a new year without worrying about electricity and computers. This will be a much more spirited and joyous New Year's celebration than the last, as we will have a great deal to be thankful for.

Western civilization will be alive and well. We will all have come through an experience that taught us a lot, and that brought us closer together in our communities.

Amazingly, we will have learned (or at least many of us will have learned) that putting our faith in technology and government and bull markets is misguided. We will have learned that when they fail us, we can survive and do quite nicely, thank you. The values that we grew up with will come into prominence in our lives. God, family, friends, and our own two hands will become the basis for organizing our lives and our country.

As one of my early mentors told me, "Relationships are more important than things."

Things That Go Bump in the Night

I keep telling you that I am an optimist. Some of you may be starting to doubt that, but I am trying to give you a heads-up, real-world assessment of the facts and situation as we know them today. I do not expect many startlingly new facts in the first few months of 1999, but by late spring or early summer I hope that we start getting more facts instead of mostly anecdotes and happy-face press releases. I still believe that faced with the looming deadline, we will see Herculean efforts in 1999. Not enough to avoid a recession, but enough to avoid a depression, collapse, or systemic breakdown.

Now, I want a promise from you. If you read this chapter, please read the last chapter as well. This chapter contains discussions about possible events that will make you uncomfortable. I have no data that suggests that these events will ever take place, but they are concerns. The last chapter will look beyond the short-term problems, and explain why I am a long-term optimist.

That said, there are some things that worry me. The worries in this chapter are like the monsters in the closet or under the bed when we were kids. Every bump, every dog barking, every tree scraping against the window seemed to confirm our fears. Of course, no monsters ever showed themselves, but that was because our mothers' stern instructions to the monsters made them all behave.

The real problems that we face will stem from a recession, and especially a global recession. Lost jobs, reduced incomes, and stress from a tight economy are longer-term problems than a few weeks of chaotic hassles.

But what really worries me—the things which go bump in the

night—are the possibilities that can take us from a recession into a global depression. I am worried about the possible negative effects these events could have on the future we are leaving to our children. There is the potential for a generation to have their dreams shattered.

So, let's look at some of the monsters in the closet, and hope that they are only as real as the monsters we feared when we were kids.

The Counter-Party Exposure of the Largest U.S. Banks

For almost ten years, I have been a consultant to several large investment funds. I have nothing to do with the trading activities of any of the funds, but I do get to look over some large shoulders every now and then. I have gone to industry conferences, listened to seminars, and spent more than a few dinners with some of the best money managers in the world. This doesn't qualify me to trade soybeans, but I have learned a lot.

While speaking at high-level investment conferences (mostly for hedge funds), I have been exposed to discussions about "derivatives." For the most part, I am a big proponent of derivatives. Basically, they allow two parties to trade risks. If one party wants to get rid of its currency risk, and another wants to get rid of its interest-rate risk, some clever investment banker will figure out how to produce a transaction that gives them both what they want for the customary small fee.

And this works well, most of the time. It works probably 99 percent of the time.

But what makes it work is the ability of each of the institutions doing the transaction to actually hold up its end of the bargain. If one party were to experience financial difficulties and not be able to deliver on its part of the bargain, this could be a real problem to the other institution.

I want you to be clear about my concern. I am not worried about the hedge positions that banks use to limit their risks. I am not worried about derivatives per se. (In fact, I would be worried if banks didn't have them.) I am not concerned about the currency trading that banks do. Most of the things called derivatives are not bothersome if you understand them. There are some writers who play fast and loose with the facts about derivatives and try to scare people about business practices that are actually quite sound.

My concern is an international Y2K scenario in which normal assumptions about business and markets may not hold up. I am concerned about *counter-party risk.*

Our largest international banks have a combined exposure of tens of trillions of dollars in derivatives. These banks will enter into numerous transactions in efforts to reduce risk. Most of them are quite benign and hedged.

Measuring the actual risk is difficult, to say the least. For instance, if a foreign counter-party to one of our U.S. banks went bankrupt, the U.S. bank might be stuck with assuming the risk that they thought that they had gotten rid of. I say "might be," because the new owners of the bankrupt bank might decide to honor the contract, or if it has gone in the bankrupt institution's favor would keep it as a positive asset.

In normal times, the failure of a few foreign banks poses no real threat to an individual bank or country. Banks presumably make sure to distribute their risk over many countries and many institutions.

But 2000 will not be a normal time. We are going to see the potential demise of hundreds of foreign banks once thought sound, as their countries go through Y2K-related economic crises that they simply have not prepared for. And as their national economies are experiencing a collapse of services and a full-scale depression, those foreign voters are not going to look favorably on paying taxes to bail out their banks just so that our U.S. banks can get their money.

There is no way for me to quantify this risk. There is no way to know how real it is. Will U.S. banks experience some losses resulting from failed contracts with foreign banks? Absolutely. But will they be significant enough to bring down some U.S. banks? That is hard to say.

Until a few weeks ago, I had consigned this bump to the back of the closet. But the problems with the hedge fund called Long Term Capital exposed a chilling weakness in the system.

This large and well-known hedge fund imploded, causing severe problems in the world markets. Basically, they borrowed tens of billions of dollars and invested in sophisticated transactions. They borrowed about $40 for every dollar of actual capital they had.

But supposedly the investments they made were low risk. The head of the fund was a famous manager. They had not one but *two* Nobel Prize–winning economists who had designed their trading strategy. And they had compiled one of the most impressive track records anywhere. The crème de la crème of the investment world lined up to invest tens of millions in the fund. The largest banks and institutions in the world opened their loan windows, giving the fund whatever they asked for, clearly without asking too many questions. (The attitude of the fund was that if a bank asked too many questions, they would just go somewhere else. In those days, there was always somewhere else.)

The investment strategy that they employed apparently was vulnerable only if a combination of things happened, all of which were very unlikely and had never yet occurred. Times were good.

And then a funny thing happened. The circumstances that were only remotely possible actually came to pass. The investment strategy began to unravel. Rumors in the marketplace began to grow, and traders lined up to take advantage of the huge bets that Long Term Capital had placed. The problem was not necessarily the bets themselves, but the size of them. Once things began to go bad, the fund could not unwind (sell) its positions without making things worse. And it did not have enough capital to back up its positions.

Normally, when a hedge fund dies, very few people care. The Federal Reserve is notorious for its callous attitude about hedge funds. The Fed simply does *not* get involved. I can't emphasize that point enough, because when Long Term Capital had problems, they did get involved. I am convinced that it was not because all the big insiders were losing money, or that the Fed wanted to save John Meriweather, the head of the fund.

The Federal Reserve president does not call an emergency night meeting, "request" the presence of the biggest bankers and brokers in the world on a moment's notice, and tell them, "Gentlemen, we have a little problem, bring your checkbooks." Not unless there are real problems.

About two weeks after that near-meltdown, I was flying to Bermuda to speak at a hedge-fund conference. Sitting next to me was the chairman of one of the largest insurance organizations in the world. We struck up a conversation, and after awhile the conversation turned to the Long Term Capital situation. This gentleman is a power in his own right in the marketplace, and is as well connected as one could possibly be, having been on Wall Street and in its environs for over forty years.

He was well aware of what had really happened over the past few weeks, knowing many of the corporate leaders who had been in those private meetings. And his summary sent chills down my spine. To quote, "For the first time in my career, we went to the abyss and looked over. We were close to going over the edge and seeing the collapse of the banking system."

But of course the Federal Reserve stepped in and saved the day, the markets recovered, and life went on.

Why is that story important to banks and to Y2K?

In Long Term Capital we had a brilliant investment strategy designed by the best and the brightest. The investment strategies designed for our major international banks are also designed by the best and the brightest.

It took a highly improbable set of unanticipated events to bring Long Term Capital down, and in the process these events almost brought the banking system down. It would take a highly improbable set of unanticipated events to damage the large U.S. money-center banks and threaten the U.S. and world banking system.

I can tell you that Y2K is an unanticipated event. That weekend when I attended the largest hedge-fund conference in the world to talk about Y2K, the number of hedge-fund managers who took the problem seriously was a definite minority. Many told me that they thought it was either a hoax or a nonevent.

The boards of directors of the world's largest financial institutions are not anticipating the collapse of significant counter-party foreign banks.

They are not yet reserving capital for potential Y2K-related foreign loan defaults and losses. They have not considered the potential losses from the default on the national debt of countries whose Y2K status is questionable at best.

Either GartnerGroup and other research firms are wrong in their data on the international situation, or many financial institutions are asleep at the wheel.

I keep telling myself that there is not a problem. That the heads and brains in our largest institutions know what the %#^% they are doing. That the Fed will step in and do whatever it takes to make sure the system remains sound. It is simply outside of my comfort zone to really imagine that there could be a problem bigger than these wise and powerful people can figure out how to solve.

But Long Term Capital keeps bumping around in my closet.

(Do not interpret the above as a blanket criticism of "hedge funds." I am a big fan of hedge funds. They are financial vehicles that offer the potential for investors to participate in creative and profitable investment strategies managed by some of the best money managers in the world. In one respect, hedge funds are like mutual funds: there are good ones, and there are bad ones, and there are a lot in between. Investing in anything, whether mutual funds or hedge funds, requires study and due diligence. You need to know whom you are investing with and what they are doing with your funds.)

Trade Wars

There have been recessions since the Babylonians started trading with the Medes. There will always be recessions. It is a natural process, much like breathing. You cannot continue to grow forever. Eventually, optimism gives way to exuberance, and exuberance yields excess, and excess leads to headaches and recession.

But recessions, if properly planned for in the business cycle, are not without a few silver linings. A recession makes us look long and hard at our core businesses, and offers us the opportunity to make the hard decisions that we avoided during a time of plenty. Recessions help keep companies lean and more profitable over the long haul.

That said, recessions are no fun. I don't like them, and neither does anybody else, except for a few bear-market funds. Fortunately, recessions generally only last a few years, and then the boom starts again.

But sometimes, recessions turn into depressions. There is no redeeming purpose or rationale for depressions. But I know what causes them.

Government.

Or, more specifically, depressions are caused by bad policies pursued by governments in an effort to fix a perceived problem. As is often the case, when a government decides to fix a problem, it creates two more problems, often with quite unintended and unexpected consequences. Generally, these bad policies are instituted to help some group get an advantage over another group. Sometimes it is a small, insider clique that manipulates money supply, loans, and national assets to benefit a few royal families or friends of the president (*a la* Indonesia). This type of corruption always ends in disaster, as eventually the insiders start to see themselves as deserving their lifestyles and privileges and get too greedy.

Sometimes it is a war. Few things can ravage a country like war. Sometimes it is one group of voters deciding to take advantage of another. This is especially easy when the other group is in another country altogether and doesn't even get to vote.

An example of this is the urge of one country to erect trade barriers against foreign businesses, because foreign businesses are taking away jobs or are being unfair by selling that country goods and services more cheaply than it can make them.

In the late twenties and thirties, our government and the Federal Reserve leadership did some foolish things. The leaders of our country, in a series of disastrous decisions, threw the country, and then the world, into a depression. Let's quickly look at what policies caused the Great Depression.

"By early '29, the Fed was concerned about rising consumer prices and speculation in the stock market, and it started raising interest rates," said Richard Ebeling, an economist at Hillsdale College in Hillsdale, Michigan. This started choking business activity, and profits fell. By September 1929, the stock market had started to stumble. In October, it crashed.[1] Of course, part of the problem was that the Federal Reserve had artificially made money too easy to borrow and were to a large degree responsible for the excesses of the Roaring Twenties.

And in the face of a world recession, we passed the Smoot-Hawley Act and erected significant trade barriers to try to protect jobs in the U.S. that were being lost to foreign competition. We did this even though other countries had clearly indicated that they would retaliate with similar policies. In one of the most disastrous political decisions in our country's history, we sent the signal that started a wave of protectionism all over the world. In the name of protecting a few American jobs, we destroyed the global economy.

To add insult to injury, we greatly expanded the size of government and passed the largest peacetime tax increase in history. Income-tax rates went as high as 91 percent.

In the process, we pushed ourselves into a depression and the rest of the world into an even worse depression, and set the stage for dema-

[1]*Investor's Business Daily,* October 10, 1998, from an article by Charles Oliver.

gogues like Hitler, Mussolini, and Tojo to preach their form of national salvation.

It is hard for us to grasp today how bad the Depression was. The output of U.S. factories, mines, and utilities fell by more than half from 1929 to 1933. Real disposable incomes dropped by more than a fourth. The Dow Jones Industrial Average crashed to one-tenth of its pre-Depression high. Unemployment was in the high double digits for over ten years, and was as high as 20 percent. In 1939, ten years after the crash, it was still 15 percent.

I hope that we have learned our lesson. *But I am hearing bumping noises in the closet.*

Other countries' readiness for Y2K is much worse than that of the U.S. Even if we completely get our Y2K act together, I think that the international situation will be enough of a problem to throw us into a recession.

What concerns me is that as many economies around the world begin to suffer through an economic crisis and recession, their currencies will fall, and the dollar will correspondingly rise. This will give them the advantage of being able to sell their products to us more cheaply. Further, since they will be in a recession or even in a depression, they will *really* want our dollars, and will do what they have to do to get them.

Foreign competition is a good thing for consumers, because it means that they get cheaper goods. But it is bad for companies competing with these foreign companies, because they have to lower prices. The only way that they can do this is to cut costs or profits. And since we have just come through a period of "restructuring," we are supposedly already lean. All things being equal, it is possible that we'll lose a few companies (maybe a lot of companies) to global competition.

Now, in the growth periods of the eighties and nineties we have faced foreign competition in several ways. Some companies simply figure out ways to lower costs and increase productivity. Some companies lower costs by cutting jobs. Others move some or all of their production offshore to get access to cheaper labor. Some companies simply go out of business.

But since the economy has been growing so fast, there has not been a discernible overall job loss. Net job creation has been at an all-time high. In fact, in many areas of the country it is tough to find good help. You might not be able to get a job like the one that you lost, but there is a job often a better one. Good economies can mask these dislocations.

But what happens when there are no other jobs to go to? What happens when we have a recession and there are fewer jobs, and they pay less, and it is rare to find a better job? Unfortunately, that is what happens in a recession.

For the last few years there has been a growing protectionist movement in this country led by Pat Buchanan on the one side, Bob Gephardt on the other, and Ross Perot on his own side. Most of us in the Free Market School have smiled at these guys as being quaint, maybe a little dangerous, but nothing that Republicans and centrist Democrats couldn't hold at bay. (I have to give Clinton his due here: he has pushed for more-open markets, even if they are not as free as I would like them to be.)

But lately, strange alliances of liberal Democrats and conservative Republicans have been uniting to stall fast-track free-market initiatives. We see Big Steel pushing hard for trade barriers against that nasty foreign steel, and actually being listened to and publicly sympathized with by a number of former free-market proponents. And the level of rhetoric from trade unions, Ross Perot, and others has been turned up.

The bumping sound in my closet is my concern over the national elections in 2000.

First off, we will be holding primaries during the Y2K Recession, and the voting public is going to be blaming politicians (rightly enough, to a great degree) for not showing leadership and for ignoring, let alone fixing, the problems—especially the government-service problems. We will start to see real job losses, and government services will be spotty in some states through *at least* the early part of the primary season.

This is a situation ripe for "America First" campaign rhetoric from all sides of the political spectrum. Speaking bluntly, I do not think that Pat Buchanan could win a GOP primary, but he will scare the pants off less populist Republicans. His combination of protectionist policies with social conservatism will give him a strong base in 2000.

In my nightmare, it does not really matter who wins the GOP nomination (unless it is Buchanan), so I won't speculate as to who will win. I will point out that this will be a different primary season, since California's primary will be on March 6, 2000 and Super Tuesday, with Texas and Florida, will be the next week. I think that it is likely that only those candidates with the ability to raise serious sums of money will make it past the California, Texas, and Florida primaries.

On the Democratic side, all the Big Money is still talking Al Gore. But during the Y2K Recession, I think that Gore's pseudotechie profile will hurt him. He will be blamed for doing and saying nothing early on about the crisis, as he should be (as should a lot of Republicans, too). Unless someone else steps forward with the support of the traditional Democratic base, Gephardt could surprise the pundits by winning the Democratic Party nomination.

Gephardt will be running on a platform of saving America's jobs. This platform will be very appealing to the traditional Democratic base.

And once again, Ross Perot will hear the siren call of politics. It will not be like his last run, where his numbers went down because voters were not in a mood to change things too much. This time, we will be in a recession. We will be losing jobs to companies around the world. When he talks about a "giant sucking sound," people will be hearing that sound in the form of their friends or themselves losing jobs. Larry King will give him all the free time he wants. Perot is getting older, this is his last hurrah, and he will open his checkbook. (I bet he isn't long the stock market!) During a recession, his message will be more potent, and his dollars will buy more advertising time.

By November 2000, the country will be in a full recession, and though things may be turning around, the numbers demonstrating the turnaround won't show up until after January 2001. *And the country will have heard ten months of a potent "America First" message.* The mood will be dark. My fear is that many former free-market politicians on both sides of the aisle will begin to soften their stances to appease their electorates.

Will there be a strong free-market voice to counterbalance the protectionist argument heard from all sides of the political spectrum? I am afraid that there might not be.

If Perot gets enough votes, is it possible that as in 1992, a Democratic nominee will get into the White House with only 43 percent of the popular vote? President Dick Gephardt will then assert that he has a mandate to protect American jobs. And he will have a Congress that just might agree with him.

President Gephardt, with a growing coalition of protectionists, could begin to erect trade barriers in the name of "fairness." Especially if the demagoguery of both Perot and Buchanan is added to Gephardt's own rhetoric, we could see the electorate begin to believe that our recession problems are not of our own making, but rather created by those unfair foreign companies. And as the polls show a growing protectionist sentiment, our "strong-willed" politicians could see the wind and tack into it.

Just as in the 1930s, other countries will begin to respond in kind, and we will begin to lose our export base and go further into recession, and the cycle will continue, and before we know it, we will be in a depression spiral too steep to climb out of in less than a decade.

The last time we went into a protectionist mode, we gave rise to Hitler, Mussolini, and Tojo. I don't know if anyone is looking, but the world is getting very dicey. There are hot spots everywhere. It will get worse because of Y2K. If a world depression were to develop, who knows what sort of mischief might come from little demagogues wanting to use the misery of others to grab power and make themselves into big demagogues.

In my closet, trade wars are the biggest monster.

A Few Smaller Monsters

INTERNATIONAL DEBT

Foreign countries and companies borrow money from U.S. banks, the International Monetary Fund (IMF), European banks, and other international lending agencies. During a serious global recession there are going to be a lot of problems because many Third World countries will have difficulties earning the hard currencies (dollars, marks, yen) necessary to pay their debts. There are a number of countries already having difficulties.

Table 16-1 is a partial listing of the debt from countries in Status Groups 3 and 4 as determined by the GartnerGroup survey. The debt to international institutions is money owed to world lending agencies such as the World Bank or the IMF. Bilateral debt is money owed to other countries, and outstanding bonds and private debt are owed to banks and individuals. Note that the three columns do not add up to total debt, as there are other categories (such as short-term debt) that make up the grand total.

The investment markets became extremely volatile when Russia defaulted on its debt in 1998. What would happen if a series of Status 4 countries defaulted on their debt?

The good news is that when we saw a series of real problems with debt stemming from the Asian crisis, apparently the private banking community had not overextended debt to the point where it would threaten the banks themselves. It may be that much of the problem had been isolated, written off, or taken care of already.

But there is a potential for a liquidity or credit crunch if money-center banks are overexposed to countries and foreign companies that were once considered safe and that because of Y2K start to have problems. If banks have to take losses to their capital, they must then have to scramble in order to meet reserve requirements. One way to do this would be by loaning less money, even to good customers, as I mentioned earlier.

It seems likely that if government services in Status 4 countries as rated by GartnerGroup are really going to be widely and severely disrupted if exports are seriously impacted, and if electric and phone services are down, then those countries and their companies are going to have difficulty in producing the goods needed to service their foreign debts.

Much of that debt is owed to U.S. and European money-center banks, and a great deal of it is "cosigned" by U.S. taxpayers. In the past, the general trend has been to not declare the loan bad, but to "restructure" the loan, which means that the countries agree to pay the loan some day, just not today, and under new terms, which usually means that we give them even more money so that they can pretend to pay the old loans. And usually the IMF or lending agency requires the country to undergo strenuous economic restructuring, which makes the people of the country suffer a great deal.

What happens if this shell game stops? What happens if countries get so far in the hole that they see no reason to pretend that they are ever going to pay?

How can this happen? Let's use a simple analogy. Suppose that a busi-

TABLE 16-1 ▨▨▨▨▨▨▨▨▨▨▨▨▨▨▨▨▨▨▨▨▨▨

Debt Obligations of Status Group 3 and Status Group 4 Countries (U.S. millions)

	International Institutions	Bilateral	Private	Total Debt
Status Three				
Argentina	$ 16,814	$ 10,028	$ 55,429	$ 93,841
Armenia	429	122	0	552
Bulgaria	1,825	1,403	5,692	9,819
Colombia	4,765	1,738	16,472	28,859
Czech Republic	970	364	12,811	20,094
Guatemala	1,036	1,132	719	3,785
India	30,644	23,916	28,541	89,827
Jordan	1,724	4,072	1,725	8,118
Malaysia	1,404	2,816	24,489	39,777
Poland	2,175	28,335	10,309	40,895
South Africa	884	0	13,906	23,590
Sri Lanka	3,473	3,426	530	7,995
Turkey	8,370	7,494	43,389	79,789
Venezuela	4,985	1,269	26,209	35,344
Yugoslavia	1,316	3,112	6,892	13,439
Total	**$80,814**	**$89,227**	**$247,113**	**$495,724**
Status Four				
Bangladesh	$ 10,376	$ 5,323	$ 220	$ 16,083
Cambodia	261	1,821	10	2,111
Chad	799	163	17	997
China	17,696	21,737	63,977	128,817
Costa Rica	1,286	965	832	3,454
Ecuador	3,054	2,198	7,647	14,491
Egypt	4,207	23,371	1,482	31,407
El Salvador	1,552	617	129	2,894
Ethiopia	2,578	6,643	354	10,077
Fiji	130	16	53	217
Indonesia	17,250	28,911	50,642	129,033
Kenya	3,273	2,134	952	6,893
Laos	807	1,445	0	2,263
Lithuania	516	177	436	1,286
Morocco	6,532	8,840	5,797	21,767
Mozambique	1,670	3,917	70	5,842
Nepal	2,022	325	41	2,414
Nigeria	4,494	14,151	7,086	31,407
Pakistan	13,590	10,262	3,233	29,901
Philippines	8,343	12,085	12,817	41,214

	International Institutions	Bilateral	Private	Total Debt
Romania	2,697	1,994	2,785	8,291
Russia	15,270	59,924	37,777	124,785
Somalia	924	1,119	36	2,643
Sudan	2,976	5,692	2,090	16,972
Thailand	2,985	7,623	42,603	90,824
Uruguay	1,213	266	2,761	5,899
Vietnam	1,063	20,257	1,562	26,764
Democratic Republic of Congo (Zaire)	2,752	6,082	861	12,826
Zimbabwe	2,021	1,180	1,003	5,005
Total	**$132,337**	**$249,238**	**$247,273**	**$776,577**
Three and Four Total	**$213,151**	**$338,465**	**$494,386**	**$1,272,301**

ness is in debt, and is using 40 percent of its income to pay for the debt. Then a crisis hits, and the business income is cut in half. The banks tell the business, "We will lend you more money so that you can grow your way out of the problem."

But the business owner looks at the debt load, and the really harsh requirements that the banks want to impose (moving out of his home into a small apartment, old cars, beans and rice, eighty-hour weeks) and decides that he would be better off walking away and starting all over again. The owner knows that he will not be able to get any more loans, at least for a while, but he will be better off financially and living standard–wise if he simply declares bankruptcy.

The situation for a country is more complex, but at some point, in a crisis, who knows what decisions will be made in these Status 4 countries? Will international lenders allow countries to essentially not pay and still carry the loans as performing on their books? At what point is a country better off taking what cash flow it has and self-financing its recovery rather than paying the majority of its earnings to foreign banks and international lending agencies? Especially when those institutions do not vote, and the citizens have their backs against the wall because of Y2K?

There is a point at which some countries may simply decide that they are better off simply repudiating the debt entirely. This means, of course, that they will not be able to get new loans. (This threat is the only reason that they agree to continue the shell game at great cost to their citizens.) But there is a point where the costs and policies required to continue the game could be too much.

It is not inconceivable for countries to declare bankruptcy just as individuals do. To date, international lenders have found ways to keep this from happening, usually in the from of "restructuring." My guess is that they will continue to do so in the future, as banks and governments do not want to contemplate the possibilities of default. *But there is a bumping noise in my closet that makes me wonder if the game is about to come to a halt.*

LACK OF PROPER GOVERNMENT ACTION

The cornerstone of civilization is confidence. Because I have confidence in the overall scheme of things, I feel free to act and work and go about my business.

I am confident that when I write a check, my bank will move the money from my account to someone else's. I am confident that the money in my bank will be there when I need it. I am confident that my stock is at my broker's and that the trust company knows where my pension funds are.

I assume that the electric company will give me power when I want to turn on the lights. Ditto for the water, gas, and grocery store. I expect the police to patrol my neighborhood and to lock up bad guys. I expect you to drive on the right side of the road. My children expect me to provide them with food, clothes, and an education (until they become teenagers, and then they expect more).

Our culture cannot exist if we do not have confidence in things working the way they should, or at least have reason to think that they will get fixed quickly if something happens.

If our government leaders do nothing in 1999, our confidence in many systems could be severely tested.

Two things hint to me that I am not alone in my concern about confidence.

In the late summer of 1998, the Federal Reserve decided to tell the world that they have a stash of $150 billion in paper money and are planning to print another $50 billion. I can find no one who was aware of this reserve prior to that announcement. Presumably, this reserve has been around for quite some time. Frankly, this is a good thing, because it tells me that someone at the Fed was doing some worst-case-scenario contingency planning at some time in the past.

But why bring it to the public's attention? In my more cynical moments, I think that someone at the Federal Reserve was monitoring cash flow and decided that a problem was developing. The leaders of the Fed then decided that it would be appropriate to make an announcement to make sure you remained confident that if you wanted your money, you could get it.

Then, in late October, Federal Reserve governor Edward W. Kelley, Jr. seemingly reversed his position on the Y2K problem. During roughly the same time period that Lou Marcoccio was testifying to the Senate about the extent of the Y2K problem, Kelley decided that Y2K would cause no major problems. In the same statement, he did point out that if there was a liquidity crisis due to this nonproblem, the Fed was ready to step in and provide liquidity.

Both of these actions were made to help maintain confidence in the system.

Congress passed some laws in October, but there is a lot of work to do yet. Most of Congress has not yet understood the nature of the problem, and the issue is way down on the list of things to be taken up in the beginning of 1999. I hope that all of the issues below will be top priorities.

Congress must mandate that the Federal Reserve tell us which of our individual banks are compliant. They must step in to assure businesses that their deposits above $100,000 will not be at risk due to Y2K-related problems.

Congress must demand full disclosure from all public institutions, both businesses and governments, at all levels. Congress must create an environment for Y2K legal sanity so that businesses can make plans and cooperate without looking over their liability shoulders. The Securities and Exchange Commission needs to audit Y2K compliance of our public companies.

In short, we need to know what we are facing so that we can make plans to deal with whatever will happen, good or bad.

The fear of possible problems is probably much worse than the reality of what will actually happen.

That bumping sound is Congress fiddling while our confidence burns.

MEDIA SENSATIONALISM

When I asked Y2K expert Peter de Jager what was his chief concern about Y2K, he did not hesitate. He immediately said the media. Considering that he probably knows as much as anyone about the extent of Y2K problems, that answer surprised me. That question developed into a long conversation, and I had to agree that he had noticed a serious potential problem.

It is related to my concern about confidence. The media have a great deal to do with our perception of the world. How they cover a particular story will affect public perceptions about that story.

How the media cover the Y2K story will have a great deal to do with our perceptions of the problem. If they sensationalize the story, always looking for the worst case, developing the most controversial theme, or only dealing with worst-case scenarios, there is the potential for the self-fulfilling prophecy syndrome.

If we keep repeating that there is going to be a problem, we will create the problem.

I am not talking about discussing the fact that there *is* a Y2K problem, or discussing its consequences. My concern is that the media will keep predicting a cash run and in doing so motivate enough people to action and actually create a cash run on local banks. Or the media will talk about the possibility that there will be no food, so we will go from a positive storage mentality into a hoarding mentality.

Those of us who are interviewed about Y2K have noticed the tendency of some reporters to all but finish their story and then look for support for their thesis. And often, that story is crisis-oriented and sensational.

Analytical stories evidently do not appeal to many editors unless they can attach an urgent or sensational element to them. Urgency is okay, but there is a fine line between inspiring urgency and instigating panic.

And Finally

As I stated at the beginning of this chapter, there are no statistics or data that can logically promise that these possibilities will come true. But they are things that could greatly alter the course of our future. By being aware of these potential problems, we might not have to face the reality.

When you began this chapter, I asked you to promise to read the last chapter. You need to know why I am an optimist, in spite of Y2K problems and things that go bump in the night. There are more positive things happening in the world than negative ones. We need to look at how far we have come and where we are going.

Actions Government Should Take Now

For the previous sixteen chapters we have looked at how the Y2K Recession is going to affect your family, your investments, and your community. We have also looked at ways to protect yourself and to actually prosper in the face of the recession. I am sure that you join me in wishing there were something we could do to avoid this recession or reduce its effects upon our country.

Frankly, I think that it is too late to completely avoid a recession, due mainly to international problems over which we have little control. But there are a number of steps that we can take to greatly lessen the strength and duration of the Y2K Recession.

The first is obvious. We simply must fix more code. The more we fix prior to 2000, the fewer problems we will have. Those businesses and government entities that do finish their code should help their suppliers, customers, and government peer groups achieve compliance. There will be many businesses that achieve compliance well in advance of January 2000. They will have excess programming capacity. Instead of starting a new software project, perhaps these compliant firms could consider "renting" excess programming staff to their suppliers, or customers or to government agencies in an effort to insure that those entities that most directly affect their well-being are compliant as well. We should treat this just as we treat a hurricane or an earthquake. During natural disasters, communities and businesses work together in an extraordinary manner to get things back to normal.

Second, since it is unrealistic to think that we can fix all the code, the business community and governments must develop contingency plans to maintain their ability to provide their customers and citizens with goods and services. We must not wait until the last minute hoping for programming miracles. If it is clear that there is a possibility of a business service or government program being interrupted, then the earlier that we plan for the problems stemming from that interruption, the better off we will be. While this will require complete disclosure and perhaps a painful admission that some firms and agencies may not be ready, the more honest we are with each other, the better off we ultimately will be.

Those are the easy steps. Most businesses and governments are going to be taking them to some extent anyway. But there are things that government can do now to lessen the impact of a recession on this country. Waiting until October of 1999 or even worse, doing nothing, will only make things much worse than they have to be.

I am going to list some "action items" that governments and government agencies should do as soon as possible. This is by no means a complete list. It also does not provide an exhaustive explanation of the rationale for each item. It is meant to foster thought and debate. Some items are more important than others. The list does not go by order of importance, but by category of action.

Pulling Back the Curtain

One of my favorite characters on television was Vinnie (John Travolta) on "Welcome Back, Kotter." Vinnie was a little slower than some of the guys, and frequently he would exclaim in a high-pitched whine, "I'm so confused!"

There is a great deal of confusion about the Y2K Crisis. Far too many people simply do not see it as a problem. The first thing our governments should do at all levels is to make people aware of the seriousness of the problem. Federal government leaders especially should stop treating us as children who need to be comforted or kept in the dark about problems.

Besides a few brave souls like Senators Bob Bennett, Chris Dodd, and Patrick Moynihan and Congressmen Steve Horn, Pete Sessions, and a few of their congressional peers, most of what we hear is happy talk, or "lip service" in somber tones about the gravity of the situation.

If there had been realistic acknowledgement of the problem on the part of our national leaders, Congress would have passed a great deal more legislation last session. Instead, they were more concerned with stains on blue dresses on one side and the vast right-wing conspiracy on the other. There were congressmen and senators who wanted to do more. But they couldn't get enough attention focused on these issues to pass more than a stop-gap, halfway-measure liability bill.

Washington is fiddling while our nation burns.

President Clinton has appointed a very energetic and capable gentleman, John Koskinen, as the head of the President's Council on Year 2000

Conversion. The problem is that the office holds no power, has no authority, and can actually do little more than act as chief cheerleader.

The various congressional committees have done what they can to publicize the problem, short of yelling "fire" in the Senate chambers. But the Senate and House leadership have not stepped up. The Senate Majority Leader and the House Speaker must give Y2K a high and vocal priority.

We need President Clinton to address this issue in more than a sound-bite manner. He must issue a call to arms and put Y2K first on our national agenda. Every day that we procrastinate as a nation means more people out of work in 2000. Vice President Al Gore supposedly has technology as one of the chief items in his portfolio. As of the final printing of this book, he has been curiously silent.

President Clinton and the State Department must step up the level of international awareness. The leaders of the G-8 countries have met and discussed the problem, but considering the sorry Y2K-readiness state of many of those countries (Germany and Japan in particular), very little has happened. Meetings are not enough. We need actions. I'll believe that something is happening when I stop seeing press releases about "shared concerns" and "significant problems" and start seeing press releases about budgets and action plans.

There may be as many as 8 million more Americans without jobs in 2000. Every single one of those people deserves better than we are getting from our national leaders. Anything that we can do to keep even one more family employed is worth the effort. There are things that we should have done already and need to do now that can help millions of people stay employed.

The first thing that we need to do is start a national awareness program. It needs to be more than one man and a small staff. It needs to start at the top.

My advice to the politicians who want to run for president in 2000? We will be in a recession when we go to the polls in 2000. If you want to win the primary nomination and then the national election, you are going to have to point out what you did about the Y2K problem. If you did not see it coming, I think that voters are going to be dubious (and rightly so) about your qualifications for office. If you saw it coming and did not stand up vigorously and call national attention to the problem, then what type of leadership did you show?

And if you were responsible for government agencies being ready, what did you do? Were your agencies ready? Were you out in front and leading? Or were you letting others do the work while you stood by and watched?

We need leaders who will *lead* and not wait for polls to tell them what to do. It is not good enough to wait and see which way the crowd is going and then run to the front and pretend to be leading. Real leaders say "Follow me" and start moving.

What Should Government Do?

▎Require Compliance from Government Suppliers

The first thing that governments must do is demonstrate that they understand the seriousness of the problem. They can communicate their concern by passing legislation that says, "All companies that wish to do or continue to do business with our city, state, or federal agency must demonstrate that they will be Y2K compliant or provide a contingency plan that details how they will be able to continue to produce the services or products provided by their firm." These documents should be made available to the public.

▎Provide a Detailed Outline of Their Compliance or Contingency Plan

Most cities, states, and federal agencies will not be ready themselves. Nevertheless, they must do as they ask their vendors. They must demonstrate their compliance and ability to continue performing, or they must provide detailed contingency plans to show how they will provide services to their clients.

▎Pass No New Laws that Impact Y2K Preparations

Government agencies at all levels have enough to do getting ready for January 1, 2000. No laws should be passed unless it can be demonstrated that they will not have an impact on Y2K readiness.

▎Pass Laws Mandating Full Disclosure

After public companies basically ignored the requests by the SEC for Y2K disclosures, in the summer of 1998 the SEC issued new guidelines requiring disclosure about Y2K compliance for all public companies. I testified before Congress a few weeks after these new guidelines were issued. I told the committee that the proposed guidelines did not have the teeth that they needed to have. I predicted that until we got strong legislation with serious penalties we would see disclosures written by lawyers that told us as little as possible. Both Chairman Horn and Vice Chairman Sessions said that they would be watching.

The first round of disclosures are coming in as I write this book. It appears that I was right. While some companies are commendably coming forward and trying to comply with the intent of the guidelines, others are simply dodging the issue.

Shareholders are the owners of the company. They deserve full and complete disclosure of all material facts about a company in order to be informed investors. And while companies can and do state that the amount of money that they are spending on Y2K issues is "not material," the costs of *not* being compliant are *far more significant* than the money spent to fix the problem. The SEC ruling leaves open the possibility for companies to not disclose issues, or to selectively decide what to disclose and how to spin their disclosures.

Companies should not only be required to disclose information about their Y2K status, but should also file quarterly progress reports, assessments of risk from their vendors and customers, and an analysis of any particular litigation issues facing the company.

The byword for disclosure should be more rather than less, sooner rather than later. This legislation must be passed quickly. There should also be provisions for random audits and funds provided to hire consultants to do those audits. It goes without stating that waiting until the summer of 1999 to pass this law is almost pointless.

And while Congress is writing these laws, it would be helpful to require full disclosure from all government agencies, from the largest federal bureaucracy down to the smallest cities.

▌ *Limit Liability and Legal Costs*

In all fairness to the companies worried about disclosure, the legal liability surrounding Y2K is enormous. When Lloyd's of London predicts $1.1 trillion in legal costs and damages, companies are rightly scared. Congress did pass laws limiting legal liability to some extent, but I think that if we are going to require full disclosure, we cannot allow companies to be sued using the contents of the disclosure. It is the same principle as not being required to testify against yourself.

The laws that we passed were a good start. We need to go further. We need to also talk about how to limit the legal liability and damages. If we add $1 trillion in damages and legal costs on top of a major recession, we could prolong the recession for a long time. I do not believe in allowing fraudulent or irresponsible behavior to go unchecked, but I am afraid that lawyers will be suing every supposed deep pocket looking for settlements. That is the way many lawyers play the game.

One very good way to hold down the frivolous lawsuits is to require that the loser pay the legal costs of the winner. While this would be a good practice to have for the whole of our legal system, we should at least enact it for Y2K-related lawsuits. We might find that it works very well and want to expand the concept, which is why every trial lawyer in America will fight this tooth and nail. But we must not allow the trial lawyers' lobby to prolong the Y2K Recession and keep innocent people from keeping their productive jobs.

We should also aggressively press the other nations of the world to enact laws similar to ours that will limit the liability and legal costs associated with full disclosure. It is not fair to require full disclosure in the U.S. that will result in a lawsuit in Europe. The playing field should be made level throughout the world.

Require Independently Audited, Full Disclosures from Utilities and Telephone Companies

We need to pay special attention to our utilities and telephone companies. I think that it would be better for these issues to be handled on a state level by the local public utility commissions in each state.

Utilities and telecommunications companies have benefited from monopoly or near-monopoly status. The services that they provide are basic to our lives. We need not only disclosure but in-depth outside auditing of these institutions. If there is going to be a problem, we need to know as soon as possible, and if there isn't, then we need to concentrate our contingency efforts elsewhere.

Frankly, having to worry about my power company is a major pain. I would like an independent audit that can tell me whether or not to expect a real problem. I can see no reason why we shouldn't have such an audit. I expect the companies will not be thrilled to have to go through the process, but considering the position they hold and the importance of their service, I don't have a lot of sympathy for anything less than complete cooperation with independent audits.

Require Complete Disclosure from the Federal Reserve

In chapter 5 I addressed the need for the Federal Reserve to disclose which banking institutions are not compliant. I think that this should occur no later than September of 1999. These institutions can either be merged, sold, shut down, or taken over. We must not risk public confidence in the banking system at large in order to protect a small percentage of banks whose management did not have their act together.

This is absolutely critical, in my opinion. To put it bluntly, we are putting at risk the entire fractional reserve banking system. I have cited various studies that show that alarming numbers of people are planning to pull all or substantially all of their deposits from the banking system prior to the end of 1999. They are doing this out of a studied self-interest. They are doing it because they do not trust the banks to maintain their computer systems.

We must do everything possible to assure the people of this country that their money is safe. The only way to do this is complete, transparent, and independent disclosure. For the Federal Reserve to wait until there is a crisis *will only insure* that there will be a crisis.

Further, the Federal Reserve must act to provide special accounts from mid-December 1999 through February 2000 that allow banks to maintain customer assets but that do not expose business deposits over $100,000 to the FDIC liability limits. If something on this order is not done, we are risking a severe credit crunch and liquidity crisis. Congress needs to pass laws allowing the Federal Reserve broad authority to maintain liquidity during the rollover period, including the establishment of these special accounts.

(For a more complete review of the necessity for these actions, see chapter 5.)

Cut Taxes Now

One proven recession-busting action is a deep, across-the-board tax cut. We need to do this preemptively, and not wait until we are already mired in recession. We need to slash capital-gains taxes, institute programs to encourage new businesses (and thus new employment), and rescind the 1994 Clinton tax surcharges, making more money available for taxpayers to spend.

Waiting until 2000 when we are in a recession will only postpone the recovery, prolong high unemployment, and serve to increase government deficits, as profits and incomes will be down longer than necessary.

Open Up Immigration for Those with Programming Skills

We are short 300,000 programmers. We should allow any foreign national with programming skills who would like a work visa and has a job commitment to come to the U.S. as soon as possible. While this will deplete programming skills in foreign countries, we must balance this depletion with the fact that we are the economic engine for the world. The sooner we are back to full compliance status, the sooner we will begin to come out of our recession, and the sooner we can pull other countries out of their recession.

Put the National Guard on Alert

Canada has done it. England has done it. Watch as every nation in the world does it. Will we need the National Guard? I don't know, but I want them ready with contingency plans for a variety of scenarios, such as civil unrest, transportation difficulties, communication problems, water shortages, and power loss. It will be nice if we don't need them. But if we do, they need to be prepared and have a well-thought-out plan.

International Issues

The remaining proposals deal with the risk posed by Y2K from outside our borders: loss of imports and exports, global recession or depression, military crises, and the simple problems of helping Third World countries come back from the loss of serious infrastructure breakdown.

Eighty percent of the world's population lives in countries that are going to experience severe problems. If I lived in those countries, I would be part of the doom-and-gloom crowd. I would be trying to figure out how to take my family and leave. These countries are going to suffer severe losses of power, telephones, transportation, and other infrastructure systems. The problems will have severe economic consequences, and in some cases will result in shortages of food and basic medical services. The temptation for revolutions, military coups, and outside aggression will be high. The Y2K problem in many countries is going to produce a highly unstable environment with consequences that we can only guess at. But many of the guesses are not pleasant to contemplate.

It is in the best interest of the United States and the rest of the developed world that the problems from Y2K be as limited as possible, and solved as quickly as possible in the developing world. Otherwise, the loss of world trade and strategic materials could be serious, and the costs of military action could be budget-busting. I am reminded of that line from the old commercial, "Pay me now or pay me later!"

Establish a Central International Y2K Commission

Just as every business needs to check how Y2K problems are affecting their suppliers and customers, and if necessary help them become compliant, the U.S. needs to make sure that the nations of the world that are our customers and suppliers get the help they need.

The U.S. immediately needs to establish a central office that will help developing nations solve their Y2K problems in the areas of power, telephones and transportation. U.S. exports and imports combined are over

$1 trillion! Spending a few billion now to make sure that these countries are impacted for as briefly as possible is crucial.

We need to provide technical assistance, funds, and training. In some cases, emergency equipment for power and phones may be required. We need to help the world's governments develop and implement contingency plans that will maintain minimal operational services until the various elements of the infrastructure are fixed.

While there are some minimal assistance programs available managed by various world organizations, nothing of any major impact is currently observable. Most of the programs deal with "education" or "awareness" and produce little substance.

Part of the project must be a major effort by the president and our leaders to communicate the urgency of the problem. The project must be headed by a high-profile leader, who must be given the resources to do as much as possible in as short a time as possible.

I understand that there is not enough time to fix the problem. But the sooner the effort is started, the sooner it will get fixed. Waiting until January 2000 and reacting to emergencies in scores of countries throughout the world are not acceptable. We will not have the resources to deal with all of the problems unless we begin to plan now how to respond. We will not know how to effectively respond unless we make some effort today to determine the depth of the problems in every country at risk.

I can see four real objections to this sort of program:

a. If we do not seem to be able to get our own governmental software fixed, how can we hope to help other countries?

The fact is that we are in better shape, as poor as it is, than any other country. Helping other countries get their problems solved should not detract from our internal efforts.

b. Just as we cannot be the policeman to the world, so we cannot be the world's Y2K savior.

I would suggest that just as there are times (albeit quite few) that military force is justified, there are also times when we must recognize a certain sense of responsibility as the largest party in the world's economy and the leader of the free world. I find it morally reprehensible that we could stand by and watch hundreds of millions suffer and do nothing.

c. This program could conceivably cost several billions of dollars and will be just one more example of government waste.

The answer is a straightforward economic cost-benefit analysis. How many billions of dollars of tax revenues will we lose as a result of lower corporate profits and lost income due to direct export losses and the difficulty of importing strategic materials? How many billions of tax dollars will we spend on unemployment, Social Security, and welfare? How many billions of lost tax revenues from lower income and Social Security tax receipts will result from unemployment due to export losses?

Further, funds could be diverted from the current budgets of a variety of agencies. The obvious point personnel in each country would be the commerce and state department personnel stationed at embassies and consulates. I would argue that we have no more pressing diplomatic or commercial agenda than the continued economic survival of the nations of the world.

d. This project should be done as a joint effort with the United Nations or the G-8 countries.

With all due respect, the UN or a coalition of the G-8 countries could not organize a three-man parade in the time we have remaining. We should enlist their support, and work with anyone, but this is one time when we need to act and lead unilaterally. If the rest of the world wants to get involved, fine—the more the merrier. But trying to organize a "world Y2K coalition" is a waste of time that we don't have. That is why we need a high-profile leader like former president Bush, General Colin Powell, or General Norman Schwartzkopf who can command the attention of the world's leaders and elicit cooperation because of their international stature.

Assess Our Dependence on and Supply of Strategic Materials

There are minerals and products that our nation needs to function properly. We import 50 percent of our oil. In chapter 8 (Table 8–1) I listed numerous materials absolutely vital for U.S. industry. We need to assess the ability of our trading partners to continue to provide a smooth flow of these strategic materials, and if it appears that there will be a problem, we need to move to alleviate it as soon as possible. This is especially true for items of military importance and agricultural importance.

Free Trade Is the Solution, Not the Problem

In 2000, the world is going to be mired in a recession, the worst in more than sixty years. Much of the world will be in outright depression. The best way to shorten the period of this recession and the inevitable pain is to expand, not diminish, free trade. Congress needs to grant "fast-track authority" for trade agreements as quickly as possible, and the president needs to move on establishing new free-trade agreements. The best free-trade agreements are those that are short and have few limits.

It is unthinkable that Texas would impose economic barriers against products from California simply because those products hurt Texas workers. The U.S. at large benefits from free trade within its borders. We should expand those economic borders to include as many countries as will reciprocate with true free-trade agreements. We all will benefit, just as Texas and California benefit from free trade with each other and with the rest of the states. Freer trade will lift the world out of recession sooner and give our U.S. consumers access to cheaper products, thereby raising our standard of living.

Agree to Military Cooperation

The U.S. should exchange high-ranking officers with other nuclear powers and station them at nuclear facilities throughout the world. These officers should have the ability to communicate independently with their counterparts in their home countries. As we have already documented, there is reason to be concerned about the early-warning systems of other nuclear powers. The exchange of officers will allow physical verification of no missile activity no matter what the computer screens say, or even if they go blank.

The opportunity will exist for some rogue nations to start military actions against their neighbors while there is confusion stemming from power and communications losses. We should consider enlisting the G-8 countries and the UN in imposing a period of time after 2000 (say, six months) in which no military actions may be taken by one country against another. Of course, in order for this to be effective, there must be real sanctions for any military activity up to and including a no-warning response by combined military forces. Negotiating with one country while it is taking over another country is not going to be effective. There would have to be immediate and severe responses to those who start wars in this period. (The name Saddam Hussein specifically comes to mind.)

It would be interesting to see which countries would oppose such a measure.

Devise Contingency Plans for Food Shortages

Many countries depend upon imports of food for their survival. Y2K may pose an extra element of risk to some of these countries. We should assess the problem and in conjunction with world relief organizations and world governmental bodies develop contingency plans for making sure that no country is without the food to feed its people. It is quite possible that we will be confronted with more crisis situations in a short period of time than ever before. If the world waits to develop plans for response, there is the potential for a great deal of suffering and many lost lives. The U.S. should lead in organizing a coordinated response to possible crisis situations resulting from Y2K problems.

The Millennium Wave

Let others praise ancient times,
I am glad that I was born in these.

—Cicero (106–43 b.c.)

There are forces and events that change the course of history. Countries rise and fall, markets grow and collapse, from the effects of these forces. I like to think of these forces as waves.

Like the tide, a true wave can't be stopped. It becomes a force in itself. It will run until it finally spends its power. Large waves can have an effect upon human affairs for centuries.

To show you what I mean, let's look at just a few of the dozens of major waves of the past millennium.

Gunpowder changed the way that wars were fought. No longer could a feudal lord stay securely in his castle during a siege. Gunpowder was a great equalizer between the well-armored knights and the commoner. Old feudal empires fell, and new nations arose, because of gunpowder.

The Reformation shaped the way that the Western world approached life and business by infusing a new ethic of productivity and a positive, progressive, and linear view of time.

Harnessing the power of *electricity and the internal combustion engine* made it possible for one man to do the work of many, thus dramatically changing the division of labor. Because of these discoveries, our country moved from a rural, agricultural nation to an urban, business, and enterprise-oriented society.

The Industrial Revolution changed the way that whole economies were organized and paved the way for a great economic expansion.

Some of the power of the above waves is still being felt today. Over the last twenty years, we have seen the introduction of new waves and an exponential increase in the power of already-existing waves that are bringing about change at a pace and on a scale never before seen in history.

For seventeen chapters we have looked at the causes of the Y2K Recession and what our responses should be. We have tried to get a picture of what is likely to transpire as we move into the next millennium.

I believe that the Y2K Recession is just a passing moment in history. Clearly, it has the potential to be an intense moment, and for the unprepared it will be a difficult and seemingly endless moment. But it will pass. It is just a recession, and there are forces of growth at work that will overwhelm the forces of recession.

The Y2K Recession is an aberration. *It is not a wave.* It shouldn't have happened. Historians will look back one hundred years from now and note the irony of a brief, but severe, global recession caused by a simple programming decision that interrupted an ongoing global expansion.

There are six waves combining to produce the growth and prosperity that we see in the world today. I call this combination the *Millennium Wave.*

The same forces that produced the current period of growth and prosperity are not going to go away because of a recession or even a depression, for that matter. The Millennium Wave will come up to the Y2K Recession and roll right past it.

I am not unaware of the tragedy and losses that will be produced by a recession in the U.S. and a depression in the rest of the world. I do not want to make light of the effects of the Millennium Bug.

But I truly believe that the effects will be short-lived *if governments do nothing to prolong the problem.* If you prepare properly for the Y2K Recession, you should be ready to take advantage of the Millennium Wave.

Six Inexorable Forces That Will Shape the New Millennium

GROWTH OF FREEDOM WORLDWIDE

Beginning in 1776 with the Declaration of Independence, the nations of the world have been changing their forms of government to that of democracy. With the fall of the Berlin Wall and the collapse of Communism, the number of countries free to move toward full-fledged democracy has increased dramatically.

Very rarely do countries move overnight to a free-market democracy. It takes time for all the internal forces to come together. But many countries that only a few years ago were mired in what seemed like hopeless dictatorships are beginning to take steps down the road to democracy.

Russia, which is an economic basket case, holds elections. We may not like the outcomes, but they are elections nonetheless. Dictatorships in Latin America, once the norm, are now the exception. Oligarchies in Asia are one by one surrendering to democracy.

It is not always a straight-line parade of progress. Sometimes it is the two-steps-forward, one-step-back form of progress. But measuring progress over decades and not from year to year, we can see a clear movement toward greater and greater personal freedom. The exceptions prove the rule.

I remember doing emergency drills in elementary school as a preparation for nuclear attacks. No one dreamed that the Soviet Union would one day collapse and that some of its satellites would be moving to free-market democracies and pressing to join NATO. Today, it is hard to imagine Iraq or North Korea as anything but monolithic dictatorships, but one day those regimes too will fall.

Our American forefathers loosed the democratic wave upon the world. It is a wave that will continue to roll forward, because the benefits of being free, when contrasted with the costs of dictatorships, are truly overwhelming. The benefits are there for all the world to see.

GROWTH OF FREE MARKETS

Just because a country begins to hold elections and allow more freedom to its people does not mean that it will have free markets. In fact, at the beginning stages of democracy there are usually tight controls on markets. The trend as of the past few decades, however, has been clear. The growth of true free markets and free trade in the world's economy today is dramatic when compared to that of forty or twenty or even ten years ago.

Free trade has been the foundation for the economic growth that we have seen in the world. And little by little free trade is expanding. China has let the free-market genie out of the bottle. The Chinese people seem particularly adept at pursuing free enterprise and entrepreneurial activities. As the Chinese slowly free themselves from market controls, they are experiencing rapid growth and a newfound level of personal wealth.

Free markets work. Admittedly, as markets are opened, there are winners and losers, but the winners always outnumber the losers.

One nation after another is entering into free-trade agreements with their neighbors. This trend will continue. The North American continent is for all practical purposes becoming a giant free-trade zone. Europe is moving toward a true free-trade zone. Countries in Latin America, Africa, and Asia are establishing their own free-trade zones.

As free trade expands, the world's economy will continue to grow, and so will our own prosperity. Our exports will grow, our access to less-expensive foreign goods will enhance our economic lifestyle, and exciting new investment opportunities will arise.

THE INFORMATION REVOLUTION

Computers are a tool, but knowledge is power. Five years ago, researching a book like this would have taken years, and I would have missed scores of important sources. Today, I can have my search engines bring me dozens (sometimes hundreds) of Y2K-related stories from all over the world every morning. I can exchange ideas with authorities on a variety of topics. I can send out a chapter for comments to twenty different experts and get back comments in a few hours or the next day.

If you are an investor, you can research a company in detail. There are web sites that allow investors in even very small companies to communicate with each other and share what they know. You can follow your investments on a minute-by-minute basis if you want to, learn of potential new investments, find less expensive ways to place orders, and execute complex transactions directly over the Internet.

You can buy this book and hundreds of thousands more on the Internet. You can buy cars, homes, tools, and almost anything else that you can imagine, often saving significant percentages over regular retail buying.

You can move your money from your local bank to another country in the blink of an eye. You can bypass traditional news services and get information directly from the original sources. You can instruct your computer to look for stories on specific topics of your choosing. If you are a student, the libraries of the world are open to you on the Internet.

I could go on and on. But as far as we have come in the past ten years, we have just scratched the surface. The availability of information is increasing exponentially. For all the hype about the Internet, it really is going to change the way that the world does business. It will open up opportunities for everyone, regardless of race, sex, age, physical appearance, or handicap. It is perhaps the greatest equalizer in the history of the world. It makes small one-man operations potentially as significant as large corporations. One of my favorite cartoons is a picture of a Labrador retriever talking to another dog as he types into a computer, telling him, "On the Internet, nobody cares if you are a dog."

The Internet is inherently deflationary. Now you can shop prices on products all over the world, and not just around the corner. Business structures are going to change. Retail systems are going to change.

The *information revolution* makes the growth in freedom and free markets even more powerful. Freedom of information isn't conducive to controlled markets and totalitarian governments. Totalitarian regimes have to either totally isolate their citizens, thereby severely limiting their economies, or deal with an increasingly informed citizenry. As citizens in repressed societies learn about the options that people like them have in other countries, and see their wealth and the other benefits of freedom, their hunger for freedom and free markets grows.

In today's world, it is difficult to compete unless you are willing to join the information society. In ten years, it will be impossible. The nations of the world will start to divide along the lines of those with totally open and relatively cheap access to information and those without it.

Authors James Dale Davidson and Sir William Rees-Mogg point out in *The Sovereign Individual* that in the future governments will be limited in their taxing ability as more and more people are no longer limited to living in any one country in order to earn a superior living. Countries will begin to compete with each other for new business on the basis of low taxes. I recently spoke at a conference where ten countries (including one European country!) aggressively courted new job-producing business enterprises, and each country featured their lower taxes and reduced regulatory environments as inducements.

One hundred thousand dollars in saved taxes grows to $6 million in forty years at only 10 percent compound tax-free growth. At 15 percent compound interest it grows to over $25 million! The sheer magnitude of these numbers is going to increase the motivation for those who can escape oppressive tax regimes to do so, and the pressure on governments to lower taxes is going to increase so as to not drive away these productive people. The last holdout will probably be the U.S., but it will happen even here.

THE DEVELOPMENT OF NEW TECHNOLOGIES

As much as technology has changed our lives in this last century, the next few decades will hold changes more dramatic than all the changes in the twentieth century combined. I can think of no more exciting time to live than now. The only time more exciting will be that of my children.

There are three technologies that hold tremendous promise in the next few decades.

The *computer revolution* is barely into its fourth decade. The difference between the power and the cost of the computers of only ten years ago, not to mention forty, is dramatic. The difference over the next twenty years is going to be even more so. Increased power combined with decreased cost will allow for tremendous new cost-saving technologies. Plus, as automation of assembly and manufacturing lines increases, we will have the ability to customize everything from clothes to cars to manufacturing equipment.

The *biotechnology revolution* has the potential to be every bit as powerful as the computer revolution has been, generating a wide array of new companies with technologies for extending our lives, preventing and healing diseases, and more efficiently feeding and clothing us. There are many of us at midlife today who will live to see a robust one hundred years. My children will be part of the first generation to celebrate the coming of two centuries, thanks to the life-enhancing and life-prolonging drugs and biotechnologies that lie just around the corner.

The *quantum revolution* (the change in the way that we think about the forces of the molecular world) will allow us to build increasingly smaller and cheaper machines, opening the way for a vast array of new technologies. Later in the third or fourth decades of the twenty-first century, fusion-powered electric plants will give us unlimited clean power at a fraction of the current cost. There are a number of new low-cost power sources that offer the potential to rival the internal combustion engine early in the next century. Plus, there are dozens of new developments in lasers, ceramics, and metals that will offer significant improvements in our quality of life.

This wave of new revolutionary technologies will produce the next major wave affecting our world, *deflation.*

DEFLATION: LOWER PRICES DUE TO IMPROVED PRODUCTIVITY

With each advance in technology, new products and processes become possible. As the free market expands and as information about new research is more quickly disseminated, businesses will be quicker to adopt new ideas that can make them more efficient and thus more competitive in global markets.

While this will mean that companies will be constantly reinventing themselves in order to stay profitable, it will also mean that consumers will be offered more goods and services at ever-lower prices. In an inflationary world, the losers are those who save and are on a fixed income. In a deflationary world, these same people become the winners. In deflation, the losers are those who fail to adapt.

THE REESTABLISHMENT OF VALUES

There is little doubt that the twin pressures of modern technology and a modern lifestyle have eroded the family unit, seemingly lowered acceptable standards of civilized behavior, and redefined the nature of relationships at all levels, from civic relationships (the way we relate to our community and our country) to personal and family relationships. The twentieth century has not been kind to the human spirit.

There is reason to believe that this trend is beginning to reverse itself. I think that historians will look back on our time and see the reemergence of the importance of values and character as the basis for relationships. If there is a silver lining to the Y2K problem, it will be that it causes us to think about those things in which we place our trust.

Davidson and Rees-Mogg, cited above, see that in our future world, as relationships are forged across continents through electronic means, a person's reputation will ride on his or her ability to develop trust as well as on his or her technical abilities. If you cannot be trusted, you will not find anyone to work with you.

The scholarly and celebrated authors of *The Fourth Turning* (see appendix A) predict that the new generation that will achieve ascendancy early in the next century will place a high premium upon character and values.

This is a book about economics and finance. I do believe that character and values will have a great deal to do with how prosperous we will become in the future. I am going to resist the temptation to discuss this topic at length in the book proper. For those interested in a brief discussion of this point, please see appendix D.

A Few Final Thoughts

We have covered a lot of territory in this book. I am sure that much of what you have read is troubling to you. I have tried to present to you the facts as we know them today so that you can understand the basis for my advice.

You are going to hear a lot of conflicting information over the next year. On the one hand will be the Pollyannas. Pay no attention to them until they have hard data disputing software-delivery times or news that the nations of the world have fixed their systems. Y2K will not go away by wishing upon a millennial star.

You will hear and read even more doomsday stories. My sincere suggestion is that every time you get depressed about Y2K, you get the most recent *Forbes* magazine and read every article about how some business is succeeding. It will remind you that America is a nation of powerful, creative entrepreneurs and competent, concerned managers.

Fear is paralyzing. If you begin to live in fear, you will not do the things that you must in order to deal with the Y2K Recession. Y2K may set us back, but it won't knock us out.

I simply cannot understand those who think that the forces described above will simply disappear. Will we forget the technological advances of the last century? Will the spirit that built this nation evaporate in the face of a simple, known problem? I look back in our history, and it seems to me that we have faced much worse situations before. Given the choice of any of our wars or depressions of the last two centuries or Y2K, I would choose Y2K every time. We came through those crises, and we will survive this one and go on into the new millennium with more promise than any country has ever had in the history of man.

The message of this book is simple. *Y2K is not a matter of survival. It is an economic problem.* There is a recession coming. Yes, there will be a brief period at the beginning of the next millennium in which it will cause some serious disruptions in our normal lifestyles.

But you can *survive* the period of disruptions and *prosper* in the recession if you *start now* to make a plan and then execute it.

If you do, you will be in excellent shape to take advantage of the next long period of prosperity: the Millennium Wave. But that's another book.

Information Resources

This appendix has three main sections: Y2K Information Resources (web sites and books), Investment Resources (web sites and newsletters), and Suggested Reading. Where appropriate, I have added my personal comments.

Y2K INFORMATION RESOURCES:

WEB SITES:

Web sites of the author:

My public web site is *www.2000wave.com*. Throughout this book I have told you that I would keep you updated on a variety of public issues. I will follow the promised stories, plus provide the following:

1. Links to the sites featured below, plus links to dozens of other sites, and a lengthy section on Y2K resources.
2. My own commentary on recent Y2K news stories of public concern.
3. At least once a week we will do a digest and links to the most important Y2K stories to those who will give me their e-mail address.
4. *The Mauldin Millennium Interviews,* which feature interviews with a variety of Y2K experts.
5. Links to the various web sites of state and federal agencies so that you can gauge the progress of government agencies which affect you the most.
6. My speaking and radio/television appearances.

The *Year 2000 Alert Newsletter* web site is for subscribers to the investment newsletter that I edit (see below). In general, this is where I write about investments. Readers of this book may subscribe to the newsletter at a discount (see below). The address is *www.2000alert.com*. In addition to the above:

1. Specific advice on investment opportunities, discussion of timing issues on investments, plus my commentary on how Y2K is affecting the investment markets.
2. Subscribers can e-mail me at this site and I or my staff will try to answer your questions.

I have a web site for accredited investors at *www.accreditedinvestor.com*. This web site deals with issues and opportunities affecting accredited investors (see chapter 12), including general information on hedge funds. There is a general section and a password-protected section for accredited investors. Inside the password-protected section are links to numerous sites of interest to high-net-worth individuals. The password protection on this section is a requirement of U.S. security laws. I have no desire to exclude anyone, but the rules are such that you must be an accredited investor to get information about private offerings. In the interest of full disclosure, I am a partner in a firm that is a general partner in several privately offered hedge funds. The web site is not a promotional site for our funds, but a general information site and a service to the accredited-investor community at large.

Other Y2K information web sites:

Westergaard 2000. *http://www.y2ktimebomb.com/*

One of the best Y2K sites on the net. The Westergaard site is becoming a very good site for sparking debate, and since almost everyone involved with Y2K reads it daily, it is a good place to find out what Y2K gurus are thinking. They have assembled a broad range of writers, some who contribute weekly and others sporadically. I write columns from time to time, as it is a good way to disseminate information and/or opinions about Y2K issues quickly. Westergaard will send you a daily e-mail with summaries of—and links to—the new articles. When I said that there is a wide range of writers, that means that there is not agreement among the contributors. I am not endorsing the editorial content of any one writer, but the site in general.

Dr. Ed Yardeni. *http://www.yardeni.com*

Dr. Ed Yardeni is the chief economist for Deutsche Bank Securities. He was the first significant Wall Street economist to address the Y2K issue. To date, none of his peers have elected to join him. Yardeni is one of the more quoted authorities on Y2K and is often seen on various TV shows. He has a lengthy report on the web, which he updates, on a variety of Y2K topics. His site also has a wealth of economic data unrelated to Y2K. He only does a new update on Y2K every few weeks, but when he does, I immediately read it.

CBN (Christian Broadcasting Network). *http://www.cbn.org/y2k/ index.asp*

This site has a good daily information update, edited by Drew Parkhill, the CBN News Y2K editor. In it, you can find not only current stories, but an archive of stories covered by CBN on Y2K. CBN has given the Y2K issue more coverage than other television networks. I enjoy reading Parkhill's comments, even when I don't agree with him.

Y2K Press Clippings. *http://www.year2000.com/y2karticles.html*

Peter de Jager is a leading figure in Y2K circles. He was the first to really publicize the extent of the problem and create awareness of the issue. This portion of his web site is like a traditional newspaper "clipping service." Each day links to nearly every one of the articles on Y2K from papers all over the world are posted on the site, along with their headlines. Reading through all of the articles can be daunting. If you want someone to sift through them for you and pull out the important ones, come to my site. If you are doing original research, though, this is one of the best sites. You can go to the home page for more of de Jager's writings.

General Accounting Office (GAO) Year 2000 Computing Crisis. *http://www.gao.gov/y2kr.htm*

The GAO has a good web site and is pretty good about trying to give us their real opinion about the progress levels of various government agencies. It will be interesting to see their analysis as we get closer to the end of 1999 and there are still half a dozen major agencies way behind. I hope they don't succumb to the pressure to toe the happy-face party line. We need to know exactly what to expect.

House Subcommittee on Government, Management, Information, and Technology. *http://www.house.gov/reform/gmit/y2k/*

This is the Y2K site maintained by the U.S. House of Representatives. It contains committee testimony and the ever-popular Federal Government Y2K Report Card. Congressman Stephen Horn (Republican of California) chairs the committee and Congressman Pete Sessions (Republican of Texas) is vice chair. These gentlemen are solid and outspoken. I testified before this committee in August 1998, and they were kind enough to mention some of my remarks in their latest report. Horn and Sessions are straight shooters, and I doubt that they will allow any pressure to color their analysis.

Senate Special Committee on the Year 2000 Technology Problem. *http://www.senate.gov/~y2k/*

Maintained by the U.S. Senate, this site contains committee testimony, press releases, and survey results. It is organized by industry segment, which is how the hearings have been grouped, and it is useful for that reason, although most of the presentations by industry spokesmen are happy talk. Senator Bob Bennett (Republican of Utah), who calls himself "the Paul Revere of Y2K," chairs the committee. The vice chairman is Senator Christopher Dodd (Democrat of Connecticut). Both these gentlemen have shown some backbone and a willingness to get in the face of industries who are slow in giving us full disclosure. Ninety-eight more senators need to follow their lead.

President's Council on Year 2000 Conversion. *http://www.y2k.gov/*

This is the Clinton administration's official Y2K site. John Koskinen is the president's Y2K czar. This site is remarkable for what it doesn't contain. Read it and get a grasp of why we are in trouble.

Apocalypse Now

There are two sites that I read that are authored by people far more apocalyptic than I am. If you can't deal with someone who will challenge your thinking, I suggest you avoid these sites.

The first is a site by Dr. Gary North. He has become the de facto leader of the doom-and-gloom camp. Since I believe in full disclosure, I will tell you that I have been a friend of North's for over fifteen years and twelve years ago was CEO of the corporation that published his investment newsletter. I disagree with him about his Y2K approach and his analysis of the extent of the problem and of the response to the problem. That said, he has a terrific web site if you are doing research on Y2K. Since he is a researcher, he has built a web site for those who want to do research. He has more links to news stories and articles than anyone. He conveniently groups them by general category and by date. He also comments on them, and his comments are acerbic, to say the least. They can also be humorous. This web site is why North is quoted so often, because any reporter wanting background on a Y2K story will usually end up on this site. I read North because he makes me think. He is especially good at making me examine my presuppositions, which is where I generally find that my disagreement with the doomsday approach stems from. Web site: Gary North's Y2K Links and Forums. *http://www.garynorth.com/*

I do not know who writes the second site, *y2knewswire*. He or she wants to remain anonymous. This person has a first-rate mind, and poses some very hard questions that need answers. There are usually a few references to current stories, which is typical of lots of sites, but the author's comments I find interesting. You can get them sent to you daily. The site is supported by a supplier of survivalist items. Web site: *http://www.y2knewswire.com/*

There are dozens of other sites, and new ones popping up every week. The above are the ones I go to frequently. I have links to others on my web site.

Y2K Preparedness

Many of my readers may want or need to take a more aggressive approach to physical preparations. For instance, if I lived in the country and my rural electric coop had not yet started an assessment of its Y2K situation, I would be far more concerned than I am now, living where I do. For that matter, if I lived anywhere and my utility companies were behind in their remediation efforts, I would be quite concerned. More extensive preparations would be quite appropriate. There are dozens of sites that I could recommend. Here are three sites that I suggest you start with, and they have links to many more sites. From these three sites and their links, you will be able to find anything you could possibly want to know about Y2K preparedness and survival. I personally know Mike Hyatt and Karen Anderson, and Yourdon's reputation and credentials are impeccable. I think that when you are dealing with something as controversial as this topic that it is important to start with people you know are levelheaded. You can spend days planning to get prepared just reading these.

Ed Yourdon's preparation site: *http://www.readyfory2k.com/*

Yourdon (see site review below) has an excellent preparedness site. He is the author of *Time Bomb 2000*. I am not a survivalist, and I still spent a lot of time reading the information and searching the links. He has lots of links and has done a lot of homework for you.

Mike Hyatt's preparation site: *http://www.michaelhyatt.com/*

Mike Hyatt is the author of the best-seller *The Millennium Bug*. We correspond and talk occasionally, and I admit that I am more optimistic than Mike. That said, he has an excellent site with lots of good material, and probably the best preparation site links and reviews that I have found. He also sells some preparedness materials.

Y2K for Women by Karen Anderson. *http://www.y2kwomen.com/*

This is an excellent site with more practicality than any other preparation site that I have seen. Don't go buying a lot of "stuff" until you have read this site. She writes it for women, but men need to read it too.

Y2K Technical Preparation Sites

Greenwich Mean Time. *http://www.gmt-2000.com/main.htm.*

If you are looking for software to fix your PC and analyze your potential software problems, here is a good place to start.

Ed Yourdon. *http://www.yourdon.com*

Ed Yourdon is one of the most knowledgeable programming authorities in the world. He has literally written the book (some twenty of them) on programming. Reading his web site and studying all the things that he does (consulting on Y2K and programming issues), the places he travels to, and the books, newsletters, web sites, and articles that he writes makes me tired. In addition, he does book reviews in his spare time. (Anybody who reads Orson Scott Card shows good taste in science fiction.)

Here you will find links to technical books on Y2K and articles he has written on the problem. This is a good place to start if you have technical problems.

Capers Jones. *http://www.spr.com/*

This site has excellent articles on the costs and software problems stemming from Y2K. Jones is the head of Software Productivity Research and is one of the most quoted figures on the global impact of Y2K, software productivity, and other programming matters.

Y2K Books:

The Year 2000 Software Problem by Capers Jones, published by Addison Wesley. Y2K skeptics should be made to read this book. Jones very clearly lays out the problems, quantifying the costs and assessing the consequences.

The Year 2000 Software Crisis by Ian Hayes and William Ulrich, published by Prentice Hall as part of the Yourdon Press Computing Series. Businesses which are dealing with Y2K issues should read this book. It has a very good section on contingency planning, triage and crisis management, as well as commentary on legal issues, testing, risk management and supply chain issues. Hayes and Ulrich are knowledgeable gentlemen, and the book is clear reading. (I have interviews with them on my web site.)

The Millennium Bug by Mike Hyatt, published by Regnery Publishing. Hyatt has produced a well-written book slanted to the survivalist side of the Y2K issue. Lots of practical advice makes this book useful even if you agree with my more sanguine approach.

Time Bomb 2000 by Edward Yourdon and Jennifer Yourdon, published by Prentice Hall. The father-and-daughter team have collaborated to write this bestselling book. It has been updated and I have not seen the new version, but the original is the best easy-to-read explanation of the technical problems as well as a description of several scenarios as to what might happen. The Yourdons write in a clear style. Jennifer Yourdon is an analyst in a major Wall Street investment bank. For those interested in more on the topic, this is a great book.

Investment Newsletters:

Year 2000 Alert, John Mauldin, editor; published by Weiss Resources ($98 per year; $49 introductory price). This is my investment newsletter, where I deal monthly with the investment implications of the Y2K Recession and offer specific advice, timing, and how-to tips on investments. A sister company of Weiss Research also rates banks not only as to their financial strength but also for those banks which respond to their surveys on their Y2K status (a surprising number do). Readers of this book can get a half-off introductory price, and if you order by phone, Weiss will also tell you the rating of your bank. Of course, there is a 100 percent money back guarantee. Call 800-871-2374, and tell them you saw this offer in *How to Profit from the Y2K Recession.*

Sometime in 2000, when I believe we are at the bottom of the market, I intend to change the name of the newsletter to *The Millennium Wave* and become bullish as we move back into the stock market.

Fabian Premium Investment Resource, Doug Fabian, editor ($179; first-time subscribers get a special price), 800-950-8765. Doug Fabian has one of the better track records for newsletter market timers. His methodology is simple. Mutual-funds investors should consider his approach.

Forecast and Trends, Gary Halbert, editor, 800-348-3601. Halbert has been writing F&T for over twenty years. It is only available to his clients. I am a long-time business associate of Halbert's and an avid reader of his excellent newsletter. He writes about economic and political issues and provides a real insider's view of how these events affect the markets and investments. He has graciously offered to send readers of this book three issues for free. You can also read current and back issues at *www.profutures.com.*

Sagami's Mutual Fund Alert, Tony Sagami, editor ($99 per year), 800-827-0940. Monthly letter on mutual funds. I am a big fan of Tony Sagami. He really knows his mutual funds. If you invest in mutual funds, you should make Tony a prime source of information.

Safe Money Review, Martin Weiss, editor ($96 per year), 800-289-9222. This newsletter is excellent for tracking bonds and bond timing.

Profitable Investing, Richard Band, editor ($149 introductory), 800-211-8566. Band is one of my favorite writers. I like his contrarian approach, and he takes his job seriously.

Gold Mining Stock Report, Bob Bishop, editor ($119 per year), 800-759-7677. Call for free sample. My favorite gold-stock newsletter. Don't invest in gold stocks without it.

The MoniResearch Newsletter, Steve Shellans, editor ($139 per year), 1-800-615-6664. This newsletter publishes the track record of investment advisors.

Funds recommended in this book:

Rydex Funds: Rydex Ursa	800-820-0888
ProFunds Ultra Bear	888-776-3637
Potomac US Short	800-851-0511
Prudent Bear Fund	888-778-2327
US Global Government Savings Fund	800-US-FUNDS
Vanguard Treasury Money Market Portfolio	800-662-2739
American Century Target Maturity Trust 2025 Portfolio	800-345-2021
American Century Capital Preservation Funds	800-345-2021
Fidelity Spartan US Treasury MMF	800-544-8888
US Global Treasury Securities Cash	800-USFUNDS
Vanguard US Treasury Portfolio	800-662-7447
Weiss Treasury Only Money Market Fund	800-289-8100

INVESTMENT ADVISORS RECOMMENDED IN THIS BOOK:

Central Plains Advisors; Cooper Linse Hallman; and Hampton Advisors can be reached through ProFutures Investments at 800-348-3601. Please note that I have personal investments with these advisors and have also been a consultant to certain ProFutures subsidiaries and funds for many years.

SUGGESTED READING:

These are books whose primary purpose is to help you understand the changes we will be experiencing in the future. It is important for investors to have a sense of the future as well as of history. The simple fact that most investment analysts are completely missing the implications of Y2K on investing demonstrates that too many of our experts have a much too narrow analytical focus. These books will help you broaden your perspective.

The Sovereign Individual by James Dale Davidson and Sir William Rees-Mogg, published by Simon and Schuster. This is one of the those *important* books that you should read. In their previous books, Davidson and Rees-Mogg established an uncanny record of predicting seemingly improbable events. In 1987, they predicted the fall of communism, the S&L bankruptcy crisis, and the military disarmament at the height of the Reagan build-up. In 1991, they foretold the Japanese real-estate bust, the collapse of the Soviet central command, and the rise of Islam as the main ideology of confrontation. This latest book takes a more sweeping view of the future and postulates a world order dramatically different from the present—one in which individuals gain more autonomy and financial freedom and governments actually decrease in size. This book should be read and pondered.

Deflation by A. Gary Shilling, published by Lakeview Publishing Company. This is a must for investors. Whether or not you agree with Shilling, he offers the best explanation of deflation I have read. The future is uncertain, but it now appears that deflation is the concern that we should have and not inflation. If that is the case, then our investing patterns must change. The book is thankfully easy to read, with lots of charts and graphs explaining Shilling's thought process as he takes you point by point through his arguments.

Visions by Michio Kaku, published by Anchor Books. The single easiest-to-read explanation of how science will change the twenty-first century. Kaku takes difficult topics and makes them practical and understandable. Anyone curious about the future should read this book.

The 500 Year Delta by Jim Taylor and Watts Wacker, published by Harper Business. Taylor and Wacker come from a completely different set of premises than Davidson and Rees-Mogg in making predictions about the future. The two sets of authors are pretty far apart philosophically and politically. But they come to amazingly, almost eerily, similar conclusions. Read this after you read *The Sovereign Individual*.

The Fourth Turning by William Strauss and Neil Howe, published by Broadway Books. This is another *important,* very scholarly, book. The authors demonstrate a cycle in the generations of American families that keeps recurring. We are getting ready to enter into the fourth cycle of turning (their term). This book will give you some serious things to ponder and has enormous implications if they are right.

I should also mention *The Millionaire Next Door* by Thomas Stanley and William Danko (Longstreet Press).

APPENDIX B

This is the best example of a contingency-planning document that I have seen. You need to read it for two reasons. First, you will see what your community faces and what should be happening in your community. The odds are very high that nothing approaching this scenario is taking place. That means that it is up to you to get the project started. Start by copying this plan and distributing it to every city official, local activist, and pastor, and to businesses and the chamber of commerce. Find allies, and get started. You will notice that you're already behind. Don't despair, just do what you can. Every bit of preparation will make the 2000 transition easier.

Secondly, this will show you what a contingency plan should look like for your business. It should be this detailed. If it isn't, then look at this document, find the analogies between planning for cities and your business, and add those points to your business plan. I have listed additional sources for community planning help in appendix A.

YEAR 2000 Contingency Planning for Municipal Governments

October 1, 1998
Version 2.0

Abstract
The year 2000 software problem can have a very unfortunate impact on municipal governments in the United States and abroad. Urban government year 2000 problems may be severe, and many governments will not be able to repair all of the problems before the end of the century. In addition, the year 2000 problem has the potential to damage urban infrastructures and temporarily disable public utilities such as electric power, water supplies, and sewage.

The year 1998 is a critical transition period in year 2000 planning. Prior to 1998 most year 2000 plans concentrated on repairs and remediation. From now on, most year 2000 plans will concentrate on damages and recovery actions. This generic municipal planning template sketches out some of the considerations for year 2000 contingency plans in the context of urban governments in the United States.

Capers Jones, Chief Scientist
Artemis Management Systems
Software Productivity Research, Inc.
an Artemis company
1 New England Executive Park
Burlington, MA 01803–5005
Phone: 617-273-0140 ex. 102; FAX: 617-273-5176; e-mail: *Capers@spr.com* or
CompuServe 75430,231

YEAR 2000 CONTINGENCY PLANNING AND MUNICIPAL GOVERNMENTS

The needs of municipal governments for year 2000 repairs are more complex than corporate needs, due to several factors. Municipal governments will be tasked with coordinating damage control for many infrastructure problems, such as loss of electric power and perhaps interruption of public water supplies. If these infrastructure problems occur and last more than a day or two, then they will trigger needs for police and fire department involvement. Should these problems last more than about ten days, then National Guard assistance may also be needed.

If the year 2000 infrastructure problems such as loss of electric power last more than about a week, then secondary impacts will also occur. These collateral damages include transportation problems, weather damages such as burst pipes for cities in cold climates, and possible food shortages if transportation is interrupted. Thus public shelters may be needed.

In addition, the municipal costs of year 2000 damage control and recovery will be large and may exceed planned budgets. This may necessitate unpleasant increases in local taxes or reductions in urban services, or both. In fact, urban bankruptcies are a significant possibility.

This brief outline merely summarizes some of the factors that should be included in municipal government contingency and recovery plans for the year 2000 problem. It is no longer possible to achieve 100 percent year 2000 repairs, so the time to begin serious contingency planning is right now in 1998. It would be imprudent and irresponsible to delay contingency planning until it is too late to stock necessary emergency supplies.

GOALS FOR MUNICIPAL YEAR 2000 CONTINGENCY PLANNING

1. Minimize urban damages from unrepaired year 2000 problems
2. Minimize risk of infrastructure damages due to power or water failures
3. Optimize the speed of recovery from unrepaired year 2000 problems

4. Minimize the risks of litigation against government units
5. Provide accurate status information to concerned citizens
6. Coordinate local Y2K status with other governments

Municipal Year 2000 Advisory Board Members

The year 2000 problem is pervasive and affects financial applications, telephone systems, electric power generation, water supplies, sewage treatment, and all other computer-controlled activities. This means that year 2000 coordination for urban governments must involve every bureau and operating unit. A municipal year 2000 advisory board should be set up in mid 1998 to handle the overall coordination of year 2000 information and repairs.

MANDATORY MEMBERS

Mayor's office or city manager's office
City council representatives
Operating unit representatives
    CIO or data processing
    Police department
    Fire department
    Tax office
    Public health
    Transit authority
    Port authority (if any)
    School board
    Social services
    Personnel
    Finance or CFO
    Legal or town attorney
    Emergency preparedness
    Engineering
    Planning/Real-Estate

OPTIONAL MEMBERS

Liaison—federal government
Liaison—state government
Liaison—county government
Liaison—other urban governments
Chamber of Commerce
Local Year 2000 groups
Local business associations
Local universities
Year 200 experts (pro bono basis?)

Note: The municipal year 2000 advisory board will be about twenty-five members in size for both towns and cities. It is important that the advisory board be non-partisan and non-political. The year 2000 problem can be as pervasive as a natural disaster such as a hurricane or earthquake.

YEAR 2000 CONTINGENCY TEAM MEMBERS

The role of the contingency team is to be ready to deal with year 2000 problems that are not repaired before the end of the century. There will be unrepaired year 2000 problems and it is folly to deny it. The software industry has never repaired 100 percent of any kind of problem, and the year 2000 problems are more complex than most.

Because fiscal years and calendar years are not always the same, it is necessary to assume that problems may begin to occur as early as January of 1999 for applications that "look ahead" for a twelve-month period. In particular, the U.S. Federal government's fiscal year starts in October, so any software applications or data base connections between Federal and municipal governments may experience problems. Other fiscal years can also be troublesome.

The contingency team members will largely be derived from the pool of personnel who are already working on year 2000 repairs.

APPROXIMATE SIZE OF YEAR 2000 CONTINGENCY TEAMS

Software expert(s)	1 per 5,000 function points deployed
Data base expert(s)	1 per 10,000 function points deployed
Embedded system expert(s)	1 per 2,500 function points deployed
Public utility experts	1 per 100,000 population of city
Electricity	
Water	
Sewage	
Police department	1 per 25,000 population of city
Fire department	Unknown
Legal department	All available attorneys
Public health	1 per 5,000 population of city
Transportation	Unknown
School board	Unknown
Social services	1 per 5,000 population of city

Note: The size of the contingency team may require a total of ten to fifteen staff members per 100,000 population of the city. This means for a city with 1,000,000 people there may be 100 to 150 civil servants and contractors dedicated to emergency repairs. These personnel must be included in city budgets and hence the contingency staff may reduce other urban activities.

For several kinds of representatives on the contingency response team, there are no current rules of thumb for ascertaining how many participants may be needed. These areas of uncertainty include the fire department, the school boards, and local transportation authorities (if any exist in the municipality).

Many cities have formed local citizens action groups that are able to assist elected officials and city officers in dealing with aspects of the year 2000 problem. These citizen action groups can be very helpful and should be supported to the fullest.

Year 2000 Contingency Calendar

This generic contingency calendar is organized by month from September of 1998 through March of 2000. The calendar is not aimed at any specific city, but merely indicates some of the topics that municipal governments need to consider when dealing with year 2000 problems.

Among the worst kinds of problems might be the loss of electric power for cities with cold winter climates. For arid cities, another serious problem might be temporary disruption of water supplies. For all cities, there is a shared concern that year 2000 expenses may be so high that city finances cannot cover them, so special taxes may be needed.

Calendar Year 1998

September 1998
Local advisory board appointed
First meeting of advisory board
Town meeting #1 on year 2000 contingency plans
Press release #1 on year 2000 contingency plans

October 1998
Head of contingency planning named and begins work
Year 2000 contingency cost estimate prepared
Year 2000 preliminary budget:
    A) What if insufficient funds exist?
    B) What about political opposition?
    C) What about cuts to other urban services?
    D) What about state or federal funding?
    E) What if experts are unavailable for local assistance?
Salaries and benefits of contingency team members set
Civil service status of contingency team members set
Use of contractors/consultants for contingency work discussed
Survey of other urban governments for useful planning templates
Survey of state and federal sources for useful planning templates
Local year 2000 web site established

November 1998
Contact established with volunteer citizens groups
Contact established with local year 2000 association

Preliminary survey/audit of all urban software applications for year 2000 status
Preliminary survey/audit of public utilities for year 2000 status
  Electricity
  Water
  Sewage
  Natural gas
Preliminary survey of communication channel year 2000 status
  Local telephone companies
  Long-distance companies
  Cellular companies
  Radio stations
  Television stations
  Ham radio operators
Preliminary survey of transportation into and out of area
  Air services
  Railroads
  Trucking
  Highways
  Water transport
Preliminary survey of emergency equipment and supplies
  Electric generators
  Fuel supplies
  Emergency food and water
  Batteries for electrical equipment
  Medical supplies
Preliminary survey of weather-related supplies
  Heating oil
  Natural gas
Preliminary survey of available experts for Y2K emergency work
  Software experts
  Data base experts
  Embedded system experts
  Electrical engineers
  Civil engineers
  Transit and transport specialists
  Nursing and medical personnel

December 1998
Criteria for joining contingency team worked out
Budget approved to fund contingency group
Contingency team nucleus begins to form
  Group leader
  First software experts
Contact list of all year 2000 offices created
Liaisons established with other governments (urban, country, state, federal)

First draft of urban contingency plans created
  Fiscal year contingency plan
  Calendar year contingency plan
  Probable local damages
  Estimated time to repair
  Estimated costs of year 2000 repairs
Preliminary contingency budget approved
Funding shortages addressed
Requests for proposals from outside vendors
  Generators and emergency equipment
  Radios and two-way communication equipment
  Year 2000 testing and compliance audit

CALENDAR YEAR 1999

January 1999

Monitoring all applications for twelve-month fiscal "look ahead" year 2000
    problems
Letters/phone calls to all vendors whose software failed
First tryout of year 2000 problem notifications
First actual year 2000 problems repaired
Year 2000 "hot line" established (one shift)

February 1999

Full contingency team selected and training begins (part time)
Contracts for year 2000 consultant prepared
Possible filing of litigation against unresponsive vendors
Contract let for external audit of year 2000 testing

March 1999

Monitoring all applications for nine-month fiscal year 2000 problems
Orders placed for emergency supplies (generators, batteries, etc.)
Town attorneys review possible litigation status against town agencies
Unrepairable, unreplaceable applications identified
Manual backup plans for unrepairable applications

April 1999

Revised contingency plans based on failures during first three months of 1999
Note: 65 percent chance costs will go up; 35 percent chance costs will come
    down.
Town meeting(s) on municipal year 2000 status
Press release on municipal year 2000 status
Web site updates on municipal year 2000 status

May 1999

External audit of urban year 2000 testing and repairs
Audit report on methods and liability issues

June 1999
Monitoring all applications for six-month fiscal year 2000 problems
Year 2000 hot line expands to two-shift operation
Major town meeting on local, state, and federal year 2000 status

July 1999
Briefings to police and fire departments on anticipated year 2000 problems
Weekly year 2000 status reports released to press, radio, TV

August 1999
Revised year 2000 damage cost estimates
Updates to fiscal year and calendar year contingency plans

September 1999
Monitoring all applications for four-month "look ahead" year 2000 problems
Multi-city/state/federal testing to guard against reinfection

October 1999
U.S. Federal government fiscal year begins: *major problems can occur*
Town meeting in response to Federal government year 2000 problems
Press release in response to Federal government year 2000 problems
Emergency supplies and backup equipment stocked and available
Final survey of key local businesses for year 2000 status
    Banks
    Local phone companies
    Insurance companies
    Hospitals
    Supermarkets

November 1999
Contingency team "dry run" to check response speed
    Loss of electricity
    Loss of telephone services
    Reinfection from external sources
    Liaison with citizen volunteer groups
    Liaison with state and federal year 2000 contingency teams
    Liaison with other municipal year 2000 contingency teams

December 1999
Contingency team in place and ready for twenty-four-hour operations
Volunteer citizens groups trained and ready to assist
Emergency supplies fully stocked and available
Police and fire units standing by
Year 2000 hot lines open and staffed
Year 2000 radio/tv coverage prepared

Police and fire emergency teams ready on 12/31
Year 2000 contingency team ready on 12/31
Radio contacts with state and federal emergency groups
Final town meeting on year 2000 status
Final status reports released to TV, radio, newspapers

Because many government fiscal years start prior to calendar years, the last half of 1999 will provide a good overview of how serious year 2000 problems may be in a government context. In particular, October of 1999 will be a major milestone because that is when the U.S. Federal fiscal year begins. Major problems can be expected.

CALENDAR YEAR 2000

The worst-case scenario for January of 2000 would be protracted loss of electrical power and telephone services for a period of two weeks or more, coupled with disruption of public water supplies. For cities with cold climates, extended loss of electric power could lead to substantial collateral damages such as burst pipes and deaths of homeless persons.

Once the year 2000 event has occurred, it can be expected that at least several months of emergency work will be needed to repair software and data base applications that were not repaired in time. In addition, substantial manual backup work will be needed to perform activities that would normally be done by computer: preparing W2 tax forms and issuing municipal paychecks, for example.

By about March of 2000, assuming twenty-four-hour-a-day emergency software repairs, most of municipal software and computerized applications should be restored to service. However, this assumes that electric power outages, water shortages, and other infrastructure damages are not too severe, and will be rapidly repaired.

The spring and summer of the year 2000 will be spent in attempting to restore municipal government operations to pre-2000 levels of performance. The more serious issues during this period will be the economic damages and tax revenue reductions.

Municipal governments face a possible four-fold set of damages from the year 2000, as pointed out in Capers Jones's book *The Year 2000 Software Problem— Quantifying the Costs and Assessing the Consequences* (Addison Wesley, 1997).

1. Municipal year 2000 repair expenses will be high, and exceed planned budgets.
2. Municipal repairs will be less than 100 percent, leading to possible lawsuits.
3. Year 2000 problems may well lower municipal bond revenues.
4. Local tax revenues will be reduced due to corporate year 2000 problems.

The aftermath of the year 2000 problem may result in some municipal bankruptcies. Even if bankruptcy does not occur, there will probably be a need to raise local taxes and reduce some local services to pay for year 2000 damages. There may be State and Federal year 2000 relief, but none is currently committed as this is written.

There will also be negative political fallout from the year 2000 event. Elected officials who were not proactive about year 2000 repairs will probably not be reelected. For several years, a political leader's stance on year 2000 problems will no doubt play a significant part in election results.

January 2000
Police and fire emergency teams on twenty-four-hour duty for first week
    Guarding food stores
    Guarding banks
    Guarding public facilities
Volunteer citizens groups assist police and fire departments if needed
Contingency team on twenty-four-hour duty for first two weeks
Year 2000 hot line on twenty-four-hour duty (if phones are working)
Surveillance against reinfection (if computers are working)
Daily status reports and press releases
Decision whether or not to declare city a "disaster area"
Decision whether or not to ask for National Guard assistance
Year 2000 emergency physical repairs
    Electric power
    Water
    Sewage
Emergency communication cut in
    Radio contacts with contingency team
    Radio contacts with state and federal year 2000 offices
Year 2000 emergency software repairs
    Payrolls
    Taxation
    Accounts payable and receivable
Manual backups for key activities
    Manual issuance of payroll checks
    Manual payment of accounts receivable
    Issuance of W2 forms and 1099 forms for tax reporting
Emergency shelters open if needed
    Stranded travelers at airports
    Travelers running out of gas
    Anyone if temperatures are below freezing and power is off
Initial assessment of year 2000 urban damages
    Physical damages due to freezing, fire, riots, etc.
    Status of all urban software, data bases, hardware, etc.

Collateral damages (burst pipes, polluted water, etc.)
Social problems (civil disturbances, evacuations, etc.)
Litigation filings against vendors whose products caused serious damages
Litigation defense against claims by citizens and businesses

February 2000

Accumulation of municipal year 2000 damage costs
Survey of infrastructure damages and repairs
Water supplies
Electric power
Sewage
Continued filing of litigation against vendors whose software failed
Continued defense against litigation filed against town agencies
Negotiations with IRS on dealing with incorrect W2 and 1099 forms
Hopefully all public utilities restored and fully operational
Electricity
Water
Sewage
Telephones
Hopefully all modes of travel back at full capacity
Year 2000 aftermath town meetings

March 2000

Survey of local business failures with analysis of reduction in city tax base
Manual backup methods gradually phased out as software repairs wind down
Financial health of urban government assessed
Federal and state financial assistance disbursements continue
Decisions on raising taxes, reducing services, or both to pay for year 2000
Decision on potential municipal bankruptcy to avoid damage claims
Some municipal services more or less normal
Some municipal services suspended due to lack of available funds
Litigation continues indefinitely
Contingency team begins to disband if problems are contained

The economic aftershock from the year 2000 problem may well last for years.
The worst-case assumption for a municipal government would be such severe
reductions in tax revenues coupled with lawsuits for urban year 2000 damages
that municipal bankruptcy occurs. The worst case situation would occur if
electricity and water supplies were shut down long enough to cause major
infrastructure damages and local business failures.

The expected case for municipal governments would be a stressful period that
lasts from mid 1999 through the end of fiscal year 2000 and perhaps into 2001.
During this period emergency repairs and recovery would be dominant activities,
but the year 2000 problem would not be severe enough to trigger bankruptcy.

The best case for municipal governments would be only minor problems
between about October of 1999 (when the Federal fiscal year begins) and June of
2000, by which time unrepaired year 2000 problems would be under control.

Fixing Your Personal Computer

The biggest Y2K question that most people have to deal with is "What do I do about my personal computer?"

Nearly every personal computer (PC) has Y2K problems. Ninety-eight percent of personal computers have yet to be fixed. The good news is that fixing them is relatively simple. There are inexpensive software programs that can fix the problems on your PC and even tell you what software on your PC has Y2K problems. You can go to your local computer store and buy these programs.

I personally like the program from Greenwich Mean Time, but there are other programs that will essentially do the same thing. The key is to get one of the programs (that are on disk), put the disk into your computer, and run the very simple program to fix your computer. I think that you need to do this for every computer that you have, no matter how new it is! There are numerous verified stories of new computers not being Y2K compliant.

I do not pretend to be an expert on the PC problem, but Karl Feilder of Greenwich Mean Time is. I asked him to give me a simple explanation of the problem. He very graciously sent me the article below. I think you will find it very informative.

The Five Layers of the PC Year 2000 Problem

By Karl W Feilder,
President and CEO, Greenwich Mean Time

The Millennium Bug is likely to affect all PCs in one way or another. The key to minimizing your risk is to first understand the problem and how it may show itself in your PC.

WHAT EXACTLY IS A PC?

PCs are common in most business environments, either as free-standing work-stations or, in larger companies, networked together with servers to improve information sharing through common diaries or electronic mail. The term *PC* covers any desktop or portable computer but the same year 2000 risks may also apply to some hand-held or palm-top hardware, where the system components are similar to the larger models.

Do not overlook unattended PCs which quietly get on with seemingly unimportant routine tasks—they too may be affected by the Millennium Bug, and may still have a role to play in a business process.

WHEN IN DOUBT, CHECK IT OUT

As with all areas of year 2000 risk assessment, it is safest to assume that you have a problem, and then proceed to prove that you do not. Your investment in PCs, software programs, and data will be wasted if you cannot make use of them in the future.

Most PCs are IBM-compatible but some manufacturers build to an individual specification and vary the internal components during production runs. This means that two PCs that look identical on the outside may not be the same on the inside, and hence may house different year 2000 risks.

You may have opted for an unusual or customized computer or software, or had programs written for you. These will have to be checked because they will not be covered by generic statements from your other computer or software suppliers.

Apple Macintosh computers have their own operating system which in itself may not be vulnerable to the Millennium Bug. However, AppleMac software packages and your data are likely to be affected in much the same way as PC software and data. You should assess your risk for each software application. Remember that PC systems which process data transmitted from other sources may have a problem if the date functions have not been corrected at the sender's end.

HOW YOUR PERSONAL COMPUTER CAN BE AFFECTED

The year 2000 problem affects all five layers that make up PCs: hardware (BIOS), operating systems, software programs, data, and data sharing. The complexity of the problem increases at each layer, so the least complex problems occur at the hardware layer and the most complex at the data sharing layer.

1. HARDWARE LAYER (BIOS)

This refers to your PC itself, which in many cases will fail to correctly change from 1999 to 2000. Statistics show that this failure is common in 1996 and older PCs (93 percent), and even at the end of 1997 some 21 percent of new models were failing the test. The failure is the result of a two-digit date (YY) from the real-time clock (RTC) chip being incorrectly expanded to a four-digit date (CCYY) by the basic input/output system (BIOS).

The internal layout of the real-time clock (RTC) was part of the original Motorola MC 146818A specification, first released in the PC/AT in 1984. This chip and its derivatives continue to be used in over 90 percent of PCs today.

Although this chip clearly does not count in centuries, it will continue to work in the year 2000 and beyond, as it will treat 00 as 2000.

The RTC (like your wristwatch) does not count in centuries, but will work fine into the next century as long as the BIOS is year 2000 compliant.

The RTC passes a two-digit year (YY) to the BIOS when your PC boots up, and the BIOS should then convert this to a four-digit year that includes the century (CCYY) to be passed to other programs and the operating system (OS). The good news about this layer is that it is simple to diagnose and relatively simple to correct in the vast majority of cases. There are a number of affordable tools available that can test and correct your BIOS problems.

2. THE OPERATING SYSTEM LAYER (OS)

Most common operating systems are able to deal with the year 2000 provided they are set up correctly. Unfortunately, the normal installation of most Microsoft Windows–based OS is incompatible with the next century, but can be easily diagnosed and corrected. There are also some minor display problems with two Windows OS components—File Manager and Explorer—for which Microsoft has produced patches.

You should check the way your Windows operating system is set up. This is relatively easily done by looking in "Control Panel" and then in "Regional Settings" where you will find the choice box.

It is generally recommended that you change the "Short Date Style" to MM/DD/YYYY or DD/MM/YYYY, but there is a small chance that some of your programs will not accept this change or react badly to it. To be safe try this on a test PC before using one of your important PCs.

3. THE SOFTWARE PROGRAM LAYER (SOFTWARE)

Reserach published in 1997 showed that of 4,000 commonly used PC software programs more than 64 percent had the potential, during normal usage and operation, to be adversely affected by dates at the end of this century and into the next. This does not mean that you need to replace all of these programs, but you may need to change the way they are installed or the way you use them. Testing for these problems is difficult and can be dangerous, but may be easier if the program name and manufacturer (and its year 2000 status) can be identified on a per-PC basis.

An example of a simple software year 2000 problem is the leap year problem. Other problems are more complex. For example, a popular accounting software package is able to display dates into the year 2000 but it incorrectly shows only twenty-eight days in February 2000. Pope Gregory XIII declared the year 2000 a leap year in 1582, and hence February should have twenty-nine days.

4. THE DATA LAYER (DATA)

As most of us prefer writing year dates as two digits (98 rather than 1998) the YY format has been commonly used in PCs. However, most software programs actually calculate in four digit years (CCYY). Many software programs automatically expand these YY dates to CCYY dates without notifying the user of the underlying assumptions used. Your data should be checked for the occurrence of such "short dates" (YY), and spreadsheets and data bases cleaned in preparation for the end of the century.

For instance, your spreadsheet program may be year 2000 compliant as long as you know how to use it like that, which in most cases means always using CCYY dates, but your specific spreadsheet applications may not be compliant. Every date reference needs to be checked.

5. THE DATA SHARING LAYER

PCs are now regularly used to exchange data, both between PCs and between programs resident on the same PC. The data problems described previously obviously compound the data sharing problem and make creation of a truly "safe" PC very difficult. Data is shared in many ways, such as over the Internet, via e-mail, floppy disk, and EDI. Your colleagues probably share data with you across your company's PC network, and you should be careful that all data only contains years in the CCYY date format.

If you are running your own programs created in one of the commonly used languages such as Visual Basic, Delphi, or C++, you will need to check that they perform date processing correctly beyond the end of this century. Most of these programs have used a technique known as "Date Windowing" to expand YY dates to CCYY dates, and in many cases this can cause problems for the correct operation of your own programs in the next century.

FIX OR WAIT?

The year 2000 problem affects all of us, so you must begin immediately to check how it affects you. You should also be aware that the Millennium Bug has already started to appear in some PC software programs as they start to deal with dates forward into the next century. We advise you to put a checking process in place immediately. The three key stages to any year 2000 project are:

ASSESS the impact of each of the five layers to your business and make decisions about which risks are most serious, and which you can afford to ignore. You will undoubtedly find this quicker and more reliable if you use one of the affordable PC year 2000 tools on the market today. Ideally, you need a tool that allows you to assess your risks at each of the five layers.

CHANGE the way you use your PCs. For example, never casually accept data from other sources unless you can first check that it features only four-digit years (CCYY). Also change the way you enter dates, from YY to CCYY. If necessary you may have to replace some of your hardware or software, and you will have to correct your critical data to CCYY years.

TEST that the changes you have made have addressed the most critical areas of your business. Remember that a year 2000 project is not a one-off audit, and you should have weekly progress reports and meetings with your colleagues to ensure that your entire business network is operating correctly for 2000.

ACT Now! Check every single PC.

APPENDIX D

The Cultural and Religious
Implications of the Y2K Crisis

The Millennium Bug has profound implications for our economy. I have spent a whole book outlining the economic and financial problems that we face as a result of the Y2K Crisis.

As serious as these are, I believe that it is possible that the cultural and spiritual implications may be far more pervasive and lasting. On this side of the millennium, it is not altogether clear whether the cultural fallout will be positive or negative. It has the potential to be either, depending upon how we choose to respond.

Specifically, I think the responsibility for directing the nature of our corporate response lies with our religious institutions. History teaches us that when economies perform poorly there is clearly the potential for the resulting cultural reaction to be negative, leading to a plague of despair, mistrust, and hopelessness. If the overriding emotional reaction becomes an "us-against-them" mood in our country and the world, the possibility for a worldwide crisis increases.

In such crises, demagogues proliferate and scar the world with their messages of hate, superiority, distrust, and anger as they lay the blame for whatever problems a nation is experiencing at the feet of those who are "different." Often this blame is heaped upon minority populations, foreigners, and foreign nations or groups that have seemed to prosper in the face of crisis.

But this dark scenario does not have to be played out. In fact, I think that we could see a renaissance of spiritual growth and coming together of peoples and nations. But it will only happen if the religious leaders of our world decide to take this crisis and use it as an opportunity to foster a climate for spiritual growth and reconciliation between individuals, families, and peoples at all levels.

What is it about Y2K that holds a potential for negative cultural impact? To understand the full scope of the problem, we need to look briefly at changes in our culture that began during the last century.

(I come from a Judaeo-Christian heritage, and my remarks will primarily be directed to that tradition, and primarily to those who reside in the U.S. But the broader implications of what I am saying reach across all religious traditions and national borders.)

Over one hundred years ago, a subtle change began to develop in our national thinking. At the time of the founding of our country, and for most of the next century, there was:

1. An expectation that religious values should influence our government. Any reading of the letters, books, and speeches of the leaders of the eighteenth and nineteenth centuries clearly demonstrates this. While there was a wide variety of religious expression, and even while acknowledging that some of those expressions were not beneficial, there is no escaping the fact of the influence of religious values and more specifically of the Christian church upon our nation. The religious leaders in the pulpits of our nation exerted great influence upon the issues of the day.
2. An expectation that the primary institution responsible for the welfare of individuals was the church and its related institutions. Welfare was handled on a local and individual basis, with first families and then religious institutions taking the lead in helping the aged, the poor, and the sick and children in need.
3. An expectation that even if the local church was not the actual provider of education (and in many cases it was), that education was to have religious flavor and character.

But in the late nineteenth century, a significant change occurred in the way that people viewed religious values and the role of religious institutions in society. Two broad streams emerged. One stream turned inward, slowly at first and then with increasing force, divorcing the implications and influence of personal religious experience from ideas about governments policy and practices. As society increasingly turned secular, the influence of religious values (what some call a biblical worldview) on the philosophy of government became weaker.

The second stream believed that government should have a greater role in education and welfare. In fact, as the twentieth century progressed, government played a greater role in almost every aspect of our personal lives. The role of the church and religious institutions was diminished.

If a visitor from another galaxy visited the United States in the early nineteenth century, he or she would have observed that the primary focus of "faith" was toward God and that the primary shaper of corporate and personal values was the churches.

An extra-galactic visitor today would not come to the same conclusions. Our corporate faith is now invested in a variety of smaller, lesser gods, and the shaper of our values is no longer primarily the churches. While I would not deny the signs of growing interest in spirituality, I think those of us in the religious (and especially Christian) community are only kidding ourselves if we believe that we are the major influence upon society today.

Strangely enough, I think the Y2K Crisis could give the church an opportunity to increase its influence and resume a more influential role in society. That is because the Y2K Crisis is going to pose significant questions for the institutions that now enjoy the public trust.

As a society we have placed a significant amount of faith in three major institutions.

We have elevated *government* to a godlike role. The government is now responsible for our health (through various programs), our economic well-being, and our welfare and serves as our protector—roles that our forefathers would have ascribed to God. Government leaders routinely take credit for providing whatever blessings our economic hard work and endeavors endow upon us.

The Y2K Crisis has the potential to seriously disrupt the ability of governments to deliver services.

Secondly, we have an almost childlike faith in *technology*. We have come to expect the benefits of an ever-increasing array of services provided by technology, assuming that the answers to our problems are only a discovery or a new invention away.

The Y2K Crisis has the potential to reveal that technology is nothing more than a tool, and certainly nothing upon which we should place our faith.

Thirdly, we have come to rely upon the *economy* (our jobs and investments) as a source of well-being, rather than realizing that God is our source no matter what the economy or our personal circumstances dictate.

The Y2K Crisis has the potential to reveal that the economy is important but not the ultimate foundation upon which our lives are built.

I believe that we could see the rug pulled out from under those who have placed their faith in the three lesser gods of modern society. Few people would admit that they have placed a religious-like faith in these three icons, but the actions and emotional attachments of our society clearly demonstrate otherwise.

The rapid loss of faith will produce a vacuum. We will quickly see a culture, not only in the United States, but throughout the world, in search of something in which to place its faith. If this vacuum is not filled with something worthy of trust and faith, with something that produces positive values and actions, my fear is that people will be seduced by more malevolent, less benign institutions than the three mentioned above.

Those of us in the community of faith often sadly bemoan the fact of our loss of impact upon today's world. The Y2K Crisis may very well give us an opportunity to begin to reverse a century of moral and social drift.

This will not be accomplished by "I told you so's" or other standard religious fares. It is not the time for thunderous sermons. What will be needed is for the church to simply serve those hurt by the Y2K Crisis and to present those hurting with the fact of their acceptance in the household of faith.

The poor, the elderly, children, those who have lost their jobs, and others who depend upon government, technology, and the economy to sustain them are going to need someone to make sure they are taken care of. It is my hope that communities respond to these needs and that the lead in providing aid is taken by the local churches in cooperation with one another.

It is when people of faith demonstrate the ability to make a difference by serving those who most need help that we will be afforded the opportunity to once again influence our culture in a significant and positive manner. Words are not enough. There must be visible, widespread actions accompanying our words, or we will slip even further into cultural irrelevancy. And frankly, we will deserve that fate if we fail to seize this opportunity.

To respond correctly, to be most effective, will require cooperation throughout the entire spectrum of the community of faith. A great part of the cultural irrelevancy of the church is due in no small way to the divisions (and often outright conflict) within the church. In this I am not thinking of just denominational divisions, but primarily of racial, economic, nationalistic, and cultural divisions.

What better way to demonstrate to the world the reconciling power of the gospel than to show that we can reconcile these divisions within our own communities? If we cannot demonstrate evidence of the power of Love by working together, demonstrating true unity in the midst of crisis, then why should we expect society to follow our standards of behavior in times of peace and plenty?

Please do not think I am suggesting that centuries of problems can be changed overnight. They can't. But the catalyst for real change is often produced in times of crisis when people rise to the occasion. And frankly, if we miss this opportunity, it may be a generation before we are given another.

There are five responses that we must avoid. The first is to do nothing. It should be obvious after reading this book why this is inappropriate.

The second is to respond in an ad hoc, uncoordinated manner. Not only will this add to the confusion in the midst of crisis, it will surely mean that many of those in need will slip through the cracks.

The third wrong response is one of millennial hysteria and/or a withdrawal into a selfish, survivalist mode. The Y2K Crisis is an opportunity for ministry, not an excuse for retreat into isolated shelters. It is not the end of the world, but perhaps the beginning of a period of spiritual renewal.

The fourth wrong response is to only respond to the crisis within our national borders. While we must care for those in our own backyards, we must not lose sight of the suffering that the rest of the world will be going through. Each church should consider how it will help those outside of our national community.

The fifth wrong response would be an improper attitude and motive for our actions. When I think of churches *leading*, it is not by taking charge but *by leading in service*. A servant's actions require a servant's heart. In some cases, the best thing that a church can do is to place its facilities and members at the disposal and direction of community leaders. It will be up to the leaders of each church to determine what role of service it should play. It will be up to the leaders of the churches in each community to best determine how to cooperate and support each other and the community at large.

The benefits of preparing for a crisis should be obvious. And as you organize, remember that it is the economic effects of the Y2K Recession that will last long after a few days of random infrastructure problems. Even if the Y2K Recession/Crisis turns out to be less serious than I believe it will be, the positive results from coming together as a community of faith will be felt for a long time. And if it is as bad or worse than I believe, then lives will be saved. In either case, we could see a culture transformed.

I sincerely pray that this will be the case.

(Two books that I highly recommend and that are helpful reading in this context are *Healing America's Wounds* by John Dawson, available in most religious bookstores; and *The Samaritan Strategy* by Colonel Doner, available by calling 888-781-1585.)

Special Offer for Readers of This Book

The author of *How to Profit from the Y2K Recession* is also the editor of the *Year 2000 Alert* monthly newsletter. Since it provides regular updates on many of the topics covered in this book, we would like to make the newsletter available to you at a special rate.

A year subscription (12 issues) to *Year 2000 Alert* is regularly $98.00. However, we are making it available to you at a 50 percent discount of $49. As an additional bonus, new subscribers will also receive a free Weiss Y2K Safety Rating of their bank or financial institution. This offer is good through December 31, 2000.

To take advantage of this offer, clip the coupon below (photocopies are okay) and mail to Y2K Alert, Box 109665, Palm Beach Gardens, FL 33410. Or order by calling 1-800-871-2374 and get a instant Weiss Safety Rating on your bank.

Please enter my subscription to the *Year 2000 Alert* newsletter. I understand that as a reader of *How to Profit from the Y2K Recession,* I receive a special $49 rate for twelve monthly issues (a 50 percent discount off the regular price). I also understand that with my paid subscription I will also receive a free Weiss Y2K Safety Rating of my bank or financial institution. Please attach your mailing address to this coupon.

Name of Bank (for rating)_____

___My check or money order for $49 is enclosed.

Bill My: ___MC   ___Visa   ___AMEX   ___Discover

Card #_____Exp. Date_____

Signature_____

Make checks payable to Year 2000 Alert. Florida residents please add 6 percent sales tax. Non-U.S. residents add an additional $20 per year for postage and handling. Please make checks payable in U.S. dollars. With checks drawn on non-U.S. banks, add an additional $30 for processing.

Year 2000 Alert, Box 109665, Palm Beach Gardens, FL 33410,
1-800-817-2374

Offer good through Dec. 31, 2000